Landfalls of Paradise: The Guide to Pacific Islands

Earl R. Hinz

Landfalls of Paradise: The Guide to Pacific Islands

Earl R. Hinz

Covering 33 island groups including
Polynesia, Melanesia, Micronesia
and the other islands of Oceania.
With 150 photographs, 90 charts
and 56 Ports of Entry.

Western Marine Enterprises, Inc.
Ventura, California 93002

By the Same Author:

The Offshore Log, 1974
Sail Before Sunset, 1979

©1980 by Earl R. Hinz

Second Printing — 1981

Library of Congress Cataloging in Publication Data

Hinz, Earl R.
Landfalls of paradise.
Bibliography: p.
Includes index.
1. Yachts and yachting — Oceanica.   2. Oceanica — Description and travel — 1951.   I. Title.
GV817.027H56   919   79-17600
ISBN 0-930030-13-3

Book Design: Fred Colcer and Lil Fox
Charts drawn by Merlin Kastler

PUBLISHED BY WESTERN MARINE ENTERPRISES, INC.
Publishers of the *Pacific Boating Almanac*
and other marine books. Catalog on request.
Box Q, Ventura, California 93002

In Canada:
Gordon Soules Book Publishers
525-355 Burrard Street
Vancouver, B.C. V6C 2G8

Acknowledgments

During the preparation of this book the author on more than one occasion sat back and wondered how he could have the effrontery to offer himself as an authority on the vast Pacific Basin. The very thought of anyone attempting to make a cruising guide for the entire Pacific Ocean was without precedent. Four years of research, two years of cruising these very same waters, two Transpacific yacht races, and three years of living in Hawaii finally stiffened his editorial backbone enough to put between covers most of the facts needed by the cruising yachtsman.

In doing so, the author has also drawn on a number of authoritative government publications for supplementary facts which appear herein. In particular, acknowledgment is made of help from the following publications:

Area Handbook for Oceania, U.S. Department of State
Health Information for International Travel, U.S. Department of Health, Education and Welfare
Pilot Charts — North and South Pacific, United States Naval Oceanographic Office and National Oceanic and Atmospheric Administration
Mariners Worldwide Climatic Guide to Tropical Storms at Sea, Naval Weather Service Command
Sailing Directions, U.S. Hydrographic Office
Pacific Islands Pilot, British Admiralty

Some excerpts have been taken from the following public documents where the interest of the cruising yachtsman would be best served:

Chapter
3 *Mariners Worldwide Climatic Guide to Tropical Storms at Sea*, Naval Weather Service Command
5 *Hawaii, the Aloha State*, Hawaii Visitors Bureau
10 *American Samoa Annual Report*, Office of Samoan Information, and, *Western Samoa Background Notes*, U.S. Department of State
12 *Tonga Background Notes*, U.S. Department of State
15 *Facts About New Zealand*, New Zealand Information Service
17 *Fiji Background Notes*, U.S. Department of State
19 *Papua New Guinea Background Notes*, U.S. Department of State
21 *Area Handbook for Oceania*, U.S. Department of State
23 *Area Handbook for Oceania*, U.S. Department of State
24 *Area Handbook for Oceania*, U.S. Department of State, and, *Micronesia Guidebook*, Micronesia Office of Tourism
25 *Area Handbook for Oceania*, U.S. Department of State

Special thanks are due the Pacific Area Travel Association, Pacific Travel News, and the American Radio Relay League for their generous assistance.

Personal thanks are also due the representatives of the many Pacific island governments who contributed to local facts and in many cases also reviewed the manuscript concerning their areas. It is sincerely hoped that *Landfalls of Paradise* will strengthen the bonds of friendship between their countries and the cruising yachtsman.

Foreword

You are about to set sail on the largest of oceans, the Pacific, seen for the first time by European eyes in 1513. At that time Vasco Nunez de Balboa had arrived at the western side of the Panamanian Isthmus and, because the shoreline runs east and west at this point, Balboa called the waters Mar del Sur or, South Seas, to differentiate them from the Caribbean to the north which he termed the North Sea. While the term North Sea for the Caribbean has disappeared from common use, it is still common, especially in a romantic sense, to refer to the tropics and near-tropics of the Pacific as the South Seas.

Inasmuch as cruising is a return to romance, anyone contemplating a cruise to the South Seas could be visiting any of the islands of the Pacific Basin including Polynesia, Melanesia, Micronesia, or the islands of the eastern and western Pacific. In fact, this is all Oceania, a term often used by geographers to describe collectively the islands of the Pacific. Whatever you choose to call it, there awaits a touch of romantic adventure for the cruising sailor.

Cruising is an experience in sailing new seas, seeing new lands, and meeting new people. It can be done with ignorance and fortitude as the sailors of old, or it can be planned to make it the happy adventure of a lifetime. Considering your investment in time, boat, and supplies, you should settle for nothing less than the best knowledge of what is ahead. There is nothing sadder than a broken voyage and an able boat put on the block for lack of proper planning.

Landfalls of Paradise has assembled the most current information on the countries of the Pacific Basin and given procedures for planning passages, making entry into those countries, conducting cruising business ashore, and feeling at home in a foreign port. With it you can prepare yourself and your crew for the delights of cruising the vast Pacific Ocean.

You will recognize many familiar ports of call such as Honolulu, Papeete, Pago Pago, Suva, and Auckland. But you will also find many more equally interesting places such as Raivavae, Apia, Funafuti, Noumea, and Majuro. Don't be constrained to places that your friends have visited — get off the beaten path and introduce yourself to unspoiled and uncrowded parts of the Pacific. There are more than 10,000 islands in the Pacific so you can be a modern day Captain Cook and explore new places. The only difference is that you have *Landfalls of Paradise* to make it easier.

The author has made every attempt to keep the facts of the Pacific up-to-date as the years of manuscript preparation went by so that on publication it was correct. However, there are continuing social and political changes taking place throughout the Pacific, some of which could effect the information contained herein. One must expect these changes as the peoples of the Pacific accept the challenge of the 20th Century. So take this book for what it is, a planning guide, and add your own common sense as you enter the domain of the friendliest people on earth.

May your winds be fair and your seas smooth!

Earl R. Hinz, WD6 EYJ
Yacht Horizon
1980

Table of Contents

ACKNOWLEDGEMENTS		5
FOREWORD		6
YOUR PACIFIC OCEAN	Chapter 1	13
ROCKS AND SHOALS	Chapter 2	17
PACIFIC WEATHER	Chapter 3	23
PASSAGE PLANNING	Chapter 4	33
PART I. ISLANDS OF POLYNESIA		47
HAWAII	Chapter 5	51
FRENCH POLYNESIA	Chapter 6	75
MARQUESAS ISLANDS	Chapter 6-A	79
TUAMOTU ARCHIPELAGO	Chapter 6-B	88
SOCIETY ISLANDS	Chapter 6-C	95
AUSTRAL ISLANDS	Chapter 6-D	105
EASTER ISLAND	Chapter 7	111
PITCAIRN ISLAND	Chapter 8	116
COOK ISLANDS	Chapter 9	121
SAMOA ISLANDS	Chapter 10	131
AMERICAN SAMOA	Chapter 10-A	135
WESTERN SAMOA	Chapter 10-B	143
TOKELAU ISLANDS	Chapter 11	149
TONGA	Chapter 12	153
TUVALU	Chapter 13	165
NIUE	Chapter 14	170
NEW ZEALAND	Chapter 15	173
KERMADEC ISLANDS	Chapter 16	195

PART II. ISLANDS OF MELANESIA   197

FIJI	Chapter 17	199
WALLIS & FUTUNA ISLANDS	Chapter 18	213
PAPUA NEW GUINEA	Chapter 19	219
SOLOMON ISLANDS	Chapter 20	235
NEW CALEDONIA	Chapter 21	245
NEW HEBRIDES	Chapter 22	257

PART III. ISLANDS OF MICRONESIA   265

MARIANA ISLANDS CHAIN	Chapter 23	267
GUAM	Chapter 23-A	271
COMMONWEALTH OF THE NORTHERN MARIANA ISLANDS	Chapter 23-B	279
TRUST TERRITORY OF THE PACIFIC ISLANDS	Chapter 24	283
MARSHALL DISTRICT	Chapter 24-A	295
KOSRAE DISTRICT	Chapter 24-B	303
PONAPE DISTRICT	Chapter 24-C	307
TRUK DISTRICT	Chapter 24-D	315
YAP DISTRICT	Chapter 24-E	321
PALAU DISTRICT	Chapter 24-F	331
KIRIBATI	Chapter 25	337
REPUBLIC OF NAURU	Chapter 26	345

PART IV. ISLANDS OF THE EASTERN PACIFIC   349

GALAPAGOS ISLANDS	Chapter 27	351

APPENDICES   361

TRI-LANGUAGE DICTIONARY FOR PORT ENTRY	Appendix A	362
GLOSSARY OF CRUISING WORDS	Appendix B	365
MASTERING THE THREE Rs AT SEA	Appendix C	367
AMATEUR RADIO OPERATION IN FOREIGN WATERS	Appendix D	371
CHARTER BOATS IN THE PACIFIC	Appendix E	373

INDEX   381

Chart Index

Introduction

Cultures and Time Zones of Oceania 14
Tropical Cyclone Areas 27
Oceania 32
Wind and Pressure Patterns 35
Sample Cruising Tracks for the Pacific 38
Major Pacific Shipping Routes 40
Air Routes Over the Pacific 42

Part I

Hawaiian Islands — East End 50
Hilo Bay 66
Kahului Harbor 68
Honolulu Harbors 69
Nawiliwili Harbor 70
French Polynesia 74
Marquesas Islands 80
Nuku Hiva Island 83
Hiva Oa Island 84
Tuamotu Archipelago — West End 86
Tuamotu Archipelago — East End 87
Avatoru, Rangiroa 94
Tiputa, Rangiroa 94
Rotoava, Fakarava 94
Society Islands 96
Papeete Harbor 100
Bora Bora Island 101
Tubuai Island 106
Raivavae Island 108
Easter Island 110
Pitcairn Island 117
Cook Islands 122
Avatiu and Avarua Harbors 129
Samoa Islands 133
Pago Pago Harbor 134
Apia Harbor 142
Tokelau Islands 149
Nukunonu Atoll 151
Tonga Islands 154
Nuku'alofa Harbor 161
Vava'u Islands 163
Tuvalu Islands 166
Funafuti Atoll 168
Niue Island 170
New Zealand 174
Bay of Islands 188
Whangarei Harbor 189
Auckland Harbor 191
Raoul Island 194

Part II

Fiji Islands 200
Suva Harbor 209
Lautoka Harbor 210
Levuka Harbor 211
Wallis and Horne Islands 214
Wallis Islands 216
Papua New Guinea 218
Port Moresby 229
Rabaul Harbors 231
Kavieng Harbor 232
Solomon Islands 234
Honiara Harbor 240
Ndende Island 242
Gizo Island 243
New Caledonia 246
Noumea Harbor 249
New Hebrides Islands 256
Santo/Luganville Bay 261
Vila Harbor 262

Part III

Mariana Islands 268
Apra Harbor 272
Saipan Harbor 278
Trust Territory of the Pacific Islands 284
Marshall Islands 294
Majuro Atoll — East End 300
Kosrae Island 302
Lele Harbor 304
Senyavin Islands 309
Ponape Harbor 310
Truk Islands 314
Moen Island 317
Yap Islands 322
Tomil Harbor 328
Palau Islands 330
Port of Palau 334
Kiribati 338
Tarawa Atoll 342
Banaba Island 342
Nauru Island 344

Part IV

Galapagos Islands 352
Wreck Bay 356
Academy Bay 358

Chart Legend

Chart Code	Source
BA	British Admiralty, Hydrographer of the Navy, London
FR	French, Service Hydrographique et Oceanographique de la Marine, Paris
NZ	New Zealand, Hydrographic Office, Royal New Zealand Navy, Auckland
US	United States, Defense Mapping Agency, Hydrographic Center, Washington

 Land area

Reef line

Edge of drying land

Approximate boundary between island groups

Roads

Route into harbor

Possible pass through reef

Ferry route

Anchorage

Port of Entry

Other cities, villages or ports

Mountain peak (height in feet)

Key building

True North

Photo Credits

Chapter 1

YOUR PACIFIC OCEAN

The Pacific Ocean offers the cruising yachtsman unparalleled advantages in space, exotic ports of call, weather, and hospitable peoples. It is the largest ocean of the world covering 64 million square miles and this does not include another 6 million square miles of adjoining seas. At the equator the Pacific Ocean measures 11,000 miles east to west and it is over 9,000 miles north to south. Approximately 30 million square miles of it lies between the Tropics of Cancer and Capricorn wherein lie the majority of all islands of the Pacific (New Zealand is a notable exception).

As a whole, the Pacific Ocean has more islands in it than all of the rest of the oceans and seas together. On a global scale the Pacific Ocean and adjoining seas cover about one-third of the earth's surface which is more area than all of the land masses of the world combined.

The Pacific Ocean is rimmed with mountains and, indeed, many of its islands are mountains or mountain ranges rising up in some cases, to 30,000 or more feet from the ocean floor. Many of the mountains on the rim as well as in the basin itself are active volcanoes providing a contemporary view of how land masses are formed. The island of Hawaii is probably the best known active volcano site in the Pacific but Falcon Island in the Tonga group may be the most intriguing. Falcon Island appears and disappears on the ocean surface as volcanic activity rises and subsides.

Earthquakes are another feature of Pacific geology occuring frequently in the mountains rimming the basin and, occasionally, in the islands of the Western Pacific. Their importance to the mariner concerns the generation of tsunamis — rapidly moving waves that traverse the Pacific and can raise havoc with shorelines and harbors. Fortunately, there is a tsunami warning system spanning the entire Pacific which alerts countries to the occurrence of an earthquake and the possible generation of a tsunami.

Magellan was the first European to cross the Pacific Ocean in his circumnavigation of the world in the years 1519 to 1522. It was he who named it "Pacifico" because of its calm nature. The Pacific also has a violent face with seasonal hurricanes off Mexico and in the southwest as well as typhoons in its western waters. South of latitude 40°S are the Roaring Forties where westerly gales almost never stop and sailing ships of yore made their record runs.

But the cruising yachtsman can avoid the cold and gales of the higher latitudes and the seasonal tropical storms at sea by proper scheduling of his passages. In return he gets to enjoy the balmy weather of the tropics with all the pleasures of steady tradewinds and balmy temperatures that invite rain-shower bathing.

In the Pacific is also found the International Date Line which regulates the dates of the world. Nominally it follows the 180th meridian and separates the eastern and western hemispheres of the world by definition. The 24-hour time change as your boat crosses the date line is certain to test the skill of your navigation. You will especially enjoy your visit to Tonga whose local time is 13 hours fast on Greenwich, giving it the distinction of being where "time begins".

Early Migrations

Pacific history is difficult to trace because the original inhabitants had no written language and accounts of their early history passed on by word of mouth have become colored by romanticism. But this should not offend your historical sense for cruising itself is a romantic endeavor quite compatible with the history of the Pacific people.

The generally accepted migration routes of the ancient peoples started from southeast Asia about 6,000 years ago and settled New Guinea, the Solomons, New Hebrides, New Caledonia, and the Fiji Islands. This region later became known as Melanesia, meaning "black islands" since the peoples were of negroid descent. The region settled was composed predominantly of high volcanic islands of great fertility. Rainfall was abundant and the atmosphere hot and humid. It was there that their migration seems to have stopped although they were known to have visited both the Samoas and Tonga in later years. Possibly the changing character of the islands and the weather further to the east deterred them from traveling any further.

Meanwhile a second migration had started north of the equator with the migrants coming from Indonesia and the Philippines. They settled in the region now called Micronesia which means "small islands". Generally speaking, the Micronesians stayed close to home although they were known to be great navigators. Their homes became the small volcanic islands and atolls of the Mariana, Caroline, Marshall and Gilbert groups.

Greatest of all navigators were the Polynesians who sailed by the stars and winds and interpreted wave patterns and other natural signs to tell them of the presence of islands. Lightest in skin color of all the Pacific islanders, their first homes were in Samoa and Tonga, probably 3000 years ago, but how they arrived there is open to question. It is not certain what prompted them to continue wandering, possibly it was overpopulation or an innate sense of adventure such as is also present in the cruising yachtsman. At any rate, they sailed north to pop-

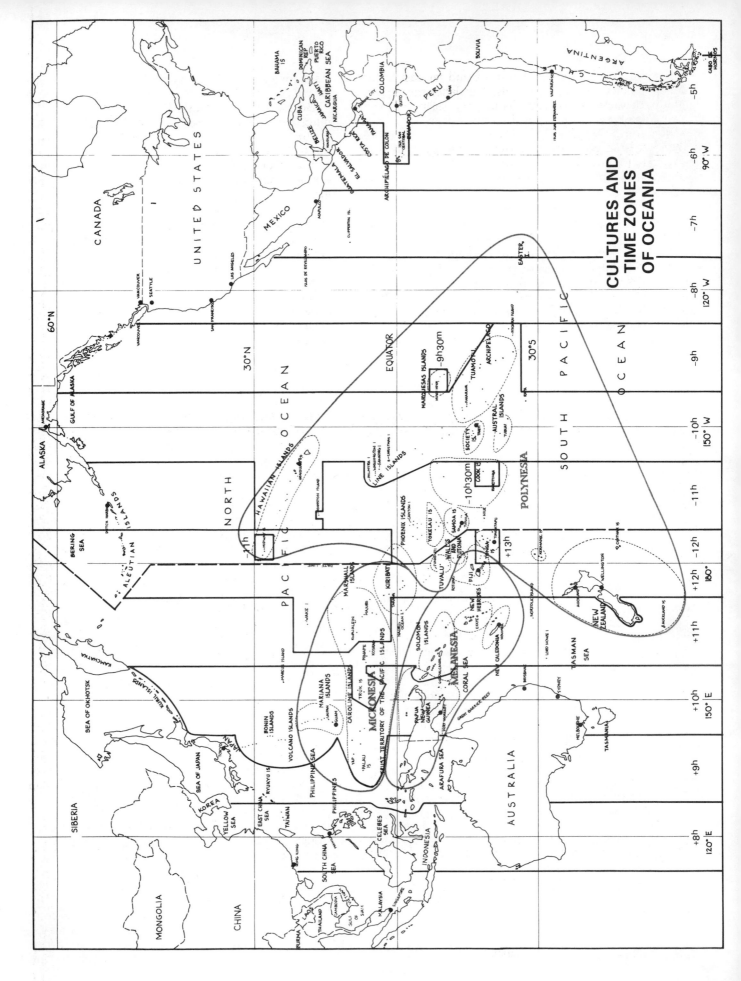

CULTURES AND TIME ZONES OF OCEANIA

14

ulate the Tokelau and Tuvalu atolls and far east to the mountainous Marquesas Islands. This latter trip against the tradewinds certainly speaks for their sailing ability.

Explorations and migrations were believed to have taken place before 500 AD from the Marquesas to all points of the compass — Hawaii to the north, Easter Island to the east, Tahiti to the south, and New Zealand to the (south)west. The boldness and ability of these ancient navigators is to be admired.

After the year 1000 AD, native exploration gave way to cultural and political development of the island societies as they were eventually discovered by the European explorers. Polynesia, in particular, developed very sophisticated tropical civilizations in Hawaii, Tahiti, and New Zealand as well as many of the other islands. Although these societies were well suited to the climate and resources of the area, they were not prepared to deal with the overwhelming and ruthless invasion of their peaceful waters by the European explorers.

European Encroachment

First to arrive were the Portuguese and Spaniards who dominated Pacific exploration in the 16th century. The Spice Islands of the East Indies attracted the Portuguese to the western fringes of the Pacific via Cape of Good Hope. But it was the Spanish who having seen the wealth of Central and South America, set the stage for Pacific exploration from the east. From the time Magellan (a Portuguese) found his way through the straits at the tip of South America and crossed to the Philippines, the mighty Pacific became crisscrossed with European explorers. The Spanish and Portuguese were soon followed by the Dutch, French and English. Most notable of the latter was James Cook whose thorough and objective explorations from 1768 to 1780 opened the way for the developers and rapists of the Pacific islands.

England, France, Spain, and later America sought riches and new colonies to support their ambitious political growth back home and this was done at the expense of the Pacific islanders. Whaling, the sandlewood trade, and black pearling were pursued to their demise. Islanders were "contracted" for guano mining labor on islands as far away as the coast of South America never to return home. This infamous form of slavery was called "blackbirding". European diseases decimated native populations who had no natural immunity to foreign disease. Finally, the conservative missionary influence spelled the end of native culture which was centered on religion.

In the late 1800s the major world powers consolidated their Pacific colonies annexing all unclaimed island groups. At the end of the Spanish-American War, the Philippines and Guam were ceded to the United States who also annexed Hawaii. Remaining Spanish possessions were sold to Germany who also acquired Samoa. But then came World War I and German colonies in the Pacific were taken over by the Allies. Australia and New Zealand became governors of much of the Southwest Pacific but, more important, a quiet ally, Japan, took over the Caroline, Mariana, and Marshall Islands setting the stage for aggressive expansion which was to trigger World War II.

Between the two World Wars the Pacific was pretty much forgotten except by the powers who were already in control. Japan quietly began arming the island of Truk in the Carolines in anticipation of military expansion while all the other powers simply governed the native peoples with little purpose other than to provide a good living for the colonial governors.

On December 7th, 1941, the Pacific exploded into an inferno which was to last for almost four years. For the first time in history communications were sufficiently well developed so that the entire world could follow the war in any part of the world and the Pacific became instantly known to everyone. It was no longer a remote place seen only by adventurers, for now millions of servicemen were to become familiar with islands, atolls, native peoples, and the intoxicating grandeur of tropical geography. They may not have been able to appreciate it while in uniform but the spell of the tropics was indelibly etched in their minds.

The war carried on, and the Japanese advanced south to New Guinea and the Solomon Islands. But the industrial might and resources of the United States and its Pacific allies turned the tables in 1944 and started an island-hopping counter-offensive that took them right to Tokyo in 1945 for the signing of the treaty that capped the Pacific war cauldron.

But things were never the same. For all of the islands of the Pacific had been touched by modern technology and politics and the islanders felt the need to advance with the rest of the world.

Postwar political developments saw Britain shedding herself of Pacific responsibilities in order to recover from the pounding that she took from Germany in the war. Australia and New Zealand again became the caretakers of many of the islands while independence moves gestated. All of the former Japanese possessions were mandated to the United States to become the Trust Territory of the Pacific Islands.

The Pacific has not been without turmoil since the end of World War II but it has been primarily political as island groups have sought to set up their independent governments. While bloodshed seemed to be the way to freedom for other parts of the world, the Pacific islanders took a more patient viewpoint in order to gain their goals without destroying people, resources, or the goodwill of the former landlords which was needed to help in the economic transition from colony to independent nation. It has been slow but steady and, when the peoples of the Trust Territory make up their minds by 1981 what form of independent governments they want, most of the Pacific island groups will have become self-governing. The cycle of political status from independence to colonies to independence will have become complete.

The Cruising Scene

But there is a new look in the Pacific which has nothing to do with politics but international goodwill. It is the free-roaming cruising yacht that is finding its way to atolls and islands spreading person to person goodwill in an informal way which cannot be duplicated at the highest level of diplomacy. Cruising yachts are a phenomenon, manned by people from all walks of life bonded together by a yen for seeing the beautiful Pacific and meeting new neighbors in the world.

It all started in 1898 when Joshua Slocum returned from his epic three year single-handed sail around the world. Slocum was no adventurer but an able seaman who proved that a small boat properly handled could sail the oceans of the world in safety. He was no diplomat in striped trousers but a common and friendly individual who was welcomed by island people for what he was and not for who he represented. Monetary gain was not his objective although he probably would have welcomed some additional funds to help outfit his *Spray* and keep her shipshape. Slocum was the first yachtie and he set standards of seamanship, navigation, and goodwill which are still examples today.

Others followed in his wake, Harry Pidgeon in *Islander*, Francis Chichester in *Gypsy Moth*, Robin Knox-Johnson in *Suhaili* who was the first to circumnavigate non-stop. But of all the singlehanders, none captured the heart of the world as much as Robin Lee Graham who started out at the age of 16 and circumnavigated the world alone in *Dove*.

Cruising has gone beyond the age of stunts and it is now a family affair. Eric and Susan Hiscock have probably done more than any other persons to make cruising a way of life for people. Their circumnavigations in *Wanderers III and IV* have set the stage for the cruising families of today.

There have been many other yachties who have sailed the Pacific Ocean. You have only to visit your nearest library to get all the particulars in books of dreams fulfilled.

Bill Robinson in *Varua*, Miles and Beryl Smeeton in *Tzu Hang*, and Hal and Margaret Roth in *Whisper*, Irving and Electa Johnson in *Yankee*, and a host of others in recent years.

With better boats, charts, and more knowledge, yachties are putting to sea all over the world and heading for the Pacific islands. The numbers are getting to be impressive. In 1975 there were 200 yachts who entered the territorial waters of French Polynesia. In 1976 the number had grown to 400. At one point in May, 1976, there were 56 overseas yachts lined up along the quay in Papeete. French Polynesia is the unquestioned leader in popularity for cruising yachts but all islands of the Pacific are seeing an increase. Between 1971 and 1976 the numbers of yachts visiting America Samoa jumped from 38 to 85.

This popularity is having the expected effect on the host islands. With limited facilities they are now charging for some services and entry formalities are tightening up. But that should not deter serious yachties, for it is only happening at a few ports of call. Honolulu, Papeete, and Rarotonga have all become more formalized, but there are dozens of other places to go for a true native welcome even in those groups.

Part of this change has been forced on the cruising boats by past excesses in the days of the beachcombers who dropped in and stayed. It carried on into the days of the hippies who were freeloaders on an economy that was barely at the subsistence level. While the Pacific islanders are probably the most hospitable of any people, even they cannot continue to host the swelling numbers of yachts at the more popular ports of call.

As the years go by we are seeing more dignity in the cruising yachts led by a rise in family groups. Hopefully, these yachties with a greater sense of responsibility will improve the image of the cruising yachtsman.

Chapter 2

ROCKS AND SHOALS
The Business End of Cruising

While a cruise in the Pacific may sound very carefree and adventurous, the fact is that much of the red tape and responsibilities dreamed up by government bureaucrats will follow you throughout your cruise. Except for the uninhabited islands of the Pacific, you will have to formally enter every country that you visit and be treated as a foreigner and a tourist. Everything you bring in on your boat and the boat itself, will be under customs regulations of the host country and must be accounted for on entering and again on departure. You are inspected much more closely than your compatriots who arrive by air on one of those sterile tour packages for you have the better means to smuggle and adversely influence the native population.

Everyone has read of the despoliation of the South Seas by the European and American whalers, traders, and missionaries in years past. This was all done by sea and the countries evolved protective measures against it happening again by enacting laws and procedures to maintain control of foreigners who arrive by ship. Even though you have only a boat and not a ship, you fall under the same ancient maritime rules of entry and must pay the price in observing official procedures.

You may feel incensed over this lack of kindness to visitors who bring goodwill and money into a retarded island economy, but there have been yachties in recent years with just as much disregard for local property and customs as the sailors of old. Stealing by living off the land, growing marijuana and peddling it to the natives, selling liquor to people who neither have the money for it nor the capacity to handle it discreetly, and taking work away from the locals in the interest of building up the cruising kitty. You may think some of these petty, which they are in the sophisticated, hardened society from which you are escaping. But to the innocent and sheltered native they are real threats to his well-being and it is for this reason that each island government has a means for controlling visitors to its shores.

Fortunately, most of the countries of the Pacific still live close to the sea and have a great interest in the yachtsman who, if he abides by local laws and customs, is welcomed into their midst. It's all a matter of respecting foreign sovereignty and protocol. Do it right and you will enjoy every landfall in Paradise.

Pre-cruise Paperwork

It starts with a passport — that all-important document for world travel that identifies who you are and your country of origin. Usually it is issued for a period of five years and is renewable unless revoked for criminal cause. Even if you are traveling as a family group, get separate passports for each member of the family. You will sometime want the flexibility of going different ways for which you will need separate passports. Be sure that you get each passport stamped and/or signed when you enter and leave a country for it not only produces interesting reading but the next country's Immigration officer will want to know from whence you came.

When a passport gets within six months of its expiration date you had better take quick action to get it renewed. Many countries will not process your entry if there is less than six months of valid time on your passport. Or they may give you only a 30 day visitors permit.

The other important paper for a yachtie to have is the "yellow card" health record issued by the World Health Organization and recognized by all countries. In it is your personal record of vaccinations and other immunizations which you have had. That card, together with your passport telling what country you have last visited, is the primary basis for granting pratique.

All countries have immigration regulations defining the length of stay for foreigners on their shores. This varies from as little as two weeks up to years. Generally, you can obtain a limited entry permit after arrival on foreign shores and this may be enough time for a brief visit to a small island. But, if you want to enjoy a languorous stay in French Polynesia, New Zealand, the Trust Territory, or Hawaii, you had better apply for a visa ahead of time. A visa is an endorsement made on your passport by proper authorities of the country you wish to visit and it denotes that you have been examined and given approval to make the visit. You can obtain this *before* entering the country by contacting an embassy or consulate of that country. It may take from weeks to months, so allow adequate time.

One problem with cruising is that you do not have a firm travel schedule so it is difficult to fill out a specific date for arrival. While your visa will specify a desired length of stay, the arrival date should be left as general as possible.

You can apply for visas before you leave your home country but that reduces the flexibility of cruising. It is better to route yourself through a second country along the way that has a consul or embassy for the country you desire to visit and then you can better ascertain when you will arrive.

Most cruising people are not intending to sever their ties with the folks back home and mail becomes a very important factor in a cruise, particularly if the younger crew members are learning their three R's at sea. Mail service is not dependable to every country of the Pacific so choose as your next landfall a country that has good mail connections with your home country and let your correspondents know when you will be there. It is best to have mail sent to General Delivery or Poste Restante since harbor masters usually take little responsibility for yachties' mail other than to collect it in a shoebox.

To avoid confusing your correspondents too much, you may prefer to have all your mail sent to a friend or relative in your home country who will then forward it to you per your destination plan. Correspondence schools are the exception. They are used to foreign mailings and will shorten the time en route if you have them mail directly to your next destination.

Travel funds are getting to be more of a problem as countries of the Pacific increase their demands for proof of financial responsibility. Travelers checks are the best way to carry your money since they are accepted everywhere and usually command a better rate of exchange than money. They should be mostly in small denominations. Credit cards have limited application throughout the Pacific islands but are useful in the more sophisticated areas such as Papeete, Hawaii and New Zealand. American Express and Visa cards seem to be the most useful at this time.

For larger sums of money which you will need in places like French Polynesia where you have to show the equivalent of thousands of dollars as a condition of entry besides having a visa, you will want to consider bank drafts on your home bank. There is a certain overhead price you pay in this kind of operation because each exchange of money into a different currency will cost you a fee. Try to keep the money in one currency at all times and avoid the buying and selling losses.

Cruising Business En Route

There is a certain protocol in entering a foreign country by yacht which should be rigorously followed. Flaunting a host country's laws or customs is a good way to get a request to leave early and spoil the opportunities for yachties following in your wake.

Territorial limits of island countries are not well defined and may extend from 12 to 200 miles offshore at their discretion. Upon entering their waters, immediately hoist a courtesy ensign of their country on your starboard spreader. It should measure one-half the size of your national ensign which, traditionally, is one inch of fly for every foot of overall length of the boat. Your own national ensign should likewise be flown in foreign territorial waters.

When you arrive at your first Port of Entry in a new country, hoist the yellow Q flag just under the country's courtesy ensign. Do this whether that particular country boards vessels for entry clearance or you go ashore for the formalities. As soon as you are given pratique, lower the Q flag but keep the courtesy ensign flying day and night while in foreign waters. Your own national ensign should be lowered at night if you are at anchor or moored.

The first entry formality that takes place is an inspection of your passport and health card to determine if you have been in a country currently having a communicable disease problem. If the Health officer believes your crew and vessel to be free of any disease, he will grant you pratique and then Customs, Immigration, and Agriculture officers take over. You will need certain documents for this

H.—Q. 5

DEPARTMENT OF HEALTH

CERTIFICATE OF PRATIQUE
Under Section 107 of the Health Act 1956

*Airport/Port of _____ URUA _____

I hereby certify that the *ship/aircraft " _____ HORIZON _____ "

_____ ER HINZ _____, *Captain/Master has this day been duly granted pratique.
Given under my hand, at _____ 11-30 _____ a.m. [p.m.], this _____ 14th _____
day of _____ OCTOBER _____ 19 75

_____
Port Health Officer.

NOTE—This Certificate shall cease to have effect if for any reason the ship or aircraft again becomes liable to quarantine while in New Zealand waters.

60 pads/11/68—56343 P   *Strike out that which does not apply.

POLYNESIE FRANCAISE
SERVICE des DOUANES
-=-=-

N°

YACHTS de PLAISANCE
-=-=-=-

DECLARATION en DOUANES
-=-=-

NOM ....*HORIZON*...... Nationalité .....*USA*......

Port d'attache *LOS ANGELES* Propriétaire (capitaine) *EARL R. HINZ*

CALIFORNIA

Jauge brute ....*17*...... Jauge nette .....*15*......

Port de Provenance ...*PAPEETE*... Port de destination ...*HILO, HAWAII*...

VIA RANGIROA AND AHE

-=-=-=-=-

PROVISIONS de BORD (Stores List)
-=-=-=-=-

TWO MONTHS STORES

ARMES et MUNITIONS détenues à bord

NIL

PACOTILLES (Search List)
-=-=-=-

A débarquer .... En transit ....
-=-=-=-

3 CAMERA
1 CASSETTE PLAYER
1 CASSETTE RECORDER
1 TYPEWRITER
1 SEWING MACHINE
-=-=-

PLANTES *NIL* ANIMAUX - OISEAUX
NIL
-=-=-

MATERIEL du BORD - EQUIPEMENT

MARCHANDISES (débarquées
(embarquées

3 COMPASS 1 CLOCK
2 SEXTANTS 1 DINGHY
1 RADIO (RECEIVE)
1 BINOCULAR 1 LIFE RAFT
1 BAROMETER
1 CHRONOMETER

Je soussigné ...*EARL R. HINZ*... certifie la véracité des déclarations ci-dessus.

PAPEETE, le *22 MAY 1976*

Signature

process so you may as well get them ready ahead of the actual clearance proceedings. These documents are often referred to collectively as the ship's papers and they include:

Your boat registration or documentation papers
Passports
WHO health cards
Crew list
The outward bound clearance from the previous port visited

Only one of these papers is prepared by you and that is the crew list. Type or neatly print it in four copies. The officials will take all four and stamp and sign them and usually give back one for your records.

In addition to the ship's papers is the matter of financial responsibility. Most countries require that all crew members have onward airline tickets to get them out of the country in case they leave the yacht for any reason. The best ticket is one back to the country that issued the passport. The captain should see to it that each crew member has such a ticket and it should be kept in his possession if there is any question about crew reliability. Occasionally the owners of the boat will also need onward tickets but that varies. The owners should have full papers to show that they are in fact the owners of the boat. That, plus a boat in good condition and money to sustain them during the stay is usually enough. Family members who are not bona fide owners of the boat are treated as crew members.

The Customs officer will have you prepare a Customs Declaration listing stores, firearms and ammunition, personal equipment, ship's equipment, plants and animals. From this and a search of the boat, he will determine whether you are carrying contraband or if you are in the business of importing.

The Agriculture inspector will examine your fresh food supplies and determine what you can retain and what must be destroyed to prevent the possible introduction of a disease to the host country.

Immigration is sometimes handled on board by the Customs officer but more often you will have to go ashore to present your visa or request a temporary visitors permit. If you go ashore, bring the ship's papers plus any documents which the Health, Customs and Agriculture officials may have given you.

After clearing in with the proper officials, it is incumbent on the skipper to pay a visit to the local island chief if there is one. This initial visit should be brief and it is a courtesy to the chief and will open many doors of cultural exchange during your visit.

Once officially cleared into the country, be certain that your boat is properly moored. The Harbor Master, if there is one, will assign you a place in the harbor for the duration of your stay. If there is no Harbor Master, ask a responsible person where you can tie up or moor out of the way of shipping which may come and go on irregular schedules. Don't block local maritime operations. It would not only be rude but if you value your boat you won't argue with steel-hulled copra schooners for dock space.

So what happens when you get ready to leave? Start by

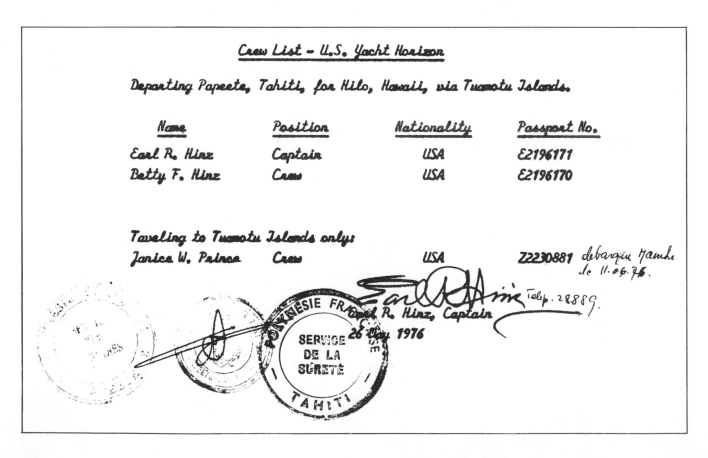

PORT OF NUKU'ALOFA, TONGA.

THIS is to certify that _EARL R. HINZ_

Master or Commander of the _YACHT HORIZON_

burthen _15_ registered tons (net) navigated with

_3_ men, _AMERICAN_ property, and bound for _RUSSELL, NEW ZEALAND_

having on board Stores as per Stores List

Cargo as per Manifest _— NIL_

Passengers as per Passenger List _— 0_

Crew as per Crew List _— 2_

has here entered and cleared his

said vessel according to law.

Given under my hand, at the Custom House, at the Port of Nuku'alofa, in the Kingdom of Tonga, this _FIFTH_ day of _OCTOBER_ nineteen hundred and _SEVENTY FIVE_.

QUEEN SALOTE WHARF
NUKU'ALOFA TONGA
−5 OCT 1975
BOARDING OFFICER
H.M. CUSTOMS

Collector of Customs.

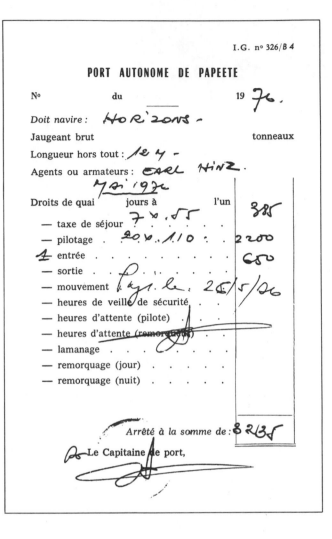

I.G. nº 326/B 4

PORT AUTONOME DE PAPEETE

Nº   du _____   19 *76.*

Doit navire : *HORIZONS -*

Jaugeant brut   tonneaux

Longueur hors tout : *124 -*

Agents ou armateurs : *EARL HINZ.*

MAI 1976

Droits de quai   jours à   l'un

— taxe de séjour   *7 x .55*   *385*

— pilotage .   *20 x .110 :   2200*

1 entrée *650*

— sortie . . . . .

— mouvement   *Payé le 26/5/76*

— heures de veille de sécurité . .

— heures d'attente (pilote) . .

— heures d'attente (remorqueur)

— lamanage . . . .

— remorquage (jour) . . . . .

— remorquage (nuit) . . . . .

Arrêté à la somme de : *8235*

Le Capitaine de port,

informing the Harbor Master who will ascertain if you owe any bills around town including wharfage or other harbor costs. Immigration will give you a clearance form and stamp your passport for the day of leaving. Your final stop is Customs where you will get an outward bound clearance (zarpe) needed for entry to your next port of call. Be certain that you get such a document as some countries will refuse entry unless you have properly cleared from your previous port of call. You are then ready to go. If for any reason you are delayed, stay on your boat and notify Customs. Otherwise you may be required to enter the country once again.

Skipper's Responsibilities

Your boat may be only a fraction of the size of an ocean liner, but you, as skipper, will have many of the same administrative responsibilities as the captain of a 30,000 ton cruise ship. In a foreign port you are responsible for your boat and crew. Failure to observe local law or regulations or getting in trouble with the local people could result in a request to leave, a fine, or worse, the confiscation of your boat.

Countries are insisting on adequate funds to sustain the crew while the boat is visiting so that living off the local people doesn't get to be a habit. Boat condition will also be important because there are already enough boats cluttering the reefs of the islands due to poor navigation without having them sink in the harbor.

The appearance of you and your crew is very important in your acceptance by the host country. Neither hippies nor nudies are welcome in most places. It is a putdown to the host country to have an ill-kept boat or a sloppy personal appearance. The formalities of entry and your acceptance by the local people will be greatly enhanced by neat appearance and proper courtesy. Yachting is informal in nature but in a foreign land a certain amount of dignity is required to maintain the goodwill needed by the cruising fraternity.

One Last Word

The level of your cruising satisfaction depends on how much you learn before you start. You have to say to yourself that I am going to do it, I am going to do it right, and I, therefore, will succeed. In other words, psych yourself up for success. You will no longer be a member of a protective society with food stores on the corner, fire and police protection a telephone call away, repairmen available to fix anything that goes wrong with the material wonders of the 20th Century, lawyers to keep you out of legal troubles, and the world's finest medical help to keep your body and soul together. You are going to leave all of that behind and go on your own to foreign lands where people don't speak your language and they, more often than not, live in a subsistence economy with few, if any, benefits of modern technology. And you are going to do all of that with a wind-propelled machine that was given up as a useful form of global transportation three-quarters of a century ago!

Yes, you will do it for that is what cruising is all about.

Chapter 3
PACIFIC WEATHER

Except for a few hardy adventurers who sail around the Horn and other colorful but cold places, most cruising yachtsmen seek the milder climates of the lower latitudes. Cruising is supposed to be fun and weather can make a big difference in how much fun you can have. But weather can be contradictory and we find that even the pleasantness of the tropics is occasionally shattered by the violence of hurricanes. Fortunately, seasonable weather patterns on the average are repeatable so that a cruise can be planned to take advantage of good winds yet avoiding the majority of the storms. While one can hope to avoid tropical storms by careful planning, you will always be faced with the possibility of gale force winds at any season, so be prepared for them.

In cruising, wind is our motive power and without it we would never leave home. But with it we can cruise the width and breadth of the vast Pacific Ocean — provided that we understand the vagaries of the wind. Winds are caused by the earth's rotation and the heating and cooling of the land, sea, and air masses. On the grand scale these effects are repetitive and produce an understandable pattern of surface winds. These surface winds are shown schematically in the diagram along with latitude variations of atmospheric pressure. .

Doldrums

The doldrums, also known as the equatorial trough or intertropical convergence zone (ICZ), is an area of low pressure situated between the tradewinds of the two hemispheres. The width of the doldrums varies daily and seasonally but average about 2½ degrees of latitude in width.

The doldrums remain north of the equator in longitudes east of 160° West. To the west of 160° West their position varies seasonally being south of the equator between December and April and north between June and October. In the western Pacific east of 150° East longitude, however, they are virtually non-existent during the northern hemisphere summer.

The weather of the doldrums ranges from light variable winds and often calms to squalls, heavy showers, and thunderstorms. West of 130° West the frequency of calms and variable winds is considerably less than over the waters between Central America and 130° West. The type of weather varies daily and seasonally and at times a boat may cross the doldrums and experience fine weather while another time there may be continuous squalls and thunderstorms. Generally, the weather in the doldrums is at its worst when the trades are strongest and where they meet at the greatest angle. This is essentially the eastern Pacific area.

During the southern hemisphere summer, the equatorial trough lies south of the equator between about December and April, reaching its southernmost position in February. The seasonal movement of the trough in the western South Pacific is large and so is its day-to-day movement in the vicinity of northern Australia and New Guinea. The width of the trough averages about 150 miles but may be anywhere from 50 to 300 miles wide. The weather is similar to the doldrums of the northern hemisphere but may be more severe due to the wider angle of the meeting southeast trades and the northwest monsoons.

Northeast Tradewinds

The northeast trades blow on the equatorial side of the large clockwise circulation of the Pacific Ocean high pressure area known as the Pacific high. The Pacific high lies farther north and is somewhat more intense in summer than in the winter. In summer the northeast trades blow as far west as 150° East and between the doldrums and about 32° North. West of 150° East, the northeast trades give way to the southwest monsoon. The northeast trades are remarkably persistent and steady over large areas of the ocean. Along the North American coast they are mainly northerly or, possibly, northwesterly. Further to the west and towards the doldrums, they are mainly easterly in the summer months.

The strength of the northeast trades averages Force 3 to 4 but occasionally freshens to Force 5 or 6. Less than 10-percent of the time will they reach Force 7.

Along the Mexican coast in the vicinity of the Gulf of Tehuantepec, north winds are particularly strong in the winter months from October to April, oftentimes reaching Force 8. The gales which may be felt 100 miles to sea may last from several hours to several days and raise a short high sea. There is less than one day per month of such winds from May to September. These are known as the Tehuantepecers. Apart from squalls, winds of this strength are unlikely within about 600 miles of the equator.

The typical weather of the trade wind belt is fair, with scattered showers, and skies half covered by small cumulus clouds known as tradewind clouds. At times the trade becomes unsteady, being interrupted by a day or two of unsettled showery weather with occasional squalls. In the northeast part of the belt, near the American coast, cloud amounts are generally smaller than elsewhere, and rain is rare.

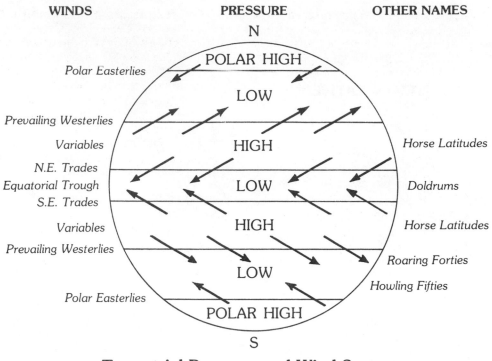

WINDS	PRESSURE	OTHER NAMES

Terrestrial Pressure and Wind Systems

Visibility over the open ocean is generally good, except in rain, but there is often a light haze which restricts visibility to between 8 and 15 miles. Showers, clouds, and haze usually increase when the wind freshens. The American coastline tends to be hazy from Mexico north due to fog and dust in the air.

Northern Variables

The northern variables are a belt of variable winds stretching across the central Pacific and located about 25 to 30-degrees north in the winter and moving to 35 to 40-degrees north in the summer. In the eastern part of this belt, winds are mainly northerly in all seasons. In the west southerly winds are prevalent in the summer giving way to southwest to northwest winds east of 150° East.

In the summer winds are generally light and are likely to reach Force 7 only on rare occasions except in association with tropical storms. East of 140° West near the American coast, north and northwest winds may reach Force 7 about 4 days a month. The weather is generally fair near the center of the Pacific high in summer and rain is infrequent. Cloudier conditions prevail east and west of the high and rain is more common to the west of it. Fog may be expected along the American coast 4 to 5 days per month in the summer.

In winter winds occasionally reach Force 7 east of 140° West but as you progress further to the west, the number of days that winds will reach Force 7 increase to 6 to 10 days per month west of 150° East. Visibility in winter is mostly good except in rain. Over the open ocean fog is not a problem.

Westerlies

North of 40° North are the westerlies fraught with gales and fog in summer as well as in winter. The main feature of this weather is its variability due to the numerous depressions that move from west to east. In winter the winds vary greatly in direction and strength and gales are frequent. The maximum number of gales occurs between Japan and the area south of the Alaskan Peninsula and winds of Force 7 or above can be expected about one-half of the time. Periods of overcast skies with rain or snow alternate with days of clear weather. Fog is uncommon but the rain and snow severely limit visibility at times.

In summer the northeasterly-moving depressions are less frequent and also less severe and their tracks generally are further north. South of 150° North gale force winds occur only 1 to 5 days per month and in July only one day of gale force winds is to be expected. The weather, however, can be cloudy and foggy much of the time. West of 160° West 5 to 10 days of fog per month can be expected. East of 160° West the number of occurences is less until you reach the California coast at which place the visibility may be impaired by fog from 5 to 10 days per month.

Southeast Tradewinds

The SE tradewinds blow on the equatorial side of the oceanic high pressure area situated about 30° South. The tradewinds are sustained by a semi-permanent high pressure area located in the eastern part of the ocean and by the migratory high pressure cells which move east from Australia. These tradewinds are also characterized by their constancy with an average strength of Force 4 but occasionally rising to Force 5 or 6 over large areas. Winds of Force 7 or greater are unlikely on more than one or two days per month. Within 10 degrees of the equator, strong winds except in short-lived squalls are uncommon.

In the vicinity of South America the trades blow from south and southeast changing to easterly as you go further west. However, in the southern winter the southeast monsoon develops over the seas north of Australia making the trades again southeast.

During the period of the steady southeast trades, the skies are usually half-covered with small cumulus clouds and there is a slight haze limiting visibility to 8 to 15 miles. Occasional showers may be expected. East of 180° and between the equator and 8° South there is a relatively dry belt that extends to the coast of South America. Although dry it is also cloudy a good share of the time and overcast is not uncommon.

West of 140° West and occurring during the period November to April but not including the foregoing dry belt, the weather tends to be unsettled and the trades unsteady. Cloudy weather with showers becomes the rule until the trades settle down again with occasional squalls from south and east.

Southern Variables

The southern variables extend in a belt from 25° to 40° South in the summer to 20° to 30° South in the winter and they are generally of moderate strength. East of 85° West the winds are an extension of the southeast trades. Winds reach Force 7 or above only 1 to 3 days per month except at the southern fringe where they may occur up to 3 to 6 days per month.

The weather is highly variable depending on where you are relative to the migrating high pressure cells that cause the variability. Near the centers the weather is usually fair but in the adjoining troughs of low pressure, cloudy, unsettled weather is the norm with more rainfall towards the southern edge of the belt. The rainfall in the eastern end of the belt near South America is very infrequent but cloud cover is usually heavy. Fog gets quite common in the vicinity of the Peru Current occurring up to 3 to 5 days per month.

Westerlies or Roaring Forties

Unlike the northern hemisphere where continental land masses interrupt and modify the flow of air, the southern hemisphere winds of the westerly wind belt can circumnavigate the earth. This unimpeded path plus a strong and constant pressure differential between the Horse Latitudes and the sub-polar low creates strong winds throughout the year of Force 5 and 6. Gales are very common especially in the winter and Force 7 winds or above occur 5 to 10 days per month. The strength of these winds has earned them the title of Roaring Forties and it was in these latitudes that the square-rigged ships of the

1880s made their fast runs from Australia back to the Atlantic around Cape Horn. One of the stormiest areas is west-northwest of Cape Horn where winds of Force 7 are likely to occur on 20 days per month during the period July to September. Summer gales are less frequent and occur further south but, nevertheless, this is not common cruising ground for small boats. The weather is variable as in the other westerlies and there are periods of overcast skies and rain or snow alternating with periods of fair weather. The fair weather does not hang around very long, however, and clouds are profuse. Some fog is common, up to 3 to 5 days per month.

Tropical Cyclones

A unique weather phenomenon of the tropics is the tropical cyclone which in its worst phase is the hurricane or typhoon. It is peculiar to the tropics since it depends on warm water as its source of energy. Occasionally tropical cyclones will pass from the tropics to the temperate zone after which they are known as extra-tropical cyclones. Of all storms experienced at sea, the fully developed tropical cyclone is the worst and one to be avoided by the mariner in planning his itinerary. Fortunately, the regions and times of year of hurricane and typhoon generation are fairly predictable, so with a little planning these can be avoided. Let's take a look at the life cycle of the tropical cyclone.

The formative stage is called a tropical disturbance and it is simply a situation wherein weather *seems* to be brewing. It is unsettled with clouds, rain, and squalls and the average wind speed is not great. There is at this time no clear cut indication of what is to come if anything. The barometer will fall very slowly and if it keeps falling, it is a sign of something significant. Strong winds will develop to the north and east of the developing vortex in the northern hemisphere (in the southern hemisphere they will develop to the south and east of the developing center). Barometric pressures will drop to the vicinity of 1010 to 1000 mbs.

A cyclone is a closed circulation with respect to the weather system (isobars). Winds cross the isobars, spiral inwards towards the center. The clouds also show this spiralling effect but on a grand scale only visible from satellite pictures. The tropical cyclone is of tropical oceanic origin, and has no weather fronts per se, it derives its energy primarily from the warm ocean waters with temperatures in excess of 80°F. Hence, they rarely generate outside of the tropics although they are known to travel poleward outside of the tropics.

When there is a definite closed circulation (in the sense of a closed isobar), and the maximum sustained wind speeds are approaching 34 knots but still less than a fresh gale, then the disturbance is termed a tropical depression. The center of the closed isobar is also the center of the depression.

As the winds further increase to sustained speeds between 34 and 63 knots the depression becomes a tropical storm. Waves, clouds, and rain are more threatening than in the depression. Not all tropical cyclones will reach this stage. Some last only a day though the winds may have

Hurricane Madeline. Satellites provide a view of weather over the vast Pacific Basin. It is late summer in the Northern Hemisphere (8 October 1976) and Hurricane Madeline with winds of 125 knots churns the ocean off of Mexico. Clouds of the doldrums follow a clear path westward along latitude 5° North. In the Southern Hemisphere it is still winter and two low pressure areas with heavy clouds lay in the Roaring Forties. The region of the Equator from the Galapagos to 180° longitude looks clear and good sailing.

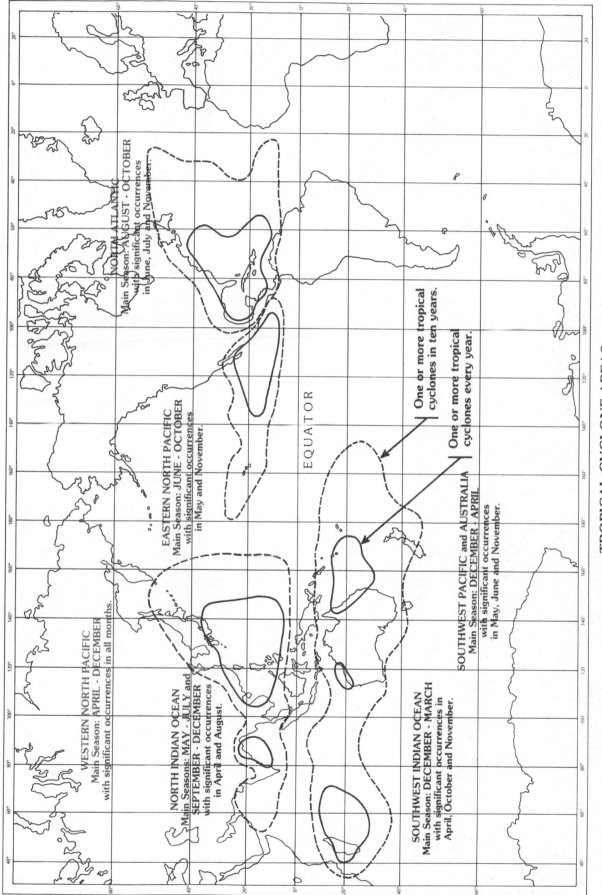

TROPICAL CYCLONE AREAS

NORTH ATLANTIC
Main Season: AUGUST - OCTOBER
with significant occurrences
in June, July and November.

EASTERN NORTH PACIFIC
Main Season: JUNE - OCTOBER
with significant occurrences
in May and November.

WESTERN NORTH PACIFIC
Main Season: APRIL - DECEMBER
with significant occurrences in all months.

NORTH INDIAN OCEAN
Main Seasons: MAY - JULY and
SEPTEMBER - DECEMBER
with significant occurrences in
April and August.

SOUTHWEST PACIFIC and AUSTRALIA
Main Season: DECEMBER - APRIL
with significant occurrences
in May, June and November.

SOUTHWEST INDIAN OCEAN
Main Season: DECEMBER - MARCH
with significant occurrences in
April, October and November.

EQUATOR

One or more tropical
cyclones in ten years.

One or more tropical
cyclones every year.

developed briefly. Others may weaken to the tropical depression stage and then travel great distances. These may grow again or they may further weaken and dissipate. If the cyclone does intensify, the barometric pressure will fall rapidly below 1000 mbs and high winds will form a tight circular band around the center. The cloud and rain pattern changes from disorganized squalls to narrow organized bands which spiral towards the center as seen from satellite photographs. Up to this point, only a relatively small area is involved.

Hurricane status is reached when the maximum sustained winds are 64 knots or greater. As long as the barometric pressure is still dropping and the speed of the gusty and squally winds is still increasing, the tropical cyclone is still developing.

The mature stage is reached when the barometric pressure at the center stops falling and the sustained wind speeds become stabilized. However, the geographic size of the storm may continue to expand for up to a week. In the immature stage the hurricane force winds may exist only within a relatively small circle of 50 miles radius. In the mature stage this radius can increase to more than 400 miles.

Fully developed tropical cyclones with winds of hurricane force tend to move towards the west in both hemispheres. In the northern hemisphere they move about 30° north of west until in the vicinity of 25°North latitude at which place they usually recurve away from the equator and head northeast. In the southern hemisphere they usually move about 30° south of west until they reach 15 to 20°South latitude and then curve to the southeast. Many storms however, do not recurve but continue their westerly course until they reach a large land mass where they quickly fill and dissipate.

Hurricanes travel at speeds of about 10 knots in their early stages increasing speed a little with latitude but seldom reaching 15 knots. A speed of 20 to 25 knots is usual after recurving with some occasionally reaching 40 knots. Not all storms follow the textbook westerly paths recurving towards the poles and east. Some are very erratic occasionally curving back on themselves but when they do, the speed of movement is usually less than 10 knots.

The hurricane stage of a tropical cyclone is known by different names in various parts of the world as follows:

North Atlantic, Caribbean, Gulf of Mexico —
   hurricane
Mexico — hurricane or cordonazo
Eastern Pacific — hurricane
Haiti — taino
Western Pacific — typhoon
Philippines — baguio or baruio
North Indian Ocean — cyclone
Australia area — willy-willy, typhoon or hurricane

When the wind speed begins to decline steadily, accompanied by an increase in the barometric pressure, the tropical cyclone is beginning to dissipate. This usually occurs after it has recurved poleward and eastward. Not all storms recurve into the temperate latitudes and they dissipate over the neighboring continent while a few even die while still over tropical waters. Sometimes the tropical cyclones will dissipate within a day while others approaching sub-polar latitudes take on a mid-latitude character and even strengthen.

Tropical cyclones generate in several different areas of the world as shown on the chart. Within the dotted line one may expect more than one tropical cyclone every 10 years while within the solid line one may expect one or more tropical cyclones every year. The exact number of tropical cyclones varies each year but the average number per month and year are given in the table for each of the basins shown on the chart. Only the western North Pacific does not have a well-defined quiescent period during the year.

The Hurricane Warning System

Hurricanes are to be avoided. The best way is to stay out of the areas in which they might appear during their usual season of occurrence. The next best way is to keep track of the weather so that you will know if there is a tropical cyclone generating anywhere in your vicinity.

The countries of the Pacific Ocean monitor hurricane activity very closely since it is damaging to land areas as well as to vessels at sea. This information is transmitted over radio and, if you listen regularly to WWVH or other weather broadcasts, you will be apprised of any hurricane activity and can take evasive action if necessary. Most of the Pacific is covered by WWVH which gets its information from the National Weather Service.

NOAA National Weather Service Hurricane Centers are located in San Francisco covering the Eastern Pacific; in Hawaii covering the Central Pacific; and the Joint Navy-Air Force Typhoon Warning System in Guam covers the Western Pacific. South Pacific hurricane information is also furnished by Fiji, New Zealand, and Australia. In general, warnings of approaching tropical cyclones which may be hazardous will include the following information: storm type, central pressure given in millibars, wind speeds observed within the storm, storm location, speed and direction of movement, the extent of the effected area, visibility, and the state of the sea as well as any other pertinent information received. These warnings are broadcast on prespecified radio frequencies immediately upon receipt of the information and at specific intervals thereafter. The broadcasting intervals and channels vary from one governing authority to another. Generally the broadcast interval is every six hours depending on the receipt of new information.

Detailed information on the radio broadcasts of all weather information and specific areas of geographical coverage are contained in the publication: *Worldwide Marine Weather Broadcasts,* published jointly by the National Weather Service and the Naval Weather Service. It is updated annually.

WORLDWIDE FREQUENCIES OF OCCURENCE OF TROPICAL CYCLONES

Tropical Storms: Winds from 34 to 63 knots   Cyclones: Winds 48 knots and over
Hurricanes and Typhoons: Winds 64 knots and over

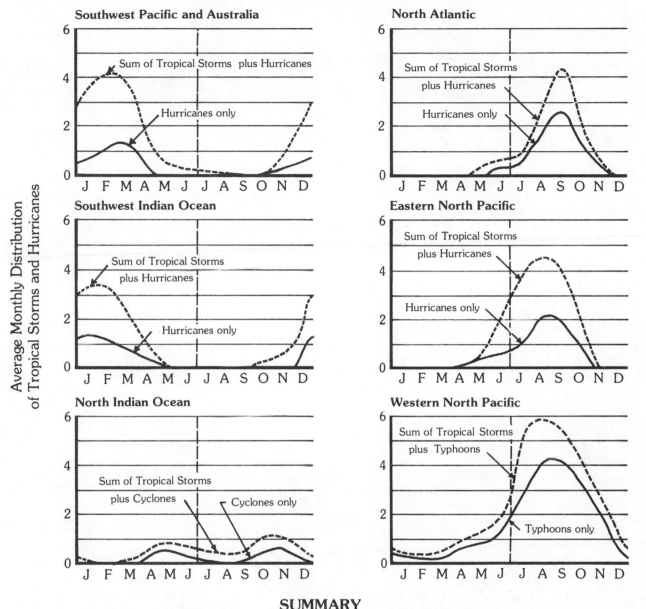

SUMMARY

AREA	Southwest Pacific & Australia	Southwest Indian Ocean	North Indian Ocean	North Atlantic	Eastern North Pacific	Western North Pacific
Average Number of Tropical Storms per Year	10.9	7.4	3.5	4.2	9.3	7.5
Average Number of Hurricanes per Year	3.8	3.8	2.2 (cyclones)	5.2	5.8	17.8 (typhoons)
Total Number of Tropical Cyclones per Year	14.7	11.2	5.7	9.4	15.1	25.3

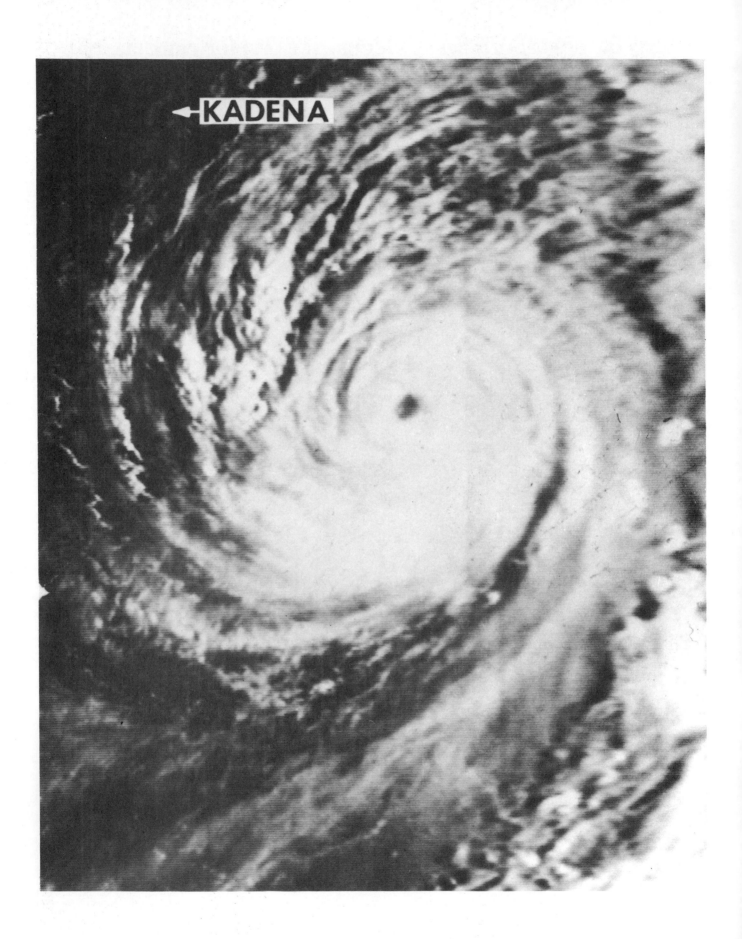

A picket line of tropical cyclones extends across the Eastern Pacific on 19 August 1978. From left to right — tropical storm Lane, tropical storm John, and hurricane Kristy: Tropical Storm Report from National Weather Service, San Francisco, Calif. (USA) at 2100 Z on August 1978: "Tropical storm Lane upgraded from tropical depression. Storm center located near 13.4N, 139.0W at 1800Z on 19 August. Position fair based on satellite image. Present movement west or 260 degrees at 11 kt. Max sustained winds 35 kt with gusts to 45 kt. Radius of 34 kt winds 60 nm. 12 hr forecast: 13.4N, 141.0W. Max sustained winds 40 kt with gusts to 50 kt. 24 hr forecast: 13.6N, 142.9W. Max sustained winds 40 kt with gusts to 50 kt. Tropical storm John with center located near 12.0N, 124.8W at 1800Z on 19 August. Position accurate within 60 nm based on satellite image. Present movement west or 260 degrees at 7 kt. Max sustained winds 40kt with gusts to 50 kt. Rad of 34 kt winds 60 nm. 12 hr forecast: 12.0N, 126.7W. Max sustained winds 40 kts with gusts to 50 kts. 24 hr forecast: 12.2N, 128.5W. Max sustained winds 45 kts with gusts to 55 kts. Hurricane Kristy upgraded from tropical storm with center located at 15.1N, 118W at 1800Z on 19 August. Position fair based on satellite image. Present movement west northwest or 300 degrees at 8 kts. Max sustained winds 65 kts with gusts to 80 kts. Rad of 50 kt winds 70 nm. Rad of 34 kt winds 140 nm. 12 hr forecast: 16.0N, 113.3W. Max sustained winds 75 kts with gusts to 90 kt. Rad of 50 kt winds 75 nm. 24 hr forecast: 16.8N, 115.0W. Max sustained winds 85 kt with gusts to 105 kt. Rad of 50 kt winds 90 nm. Next advisory 0300Z on 20 August."

←Typhoon Billie (facing page). Typhoon Billie with an intensity of 115 knot winds southeast of Okinawa on 7 August 1976. Typhoon report from the Joint Navy-Air Force Typhoon Warning System at Guam on 1800, 7 August 1976: "Based on eye at 22.3N, 132.5E at 1700Z by aircraft accurate within 15 nm. Center moving toward the northwest at 13 kts. Present wind distribution: Max sustained winds 120 kts near center with gusts to 145 kts. Radius of over 100 kt winds 50 nm northeast quadrant; 25 nm elsewhere. Radius of over 50 kt winds 125 nm northeast quadrant; 50 nm miles southwest quadrant, 100 nm elsewhere. Radius of over 30 kt winds 325 nm northeast quadrant, 125 nm southwest quadrant, 225 miles elsewhere. Forecasts: 12 hrs valid 8 August 0600Z: 23.9N, 130.2E. Max winds 115 knots with gusts to 140 kncts. Radius of over 50 kt winds, 75 nm. 24 hrs valid 8 August 1800Z: 25.3N,128.3E. Max winds 110 knots with gusts to 135 kts. Radius of over 50 kt winds 75 nm. Radius of over 30 kt winds 275 nm northeast semi-circle; 200 nm elsewhere. Extended outlook: 48 hours valid 9 August 1800Z: 27.8N, 125.5E. Max winds 100 kts with gusts to 125 kts. Radius of over 50 kt winds 75 nm northeast quadrant, 50 nm elsewhere. 72 hrs valid 10 August 1800Z: 31.8N,124.5E. Max winds 85 kts with gusts to 105 kts. Radius of over 50 kt winds 50 nm northeast semi-circle, 25 knots elsewhere. Next warning at 8 August 0000Z. Remarks: Aircraft indicates that Typhoon Billie has reached her maximum intensity and is beginning to weaken."

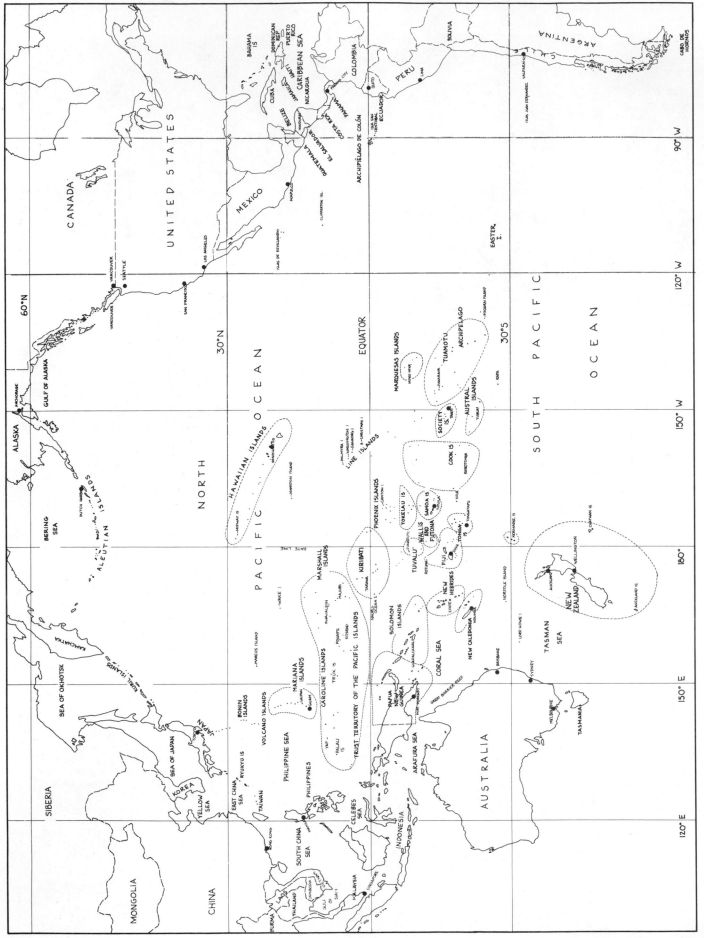

Oceania

Chapter 4

PASSAGE PLANNING

To say you are going to cruise the Pacific is to look only at the tip of the iceberg. The Pacific is vast in all dimensions—10,000 islands spread over 64 million square miles. That is a lot of opportunity for the cruising sailor and one that calls for a little planning. Not too much, though, for cruising should not be rigidly structured. But you do have to plan on self-sufficiency between provisioning ports which, because of the undeveloped nature of this cruising ground, can be quite far apart.

Then there is the matter of the time of year. Seasonal changes occur in the Pacific cruising grounds as they do elsewhere in the world. Although it may never get cold in the tropics, the seasonal changes in tradewinds and monsoonal winds can impact the ease with which you make a passage. More importantly, the hurricanes and typhoons of the Pacific are not a sailor's best friend and should be avoided by good scheduling of passages.

Winds are the motive power for the cruising boat and you are at their mercy on any passage—long or short. Your time enroute will be determined by the winds where you are, not by Pilot Charts, the experiences of another cruising boat, or your own experiences sailing in home waters. It generally takes longer than one thinks to make a passage because one plans with optimism instead of looking for the most adverse conditions. Although we may enjoy sailing, there is the matter of carrying adequate provisons for an unexpectedly slow passage. Running out of food or water enroute can spoil your outlook on cruising. And you will find that it doesn't always rain in the tropics nor are there fish waiting to be caught.

Cruising should be safe and a little thought to those factors which make up cruising safety are well worth while. Knowing when you are in heavily-transited shipping lanes will prompt you to keep a more careful lookout for traffic. While you don't want to be run down, there is also an opportunity to speak to a ship via radiotelephone and relieve the dullness of a long passage. Many boats are well equipped with electronics for safety but, except for the licensed amateur radio, few can reach the breadth of the Pacific. Consider the Emergency Position Indicating Radio Beacon (EPIRB) for announcing to aircraft that you are in distress on the sea—if you are nowhere near an air route it would be useless to put any reliance on it for recovery.

Better you should consider being able to take care of yourself under all possible emergencies that you are willing to expose yourself to. Besides a good boat properly equipped, you will want to adequately man your vessel. That means planning crew needs ahead of time—not only in numbers but in capability. There is no Union Hall from which to get crew members, furthermore, you want

friends and people with compatible personalities. And that takes some planning.

It is recommended that you do your passage planning with the following five elements in mind—destination, season, enroute time, safety, and crew makeup.

Where are you going?

You may eventually be headed for a little known South Sea island but its geography and national sovereignty require that you stop other places first. Given a choice you will want to enter an island group at the windward end so that you can sail to the other islands in the group without having to beat into the wind. One of the peculiarities of many island groups of the Pacific is that they are generally laid out running southeast to northwest. Hawaii, Marquesas, Tuamotus, Cooks, Samoas, and many others lie in this position making it of great advantage to start from the southeast and work your way up the chain enjoying scenery, sailing, and sessions with the native peoples as you go.

Unfortunately, officialdom gets in your way. All island groups and many individual islands are separate political entities requiring a visiting yacht to officially clear into its territorial boundaries. This is done at a Port of Entry and it is usually located at the major population center of the island group which isn't necessarily at the windward end of the chain. Hence, a compromise on where to enter the chain. Some island chains have Ports of Entry at the windward ends such as Hilo, Hawaii; Majuro, Marshall Islands; and Noumea, New Caledonia. But most, unfortunately, have their Ports of Entry sandwiched into the middle of the group meaning that you have to bypass many interesting outlying islands when you make your official entry. And bypass them you should, for these sovereign islands are getting pretty sticky about yachts freely transiting their waters with no regard for local custom and other regulations.

The days of casually wandering among the islands of the South Seas are over because of the number of cruising yachts on the scene. There are other reasons, too, some yachties are dope runners and have even been known to cultivate pot on isolated islands. Others are foragers who live off a land that is barely able to support the native population. Still others think in terms of the beachcombers of old who would simply settle in with the natives. No more. Island officials want to know and keep track of every yacht and crew member in their waters. While it may seem like an imposition on you, it does have its good side and that is safety. Yachts occasionally turn up missing for a number of reasons and the local officials would rather know where to look than have to mount a wide area search

So, in entering an island group for the first time, do so at a designated Port of Entry only. There are some exceptions, not in principal but in practice. Take the Marquesas islands as an example. Their official Port of Entry is Papeete, Tahiti, 760 miles away and nowhere else. But the administration of French Polynesia recognizes the awkwardness of the distances involved so they have designated sub-ports for securing a temporary entry permit of 30 days. There are two in the Marquesas, one at Taiohae, Nuku Hiva, and one at Atuona, Hiva Oa. But there the flexibility ends and the French administration will make you very unwelcome if you do not check in at one of them.

There is one other official nuance of island visiting and that is checking in at each island. Don't think for one minute that once you have cleared at a Port of Entry that you are free to roam. You must check in with the administrator of every island that has one. It may be a civilian district officer, a military representative or the island chief. In any case they are the authority and must keep track of visitors. This is hardly a penalty, for these persons living in a somewhat isolated world usually welcome visitors and more than one yachtie has found his arrival to be cause for a celebration. But don't forget that you are a guest and how you behave will have a major effect on the reception afforded the next visiting yacht. It doesn't hurt to have token gifts to offer the island chief such as coffee, tobacco, some clothing, and pictures from a Polaroid camera.

But processing official papers isn't the only reason for entering at a Port of Entry. After a long passage you are probably interested in also replenishing your supplies and maybe even having a meal in a local restaurant. Your boat may also be in need of repairs which demands that your entry be made at a big settlement with adequate facilities and parts.

To sum it up, your destination should consider the official needs of clearing into the country, replenishing supplies and setting your boat back in order for the next long passage. If your routine is to include frequent communication with the home port, you will appreciate having the postal, radiotelephone and telegram, and airline communications of the larger ports. Once you have taken care of all the ship's business and your personal needs, you can retire to the out-islands (assuming that you have a cruising permit) to enjoy the local culture in peace and quiet.

There are few good places to resupply or repair your boat in the Pacific so your overall route plan should consider those few. Your major cruising needs can best be satisfied at the following ports:

Honolulu, Hawaii
Papeete, Tahiti
Pago Pago, American Samoa
Suva, Fiji
Whangarei and Auckland, New Zealand
Guam, Mariana Islands
Noumea, New Caledonia
Rabaul, New Britain

When Are You Going?

Timing of a departure is based mainly on the weather. In fact most people cruise the tropics because they like the warm weather and the balmy tradewinds. But there is a violent side to the tropical weather as well as the weather at any latitude. Dominating your decision on when to go are the tropical cyclone patterns of the general route that you will want to take. Do not schedule a route into an area of known cyclone activity for that can be a good way to ruin a voyage. Study the patterns of tropical storms and set your routes or timing to avoid them.

If you find yourself arriving in waters during the season when tropical storms are prevalent, plan on spending a few months in a hurricane hole enjoying the local country and conditioning your boat for the next passage. Hurricane holes in the Pacific are few and far between. The better ones are Pago Pago, American Samoa; Vava'u, Tonga; and, marginally, Suva, Fiji. New Zealand is partially out of the hurricane belt and a season spent there is a reward in itself.

There is an alternative, though, to holing-up to avoid tangling with a hurricane and that is to go sailing in some other part of the Pacific. When hurricanes are in the southern hemisphere, do your cruising in the northern hemisphere and vice versa. Consider the equatorial islands themselves which are spared the onslaughts of hurricane force winds. But don't deliberately expose yourself to trouble. Tales of boats surviving hurricanes are heroic after the fact but downright terrifying during the experience. And then there are those you never hear about!

Planning of passages also involves the seasonal nature of the tradewinds. They seem to be better in some seasons than others and their general pattern in local waters is described later in the sections on weather accompanying each description of an island group. Tradewinds are quite dependable disturbed only by occasional fronts that march eastward through the area.

But remember that the best tradewinds, those in the tropics, are easterlies carrying you west in your travels. If you want to go east you either beat your way against the trades or head for the higher latitudes. Square riggers headed for the higher latitudes because they couldn't efficiently sail against the wind and also because they could make better time in the strong westerlies. But you must be prepared for gales in any season when you sail above 35° latitude. In the local winter they will obviously be at their worst.

If you have a background of racing and a boat that will go well to weather, you will say to yourself that I can tack to any destination with ease and that would be true of a short race and a dedicated racing crew. But to beat into the wind for weeks on end with a family crew is no way to enjoy a cruise.

The winds are a result of high and low pressure cells building up over the ocean or adjacent lands and a cruising yacht should take advantage of the seasonal weather patterns. Note that if you were making a passage east from New Zealand that it could be done north of 40° south in July but you would have to go south of 40° south to do the same thing in January. The effects of the

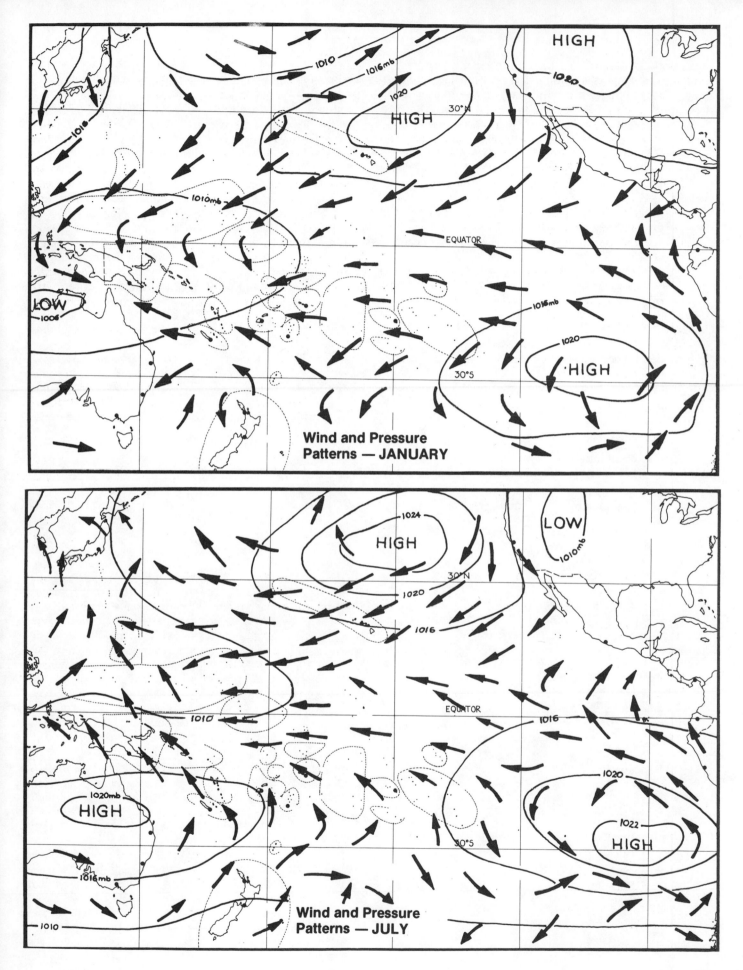

Wind and Pressure Patterns — JANUARY

Wind and Pressure Patterns — JULY

monsoons in the western Pacific are clearly evident by noting the change in wind direction between January and July. These changes are dominated by the heating and cooling of the large Asian land mass and, to a lesser extent, by the heating and cooling of Australia.

Your best source of wind data for the long passages is the Pilot Chart. It summarizes the average wind and weather conditions to be expected over the ocean and gives you the best overall pattern on which to base your cruise plan. But don't feel distressed if you eventually experience other conditions. The charts cover tens of thousands of miles and your local conditions are but a microscopic part of the whole circulation pattern.

When you are near land, radio weather forecasts may give you some idea of coming winds or rain so that you can decide whether to stay put where you are or go visit

Recorded Passage Times

Passage	Great circle distance (n.m.)	Number of days enroute		
		Minimum	Average	Maximum
Seattle/Vancouver to:				
Honolulu	2380	16	26	42
San Francisco to:				
Hilo	2020	14	21	32
Nuku Hiva	2900	24	32	39
Los Angeles/San Diego to:				
Hilo	2140	15	24	36
Nuku Hiva	2840	20	28	42
Cabo San Lucas to:				
Honolulu	2660	20	23	27
Acapulco to:				
Nuku Hiva	2900	17	23	30
Puntarenas, Costa Rica to:				
Honolulu	4240	32	34	36
Panama to:				
Galapagos	870	8	14	23
Nuku Hiva	3820	27	39	51
Honolulu	4690	36	49	62
Galapagos to:				
Nuku Hiva	2940	18	26	37
Hilo	4040	43	44	46
Honolulu to:				
Los Angeles/San Diego	2240	22	31	36
San Francisco	2090	22	24	25
Seattle/Vancouver	2410	22	29	41
Nuku Hiva	2100	18	20	22
Papeete	2320	17	26	31
Rangiroa to:				
Hilo	2130	18	21	23
Papeete to:				
Hilo	2260	14	22	38
Suva to:				
Auckland	1140	8	13	19
Auckland to:				
Papeete	2220	14	22	28
Raivavae	2100	21	23	24

the next island. On a long passage, however, there is little you can do with a weather forecast but be ready to batten down the hatches if necessary. You cannot outrun it or get out of its way. That is the primary reason for staying out of hurricane areas. It is best if you do your own weather forecasting by observing the sky and swells and tracking the barometer. A small low pressure area crossing your path can create a localized gale that may never be known to the rest of the world. But if you are prepared to shorten sail and have everything properly secured below decks then there is a good possibility that you can weather your own little gale in safety if not comfort.

Local weather forecasts can be obtained from commercial radio stations operating in the islands which you are visiting. On long passages your best weather reports (and probably all that is needed) are obtained from WWVH every hour. They describe the big picture from which you can determine whether your immediate weather pattern is localized or part of a major happening. You may want to take different survival actions in each case.

How Long Will It Take You?

If you are going to race through the South Seas, then you might as well travel by jet aircraft for cruising is not a race but a chance to enjoy an unhurried existence whether enroute or at your destination. Nevertheless, one must have some idea of length of time that it will take to make a passage.

Those used to sailing the short coastal routes of a Sunday afternoon know full well that with a good wind they can hold hull speed hour after hour, so they plan accordingly. A boat's hull speed is related to its waterline length, the longer the waterline, the higher the hull speed. Typical values are:

Waterline Length	Hull Speed
(feet)	(knots)
20	6
25	6.7
30	7.3
35	7.9
40	8.5

These speeds are the maximum sustainable speeds with good winds and moderate seas and are usually attained on a broad reach or a run with plenty of canvas flying. The rest of the time? Only the god of wind and sea will know. On an average a cruising boat can make between 100 and 125 miles per day over an extended passage. Sounds slow? Maybe, but when you consider all the times at night when the wind goes slack and long days in the doldrums or the flat that often occurs after a squall goes through, you sometimes will feel lucky to have made that good an average. While some legs will be at hull speed, others will be fraught with slatting sails. And on still others adverse currents of one to two knots will reduce your distance made good to well below what your knotmeter thinks it should be.

It is almost impossible to use speed alone to estimate the time it will take you to make a passage. Adverse cur-

rents, different points of sailing, variable winds, and navigation inconsistencies all combine to negate precise speeds made good across the bottom in the direction that you want to go. It is better to think in terms of how many days it will take you to make a passage. After you have made a number of passages and suffered through calms, squalls and changes in wind direction you will become quite good in estimating your boat's ability to make time on a passage. Until then, use the experience of others who have been just as good sailors as yourself and had just as fast a boat but learned that making a boat go its fastest day in and day out is less important than having a safe and pleasurable sail.

Recorded enroute times for 249 passages on a variety of cruising boats were compared and the results are shown in the table. There are a few interesting observations that can be made from this collection. The difference between maximum and minimum times is about 2 to 1. Crossings with long portions in the doldrums such as the legs from Panama to the Galapagos take a relatively longer time. Legs to weather such as the Honolulu-North America passages take considerably longer because you are essentially taking long tacks as you circle the North Pacific high pressure area. This on-the-wind penalty also shows distinctly in the comparison of Auckland to Papeete or Raivavae times. Going to Papeete is less of a beat than to Raivavae and, even though a longer great circle distance, the time enroute is actually less.

So what should you take as the average passage times? A boat with a long waterline and a capable crew could maybe match the minimum times. But like the statistics say, most boats will take the average time. If yours is a small boat with a short waterline, be honest with yourself and assume something near the maximum for your passage.

More important than simple calendar days, however, is the safety margin that you want to allow in planning your provisions or having your shoreside contacts wait before getting worried. A good rule of thumb is take half again the amount of time that you think it will take for the crossing.

Can you speed up your passage by using the auxiliary engine along the way? Certainly, if you carry a good supply of fuel and can put up with the noise. Unless you have a motorsailer it is not advisable to power for great distances because the average auxiliary engine installation just isn't made for that kind of service. It may be worthwhile in the doldrums or the flat of the Pacific high, otherwise save the engine for entering harbors. Passage distances are just too long for powering in the majority of cases, so you should resign yourself to becoming the best sailor possible.

This brings us to the question of how to time your arrival for a daylight entry to your destination harbor. While the principal is good, the practice is impossible. Let your arrival time take care of itself. If you arrive at night plan to stand off the harbor until daylight when you can see the navigation aids and the hazards to navigation. Time is not so precious that you should jeopardize boat and crew to save hours after you have been days enroute. Plan to drop your sails and just drift in the shadow of your

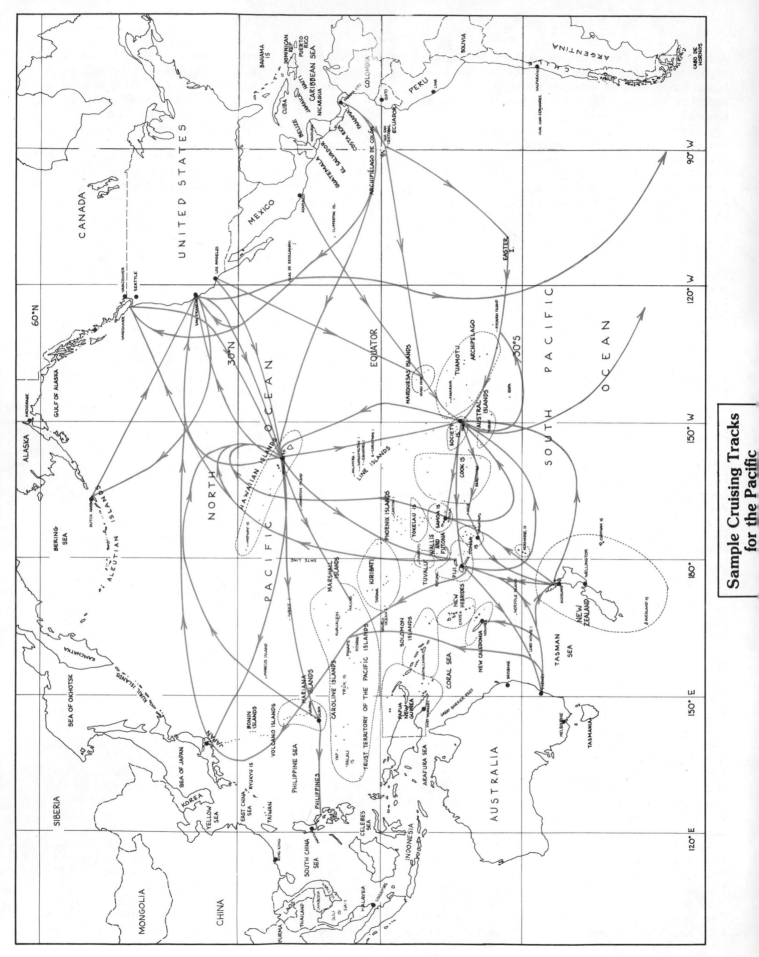

**Sample Cruising Tracks
for the Pacific**

destination if it is clearly visible. If it is not or if there is a strong current running or bad weather, don't stand in too close. Sail away from the harbor for a couple of hours and then sail back timing your arrival for daylight. Remember that your boat is safer in the ocean than near an unknown or unseen shore. Sailing back and forth allows you to correct your position for current as well as occupying the crew who might otherwise get restless.

Additional details on planning a passage from the standpoint of weather and routing can be found in *Ocean Passages of the World* published by the Hydrographer of the Navy, British Admiralty. The cost is about $US32.00

Where Do You Get Emergency Help?

Part of the fun of blue water cruising is just roaming the oceans unfettered by schedules or the traces of society. Yet, boats do turn up missing and one wonders why. Assuming that the boat is well found and the crew capable, it is hardly likely that they would come to grief because of weather short of a hurricane. And it is hardly likely that a boat properly navigated would ground on a land mass and disappear without a trace. So that leaves a collision at sea as the likely culprit in the disappearance of a cruising boat. Anyone who has traveled the oceans knows how quickly and alarmingly a ship can appear close at hand when you think you have the whole ocean to yourself. With a dependable 24-hour watch your chances of being rundown are minimal, but if there is a lapse in lookout and you are near or in steamer lanes or areas being fished by some of the Oriental fishing fleets, then trouble may be brewing.

The major steamer lanes of the Pacific Ocean are shown in the chart. But ships, like cruising boats, are not constrained to these routes and they are likely to be found anywhere, but on a less frequent basis. Should you find yourself paralleling or crossing any of these routes, keep a particularly good lookout. Most ships are running on automatic pilot at sea and their lookout may have decided to go to the galley for a cup of coffee about the time that you come into view. Likewise, don't depend on their radar to sight you. In all probability it is not on or, at least not being watched most of the time at sea. When you and they are near land, their radar is probably being monitored and your radar reflector will be noted by them, assuming that they are radar-equipped.

Many cruising boats take the opportunity to speak to ships which come into view. This is best done on VHF radio using Channel 16 which is common in all countries. Yachts have reported many friendly conversations with ships at sea who have, on request, reported the yacht's position to its home port. Don't depend on VHF for calling a ship which you cannot see, since VHF radio operates only in line of sight situations.

Selection of single sideband radio for use in Pacific cruising must take into account the vast distances and isolation of the Pacific Basin. While marine SSB has now been well developed, it does not have the range, flexibility, or price to satisfy the needs of the Pacific cruising boat. The only radio that does is the amateur (ham) rig, which, technologically, is just as advanced as marine SSB but more flexible.

Once you are licensed for this type of radio (and you have to be), you can operate it as mobile equipment on your yacht and have the capability of contacting all of the countries in and around the Pacific Basin. It also provides contact with other cruising boats through various Pacific maritime nets.

As long as you are sailing in international waters, you may operate with your home country's amateur license identifying yourself as "Maritime Mobile" according to regulations set out in detail by the International Telecommunications Union. Operating in foreign waters you will need a license from that foreign government which, generally, is obtainable on a reciprocal basis. (See Appendix D). Allowable amateur operating frequencies will be prescribed by that government.

There is only one problem with ham radio and that is every boat with a radio should have the capability to communicate on 2182 kHz, not only for their own safety but to give a hand to someone else who may be in distress. Ham rigs do not come with this frequency but some cruising boats have had their radios recrystalled to give this capability. It does not, however, constitute a legal piece of equipment in the eyes of the United States Federal Communications Commission. If you can additionally afford the price of a marine SSB radio, that would be the proper and most complete way to go.

Your best source of information on ham rigs is to take one of the courses offered by local schools or ham radio clubs aimed at qualifying you for a license. These courses will not only teach you the liecense requirements but will give you a practical background in operating a ham rig. This practical knowledge plus a well-disciplined amateur radio operator is what has kept ham radio in the United States (and probably elsewhere) from becoming chaotic such as has happened to Citizens Band and marine VHF. Let me add that not only the regulatory agencies of all countries but the ham community, in general, takes a dim view of operating without a license.

But even if you have single sideband marine or ham radio on board, don't depend on it for getting immediate emergency assistance. The ocean is vast and you may be over 1,000 miles from any land or ship. Even if they heard your call, it would take days by surface vessel to reach you. Airplanes can reach you faster if they are available but that would only be in the vicinity of major countries who can afford such life-saving operations. Better that you try to make your vessel able to take care of itself through good equipment and seaman-like operation.

Should you suffer a calamity such as a dismasting or even have to abandon your craft and take to the liferaft, then you will want to have along an Emergency Position Indicating Radio Beacon—EPIRB. The United States system works on frequencies of 121.5 and 243 MHz which are guarded by commercial airlines and military airplanes, respectively. Since most of the world is crisscrossed by airlines, there is a reasonable chance that your emergency signal would be heard by an aircraft unless you are in an exceptionally remote part of the world. The principal airline routes are shown on the chart but are

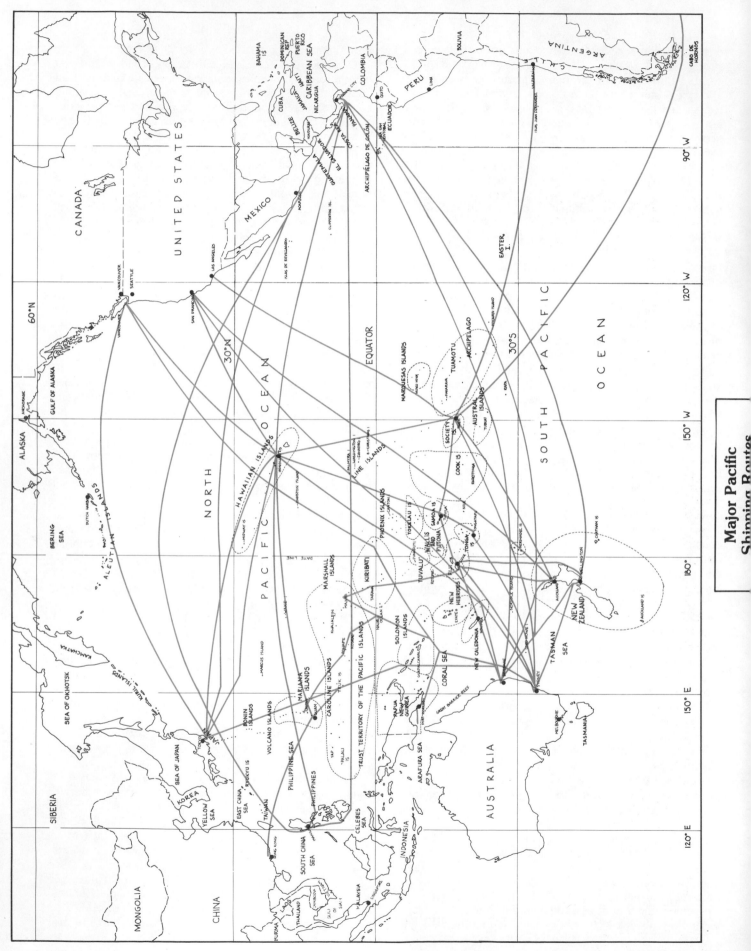

**Major Pacific
Shipping Routes**

Amateur Radio Maritime Mobile Nets In The Pacific

Net	Operating frequency	Day	Time	Control
Children's Hour (Society Islands)	2738 kHz	Daily	0800 LMT	none - marine radio
South Pacific	3815	Daily	0715 GMT	ZL1 BKD (Colin)
West Coast USA (Admirals Net)	7190	Daily	2230 GMT	unknown
		Sundays	1630 GMT	
Pacific Maritime Mobile Service	14.313 MHz	Daily	1700 GMT	WB5 DWN (Robertson)
South Pacific	14.313	Daily	0530 GMT	ZL1 CU (Noel), alternates: VK4 AEM (Ted) and KH6 EXB
Pacific InterIsland Net	14.313	Daily	0800 GMT	P29 CC (Danny), alternates: KG6 J10 (Dixie) and KC6 MJ (Mike)
Southeast Asia Net (SEANET)	14.320	Daily	1200 GMT	S79R (Carl - WB8 JDR)
Pacific Maritime Net	21.404	Mon-Fri.	2300 GMT	WB6 SYQ (Bill)

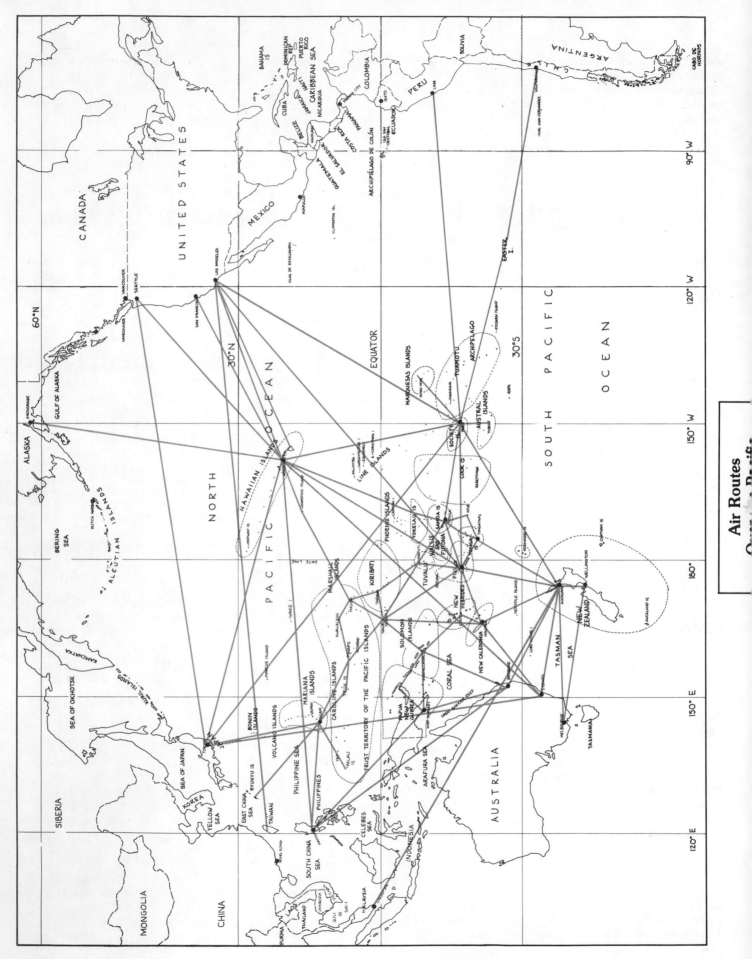

Air Routes
Oceania Pacific

subject to changes. While some of these routes have one or more flights a day, there are some that have only one or two per week. Being very optimistic and assuming that your distress signal is heard by aircraft and your location pin-pointed accurately, you could still be several days from rescue because of the logistics of getting a ship to your location. Airplanes at best can drop survival equipment to you but it will take a ship to effect the actual rescue. So you are now back to square one in your cruising game and it reads "Self Sufficiency".

Are You Looking for a Crew?

Boat size is not a determining factor for the number of crew needed in cruising. Boats to 40 feet LOA are commonly singlehanded and there are many 2-person crews sailing boats up to 50 feet LOA. Wind-vane self-steering has done much to make this possible and one cannot help but like a crewman who works uncomplainingly for long stretches and asks nothing in return but some occasional tender loving care. Although there is no minimum boat to crew-size relation, there is a meaningful maximum. Boats grow pretty small at sea and the fewer persons aboard, the fewer the problems. You will be doing no one a favor by taking unneeded crew members, particularly strangers, to share in the workload. Remember that they will also be sharing in the limited living space and each brings his own personality and habits to share with you.

The inherent problem with the multiple-person crew is compatibility over the long passages. Even good marriages and other friendly relationships have been strained to the breaking point by long passages in small boats. To add additional persons, particularly strangers, is to court trouble.

When your intentions for a dream cruise become known, you may find yourself pressed by friends for crewing berths. A most welcome situation at first blush but fraught with potential and delicate trouble. The friendships are, more than likely, of landside origin, at best marina acquaintances or weekend racing buddies. Your enthusiasm rubs off on them but when the chips are down the need for compromise becomes apparent. Mostly you will find that your friends have not conditioned their lives for an extended absence and would like only to sail a certain leg of your voyage convenient to them. This, then, results in your having to pick up replacement crew members along the way which has its difficult side. If you do take along friends, have a business-like arrangement that points out that the boat's welfare comes first and friendship second. In that way you can have a friendly parting if problems develop and your friend can (and will) pay his transportation home.

Regardless of how you acquire your crew, as far as customs and immigration officials are concerned, they are the responsibility of the skipper. Most countries insist upon each visitor having a valid airline ticket to his own country. Be sure that each crewman has this ticket in his own name and you should keep this ticket along with his passport and World Health card in your possession. Then if you want to part company, you can do so at your con-

venience and not his. If he is a national of another country, be certain of his entry eligibility to the destination country so that you, the skipper, don't become guilty of aiding and abetting illegal immigration procedures. If visas are needed be certain that each crewman gets one ahead of time.

An early understanding between crewman and skipper on how the crewman is to fit into the shipboard life may preclude some rough spots later. Besides watch-standing and sail changing, he must expect to help with the routine chores below decks such as cleaning a water closet or scrubbing down a bulkhead. He must also be put on his honor not to make midnight raids on boat stores nor use water beyond a reasonable ration. The owner should also ensure what little privacy he has on a small boat by not giving the crew members carte blanche entry to parts of the boat for which access is not required in the normal pursuit of their duties.

If you have decided that your boat does need another hand aside from your family crew, then the following advice is offered:

— Check your applicant out as thoroughly as possible beforehand since it is better to delay departure or do without than have a stranger spoil your fun.

— Be frank with your applicant at the interview and demand that he be the same, because you will both pay for deception in the end.

— If you are confident of your own abilities, don't demand experience, go for personality and a willingness to learn.

— Take only one unknown person at a time; don't load up on potential trouble.

— Agree only to take him to the next port and be sure he has a passport and sufficient finances (airline ticket at least) to travel from there on his own. If he turns out to be a good crewman, you can extend the working agreement.

— If he is on medication be certain that you know the reason for it and that he has an ample supply for the intended period.

— Try to determine if he has any hangups that may make him a liability. Can he go aloft at sea to replace a broken halyard? Is he at home on the water? Does he have a food problem? Is he a follower of a fad in meditation and trances? Above all, is he clean in both a hygienic sense and in habit?

What About Piracy and Hijacking of Cruising Boats?

Over the past years there have been a number of boats that have disappeared from sight and are believed to have been hijacked. Most of these occurred in the Caribbean or waters off Central America where boats were needed capable of hauling large amounts of drugs from Columbia and other South American countries. But there have also been some known acts of piracy in the Pacific, enough to make a sensible skipper take precautionary measures. One boat was pirated right out of Ala Wai Yacht Basin at Honolulu by armed boarders. Another was apparently pirated after arriving at Palmyra Island

and the crew disposed of.

The United States Coast Guard has investigated many known or suspected occurences and has prepared a hypothetical profile of a potential hijacked boat:

— It is a long-legged cruising boat with a large cargo-carrying capacity.

— There is more than one little known and questionable crewman aboard.

— It is outfitted for a long trip.

— There is a known large amount of negotiable paper aboard.

— It departs its last port of call unobserved.

Although this profile describes boats suspected to be placed in the dope smuggling business between the Americas, such fads seem to spread worldwide because of news notoriety. It is possible that some beachcomber may get it into his head to hijack a small boat for kicks and then all the Pacific cruising fleet could become vulnerable. So what can you do about it? The U.S. Coast Guard recommends that cruising boats take the following protective measures:

1. When taking on an unknown crewman, get positive identification from him in the form of a passport, drivers license or other photographic identification and then check references to ascertain the reliability of the individual.

2. Before departing, make up a crew list carrying the name, passport number, address, next of kin, etc. Mail to or leave with a responsible friend who will get it to the proper authorities in case of trouble. Let the crew know that you are doing this.

3. Just before leaving the dock check for stowaways. Within 15 to 30 minutes after leaving you can be out of help's way if your unstable crew and a stowaway gang up on you.

4. If you respond to a distress call at sea, which every good seaman will do, use your radio to notify someone that you are doing so. Keep the channel open while making the intercept and let the other boat know that you are in contact with a responsible station. If it is an authentic distress situation, you may want to use that radio contact to supplement what help you can give on the spot.

5. When in port don't be too eager to let strangers on your boat. They may be checking the boat for a takeover.

6. When departing on a foreign cruise, check out through your customs office whether you are required to do so or not. Leave a list of your valuables on board which could be traced if something happens.

7. Travel in the company of another yacht if possible or at least schedule a destination meeting. Regular radio contacts or radio net activity would also be useful.

8. When you are anchored in foreign ports with dubious security and suspicious waterfront characters, keep a watch on deck to minimize the possibility of a sudden boarding.

9. File a "float plan" with a friend giving all the details possible of your passage. If you don't show up at the destination, then someone can check on you. New Zealand requires such a form and it is called the "10 minute" form.

10. Use common sense—don't over react. Think twice before you use firearms, they can be a source of trouble far beyond an innocent boarding attempt.

Where to get Additional Information:

The fun of cruising is in doing it right, which means knowing what you are doing. Besides *Landfalls of Paradise* there are some very useful periodicals which expand on current conditions in the countries to be visited and the experiences of yachties who have made recent visits. Any of the following periodicals will materially add to the success and enjoyment of a cruise:

> "Commodores' Bulletin" ($US12 per year for
> Associate Members*)
> Seven Seas Cruising Association
> P.O. Box 14245
> North Palm Beach, FL 33408
> USA
> "The Spray" ($US10 per year for a membership*)
> The Slocum Society
> P.O. Box 1164
> Bellflower, CA 90706
> USA
> "Pacific Islands Monthly" ($US18 per year*)
> GPO Box 3408
> Sydney, NSW 2001
> AUSTRALIA
> "The New Pacific" ($US6 per year*)
> P.O. Box 25488
> Honolulu, HI 96825
> USA

*Memberships and subscription prices will vary between countries because of currency exchange rates and different postal rates. Inquire of the publisher for latest price.

MINISTRY OF TRANSPORT
MARINE DIVISION

"10 MINUTE FORM"

The ten minutes spent in filling in this form may save your life

WHY YOU SHOULD COMPLETE THIS FORM?

This form is designed for your safety. The information you give will help the Search and Rescue Organisation to aid you should they be called upon to do so.

WHO MUST FILL IN THIS FORM?

Yachts going on overseas voyages must complete it and hand it to the Collector of Customs at their port of departure.

WHO MAY FILL IN THIS FORM?

Any pleasure craft may complete this form if they wish. Craft going on coastal voyages are particularly recommended to do so.

WHAT TO DO WITH IT

Yachts going to ports outside New Zealand.

This form is required for customs clearance and is to be handed to the Collector of Customs at the port of departure.

Other pleasure craft.

This form is to be handed to the nearest Police Station.

NAME OF VESSEL: .... REGISTERED No. .... SAIL No. ....

From ....

By way of ....

....

....

....

to ....

DATE/TIME OF DEPARTURE: ....

Exact date/time is important. Any delay in sailing should be reported to the Police Station holding the form. Deviations from the voyage plan during passage should be reported to the nearest coast radio station for DIRMARINE, WELLINGTON.

EXPECTED DATE OF ARRIVAL: ....

If your arrangements are uncertain say so here and give general outline of your voyage.

....

....

....

DETAILS OF CREW

2

Full Name	Nationality	Experience

Shore Contacts—Relatives, persons at ports of call and destination:

Full Name	Address	Telephone Number

New Zealand's "10-Minute Form" is a model float plan

3

Qualifications	Next of Kin, Relationship	Address of Next of Kin

DETAILS OF VESSEL

A clear photograph showing the vessel broadside on, will be of great help to the Search and Rescue Organisation should they be called upon to assist you and should be attached to this form.

Attach photograph here

4

Type: .... Length: .... Beam: .... Rig: .... Masts: ....

Arrangement of Superstructure: ....

Colour—Hull: .... Deck: .... Masts: ....

Superstructure: .... Sails: ....

Any distinguishing features: ....

....

Radio equipment, name and type of set: ....

Frequencies: .... Call sign: ....

Proposed radio watch schedule: ....

Emergency set—Name and type: ....

Engines—Number and Type: .... Name of maker: ....

H.P.: .... litres. Consumption: .... litre/hour at .... knots.

Fuel: .... litres. Food for .... days.

Fresh water: ....

Emergency Equipment

Liferaft—Make and capacity: ....

Boat/Dinghy (material, colour, size): ....

Flares, parachute: .... Handheld: .... Smoke: ....

Radar reflector: ....

Lifebuoys: ....

Emergency position indicating radio beacon—Make and operating frequency: ....

IMPORTANT

Be sure to advise a reliable person of your sailing date, route, dates of arrival at ports of call and ETA at destination and tell them to advise Police if you fail to keep to the Schedule. Only on request from these people or if you make a distress call will the New Zealand Search and Rescue Organisation take action.

Report your arrival to Police at your destination.

65622G—5,000/7/75 w

Master's Signature: ....

At ....

Date: ....

New Zealand's "10-Minute Form" is a model float plan

Part 1 -

Islands of Polynesia

- Hawaiian Islands
- French Polynesia
  - *(a) Marquesas Islands*
  - *(b) Tuamotu Archipelago*
  - *(c) Society Islands*
  - *(d) Austral Islands*
- Easter Island
- Pitcairn Island
- Cook Islands
- Samoa Islands
  - *(a) American Samoa*
  - *(b) Western Samoa*
- Tokelau Islands
- Tonga
- Tuvalu
- Niue
- New Zealand
- Kermadec Islands

Island Groups
of the Polynesian Triangle

Island Group	Number of islands	Land area sq. mi.	Population (1967/71)	Government
Hawaii	8	6425	770,000	State of the USA
Marquesas	12	492	5200	French Polynesia – a French overseas territory
Tuamotu	76	343	6700	French Polynesia – a French overseas territory
Society	14	646	81,000	French Polynesia – a French overseas territory
Austral	7	63	4400	French Polynesia – a French overseas territory
Easter Island	1	30	2000	Colony of Chile
Pitcairn Island	4	2	95	A British dependency
Cook	15	93	21,600	Independent
American Samoa	7	76	28,000	United States territory
Western Samoa	8	1135	144,400	Independent
Tokelau	3	4	1700	New Zealand territory
Tonga	200	269	87,400	Kingdom
Tuvalu	9	11	5800	Independent
New Zealand	4	103,100	2,864,000	Commonwealth of British Empire

Part I -

Islands of Polynesia

The Polynesian Triangle encompasses 10 million square miles of the most beautiful cruising waters on the surface of the earth. Within this area are over 360 islands (Polynesia means "many islands") with a land area of 10,000 square miles excluding New Zealand. That gives almost 1000 square miles of water for every square mile of land and you can now begin to understand the origin of the seafaring nature of the Polynesians. Over this vast area of the Polynesian Triangle there are only 1.2 million persons (again excluding New Zealand) and over half of these people live in Hawaii.

The 360 islands are not evenly distributed over this vast area. In some cases they are chains of islands rising to the surface from submerged chains of mountains. The southern Cook islands and Austral islands are part of the same chain but others like the Marquesas are simply tops of closely spaced seamounts. Over the years neighboring islands have become politically associated and today there are eleven identifiable groups of

Polynesian islands. Except for New Zealand, all groups lie within the tropics, that is, between the Tropic of Cancer in the Northern Hemisphere and the Tropic of Capricorn in the Southern Hemisphere.*

It is believed that the first Polynesians left Asia as early as 2000 BC traveling through Micronesia and settling in the area now known as the Society Islands, from there they fanned out in all directions populating the vast Polynesian Triangle. This was probably the last great area of the world to be settled. The people are a mixture of Mongoloids and whites and have a very common culture and similar languages even though their different island homes are separated by thousands of ocean miles. Their fair features, friendly nature and the idyllic climate in which they lived, caused the European nations to concentrate their Pacific interests in this area.

* In a cartographic sense Easter and Pitcairn Islands are also out of the Tropics, but their culture and society are considered tropical.

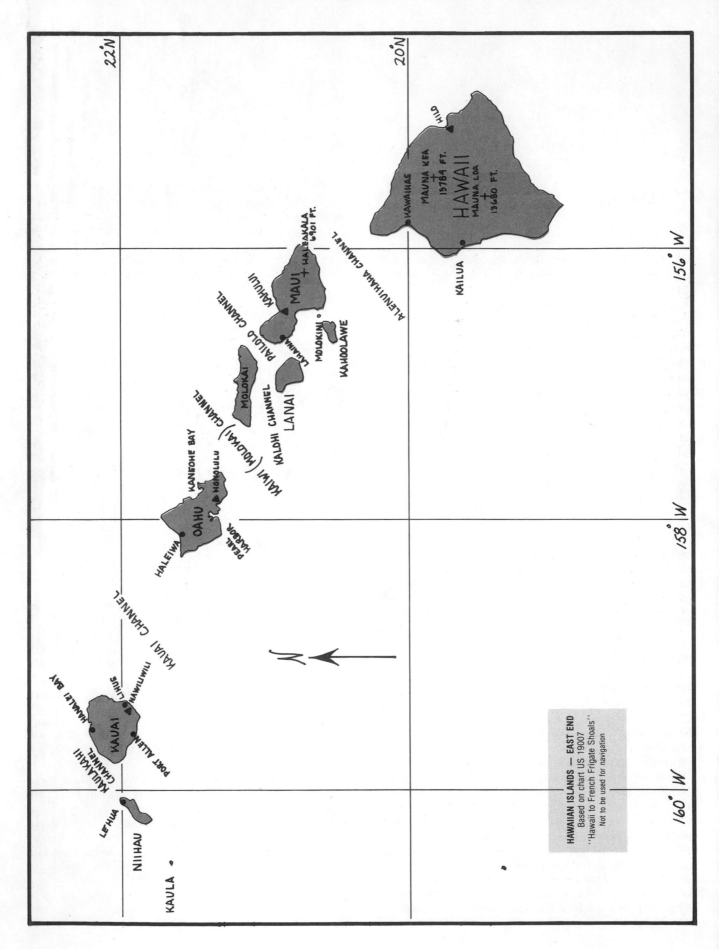

KAULA •

NIIHAU

LEHUA

KAUAI

HANALEI BAY

PORT ALLEN

LIHUE

NAWILIWILI

KAUAI CHANNEL

KAULAKAHI CHANNEL

HALEIWA

KANEOHE BAY

OAHU

HONOLULU

PEARL HARBOR

KAIWI (MOLOKAI) CHANNEL

KALOHI CHANNEL

MOLOKAI

LANAI

KAHOOLAWE

MOLOKINI

LAHAINA

KAHULUI

PAILOLO CHANNEL

MAUI

HALEAKALA

6901 FT.

ALENUIHAHA CHANNEL

HAWAIIA5

MAUNA KEA

13784 FT.

MAUNA LOA

13680 FT.

HAWAII

HILO

KAILUA

22°N

20°N

160° W

158° W

156° W

N

HAWAIIAN ISLANDS — EAST END
Based on chart US 19007
"Hawaii to French Frigate Shoals"
Not to be used for navigation

50

Chapter 5

HAWAII
(Sandwich Islands)

The Country

The Hawaiian Islands anchor the northern apex of the vast Polynesian triangle. It is a unique chain of islands which stretches for 1600 miles across the middle of the blue Pacific in a characteristic southeast to northwest direction. It is the longest and most distinctly formed archipelago in Polynesia made up of 132 shoals, reefs, and islands. In geologic history the chain began its life at the western end with, in all probability, the appearance of Kure Island now reduced by time to atoll stature. It marks the start of a volcanic fissure in the ocean floor which continued to spread southeastward creating additional seamounts whose tops surfaced above the sparkling waters to form islands. While the origin of Kure and the leeward islands of the group goes back possibly 10 million years, the chain is still growing as evidenced by the easternmost island, Hawaii, which today continues a robust volcanic growth in sight of modern man.

Between Kure and Hawaii lies an almost complete history of land formation in the Pacific Ocean. The older leeward islands have now been reduced to shoals and atolls by the irresistible weathering forces of sun and wind and erosion by rain and wave. In the middle of the chain are the last vestiges of volcanic rock such as Gardner Pinnacles which may be merely 5 million years old. But it is the eight major islands at the eastern end of the chain which form the inhabited land of Hawaii. In decreasing order of size they are Hawaii, Maui, Oahu, Kauai, Molokai, Lanai, Niihau, and Kahoolawe. They, together with the lesser leeward shoals and atolls, comprise a total land area of 6,425 square miles.

There are very few wild animals and birds in Hawaii and these were mostly imported from other places. The mongoose is probably the best known of the imported animals and it is this little fellow that is responsible for there being no snakes on the islands. In addition, there are deer, pig, and wild goats which are the targets for seasonal hunting. The Nene (pronounced nay-nay) is the largest landbird in the islands. There are also pheasants and other game birds.

Most of the flora found on other islands throughout the Pacific are also found in the Hawaiian Islands. Crops like sugar and pineapples, however, are not indigenous to the islands.

The seas around Hawaii abound in fish. Gamefish such as marlin, mahi mahi, swordfish, wahoo, skipjack, and yellowfin tuna are in the surrounding waters. Surf casting and shore fishing are popular pastimes with the local people. There is freshwater trout fishing on Kauai.

There have been various explanations of the name "Hawaii." It is said to have been named by Hawaii Loa, traditional discoverer of the islands, after himself. Hawaii or Hawaiiki, traditional home of the Polynesians, is also given as the origin. This is a compound word, Hawa, the name of the traditional place of residence, and -ii or -iiki, meaning little or small, thus, a smaller or new homeland. Since it also means raging or furious, the name is sometimes believed related to the volcanoes. It is often

Hawaiian Islands

(Sandwich Islands)
A state within the United States

Ports of Entry:

Hilo, Hawaii	19°44'N, 155°04'W
Kahului, Maui	20°54'N, 156°28'W
Honolulu, Oahu	21°19'N, 157°52'W
Nawiliwili, Kauai	21°57'N, 159°21'W

Distances between ports in nautical miles:

Between *Honolulu* and:

Apia, Western Samoa	2260
Agana, Guam	3320
Auckland, New Zealand	3820
Avatiu, Cook Islands	2550
Funafuti, Tuvalu	2250
Kwajalein, Marshall Islands	2160
Los Angeles, California	2230
Noumea, New Caledonia	3370
Nuku'alofa, Tonga	2750
Ocean Island	2480
Pago Pago, American Samoa	2280
Papeete, Society Islands	2380
Ponape, Caroline Islands	2690
Rabaul, New Britain	3360
Saipan, Mariana Islands	3230
San Diego, California	2280
San Francisco, California	2090

Suva, Fiji Islands	2780
Taiohae, Marquesas Islands	2100
Truk, Caroline Islands	3030
Vancouver, Canada	2420
Wake Island	2000
Yap, Caroline Islands	3760

Standard time:

10 hours slow on GMT

written with the glottal-stop mark as Hawai'i.

No one knows when Hawaii was first inhabited. It was long believed that the Polynesians first arrived in Hawaii from Tahiti around 1000 A.D., but new discoveries have suggested that the true date may be closer to 750 A.D.

Researchers believe that the Polynesians who conquered the Pacific in their doubled-hulled canoes came originally from Southeast Asia. Tahiti is thought to be one center of Polynesian development, but there is evidence indicating that Hawaii was first settled from the Marquesas. Regardless, to those familiar with the vast reaches of the Pacific Ocean, the seamanship of the Polynesians is a feat of staggering proportions.

Hawaii was discovered by the western world back in 1778, when British Captain James Cook sighted Oahu. Cook named the archipelago the Sandwich Islands, after his patron, the Earl of Sandwich, and for many years the islands were so known in the western world. In January 1779, Cook was slain in a fight with the Hawaiians at Kealakekua on the island of Hawaii.

At the time of Cook's arrival, each island was ruled as an independent kingdom by hereditary chiefs. One such chief, Kamehameha, consolidated his power on the island of Hawaii in a series of battles, about 1790, and then conquered Maui and Oahu. By the time of his death in 1819, Kamehameha I had united the islands under his rule and had established the Kingdom of Hawaii which survived until 1893.

In 1820, the first American missionaries arrived from New England. Not only did they bring Christianity to a people becoming disillusioned with their ancient gods, but they represented the first of several migrations which led to the cosmopolitan character of Hawaii's people today. In the years since Cook's arrival, Hawaii had become a center of whaling activity and had opened a trade in sandalwood with China, profitable for the king and the chiefs,

Radio Bay inside Hilo Harbor on the island of Hawaii offers Tahiti-style moorings along the container terminal back-up yard. Heavy surge in the winter months can be a problem. This is a Port of Entry for yachts.

Commercial ship traffic in Hilo Harbor does not affect the small boat harbor of Radio Bay behind the main wharf in the center of the picture. Blonde Reef Breakwater is seen extending to the left.

but a burden on the people who had to gather the wood. The introduction of western diseases and liquor, and a breakdown of the ancient morality, had created a chaotic situation. The missionaries gained great success because they aligned themselves with the chiefs against some of these evils.

The infant sugar industry had found a shortage of plantation labor and in 1852 Chinese were brought into the Kingdom by contract. Thus began the stream of imported labor which lasted until 1946. The first Japanese came in 1868, while Filipinos started arriving at a much later date. Koreans, Portuguese and Puerto Ricans are among the other national groups brought to the islands.

The growing importance of sugar was reflected in Hawaii's political picture during the next few decades. The sugar planters favored annexation of Hawaii by the United States to establish a firm market for the product. The Hawaiian monarchs, on the other hand, spasmodically attempted to establish and implement a policy of Hawaii for the Hawaiians. Hawaii's strategic military im-

portance in the Pacific was recognized, particularly its potential threat to the United States if another great power were to occupy the islands. By Joint Resolution of Congress, the islands were officially annexed, and formal transfer of sovereignty was made on August 12, 1898.

With annexation, the pattern for Hawaii's development during the next few decades was set. The sugar industry and the new pineapple industry were developed, and a continual stream of laborers were brought to the islands. Older workers, in turn, tended to leave the plantations for other occupations. There were some labor disputes, and even some violence, but no effective organization of labor.

The effects of the Great Depression in the 1930's were not as serious in Hawaii as they were in more industrialized areas. With growing international tensions, and particularly the aggressions of Japan in the Far East, the 30's saw a build-up of American military power in Hawaii. They also saw the binding of Hawaii closer to the mainland by Pan American World Airways' inauguration of regular commercial air flights in 1936.

Hawaii Island's only other enclosed harbor is this new facility at Kawaihae on the Kona Coast. This is a deep draft harbor but has small boat space well on the inside.

International tensions burst into flame on the morning of December 7, 1941, when the first Japanese bombs fell on Pearl Harbor causing nearly 4,000 casualties, and seriously crippling the great American fleet berthed there. Hawaii quickly mushroomed into an armed camp, and was the nerve center of America's whole Pacific war effort. The joyous celebration of V-J day on August 14, 1945 was heartfelt.

From the 30's through the 50's the dominant political-theme in Hawaii was statehood. First proposed during the reign of Kamehameha III, it became a more defined goal shortly after World War I, when Hawaii's delegate to Congress, Prince Jonah Kuhio Kalanianaole, introduced a bill to that effect in Congress. More strenuous efforts were made in the 30's, and this effort was continued after World War II.

All these efforts finally culminated in success in 1959, and both houses of Congress passed the necessary legislation on March 12. Hawaii officially entered the American Union as the 50th state on August 21, 1959.

Under Hawaii's state constitution, drawn up in 1950 and modified in 1968, executive powers are vested in Governor and Lt. Governor elected every 4 years. The state has a bicameral legislature; 51 Representatives are elected from 25 Districts for 2-year terms, and 25 Senators are elected from 8 Districts for 4-year terms. The legislature meets annually in Honolulu, the capital city.

The State Judiciary includes a 5-member Supreme Court and 4 District Courts whose judges are appointed by the Chief Justice of the State Supreme Court.

Hawaii is unique among all the states in that it enjoys only two levels of government: state and county. There are no separate municipalities, and no school districts or other smaller government jurisdictions. The city and county of Honolulu (Oahu) is governed by a Mayor and a 9-man City Council. The other counties (except Kalawao) are each governed by a Mayor and a county council.

Hawaii's people are young; more than half are under 25.

Moreover, everyone in Hawaii is a member of an ethnic

minority ... no single racial group constitutes more than about one-third of the population.

Hawaii's history has resulted in a multiracial society admired for its high degree of harmony and assimilation. In an American context, the various peoples of Asia have followed a pattern similar to that set by European immigrants to other areas of the United States. The second and third generations have become successful professional and technical people. They sit in the state legislature and in the halls of congress. They are doctors and lawyers, teachers and scientists, artists and musicians.

The people of Hawaii can trace ancestry to many ethnic and national groups of the world — Asian, Polynesian, European and others. While ancestral languages are still heard in Hawaii, English is universally used. Hawaii's citizens are Americans, nearly all of them were born under the American flag and educated in American schools. Since World War II, one out of three marriages in Hawaii has been interracial, which has further contributed to Hawaii's extremely cosmopolitan population.

Hawaii's religions are as diverse as is its cultural heritage. The missionaries who arrived in 1820 were Congregationalists. They were followed in 1827 by the Roman Catholics. In the Constitution of 1840, freedom of worship was guaranteed for all religions and there are now more than two dozen religious beliefs followed in these islands.

There are many church buildings in Hawaii, ranging from tiny one-room rural places of worship to the traditionally-styled St. Andrew's Cathedral and many churches in contemporary styles of architecture. There are also many imposing Buddhist temples and ancient Hawaiian heiaus.

Below college level, and excluding trade and business schools, there were 225 public and 120 private educational institutions in Hawaii during the 1974-75 school year, with a total enrollment of 211,702.

The University of Hawaii, with its main campus in

Kahului Harbor, Maui, is a commercial harbor and a Port of Entry. Anchorage can be taken in the unimproved areas of the harbor. The wave patterns seen here at near right angles to the prevailing wind may produce a rolly anchorage.

Lahaina, Maui, once the capital of Hawaii, has about the finest weather in the Hawaiian Islands. Visiting yachts anchor in Lahaina Roads which has good holding ground and is safe except in Kona storms.

Honolulu and a branch campus in Hilo, is a state university with a total enrollment of about 22,000 students.

Formerly under the University of Hawaii is the now independent, nonprofit East-West Center. Launched in 1960 with a $10 million appropriation from the U.S. Congress as an international training facility and an international college, it is providing education to students from Asia, Southeast Asia, the United States and other areas of the world.

In addition to the University, there are four smaller private colleges, seven public two-year community colleges and several business and technical schools.

Hawaii is one of the most prosperous states in the union. Its 1974 per capita personal income was $6,042, as compared with $5,539 in 1973 and $2,811 in 1964.

Hawaii's cost of living is higher than that of all Mainland areas, except Alaska, especially for housing and food. These higher costs are offset by the absence of heating costs and seasonal clothing requirements.

Hawaii's sources of basic income are the Federal government (particularly military), tourism, agriculture, and manufacturing.

Its great industrialized crops are sugar and pineapple, these are corporate enterprises. Hawaii has the most advanced sugar technology of any area in the world — so much so, that other countries have turned to Hawaii for assistance in developing sugar industries of their own. Among these are Iran and Peru.

Hawaiian pineapple is world famous for its quality and the industry for its technology. The total number of acres used by the industry is 57,500. Hawaii has nearly 5,500 year-round workers and more than 13,000 seasonal pineapple workers.

Among minor crops, macadamia nuts are rising in quantity and importance. New technology has permitted vastly increased shipments of fresh pineapple in recent years, and the same can be said of fresh papaya. Hawaii is the only state in the union which grows coffee; its Kona coffee is noted for its full body and fine aroma. The islands also export guava nectar, passion fruit (lilikoi) juice, orchids, anthuriums, and other varieties of Hawaiian flowers and foliage.

A variety of vegetables, as well as taro, mangoes, avocados, and citrus are grown for consumption in the islands.

A ranching industry supplies a substantial portion of the beef consumed in Hawaii. Parker Ranch, on the island of Hawaii, is one of the largest in land area in the United States.

A timber industry is considered to have excellent prospects. Recent efforts to use island timber for pallets have been particularly successful.

Now surpassing the two historic bases of Hawaii's economy, sugar and pineapple, is the visitor industry. In 1974, there were 2,786,000 visitors.

Growing rapidly has been manufacturing. Much of this constitutes manufacturing for the local market. Within the last few years, for example, there has been established an oil refinery, two cement plants, a steel mill, and pipe manufacturing plants, among others. A second oil refinery was completed in 1972. A third is planned.

An important and fast growing export industry is the manufacture of garments. "Hawaii wear" has become a world famous style, and has made Hawaii a Pacific fashion center.

While most of this economic growth has taken place on Oahu, other major islands have shown gains for the first time in decades. New resort complexes and hotels, requiring supporting industries and services, have been established in Maui, Kauai, Hawaii and Molokai.

Because Hawaii's people are Americans who can trace their lineage back to virtually every country in the world, the cultural resources of the islands are steeped with Oriental, Western and Polynesian traditions providing a colorful and fascinating environment.

A cosmopolitan influence is seen everywhere in Hawaii's architecture, music, art, theater, dress and foods. Cultures from other lands have filtered down through the generations to produce what is called today a "typical Hawaiian atmosphere."

The Bishop Museum in Honolulu is famous for its extensive collections of Pacific art and artifacts, and is a center of Pacific-wide ethnological research.

The Honolulu Academy of Arts is noted for its permanent collection of European, Oriental and Hawaiian art and it offers a wide range of educational programs to foster art appreciation.

There are noteworthy museums at Lihue on the island of Kauai and at Wailuku on Maui, at the Hulihee Palace in Kailua-Kona, and at Lyman House, Hilo.

The colorful little harbor at Maalaea, Maui, has problems with surge in all but the mildest weather conditions and becomes unbearable during Kona storms.

Jetsam and Flotsam

Currency:

Hawaii is a state of the United States and, therefore, uses the United States dollar ($). There are 100 cents in the dollar and coinage is issued in denominations of 1, 5, 10, 25, 50, and 100 cents. Notes are issued in 1, 2, 5, 10, 20, 50, and 100 dollars. It is recommended that notes larger than $20 be avoided because of the difficulty of cashing them at stores.

Language:

The indigenous language is Hawaiian which is a Polynesian dialect. It is spoken primarily by the descended Hawaiians. The official language of Hawaii is English and the unofficial language is pidgin. Japanese is also widely spoken as is Chinese by persons of those national heritages.

Electricity:

Electricity is commonly available and it is 110v, 60 Hz AC.

Postal Addresses:

Good postal service is available throughout the Hawaiian Islands. Recommended postal addresses are:

Yacht (   )
General Delivery
Hilo, HI 96720 USA

Yacht (   )
General Delivery
Honolulu, HI 96814, USA
                or
Yacht (   )
c/o Hawaii Yacht Club
P.O. Box 15931
Honolulu, HI 96815, USA

Yacht (   )
General Delivery
Kahului, HI 96732 USA
                or
Lahaina, HI 96761, USA

Yacht (   )
General Delivery
Lihui, HI 96766, USA
                or
Hanalei, HI 96714, USA

External Affairs Representative:

United States embassies and consulates

Information Center:

Hawaii Visitors Bureau
Suite 801, Waikiki Business Place
2270 Kalakaua Avenue
Honolulu, HI 96815, USA

Cruising Library:

Cruising Guide for the Hawaiian Islands, Arlo W. Fast and George Seberg; Pacific Writers Corporation, P. O. Box 1041, Honolulu, HI 96808, USA
Shoal of Time, Gavan Daws; University Press of Hawaii, 2840 Kolowalu Street, Honolulu, HI 96822, USA

The Weather

The climate of Hawaii is unusually pleasant even for the tropics. Its outstanding features are (1) the persistence of the trade winds, where not disrupted by high mountains; (2) the remarkable variability in rainfall over short distances; (3) the sunniness of the leeward lowlands, in contrast to the persistent cloudiness over nearby mountain crests; (4) the equable temperature from day to day and season to season; and (5) the infrequency of severe storms.

The prevailing wind throughout the year is the northeast trade wind, that blows for more than 90 percent of the time during the summer to only 50 percent in January.

Hawaii's equable temperatures are associated with the small seasonal variation in the amount of energy received from the sun and the tempering effect of the surrounding ocean.

Elevation is the major control factor in determining local temperatures, although location, whether in a leeward or windward position, is also a noticeable factor. The highest temperatures reached during the day in leeward districts are usually higher than those attained in windward areas. The daily range is also greater over leeward districts where, because of less cloudiness, the maximum temperatures are higher and the minimum temperatures usually lower.

August and September are the warmest months, and January and February are the coldest. At Honolulu there is an average monthly range between a low of 73°F in January and February, and a high of 79°F in August. The extreme range of temperatures at Honolulu for the 5-year period of record is from a low of 56°F for January, to a high of 93°F recorded in September. This spread of only 37°F between the extreme high and extreme low temperatures is small when compared with ranges at other Pacific coasts ports.

All coastal areas are subject to the relatively high humidities associated with a marine climate. Humidities, however, vary considerably, with high percentages over and near the windward slopes to low percentages on the leeward sides of the higher elevations.

Average water temperatures at Waikiki Beach vary from 75°F in the morning to 77°F in the afternoon during March, and from 77°F in the morning to 82°F in the afternoon during August.

Because of the persistence of the northeast trade winds, even the warmest months are usually comfortable. But when the trades diminish or give way to southern winds, a situation known locally as "kona weather" ("kona storms" when stormy), the humidity may become oppressively high.

The word "kona" is of Polynesian origin and means leeward. It refers to the southern winds and accompanying weather on the normally leeward slopes of the principal Hawaiian Islands which, because of the wind shift, have temporarily become the windward slopes.

The konas, which occur most frequently during October through April, provide the major climatic variations of the Hawaiian Islands. During kona storms, heavy rainfall and cloudiness can be expected on the lee sides of coasts and slopes, which, under the usual wind pattern, receive less cloudiness and may have almost no rain. Near gales may occur, especially in areas where the air tends to funnel into sharp mountain passes near the coasts. At such times normally leeward anchorages may become unsafe for small craft.

Intense rains of the October to April "winter" season sometimes causes serious local flash flooding. Thunderstorms are infrequent and usually mild, as compared with those of the midwestern United States. Hail seldom occurs, and when it does it is small and rarely damaging to crops. At great intervals a small tornado or a waterspout moving onshore may do some slight damage.

Except for rare 1- or 2-day disruptions of interisland airplane schedules, interference to shipping or travel because of bad weather is almost unknown.

The northeast tradewinds bring the rain-bearing clouds, which are caught by the mountains. Thus, there is an enormous range of rainfall with the windward sides of the islands being generally wetter than the leeward sides.

Waialeale on the island of Kauai has a mean annual rainfall of 486 inches and is one of the two wettest spots on earth, although there are areas on the same island, only a few miles away, which have a rainfall of less than 20 inches a year. The driest spot is Puako, on Hawaii, with a mean average of only 10 inches a year.

The complicated rainfall pattern over the islands results chiefly from the effects of the rugged terrain on the persistent trade winds. Frequent and heavy showers fall almost daily on windward and upland areas, while rains of sufficient intensity and duration to cause more than temporary inconvenience are infrequent over the lower sections of leeward areas.

In the district where the tradewinds are dominant, rains are decidedly heavier at night than during the day. This applies generally to the greater part of the islands.

Considerably more rain falls from November through April over the islands as a whole than from May through October. It is not unusual for an entire summer month to go by without measurable rain falling at some points in the Maui isthmus.

Annual rainfall in the Honolulu area averages less than 30 inches along the coast (25 inches at the airport, 24 inches in the downtown area), but increases inland at about 30 inches a mile. Parts of the Koolau Range average 300 inches or more a year. This heavy mountain rainfall sustains extensive irrigation of cane fields and the water supply for Honolulu. East (windward) of the Koolaus, coastal areas receive 30 to 50 inches annually; cane and pineapple fields in central Oahu get about 35 to 40 inches. Oahu is driest along the coast west of the Waianaes where rainfall drops to about 20 inches a year. However, variations from month to month and year to year are considerable; more so during the cooler season, when occasional major storms provide much of the rain, than in the summer, when rain occurs primarily as showers that form within the moist tradewinds as they override the mountains. Tradewind rainfall is more frequent at night, but daytime showers, usually light, often occur while the sun continues to shine, a phenomenon

59

The small boat at Manele Bay, Lanai, has depths of 4 to 6 feet at low tide and only a small number of slips. Manele Bay is known locally as Black Manele and Hulupoe Bay across the peninsula is known as White Manele.

referred to locally as "liquid sunshine."

From the dry uninhabited atolls of the west to the lush green islands on the east, the chain has a full variety of weather including snow at the mountain summits of Hawaii.

The strongest influence in the pressure pattern underlying the general circulation of air over the Hawaiian Islands area is the semipermanent high-pressure cell known as the Pacific high. The clockwise circulation around this cell, coupled with a slight deflection of the surface winds away from the high pressure, result in the northeast trades that are the dominant winds of the area.

The tradewind influence is dominant in all seasons throughout the greater part of the islands. In some local areas, winds deviate from the general pattern because of topography. In coastal areas where mountains to the east project high above sea level as they do in the kona districts of the island of Hawaii, the trades are cut off resulting in prevalent southwest winds with land and sea breezes in evidence. Such effects may be rather general in some areas and extremely local in others.

The Hawaiian Islands lie at the extremities of both the western North Pacific typhoon area and the eastern North Pacific hurricane area. Therefore, a tropical cyclone from either distant region is rare.

Typhoons can form in any month, but they rarely move east of 180°; when they do they are usually extratropical and well north of the islands. It is not impossible, but highly improbable, that a typhoon will move through the Hawaiian Islands.

It is more probable that an eastern North Pacific hurricane would hit the islands. These storms, prevalent from May through November, originate off the western Mexican coast between 10°N and 20°N. August is the most favorable month for one of these storms to reach the area, although they have occurred from July through November.

Four hurricanes have struck Hawaii since 1950, but several times that many, and a number of less intense tropical cyclones, most of them drifting west from their breeding grounds off the Mexican coast, have approached near enough for their outlying winds, clouds, and rain to affect the islands.

It is not the winds, however, which have caused Hawaii's most significant damage but tsunamis, those massive ocean swells caused by violent undersea earthquakes, generated thousands of miles away. Of no concern to the mariner at sea, they grow into immense waves in shoal waters battering shorelines and harbors. In past years damage and loss of life was so great that an extensive tsunami warning system was built in the Pacific Basin to alert the dwellers of the basin in case a tsunami develops anywhere in the Pacific. Tsunamis, like their parent earthquakes, are unpredictable, but unlike earthquakes you may have a few hours of warning time as the wave takes a finite time to traverse the broad ocean even at its great speed of up to 400 knots.

The size of a predicted tsunami cannot be estimated in advance. Most of them felt in Honolulu harbor have been relatively small; the largest of record was 10 feet high, in 1960. However, it is prudent to anticipate that even greater ones may strike.

Honolulu harbor authorities require all ships to vacate the harbor prior to the estimated time of arrival of a sea wave if possible.

Probably the only consistent sailing problem found in the Hawaiian waters is the roughness of the channels between the major islands. Straddling the tradewinds and prevailing currents, the islands form a barrier to normal surface flows with the result that the winds and currents funnel at accelerated speed through the channels. The channel waters develop steep waves which make cross-channel sailing real work when the trades are blowing strong. Night passages are generally chosen because of their quieter nature. The channels range in width from 8 miles to 63 miles and the principal ones are:

Name	Between	Miles
Alenuihaha	Hawaii and Maui	26
Pailolo	Maui and Molokai	8
Kaiwi (Molokai Channel)	Molokai and Oahu	23
Kauai	Oahu and Kauai	63

Yacht Entry

When a yacht arrives in the United States from an overseas foreign port, the first landing must be at a Port of Entry or designated place where customs service is available. This applies to *both* United States and foreign flag yachts.

If your boat has anchored or tied-up, you are considered to have entered the United States. No person shall board or leave the boat prior to completion of customs processing without permission from the Customs officer in charge, except to report arrival. If it is necessary for someone to leave the boat to report arrival to customs, he must return to the boat after reporting and remain on

In the shadows of Waikiki's famous hotels, Ala Wai Boat Harbor, is modern and efficiently run offering visiting yachts a 30-day stay. Excellent shopping facilities, marine stores and public transportation make this a good Port of Entry.

board. No one who arrived on board the boat may leave until the Customs officer grants permission to go ashore. Violations may result in sustantial penalties and even forfeiture of the boat. Customs officers will notify other departments which are involved in clearing an overseas boat into Hawaii.

There are four Ports of Entry in the Hawaiian Islands. They are Hilo, Hawaii; Kahului, Maui; Honolulu, Oahu; and Nawiliwili, Kauai. Whether coming from the continental United States or foreign ports, all yachts must clear in through one of these four ports.

Foreign yachts entering the United States at Hawaii must abide by all the Immigration, Customs, Agriculture, and Health regulations as in entering any other part of the United States. The following section describes procedures for entering yachts and non-immigrant crewmen whether on foreign or U.S. yachts.

Immigration

The immigration laws of the United States deal with aliens which includes all persons who are not citizens or nationals of the United States. In preparing for a cruise to the United States, each crewman should apply abroad to a United States consulate for a visa appropriate to his desired entry status which in all probability will be one of the two following classes of non-immigrants: (a) An alien having a residence in a foreign country which he has no intention of abandoning who is visiting the United States temporarily for pleasure, or (b) An alien crewman serving in good faith as such in any capacity required for the nor-

Medical Memo

Immunization requirements:

United States citizens coming directly from another United States port meet all the requirements. Foreign yachts or United States yachts coming from foreign ports must have a smallpox vaccination certificate less than three years old. Vaccinations for cholera and yellow fever are required if you have transited or visited within the last six days an area currently infected.

Local health situtation:

The Hawaiian Islands are free of all communicable diseases.

Health services:

Hawaii has excellent medical care in first-rate hospitals and qualified doctors on all of the principal islands. Except for the military and the Public Health Service, all medicine is privately practiced. Medical costs are very high.

Dental and optical services are also available in most towns from private practitioners.

Drug stores carry a full line of non-prescription and prescription drugs. Prescription drugs are sold only on the order of a doctor.

IAMAT*Center:

Honolulu: Queen's Medical Center
             Chief of Staff: Benjamin Tom, MD
             Executive Director: Will J. Henderson

Water:

Tap water from the public supplies is good in all the islands. Water from private wells or streams should be considered suspect and treated.

*IAMAT (International Association for Medical Assistance to Travelers):

A worldwide association of medical doctors to provide medical assistance to travelers who, while absent from their home country, may find themselves in need of medical or surgical care or of any form of medical treatment. This is done by providing those travelers with the names of medical centers in countries other than that to which they are native and the names of locally-licensed practitioners who have command of the native language spoken by the traveler and who agree to a stated and standard list of medical fees for their services.

Honolulu Harbor, Oahu, wraps around Sand Island and is the major commercial port for the Hawaiian Islands. There are essentially no yacht facilities in this port. Ala Wai Boat Harbor is off the right of the picture and Keehi Lagoon begins at the left edge.

mal operation and service on board a vessel who intends to land temporarily and solely in pursuit of his calling as a crewman and to depart from the United States with the vessel on which he arrived or some other vessel.

One problem to consider is the often unpredictable schedule of a cruising yacht since one condition for granting a visa assumes that you will arrive in the United States within the period of validity of the visa. It is recommended that a visa be gotten at the last possible port of call having a United States consulate so that the element of time uncertainty is minimized. But don't try to enter without a visa. A person requiring a visa who succeeds in obtaining transportation to the United States and is not in possession of a visa, may be denied admission and deported.

Upon arrival of an alien at a United States Port of Entry, he will be examined for admissability under the immigration statutes. If an alien is found to be inadmissible, he is not to be admitted even though he is in possession of proper documents.

Aliens, generally, must possess valid unexpired visas and passports when applying for admission to the United States. A non-immigrant must have a passport valid for a minimum of six months from the date of expiration of the period of his admission authorizing him to enter another country during that six months.

A non-immigrant may be admitted initially for whatever period the admitting officer deems appropriate to accomplish the intended purpose of his temporary stay. He is permitted to stay in the United States upon these conditions:

1. That while in the United States he will maintain the particular non-immigrant status under which he was admitted.

2. That he will depart from the United States within the period of his admission.

3. That while in the United States he will not engage in any employment unless he has been accorded such authorization.

If an extension of time is required, application should

A view of Honolulu Harbor, Honolulu International Airport and the plains of Ewa taken from the Aloha Tower.

be made at least 15 days prior to expiration of the initial admission.

A non-immigrant may be required to post a bond of not less than $500 as a condition precedent to his admission, to insure that he will depart from the United States at the expiration of his admission time and that he will maintain the immigration status under which he was admitted.

No hard and fast rule can be laid down as to the amount of money an alien should have on his arrival. Inflation is causing prices to rise in the United States as well as elsewhere. In particular, medical care is outrageously high in the United States, and medical bills could be the unfortunate yachtsman's undoing.

A word of warning to skippers of United States yachts carrying alien crewmen: Be sure that they have proper papers for entering the United States or you will be guilty of aiding and abetting an illegal entry.

Customs for Foreign Yachts

The master of a foreign yacht must report arrival to U.S. Customs within 24 hours and make formal entry within 48 hours. In the absence of a cruising license, vessels in this category must obtain a permit before proceeding to each subsequent U.S. port. The boat must also clear customs prior to departing for a foreign port.

A non-resident bringing his pleasure boat into the country under his duty free customs exemption, must formally enter the boat and pay applicable Customs duty before he sells it or offers it for sale or charter within the United States.

Cruising licenses exempt pleasure boats of certain countries from formal entry and clearance procedures at all but the first Port of Entry. They can be obtained from the Customs Director at the first port of arrival in the United States. Normally issued for no more than a six month period, a cruising license has no bearing on the dutiability of a pleasure boat. Vessels of the following countries are eligible for cruising licenses because these same countries extend reciprocal privileges to United States yachts:

Argentina	Great Britain
Australia	Honduras

Nawiliwili, Kauai, is a Port of Entry preferred by yachties because of its proximity to the principal town of Lihue. Yacht facilities are, however, minimal.

Bahama Islands Jamaica
Bermuda Liberia
Canada Netherlands
West Germany New Zealand

Once the cruising license has been granted, the yacht can freely cruise the domestic waters listed on the license. A report of arrival must still be made at each port where there is a Customhouse. But there is no requirement to go to the Customhouse or to present the vessel or its occupants for inspection. The report of arrival is generally done by telephone.

Customs for United States Yachts

American yachts must report arrival from a foreign area to Customs within 24 hours and must also report foreign merchandise aboard the vessel that is subject to duty. The report may be made by any means of communication. If an inspection is required, the Customs officer will direct the vessel to an inspection area. No notification is required when a United States boat departs for foreign ports.

Because yachts carry considerable foreign-made equip-ment on board, sometimes including the yacht itself, it may be wise to declare these items before departing, thereby eliminating any argument on return whether the duty has been paid or not. This is in lieu of trying to keep a complete file of receipts of purchase on all foreign-made equipment.

Articles imported in excess of your customs exemption will be subject to duty calculated by the Customs inspec-tor, unless the items are entitled to free entry or prohibited. Your exemptions are the same as any U.S. citizen traveler.

Firearms

Firearms and ammunition intended for legitimate hunting or lawful sporting purposes may be brought into the United States, provided that any remaining unfired am-munition is taken out upon your departure. All other firearms and ammunition are subject to restriction and im-port permits. A permit to carry a firearm is issued by a state or local government and is for a specified area. The laws of most states allow a person to transport firearms through the state provided that the firearms are not

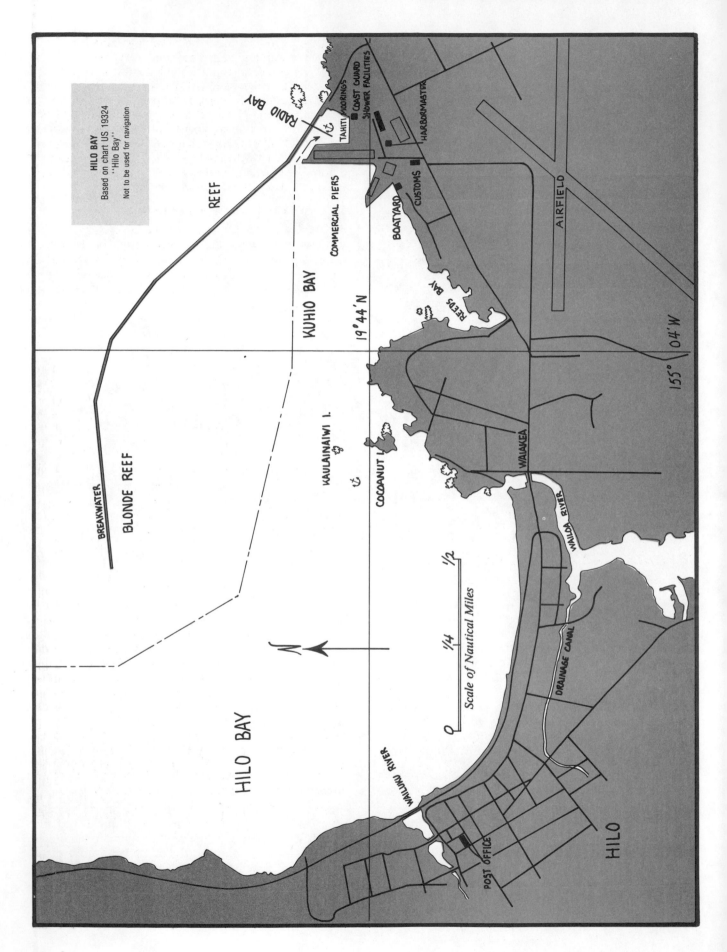

HILO BAY
Based on chart US 19324
"Hilo Bay"
Not to be used for navigation

REEF

BREAKWATER

BLONDE REEF

KUHIO BAY

RADIO BAY

TAHITI MOORINGS

COAST GUARD
SHOWER FACILITIES

HARBORMASTR

COMMERCIAL PIERS

BOATYARD

CUSTOMS

REEDS BAY

19°44'N

155° 04'W

AIRFIELD

KAULAINAIWI I.

COCOANUT I.

WAIAKEA

WAILOA RIVER

DRAINAGE CANAL

HILO BAY

WAILUKU RIVER

POST OFFICE

HILO

N

Scale of Nautical Miles

0   ¼   ½

66

readily accessible. Every person arriving in the state of Hawaii with a firearm shall within 48 hours of arrival register that firearm with the Chief of Police of the local island government. Note that hunting licenses are required in all of the United States.

Agricultural Inspection

It is illegal to bring many types of meats, fruits, vegetables, plants, animal, and animal products into the United States without approval from the Department of Agriculture. This approval extends to special products which may be harmful to a particular state's agriculture, hence it may differ slightly depending on your Port of Entry to the United States. United States yachts transiting between states are also subject to the agricultural import laws of the destination state.

The U.S. Public Health Service requires that pets brought into this country be examined at the Port of Entry to make certain that they show no evidence of disease that can be passed on to humans and that they meet the requirements of other specific regulations. Pets taken out of the United States and returned are subject to the same requirements as those entering for the first time.

There is a 72-hour quarantine period for cats and dogs aboard the arriving vessel after which they must be shipped via air to the Animal Quarantine Center in Honolulu. The animals are quarantined at the Center for a period of 120 days at a cost of $2.45 per day for a dog and $2.05 per day for a cat. You will also be required to pay an initial fee of $10.00 for the booking. The full 120 days fee must be paid in advance but, if you leave Hawaii before the 120 days is up, you can get a refund of the unused balance. Further information on bringing pets into Hawaii can be obtained from the Hawaii Department of Agriculture, P. O. Box 22159, Honolulu, HI 96822, USA.

Fishing Licenses

For salt water fishing in the state of Hawaii, there are no seasons, limits, or license requirements. This is not true in the other United States for either residents or non-residents so you must inquire when you arrive in another state.

Yacht Facilities

The Hawaiian Islands provide the best harbor and maintenance facilities to be found within the rim of the Pacific Ocean. Most of these facilities are in the Honolulu area so for other than emergency services, you will do best sailing to Honolulu. The Honolulu area with its 600,000 residents also assures a good supply of food and drink plus American-style clothing. Prices are, however, higher than on the mainland because of additional transportation expenses. There are slipways and repair facilities at Ala Wai Yacht Harbor, Kewalo Basin, Honolulu Harbor, and Keehi Lagoon. Fuel docks can supply all needed fuels and good drinking water is available at all places.

There is one fly in the ointment of paradise, however, and that is the great overcrowding of all boating facilities. The main Hawaiian Islands are still young islands and erosion and coral polyps have not had time to build many natural harbors around the periphery of the islands. This, together with the natural seafaring nature of the islanders and the attraction of the 50th United State to sailors from the Mainland, keeps all facilities occupied. If you plan on a stay longer than 30 days, be prepared to shift anchorages. Boats from the Mainland staying over 90 days may be requested to register in Hawaii but that doesn't mean that they will get any slip preference. The summer season is particularly crowded with seasonal cruising boats arriving from the Mainland as well as racing fleets descending on the islands every year from the Mainland.

Yacht Facilities at Ports of Entry

Hilo, Hawaii: Hilo is a rather large but greatly underused harbor. It faces into the prevailing winds but is protected to a large extent by Blonde Reef and the breakwater atop it. There is a designated anchorage adjacent to Kaulainaiwi Island but the Harbor Master does not want yachts anchoring out. Instead he will direct you to Radio Bay which is a snug small-boat mooring area behind the main wharf.

In Radio Bay you can anchor out or moor Tahiti-style to the quay. Unlike Tahiti, though, there is a significant tidal change preventing the close-in positioning needed for a stern gangway. Instead your dinghy is your shoreboat. Ashore there are head and shower facilities which *must* be used to keep this rather enclosed harbor clean. Small stores are within walking distance and major stores are in Hilo which is a short bus ride away. There are limited repair facilities and marine parts available. If you really need major parts or work done, you must go to Honolulu.

Charges for the Tahiti-style moorings vary according to the following schedule:

Up to 20 ft. LOA	$US2 per day
20 to 30	$US3
30 to 40	$US4
40 to 50	$US5
50 ft. and over	$US6

The first 72 hours of stay are free but if you stay longer than 72 hours then there is no free time allotted. You can live aboard your boat for up to 30 days in Radio Bay at the above costs although you can leave your boat in Radio Bay for a longer period at the same rate while living ashore. You will also be assessed an insurance charge of $US3.

Kahului, Maui: Kahului Harbor is located on the northeast coast of Maui and is a deep water shipping port. It has man-made breakwaters to protect the harbor from the swells and waves generated by the tradewinds. The harbor is approximately 1/3rd mile square and small craft have plenty of anchorage room in the unimproved areas behind the breakwaters. Yachts coming from overseas ports should seek an unoccupied spot along the wharf and call the Customs officials to initiate clearance. Do not remain along the wharf any longer than necessary to conduct entry formalities as they are needed for commerical shipping. Seek an anchorage when your clearance is effected.

The town of Kahului has good shopping facilities, laun-

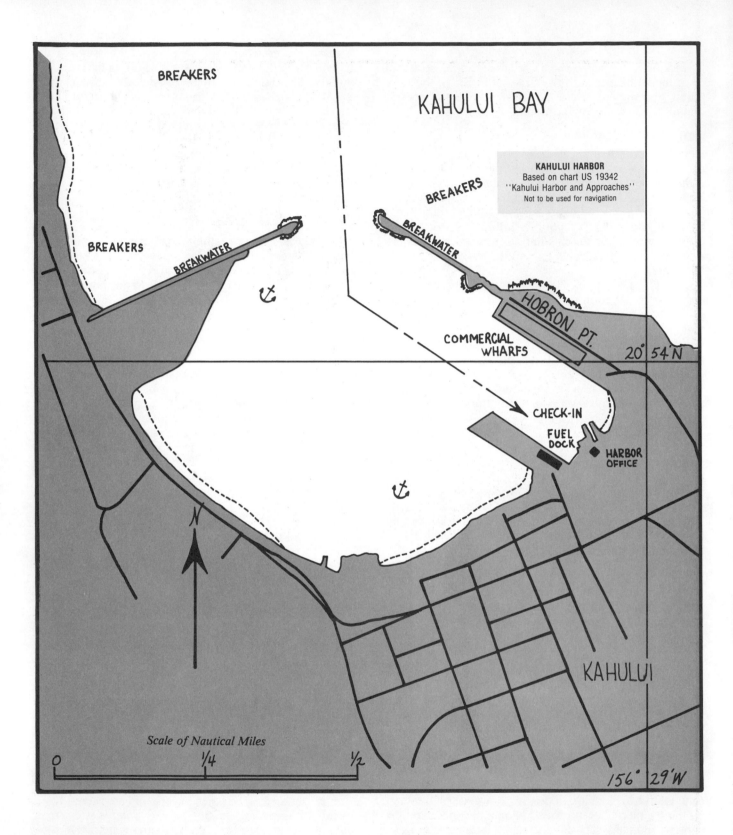

KAHULUI BAY

BREAKERS

BREAKERS

BREAKERS

BREAKWATER

BREAKWATER

BREAKWATER

HOBRON PT.

COMMERCIAL WHARFS

20° 54'N

CHECK-IN

FUEL DOCK

HARBOR OFFICE

N

KAHULUI

Scale of Nautical Miles

0   1/4   1/2

156° 29'W

dry, etc. but there are no particular amenities for yachts. Engine fuels are available. If you need any boat supplies, repairs done, or other maintenance needs you will have to go to Lahaina, if small, or to Honolulu, if large.

Most yachts favor Lahaina once formalities are completed. It is a colorful old whaling town and was once the capital of Hawaii. There is a harbor at Lahaina but it is small and fully occupied with local craft. Anchoring outside the harbor is good in all except kona weather.

In even-numbered years the Victoria-Maui race takes place and the facilities at Lahaina are overburdened by an additional 30 or so racing boats but there is adequate room in Lahaina Roads for everyone.

The Lahaina Yacht Club extends a guest membership

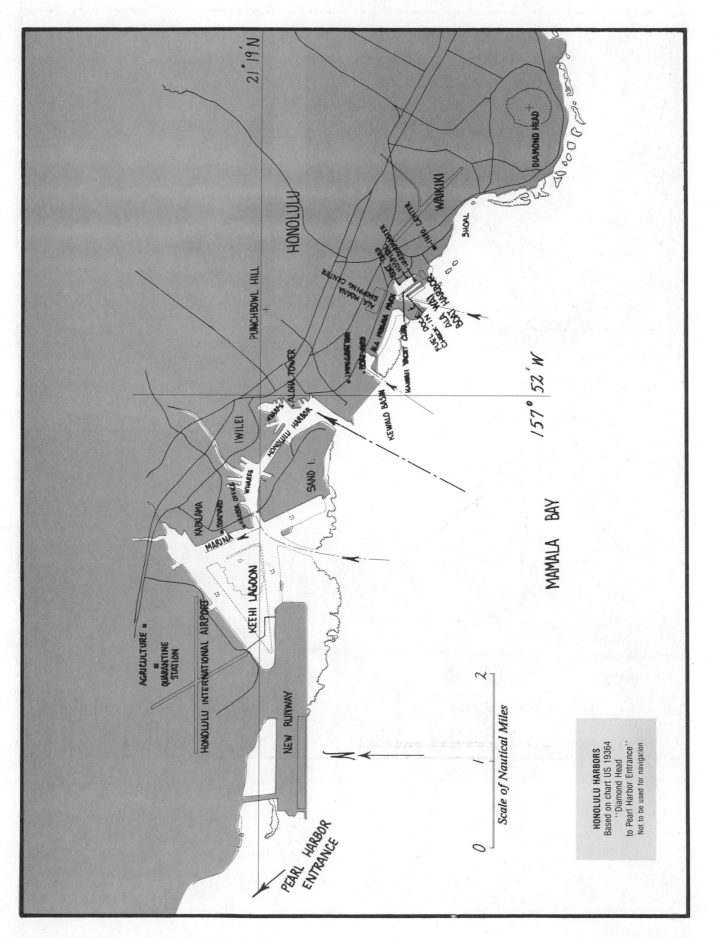

HONOLULU

DIAMOND HEAD

WAIKIKI

SHOAL

21° 19' N

PUNCHBOWL HILL

LINO CENTER

ALA MOANA SHOPPING CENTER

HARBOR OFFICE

FORT ARMY
MUSEUM

ALA WAI YACHT HARBOR

FUEL DOCK

CHECK-IN

ALA WAI
BOAT
HARBOR

IMMIGRANT TERM.

SEAPLANE

ALOHA TOWER

WHARFS

HAWAII YACHT CLUB

KEWALO BASIN

157° 52' W

IWILEI

WHARFS

HONOLULU HARBOR

SAND I.

KAPALAMA

BOATYARD

HARBOR OFFICE

MARINA

MAMALA BAY

AGRICULTURE
QUARANTINE STATION

HONOLULU INTERNATIONAL AIRPORT

KEEHI LAGOON

NEW RUNWAY

N

Scale of Nautical Miles

0   1   2

PEARL HARBOR ENTRANCE

HONOLULU HARBORS
Based on chart US 19364
"Diamond Head
to Pearl Harbor Entrance"
Not to be used for navigation

69

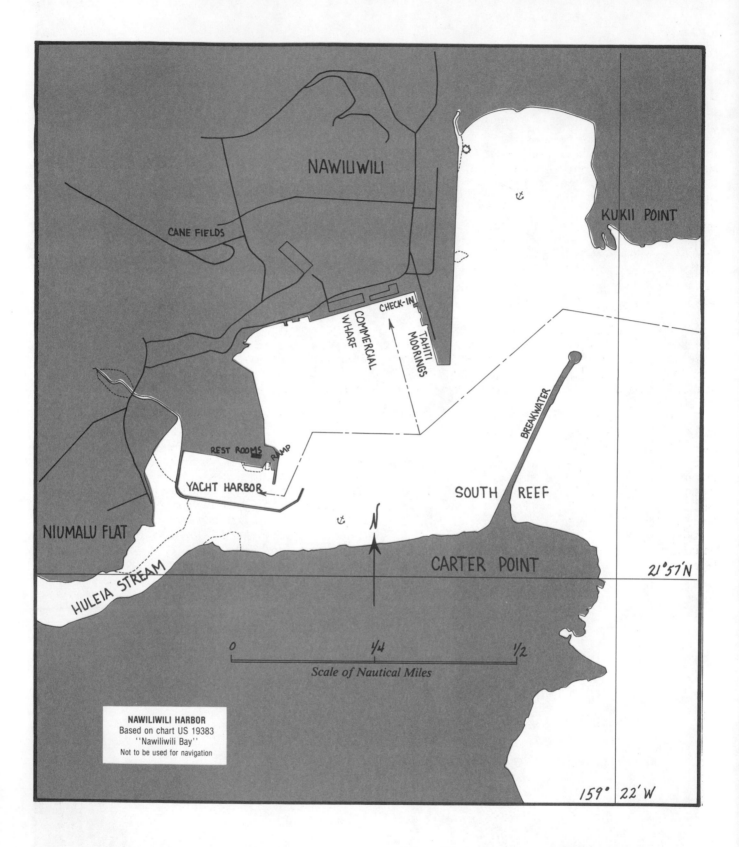

NAWILIWILI
CANE FIELDS
COMMERCIAL WHARF
CHECK-IN
TAHITI MOORINGS
KUKII POINT
REST ROOMS
RAMP
YACHT HARBOR
NIUMALU FLAT
HULEIA STREAM
N
SOUTH REEF
BREAKWATER
CARTER POINT
21°57'N
159° 22'W

0   1/4   1/2
Scale of Nautical Miles

NAWILIWILI HARBOR
Based on chart US 19383
''Nawiliwili Bay''
Not to be used for navigation

to those arriving by yacht and there is no charge for the first two weeks. Hot showers are available as well as food and refreshments. If you desire to stay longer than two weeks, a special membership at a rate of $8.50 per month for three months is available.

Honolulu, Oahu: There are actually several harbors of interest to yachtsmen in the Honolulu area. Two are specifically yacht harbors, they are Ala Wai and Keehi Lagoon. The other two are Kewalo Basin which is primarily a fishing harbor — both commercial and sportfishing, and Honolulu which is the primary deep water port of the Hawaiian Islands. Technically, entry could be made at any of these harbors but it is recommended that entry formalities be made at Ala Wai which is the most popular for yachtsmen. There is a fuel dock immediately inside the reef where you can call the Customs office and make arrangements for the clearance formalities.

Ala Wai boat harbor is overcrowded but restrictions on the length of stay of non-resident yachts keeps the transient slips rotating so everyone can have some chance of using the facilities. The Hawaii Yacht Club has Tahiti-style moorings which are available on a two week basis with the use of their club facilities for that time. Otherwise, yachts must check in with the Harbor Master who will try to locate slips for up to a month's stay. There are heads and showers available for the use of crews. Dock fees amount to $2.00 per day with a $20 deposit for the head key. Anchoring is also permissable in the turning basin opposite the fuel dock and the Hawaii Yacht Club.

There is a boatyard in the harbor which can handle craft up to 45 feet long. You can do the work yourself or hire the services of yard personnel which are very expensive. Outside the yard there are many service shops for engine, rigging, electronics, etc., which you can engage for your special needs and probably more reasonably than the boat yard.

Provisioning and shopping of all kinds can be done on foot at the large Ala Moana shopping center nearby. Everything of a personal need can be found in the vicinity.

Every odd-numbered year the Los Angeles to Honolulu race takes place with over 70 racing boats descending on Ala Wai for the months of July and August severely taxing their facilities. Plan not to be there at that time.

Keehi Lagoon is located to the west of the other three harbors and is fronted by coral reefs. The cuts through the lagoon are former seaplane landing areas. The harbor has some slips, both publicly and privately operated, and an anchorage area. It has one major drawback though, and that is it is located under the flight path of Honolulu International airport making it a noisy location.

Nawiliwili, Kauai: Nawiliwili is the principal port of Kauai and is located on the southeast coast of the island. It is well protected from all winds. The outer harbor is for commercial shipping. A small craft harbor is being developed about 100 yards to the southwest of the commercial wharfs in the Huleia stream. There are no slips or facilities of any kind but anchoring is permitted inside the basin. If you are seeking customs clearance, it is best to tie up alongside the main wharf in an area which will not interfere with commercial activities and call customs from there. After you are cleared, proceed to anchor out in the small craft basin. The Harbor Master can advise you on the best place to set your hook.

Fuel is available at the commercial wharf via tank trucks and potable water is piped to the wharf. Marine supplies of a general nature may be obtained in the neighboring town of Lihue as can most provisions. There are also some small shops to assist with repair work but there are no haulout facilities. The town of Lihue is the best place on Kauai for provisioning or obtaining marine services.

The favorite yacht anchorage on Kauai is Hanalei Bay on the north side of the island. From May to October it is a safe anchorage with just enough facilities to make yacht living easy and rustic enough to be pleasant. During the winter months, however, northers can produce surge, swell, waves and surf making it unpleasant if not untenable. You can anchor Tahiti-style to the tire-fendered commercial wharf outside the commercial working area and you can also anchor Tahiti-style in the small boat harbor. Your length of stay is limited to 30 days and the first three days are free. After that it is 20 to 58 cents per foot per month with extra charges for living aboard.

Radio Communications

Station name and call	Location	Frequency Transmit/Receive	Service hours LMT	Type of service
Hawaii				
KIPA	Hilo	620 kHz	0550-2400	Commercial broadcast
KPUA	Hilo	670 & 970	24 hours	" "
KLEI	Kailua	1130	24 hours	" "
Maui				
KMVI	Wailuku	550	0455-2400	Commercial broadcast
Oahu				
KGMB	Honolulu	590	24 hours	Commercial broadcast
KORL	"	650	"	" "
KKUA	"	690		" "
KGU	"	760	"	" "
KIKI	"	830	"	" "
KAIM	"	870	0500-2400	" "
KAHU	Waipahu	940	24 hours	" "
KHVH	Honolulu	1040	"	" "
KIOE	"	1080	"	" "
KPOI	"	1380	"	" "
KCCN	"	1420	0430-2400	" "
KUMU	"	1500	24 hours	" "
Kauai				
KIVM	Lihue	570 & 1350	24 hours	Commercial broadcast
KUAI	Eleele	720	0500-2400	" "

Port Allen at Hanapepe Bay is a second Port of Entry on Kauai and has the best-equipped small boat harbor outside of Honolulu.

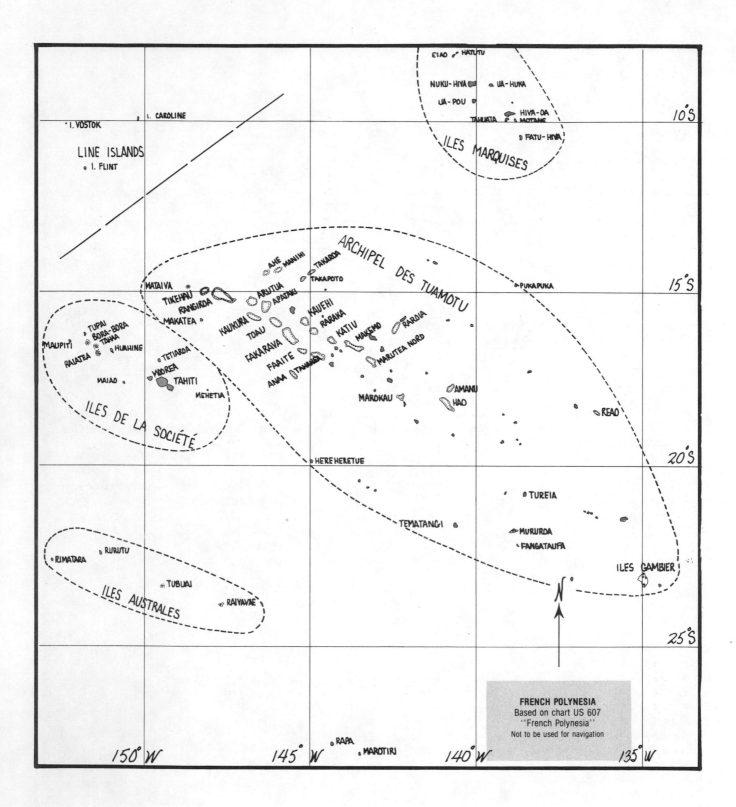

I. VOSTOK

I. CAROLINE

LINE ISLANDS

I. FLINT

ELAO   HATUTU

NUKU-HIVA   UA-HUKA

UA-POU

TAHUATA   HIVA-OA
MOTANE

FATU-HIVA

ILES MARQUISES

10°S

AHE   MANIHI   TAKAROA

MATAIVA   TAKAPOTO   ARCHIPEL DES TUAMOTU

TIKEHAU   ARUTUA   PUKAPUKA   15°S
RANGIROA   APATAKI

MAKATEA   KAUKURA   KAUEHI
TOAU   RARAKA   RAROIA

TUPAI   FAKARAVA   KATIU   MAKEMO
BORA-BORA   FAAITE   MARUTEA NORD
RAIATEA   TAHAA   HUAHINE   ANA   TAHANEA

MAUPITI   TETIAROA

MOOREA   AMANU
MAIAO   TAHITI   MAROKAU   HAO   REAO

MEHETIA

ILES DE LA SOCIÉTÉ

20°S

HEREHERETUE

TUREIA

TEMATANGI   MURUROA

FANGATAUFA

RURUTU

RIMATARA   ILES GAMBIER

TUBUAI

N

ILES AUSTRALES   RAIVAVAE

25°S

FRENCH POLYNESIA
Based on chart US 607
"French Polynesia"
Not to be used for navigation

RAPA
MAROTIRI

150° W   145° W   140° W   135° W

Chapter 6
FRENCH POLYNESIA

The Country

French Polynesia is an overseas territory of France consisting of four distinct island groups in the southeast corner of Oceania. The combined land area of all groups is a little over 1,500 square miles, and the overall population in 1970 was 98,400 persons. Except for small colonies of French and Chinese and about 10,000 French military personnel stationed in the area in connection with French atomic testing, the inhabitants are all Polynesian of rather unadulterated lineage. About one-half of the total population lives on the island of Tahiti in the Society group.

Island groups constituting French Polynesia are the Society Islands, The Tuamotu Archipelago, the Marquesas Islands, and the Austral Islands. Two small isolated areas, Rapa and Bass islands, lying far south of the main groups, are also part of the territory. The Society, Marquesas, and Austral groups are high volcanic islands; the Tuamotu Archipelago is composed entirely of low-lying atolls, except one, Makatea, which is a raised atoll.

The area has no native animals and only a few birds. Fish, both game and food varieties, abound near the reefs and seas throughout the area. Some islands of the western Society group are famous for the quality of the crabs found in their lagoons and the Tuamotus are noted for the fine pearls from the oysters in their waters.

No group of islands captures the spirit and romance of the South Seas more completely than those of French Polynesia. Known to Spanish and Dutch explorers as early as the sixteenth century, it was not until the eighteenth century that the islands came into scientific prominence with the explorations of Captain Cook. Even then, these islands half a world away from Europe, were of little consequence until the ill-fated breadfruit expedition of Captain Bligh on the HMS *Bounty* in 1788. From then on the islands were to become the unwilling hosts to a multitude of explorers, whaling ships, and missionaries. French and British rivalry backed up by naval forces soon convinced the Tahitians that they would have to pledge loyalty to one or the other of the European powers for their own protection. In 1843 France took formal possession of Tahiti and Moorea and, during the remainder of the nineteenth century, annexed all the islands of the Society, Marquesas, Tuamotu, and Austral groups into what we know today as French Polynesia.

French Polynesia lies near the center of the Polynesian Triangle and is thought to have been settled about the fifth century by Polynesian mariners arriving from the Gilbert Islands in Micronesia. Lost in an unwritten history are the real details of settlement of the four island groups comprising 109 islands of 1544 square miles area spread out over an ocean area of 1,540,000 square miles. While the original center of religious and political power was on the island of Raiatea, Tahiti, because of its large size and great fertility, became the most populous of the Society Islands and eventually gained political power over its neighbors. Today, Tahiti is the seat of government for French Polynesia which has resulted in all the peoples of this area being called Tahitians.

The islands of French Polynesia contain a cross section of the geologic history of Pacific land masses. The Marquesas are the high islands, young in age, too new to have developed any appreciable fringing coral growth. At the other extreme, the islands of the Tuomotu Archipelago are the true atolls — lagoons ringed by coral reefs which long ago swallowed up the remaining land masses. These are the low islands. Between these two geologic extremes are the volcanic, reef-fringed islands called the Society Islands, which have become the principal islands of French Polynesia. They have the fertile coastal plains of volcanic ash for growing food plus a protective barrier reef that shelters the inhabited shoreline, provides a haven for fish as well as local outrigger transportation, and now makes possible safe harbors for modern ships. Tahiti in the Society Islands is a near perfect combination of mountain, coastal plain, shoreline and reef. It is not at all surprising, then, that Polynesian civilization concentrated there. This natural environment plus an intelligent people have created a Pacific paradise to be envied by all. The French rule is accepted for its benevolent nature since the local economy is booming along with French financial aid.

French Polynesia

An Overseas Territory of France

Port of Entry:

Papeete, Tahiti	17°32′S, 149°34′W

Temporary entry can be made at the following ports:

Atuona, Hiva Oa	9°48′S, 139°02′W
Taiohae, Nuku Hiva	8°56′S, 140°05′W
Tiputa, Rangiroa	14°58′S, 147°38′W
Vaitape, Bora Bora	16°30′S, 151°45′W

Standard time:

10 hours slow on GMT (Papeete)

Currency:

French Polynesia uses the Coloniale Franc Pacifique (CFP) which is issued in coins of 1, 5, 10, 20, and 50 francs and notes of 100, 500, 1000 and 5,000 francs. At press time the rate of exchange was $US1 = 74 francs.

Language:

Tahitian is the indigenous language of the Society and Austral Islands. It is also spoken to a large extent in the Marquesas and Tuamotu Islands. There is, however, a Marquesan language and a Tuamotuan language spoken by some of the elders of those islands. French is the official language of the Territory and the only one taught in the schools. Chinese is spoken by the many Chinese shop keepers throughout all the islands. English is spoken by most persons engaged in tourist businesses.

Electricity:

Mostly 220v, 50Hz AC, but some old hotels may have 110v, 60Hz AC.

Postal Address:

Mail to any of the outlying islands is slow and somewhat undependable so it is recommended that your mail stop be Papeete:

Yacht (   )
Poste Restante
Papeete, Tahiti
FRENCH POLYNESIA

External Affairs Representative:

French consulates and embassies

Information Center:

Tahiti Tourist Board
B.P. 65
Papeete, Tahiti
FRENCH POLYNESIA

Cruising Library:

Official Directory and Guide Book for Tahiti
Bernard Covit; B.P. 602, Papeete, Tahiti, French Polynesia
Tahiti Traveler's Guide, Frank and Rose Corser;
2102 East Huntington Drive, Duarte, CA 91010, USA
Tahiti, Island of Love, Robert Langdon; Pacific Publications (Aust.) Ltd.
Technipress House, 29 Alberta Street, Sydney, NSW 2000, Australia, 1968
Typee, Herman Melville; L.C. Page & Co., Boston, MA, USA 1950
The Hidden Worlds of Polynesia, Robert C. Suggs; Harcourt, Brace & World, New Work, NY, USA, 1962
Manga Reva, Robert Lee Eskridge; Bobbs-Merrill, Indianapolis, IN, USA, 1931
Fatu Hiva, Thor Heyerdahl; Doubleday and Company, New York, NY 10017, USA, 1974
Forgotten Islands of the South Seas, Bengt Danielsson; Allen and Unwin Ltd., London, W C.1, England, 1957
Tahiti, Barnaby Conrad; Viking Press
Tahitians: Mind and Experience in the Society Islands, Robert Isaac Levy; University of Chicago Press, Chicago, IL USA, 1973

Yacht Entry

There is only one Port of Entry for all of French Polynesia and that is Papeete. An informal entry can be made, however, at many other islands having a French Government Agent present. This is usually a uniformed Gendarme who handles all official business. In their absence on the smaller islands and atolls, there may be a native chief who acts as the administrator and you are advised to seek out whoever is in authority and report your presence immediately on arrival.

Gendarmes are reported in residence at the following places:

Marquesas: Nuku Hiva, Hiva Oa and Ua Pu.
Tuamotus: Rangiroa, Apataki and Mangareva.
Society Islands: Tahiti, Moorea, Raiatea, Huahine and Bora Bora.
Australs: Tubuai, Raivavae and Rurutu.

It is reported that a $20 fine is imposed in the Marquesas if a yacht visits any other island before checking at Nuku Hiva or Hiva Oa.

A visa is required for a stay of longer than 30 days in French Polynesia. You can get a one year visa by applying for it eight months in advance outside of French Polynesia at any French Consulate. The tourist visa requires four photos and costs between $2.45 and $4.06 depending on the number of entries requested for the period.

Yachts arriving at Papeete without visas can apply for them on the spot but they will be granted for only three months to cover all of French Polynesia. Immigration officers are authorized to extend the visa three more months, but if you want to stay longer (up to one year) you will have to address a request to the Governor. Write the request in French and don't be unreasonable in your

Medical Memo

Immunization requirements:

Vaccinations for smallpox, cholera, and yellow fever are required if you have transited or visited within the last six days an area currently infected (smallpox 14 days).

Local health situation:

Cases of dengue fever have been reported in recent years in the Papeete area. Tropical ulcers can develop from open wounds infected by staph germs found in harbor waters. The nau-nau flies of the Marquesas Islands are vicious biters and can cause severe itching for days afterwards.

Health services:

In Papeete there is one government hospital and one private hospital. There are a number of private doctors in Papeete. In the outlying islands there are government dispensaries run in some cases by doctors, in others by trained medical workers, and in the smaller places by a person with some medical training. All permanently inhabited islands have radiotelephone connections with Papeete for emergency medical help.

Dental and optical services are available in limited scope from private practitioners in Papeete only.

There are four pharmacies in Papeete, one open on Sundays, which carry a full line of drugs from European sources. A few United States products are available. The dispensaries in the outlying islands stock some drugs.

IAMAT Center:

Papeete: Clinique Cardella
            Medical Director: Paul Zumbiehl, MD

Water:

Tap water is reported to be safe to drink in Papeete and the major towns of the other islands. Some of the water is treated and some of it is not. Water from other than the larger towns known to be treated should be considered suspect and treated before use.

demands, after all, they like tourist money coming in but they do not want any more beachcombers.

An onward airline ticket is required of all crew members including the owner of the boat. In the absence of an onward airline ticket, a refundable bond of $US500 will have to be posted by Americans, New Zealanders and Australians and 650 pounds by Britishers. The bond is refundable less an administrative charge at your last port of call in French Polynesia provided that there is a bank there and the necessary arrangements have been made ahead of time. In addition, all crew members will have to show evidence of having $US350 per month each of living money for the duration of the requested visa.

It has recently been reported that if you obtain your visa outside of French Polynesia, you do not have to post a bond and you can get a "green passport for yachts". By all means try to get your crew's visas before you arrive in French Polynesia.

If you are in Papeete and wish to visit the Gambier Islands in the Southeastern Tuamotu Archipelago, get your clearance at Papeete before you go. If you are arriving from the east, say Pitcairn, you get it after arrival at Mangareva. It will take about a week of waiting for it at Mangareva but you get that much time there whether it is approved or disapproved. The visitors permit will be for a nominal three weeks with a possible extension of one week. The French authorities are sensitive to yachts in this area because of its proximity to the French nuclear test site at Mururoa.

Firearms will be impounded by the Customs office when you arrive and you can recover them one hour before your scheduled departure.

Ammunition carried solely for trading purposes, such as .22 caliber shells, is strictly forbidden and will be confiscated and the yacht, possibly, denied a further stay in French Polynesia.

Chapter 6-A

MARQUESAS ISLANDS

The Country

The Marquesas group is the most northerly territory of French Polynesia and consists of six large and six small islands. All are elevated, ranging in height between 1300 and 4000 feet, and are covered with a layer of deep and very fertile soil. At one time the group had a sizable population, composed largely of blacks from Martinique and Chinese and others from Asia who were brought in to work on various types of plantations. Rainfall, which can be copious, is also erratic, and long periods of drought occurred that ultimately caused the plantations to fail. Most of the imported labor force returned to their homes, and the population in 1970 was reduced to about 5,200 native Polynesians.

The group contains no indigenous land animals, but many islands contain herds of wild sheep, cattle, and pigs left behind when the plantations were abandoned. The islands do, however, have much birdlife, the most interesting of which is a species of ground dove found nowhere else in the Pacific. Fish are also plentiful, and waters of the area contain a variety of enormous sharks.

Most islands in the group are uninhabited, but all are capable of supporting rather sizable numbers of people and in the future may be settled to take care of the expanding population. The best known of the islands is Hiva Oa, a very fertile and heavily wooded high island twenty-three miles long and ten miles wide, which reputedly was the last stronghold of cannibalism. In 1970 it was overrun with wild livestock brought in by former inhabitants. It is renowned as the last home and the burial site of Paul Gauguin, the French painter.

The five principal inhabited islands of the Marquesas group (Nuku Hiva, Ua Pu, Hiva Oa, Tahuata, and Fatu Hiva) now support a population of just over 5,200 persons. But at one time late in the eighteenth century, the population was estimated by European visitors to number 60,000 persons. At that time the island of Ua Huka was also inhabited but today it has only transient visitors at its small airport which serves all the Marquesan islands. Like most Pacific island groups, the Marquesas chain runs from SE to NW paralleling the SE trade winds. With two ports of entry, Atuona on Hiva Oa and Taiohae on Nuku Hiva, one is eventually faced with sailing to windward to see all the islands.

The Weather

These islands are in the heart of the trade wind belt, but there is much less steadiness of winds here than in the trade belt of the northern latitudes. Easterly winds are the most prevalent, but over the eastern waters of the group there is an annual tendency for the trades to be deflected a little to the north of east, while in western waters there is tendency for deflection to a little south of east. The easterly to southeasterly winds taken together from April to October are as a rule, more pronounced; while the easterly to northeasterly winds are more prevalent in the intervening months. Among the eastern islands the average wind speed is about 11 knots; among the western islands, 9 knots. The highest speeds occur in the cooler months, July and August, when the average throughout the group is 12 knots.

Gales are of rare occurrence and the few heaviest squalls, in so far as scanty records indicate, occur in December.

Yacht Facilities

There are no special facilities for yachts in any of the Marquesas Islands. There are wharfs at Taiohae and Atuona for the supply boats and you can tie up to these for taking on water and fuel. There is no treatment of water in any of these islands so be sure you are getting it from a clean source. Fuel is not readily available and, if you are going to need any, it should be ordered beforehand. At Taiohae this can be done through Maurice McKittrick and at

Marquesas Islands

Distances between ports in nautical miles:

Between *Taiohae* and:

Agana, Guam	4700
Ahe, Tuamotu Islands	510
Apia, Western Samoa	1890
Honolulu, Hawaii	2100
Noumea, New Caledonia	3180
Palmyra Island	1600
Panama City, Panama	3830
Papeete, Society Islands	760
San Cristobal, Galapagos Islands	3000
San Francisco, California	2990

Standard Time:

9 hours, 30 minutes slow on GMT

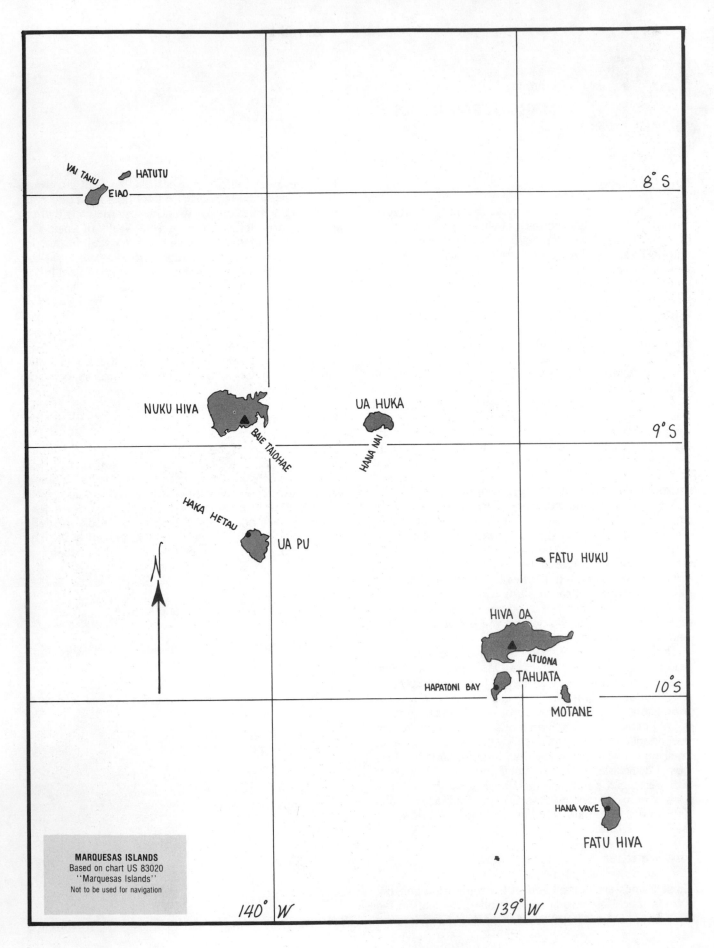

VAI TAHU   HATUTU
EIAO

8° S

NUKU HIVA   UA HUKA

9° S

BAIE TAIOHAE   HANA NAI

HAKA HETAU

UA PU

FATU HUKU

N

HIVA OA

ATUONA

HAPATONI BAY   TAHUATA

10° S

MOTANE

HANA VAVE

FATU HIVA

MARQUESAS ISLANDS
Based on chart US 83020
''Marquesas Islands''
Not to be used for navigation

140° W

139° W

The only navigation aid in the Marquesas Islands is this gas-operated lighthouse on the hill at the entrance to Taiohae Bay, Nuku Hiva. Most yachties get their clearance at this Port of Entry.

Maurice operates the most famous bar and magasin (store) in all of the Marquesas. It is located at Taiohae, Nuku Hiva.

Entering Vipihai Bay, sometimes called Traitors Bay, at Atuona, Hiva Oa. Atuona is a Port of Entry to the Marquesas Islands.

Anchored at Hana Vave, Fatu Hiva, an interisland trading vessel has a deckload of steel drums which may contain gasoline, kerosene, diesel fuel or wine! This anchorage is subject to vicious winds off the mountains but it has good holding ground.

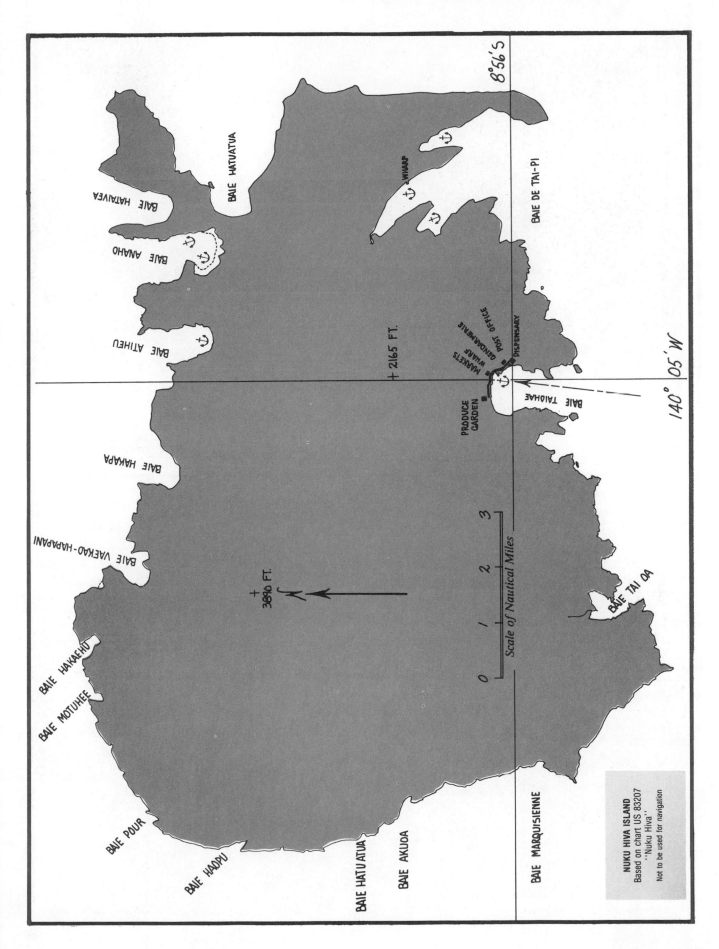

NUKU HIVA ISLAND
Based on chart US 83207
"Nuku Hiva"
Not to be used for navigation

8°56'S

140° 05' W

BAIE HATUATUA

BAIE HATAIVEA

BAIE ANAHO

BAIE ATIHEU

WHARF

BAIE DE TAI-PI

+ 2165 FT.

POST OFFICE

GENDARMERIE

WHARF

MARKETS

DISPENSARY

PRODUCE
GARDEN

BAIE TAIOHAE

BAIE HAKAPA

BAIE VAEKAO-HAAPAANI

+ 3890 FT.

0   1   2   3

Scale of Nautical Miles

BAIE TAI OA

BAIE HAKAEHU

BAIE MOTUHEE

BAIE POUR

BAIE HAOPU

BAIE HATUATUA

BAIE AKUOA

BAIE MARQUISIENNE

83

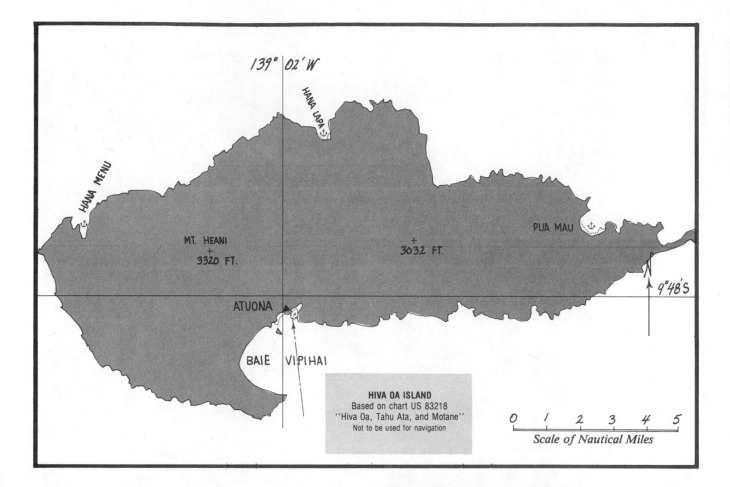

139° 02' W

HANA LAPA

HANA MENU

MT. HEANI
+
3320 FT.

+
3032 FT.

PUA MAU

N
↑ 9°48'S

ATUONA

BAIE VIPIHAI

HIVA OA ISLAND
Based on chart US 83218
''Hiva Oa, Tahu Ata, and Motane''
Not to be used for navigation

0   1   2   3   4   5
Scale of Nautical Miles

Atuona through the Donald's store.

Fruits in these islands are plentiful and grow wild in the hills but ask before you take since the property may be privately owned, the people are generous so you won't be denied. Vegetables are uncommon but there are some enterprising gardeners who grow them for the European palate. Stores carry limited canned goods and beer and some hardware incidental to local living needs but no marine hardware.

Taiohae has instituted a "water fee" for boats amounting to 200 francs for the first day in the harbor, 100 francs for the second, and 20 francs each day thereafter. There are no other charges in the Marquesas.

Butane can be purchased at Rosie's store in Atuona but you will need an adapter since the local fittings are all metric.

The Catholic Diocese at Taiohae, Nuku Hiva, in a setting of tropical grandeur.

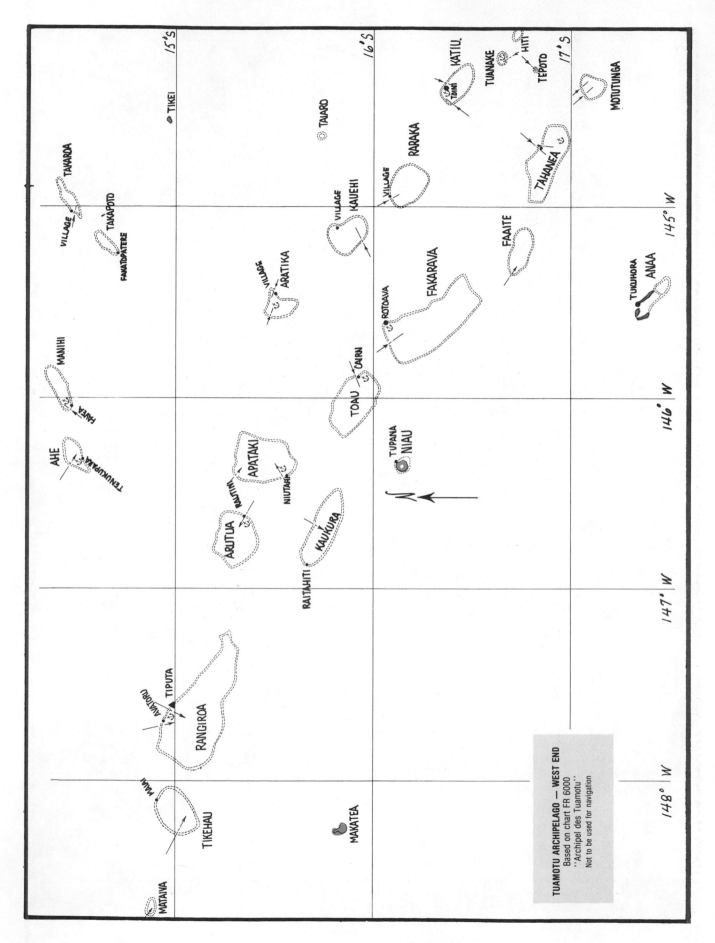

TUAMOTU ARCHIPELAGO — WEST END
Based on chart FR 6000
"Archipel des Tuamotu"
Not to be used for navigation

15°S

16°S

17°S

148°W

147°W

146°W

145°W

TIKEI

TAIARO

TAKAROA
VILLAGE

TAKÀPOTO
FAKATOPATERE

MANIHI
FAREA

AHE
TENUKUPARA

ARUTUA
RAUTINI

APATAKI
NIUTAHI

KAUKURA

RAITAHITI

ARATIKA
VILLAGE

KAUEHI
VILLAGE

RARAKA
VILLAGE

KATIU.
TONU

TUANAKE
HITI
TEPOTO

MOTUTUNGA

TAHANEA

FAAITE

TOAU
CAIRN

TUPANA
NIAU

FAKARAVA
ROTOAVA

TUKUHORA
ANAA

RANGIROA
TIPUTA
AVATORU

MAHI

TIKEHAU

MATAIVA

MAKATEA

86

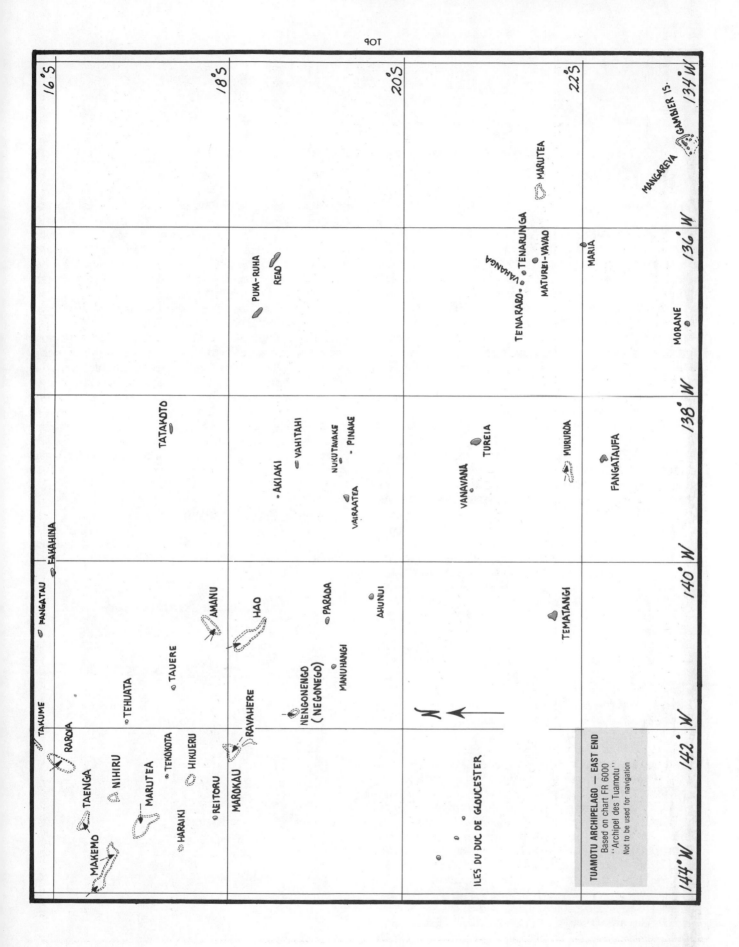

TUAMOTU ARCHIPELAGO — EAST END
Based on chart FR 6000
"Archipel des Tuamotu"
Not to be used for navigation

87

Chapter 6-B

TUAMOTU ARCHIPELAGO
(Paumotu or Dangerous Archipelago)

The Country

The Tuamotu Archipelago is an enormous arc of exclusively coral islands lying between the Society and the Marquesas groups. It consists of one raised atoll (Makatea), a dozen fairly large true atolls, and a countless number of small atolls and reefs. Many atolls have unbroken circular reefs; others, such as Fakarava and Rangiroa in the northern portion, are broken into numerous islets with good passages into their interior lagoons. Makatea was a profitable producer of phosphate until the deposits were exhausted in 1966. It, like the rest of the group, now has a copra economy. Some of the atolls have their income augumented by the fine pearls found in the extensive lagoon areas.

The Tuamotu Archipelago is made up particularly of dry "forested" atolls with rain as the only source of fresh water. The 76 islands composing the archipelago have a land area of 343 square miles and range from unbroken circles of coral surrounding a lagoon to glistening chains of coral islets with one or two navigable passes into the lagoon. As with most Pacific archipelagos, the Tuamotu chain stretches along a line southeast to northwest spanning a distance of 1,000 miles.

The Gambier group (considered here as part of the Tuamotus) is located near the southeast extremity of the Tuamotu Archipelago. It is a cluster of elevated islands collectively called Mangareva and twenty-two outlying atolls. Seven of the atolls are inhabited, and many of the others are planted in coconut palms. All are rich in birdlife, and the lagoons are the source of a richly colored pearl that is favored all over the world. More recently, five of the atolls — Mururoa, Fagataufa, Tureia, Hao, and Anaa — have been used by the French as the site of that nation's atomic tests. The actual detonations are carried out on Mururoa and are monitored by supporting installations on the other four.

Mangareva is a cluster of four principal inhabited islands and a number of outlying islets. All are elevated and enclosed in a single reef, giving them a typical almost atoll form. The group, including the atolls, has a temperate climate, an average annual rainfall of about eighty inches, and, excluding military and scientific personnel connected with the atomic tests, a total population of between 600 and 700.

Only 30 atolls of the Tuamotus are permanently uninhabited while the rest support small populations limited by food, water, and space. In bygone days atoll populations were balanced by infanticide and migration, but today big city attractions for youth is the prime balancing factor. An estimated 6,700 persons live throughout the 46 inhabited islands subsisting principally on a fishing and copra economy. In the late 1800's, pearls and mother of pearl shells were the major source of income with divers descending 50-100 feet to gather the valuable molluscs off the bottom. Soon, however, overgathering all but eliminated this income source and today only experimental black pearl cultivating remains.

Atolls of the Tuamotus were first seen by European eyes in 1615. Jacob LeMaire, a Dutchman, had sailed near the northwestern end in a passage from Cape Horn (which he had named) to Batavia, now part of Indonesia. So many other ships have since accidently and disastrously discovered the archipelago that it is also known as the Dangerous Archipelago. In recent years many carelessly navigated yachts have added further emphasis to this gloomy name. Of all the Tuamotu atolls, Raroia is probably the best known. It was here that the raft *Kon Tiki*, captained by Thor Heyerdahl, landed in 1947 after its epic 4300 mile, 3½ month drift from Peru.

Of Atolls and Coconuts

Atolls are composed of the skeletal remains of countless marine plants and animals which affixed themselves to

Tuamotu Archipelago

(Paumotu or Dangerous Archipelago)

Distances between ports in nautical miles:

Between *Rotoava*, Fakarava, (16°03'S, 145°37'W) and:

Apia, Western Samoa	1520
Honolulu, Hawaii	2360
Levuka, Fiji	2060
Noumea, New Caledonia	2740
Panama City, Panama	4260
Papeete, Society Islands	240
Rabaul, New Britain	3740
San Francisco, California	3500
Taiohae, Nuku Hiva	550

Standard time:

10 hours slow on GMT

the warm water shorelines of volcanic lands thrust up eons ago from the ocean floor. The coral polyps, each smaller than a pin head, built their limestone houses on the periphery of the then existing land, never rising completely above the surface of the warm waters nor growing downward below 150 foot depths. In time, the volcanic lands, often hollow cones, eroded away and submerged. This proceeded at such a slow rate, however, that the prolific coral polyps managed to keep their upper domain alive near the water's surface even though their host land disappeared into the depths. The accumulating coral growth, a combination of skeletons and living polyps, formed the reefs hundreds of feet above the surrounding ocean floor supported by their own living structure.

On the windward side of the atoll coral growth is most prolific as the ocean currents bring abundant nutrients to the polyps. On the leeward side gaps in the reef appear as death locally outpaces life among the coral polyp colony. Some gaps attain depths suitable for small boat passages into the lagoon. At all edges of the reef wind, wave,

The Administrative Center for Rangiroa is located at Tiputa, the second pass into the lagoon. Both Tiputa and Avatoru passes are subject to strong currents and violent rips and eddies when the current is at a maximum.

Rikatea is the principal village on the island of Mangareva in the Gambier group. It once was one of the most popular ports in the South Seas for whaling vessels who put in there for rest and recreation with their ships secure in the well-protected lagoon.

marine life, and vegetable growth together wear away at the dead surface layers to produce sand, humus, and island-like patches above water called motus. Unlike other "land masses", the atoll is alive and ever changing but at a miniscule pace.

The lagoon-encircling reef is continuous in a few instances but mostly atolls are made up of a series of motus which appear from the air as sparkling beads of a necklace. Motus vary in length from a few hundred yards to ten miles but they rarely exceed 300 to 400 yards in width.

To the unwary sailor the atolls represent danger. At best in clear weather, they are visible for 7-10 miles, but in rain or at night the visible range can be reduced to hundreds of yards. Reefs rising steeply from the bottom may be awash; motu land level rarely rises to 10 feet above the surrounding sea; while the stately coconut tree adds only another 50-75 feet of height.

Inside, the lagoon is an aquarium of marine life not sustainable in the deep, turbulent open ocean. Tropical fish abound in a rainbow of colors and a fantasy of shapes, varied coral "plants" grow with delicate forms and pastel hues, huge coral heads of ugly threatening brown rise abruptly to the surface, and a coral sand bottom reflects the jade-green rays of the sun to the quiet surface.

Vegetable life on the motus is dominated by the majestic coconut palm whose tolerance to a salt environment and poor sandy soil is beyond belief. Coconuts are the wanderers of the Pacific. Floating for thousands of miles until cast up on a shore, they have distributed themselves the world over and have made barren islets into lovely motus. Lying quiescent on its side in the warm tropical sun, the coconut soon sprouts into life, sending roots out through two of its eyes to seek water and food while simultaneously spikes or fronds shoot skyward through the third eye seeking the life-giving sunlight. In 5 to 6 years it has matured to the well known graceful palm tree whose fronds rustle musically in the gentle tradewinds.

But the coconut palm is more than romantic prose for it is the key to life for the islanders who inhabit the atolls.

Avatoru Pass, Rangiroa, is one of two entries into the lagoon of the largest atoll in French Polynesia. A schooner is anchored by the town wharf on the side of the pass where the current is the least.

The fibrous trunk is prime building material while the giant fronds are hand woven into roof thatches of geometric beauty with lifetimes of three years. Carefully stripped, the fronds yield materials for structural lashings, baskets, mats, and essential handicraft items of all kinds. The husk of the coconut forms a cushion to protect the inner nut in the fall to the ground and it also produces fibers for rope called sennit. It is the nut itself, however, that is the secret to life on the atoll.

A coconut takes a year to develop from a flower to a ripe nut. After reaching its mature size but long before fully ripening, the green nut is at the drinking stage providing more than a pint of sweet, nourishing coconut "milk". Not to be confused with the rancid fluid of the hard ripe nut sold in the supermarkets, the drinking nut furnishes the island substitute for cows milk, soda pop, and even fresh water.

More recently it has been reported that fresh coconut milk can be used in place of sterile water for some medical purposes. The addition of the proper amount of table salt compensates for the deficiency in sodium and chlorine and makes the milk suitable for oral rehydration of persons suffering from severe gastro-enteritis.

As the nut begins to ripen, a thin white pulp layer begins to form inside the hardening shell. This layer has the consistency and appearance of boiled egg white and, eaten with fingers or spoon, it makes a rare dessert treat. Left longer on the tree to ripen, the soft white pulp further hardens into a thick layer while the milk turns to a tasteless water. Shredded, this mature pulp ends up on cake frostings. Removed from the shell in chunks and dried in the sun, it becomes copra from which coconut oil is extracted to be used in such widely varied items as soap, margarine, and nitroglycerine.

A coconut which is allowed to tree-ripen and falls onto the proper surface environment (moisture, soil, light and warmth), will start the amazing process of germination. But in doing so it passes through a fourth and last food phase. Germination causes the formation of a white sponge-like substance within the nut which totally absorbs the liquid and the hard meat. This sponge has the qualities of sweet cotton candy to be eaten with the fingers. But, beware, as the life-giving sponge deteriorates, the juices become poisonous to the human system.

Besides its vegetarian contribution, the coconut palm fosters the life of the coconut crab. Fully grown he is a big fellow with a 2 to 3 foot leg span and a body the size of San Francisco sourdough bread. They are nocturnal creatures and have a vicious pair of claws. Islanders consider hunting them a real sport. These crabs are prepared

A popular atoll of call, Ahe has a short wharf for trading vessels which can be used by visiting yachts between times. In the foreground copra is being dried.

for eating simply by boiling and then they can be eaten with the fingers and a nut cracker.

Food and drink, shelter, body covering and ornamentation — such is the contribution of the ubiquitous coconut palm to life in the tropics.

The atoll of Rangiroa subsists on a coconut and fish economy. The valuable nuts grow with little assistance on nearly all of the 150 motus covering 75% of the circumference of the atoll. Native workers visit the coconut growing motus for the purpose of making copra out of the coconuts as they ripen. The outboard motorboat is used for conveyance of the workers to the motus and transporting burlap-bagged copra back to the collection points.

Fish exporting is rapidly becoming the economic mainstay of this atoll. The Tahiti Islanders traditional diet of fish can no longer be satisfied by the Tahitian fisherman since they are rapidly abandoning the sea in favor of "9 to 5" work in the new economy. Commercial fishing in the rest of French Polynesia has therefore taken on a new importance. One enterprising operator flies a small airplane daily into several Tuamotu atolls picking up freshly caught fish for the Tahitian's table that night. But it is the frozen fish business which is giving an economic uplift to the islands.

The Weather

The Tuamotu Archipelago, while in the nominal heart of the southeast tradewind belt, is strongly dominated by easterly winds. Over the eastern part, east to east-northeast winds are most prevalent; while in the western part, the majority are from east to east-southeast. The northeasterly direction is most prevalent from November to May, and the southeasterly direction, from June to October. Some 80 percent of the annual winds are from directions between northeast and southeast.

Occasional barometric depressions cross the group, sometimes resulting in squally weather and temporary reversal of the trades into winds from westerly quadrants. These are most likely to occur from January to March, but may occur earlier and later in the season. Some seven severe hurricanes are on record among the islands from 1877 to 1906. Of these, three occurred in January, two in February, and one each in March and September. There is no known record of the actual frequency of tropical cyclones in these waters. In December 1977, a tropical storm with winds of 34 to 63 knots moved southeast across the Tuamotu Archipelago.

Yacht Facilities

There are no yacht facilities in the Tuamotus. At most, many villages have copra boat wharfs and these can be used for docking when the copra boats are not present. Foods are generally very scarce except for coconuts and fish. Because of poor soil the usually common staples of the South Seas — breadfruit, bananas, and taro are not plentiful. Small stores supplied by the copra boats stock limited canned and dry goods. Water on most atolls is collected from rainfall in cisterns and during the dry season may be in short supply so don't depend on getting water in any atoll in the Pacific.

On the island of Mangareva you will be unable to buy any supplies but you will find that coconuts and fruits are abundantly available. It is reported that the fish in the lagoon are all toxic and not to be eaten.

What the atolls lack in food and amenities they make up for in beauty of the atoll and hospitality of the people.

Another popular atoll of call at the northwest end of the Tuamotus is Takaroa. This has been an important pearl fishing lagoon and experiments in growing cultured pearls are very promising.

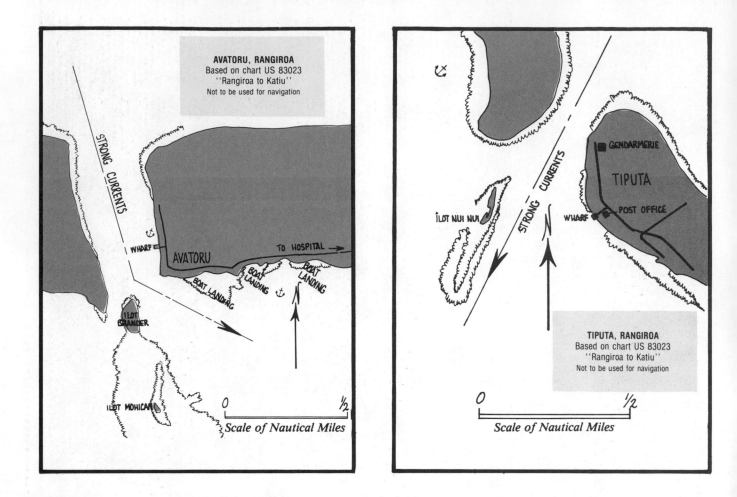

AVATORU, RANGIROA
Based on chart US 83023
"Rangiroa to Katiu"
Not to be used for navigation

STRONG CURRENTS

WHARF
AVATORU
TO HOSPITAL
BOAT LANDING
BOAT LANDING
BOAT LANDING
ILOT ORANDER
ILOT MOHICAN

0   ½
Scale of Nautical Miles

TIPUTA, RANGIROA
Based on chart US 83023
"Rangiroa to Katiu"
Not to be used for navigation

GENDARMERIE
TIPUTA
POST OFFICE
WHARF
ÎLOT NUI NUI
STRONG CURRENTS

0   ½
Scale of Nautical Miles

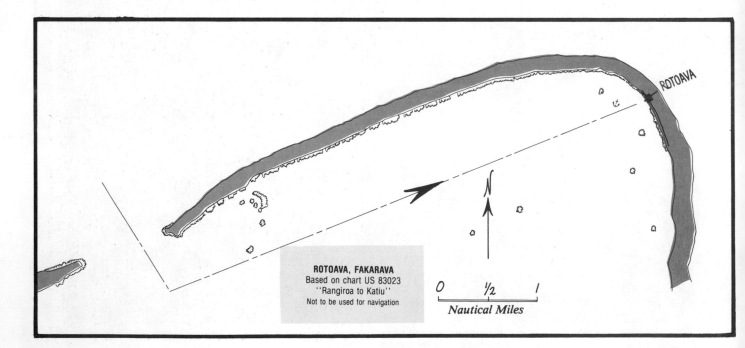

ROTOAVA

N

ROTOAVA, FAKARAVA
Based on chart US 83023
"Rangiroa to Katiu"
Not to be used for navigation

0   ½   1
Nautical Miles

Chapter 6-C

SOCIETY ISLANDS

The Country

The Society group contains twelve major islands divided into a windward cluster of five and a leeward section of seven islands. The windward group consists of Tahiti, Moorea, Mehitia (Maitea), and Tubuai Manu, which are high volcanic types, and Tetiaroa, which is a small atoll. The leeward group includes the high islands of Raiatea, Tahaa, and Huahine; Bora Bora, which is an almost atoll; and Tupai, Maupiti, and Mopihaa (Mopelia), which are true atolls.

Tahiti is the largest and best known island of the group. It has provided the locale for so many novels and adventure stories that it has come to be associated with the typical South Seas island paradise. It also was a favorite subject of Paul Gauguin, whose paintings of island people and island life made him famous. Tahiti has an area of about 400 square miles and is formed of volcanoes connected by an isthmus giving it a figure-8 configuration. The main peak, Mount Orochona, has an elevation of 7,321 feet, from which the island drops precipitously to a moderately broad coastal plain. The interior is an uninhabited, trackless upland of jagged peaks and gorges covered with lush tropical vegetation. People do not live in village groups but in homes strung out around the coastal belt. This pattern is broken only by the capital city of Papeete, a modern city of over 30,000 built around a coastal lagoon in the northwest corner of the island, that provides the area's best and busiest harbor.

Other high islands of the group are all rugged and similar in structure to Tahiti but are usually smaller and lower with peaks that rise no higher than about 4,000 feet. All are populated, and their rich soils produce considerable amounts of copra, pineapple, vanilla beans and varieties of tropical fruits. Raiatea, the largest in the leeward group, according to legend is the ancient Hawaiiki, which the original Polynesian migrants used as the base for their later dispersal to Hawaii and elsewhere.

Papeete is the distribution center for supplies to all of the French Polynesia islands which number over 100 and have a total population of about 100,000 persons. Tahiti has about 65,000 of them and Moorea is second with 5,000. Many atolls sustain only 40 to 50 persons which seem to be the threshold size for a permanent village on an atoll.

The interisland freighters, generally small — 200 to 300 tons, are diesel powered and have totally replaced the trading schooner of the romantic past. Interisland trading is conducted mainly by two companies — Donalds, which evolved from an earlier European copra trading venture, and Wing Man Hing, which is an aggressive Chinese business in import, export, and local sales. These companies' trading ships compete in purchasing copra and selling goods throughout the French Polynesia islands. Where neither feels they can make a franc, the French Navy sends its LST's to meet the needs of the islanders. In principal, the French Navy tries not to compete with the local island traders.

Papeete harbor is also home port to the French fleet supporting nuclear testing at the Gambier Islands ESE of Tahiti. While many South Pacific kingdoms decry these tests, they have greatly expanded the Tahiti economy and one wonders what the local economy will do when this source of income no longer exists.

The Weather

The prevailing wind direction is easterly throughout the

Society Islands

(Tahiti – Nouvelle Cythere)

Distances between ports in nautical miles:

Between *Papeete* and:

Apia, Western Samoa	1300
Auckland, New Zealand	2220
Avatiu, Cook Islands	620
Christmas Island	1270
Funafuti, Tuvalu	1910
Honolulu, Hawaii	2380
Noumea, New Caledonia	2500
Nuku'alofa, Tonga	1470
Ocean Island	2610
Pago Pago, American Samoa	1240
Panama City, Panama	4490
Rabaul, New Britain	3530
San Diego, California	3550
Seattle, Washington	4300
Suva, Fiji	1840
Taiohae, Marquesas Islands	760

Standard time:

10 hours slow on GMT

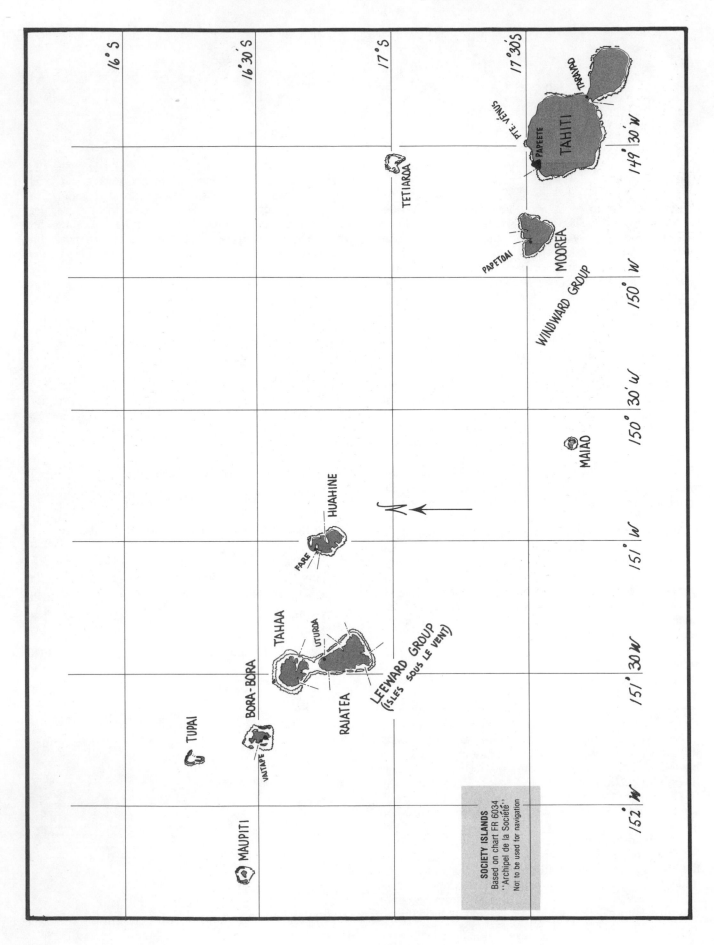

16° S

16° 30' S

17° S

17° 30' S

149° 30' W

150° W

150° 30' W

151° W

151° 30' W

152° W

TAHITI

TARAVAO

PTE. VENUS

PAPEETE

TETIAROA

MOOREA

PAPETOAI

WINDWARD GROUP

MAIAO

HUAHINE

FARE

TAHAA

UTUROA

RAIATEA

LEEWARD GROUP
(ISLES SOUS LE VENT)

BORA-BORA

VAITAPE

TUPAI

MAUPITI

SOCIETY ISLANDS
Based on chart FR 6034
"Archipel de la Société"
Not to be used for navigation

96

Papeete, capital of French Polynesia and the symbol of every adventurer's dream. Located on the leeward side of Tahiti, it is today a bustling city with the action of urban life set amidst a tropical paradise. Papeete is the only true Port of Entry for all of French Polynesia.

ocean area of the Society Islands. This holds true for every month of the year over the eastern section of the group, and for most months in the western section. Northeast winds predominate over, or are equal to, those from the southeast, in the eastern section, except in June and July, during which months the southeast winds are about twice as frequent as those from the northeast. In the western section the southeast winds are more frequent than the northeast except in March and November.

At Papeete, however, owing to local conditions, the drift is prevailingly from northeasterly, except in September, when it is superseded by both north and southwest directions; and in June, when it is equalled by winds from east and southwest. Northerly winds are frequent from September to February, and southwesterly winds from April to December. Land and sea breeze effects are definitely in evidence.

The annual average wind speed at sea is 9 to 10 knots. The strongest winds average 11 to 12 knots in the southern winter months; and the lightest, 6 to 8 knots, in the summer season.

The annual rainfall is 72 inches at Papeete, of which more than a fifth occurs in December. The rainy season lasts from November through March. The driest months are July and August. On the open sea, rain is most frequent in December and January, and least frequent in August. Thunderstorms are fairly common, particularly in January, February, and May. Fresh gales have been reported occasionally in June, but these are due only to a strengthening of the prevailing winds. Tropical cyclones are rare, but have been known to occur in September and in December to February.

The climate of the Society Islands is tempered by the surrounding ocean and is warm and sunny with only modest variation in temperature throughout the year. Seasons are best described by the number of days of rainfall in a month. December through February is the rainy season with from 11 to 14 days of rain per month. During the wet season temperatures will range between 81° and 95°F with high humidity and there will be many insects. In the dry months temperatures range between 70° and 81°F and there are virtually no insects. The frequent sud-

Tahiti's closest neighbor, Moorea, is a fantastically beautiful island with crisp mountain peaks and jade-colored lagoons. Yachts find secure anchorages and idyllic living in both Cook's Bay shown here and Opunohu Bay a few miles down the barrier reef.

den rains of this area are only of short duration and the weather is generally good the year around.

Yacht Facilities

Papeete is a very modern port and has been a port of call for ships and yachts since shortly after the days of Captain Cook. The quay (key) is a wharf along Boulevard Pomare at which yachts tie stern-to with a bow anchor set out in the stream. You step ashore on a gangway balanced between stern and the quay wall. These transom planks are

generally available on the spot. Unfortunately, there are a limited number of these berths which are outnumbered by the yachts wanting them by a factor of three or four so the rest of the yachts anchor stern-to down the boulevard with their stern lines going to bollards installed ashore along the boulevard. Your dinghy becomes your shore boat.

Papeete charges for a yacht's presence in the harbor on the following scale:

Daily charge at the quay:

up to 8 meters long	50 francs
8 to 10 meters	100

Fare, the main village on the island of Huahine, is Papeete at the turn of the century. The island is an archeological museum of maraes (altars) and ancient fish traps used to catch and store the protein of the sea.

10 to 12 meters	150
12 to 15 meters	200
15 to 20 meters	400
20 to 25 meters	600

If you are anchored down the boulevard, the fees are only 75% of the above. In addition to the daily charge there is an entry fee of 650 francs. There is electricity available along the quay (110 and 220 volts, 60Hz AC) but there is an additional charge of 25 francs per day if you connect into it. Water is available along the quay and there is a modern shower, toilet, and hand-laundry building on the shoreline.

The Port Director of Papeete rigorously controls the movement of all yachts once thay have made formal entry. He has issued the following guidelines for yachts visiting French Polynesia:

From: Director of Port Autonome of Tahiti
To: All Yachts and Boat owners visiting French Polynesia
—It is strictly forbidden to leave any equipment on the wharf or sidewalk and also to tie-up on the trees along the shore.
—Once in Port, no movement will be made without the authorization of the Harbour Captain.
—Due to shortage of room at the wharf, the Harbour Captain might designate another place to dock so therefore I suggest you do all provisioning of water and food as soon as possible after your arrival.

Moorings will be allocated as follows:
a) Upon their arrival yachts will moor for a few days along the waterfront reserved for that purpose.
b) As soon as necessity arises they will be placed in some other part of the Harbour.

Trips between Tahiti and Moorea
1. Make a verbal or written report to Harbour Captain indicating day and hour of departure.
2. Give a copy of crew list to Harbour Captain and a copy to immigration office.
3. Release will be provided to you by the agricultural services before your departure.
4. On your return trip, provide a copy of crew list

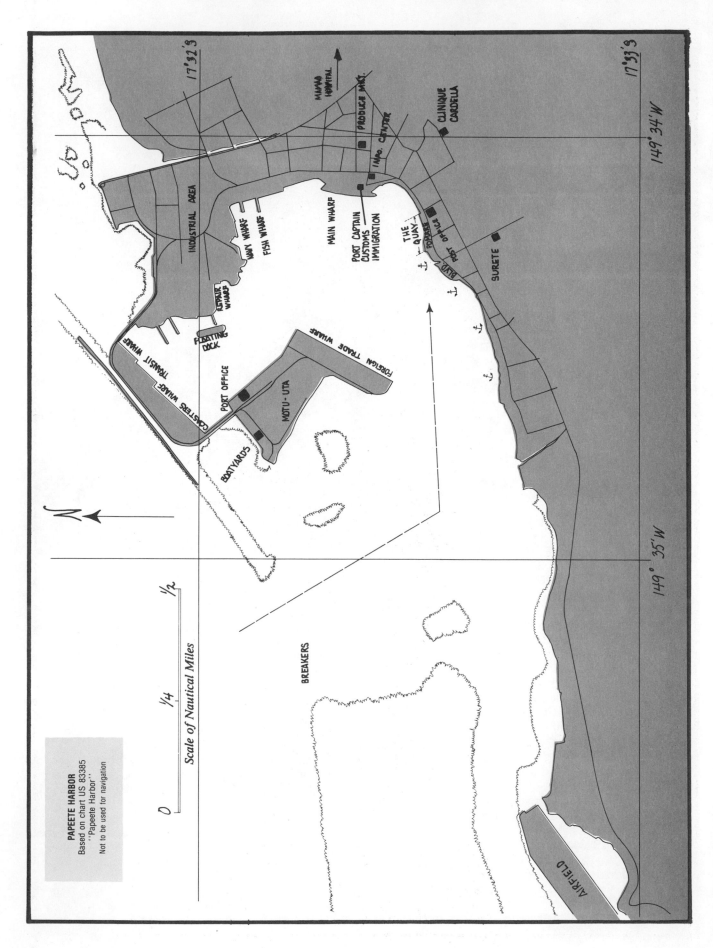

PAPEETE HARBOR
Based on chart US 83385
"Papeete Harbor"
Not to be used for navigation

Scale of Nautical Miles

0   1/4   1/2

N

INDUSTRIAL AREA

NAVY WHARF
FISH WHARF

REPAIR WHARF

FLOATING DOCK

TRANSIT WHARF

COASTERS WHARF

PORT OFFICE

BOATYARDS

MOTU-UTA

FOREIGN TRADE WHARF

MAIN WHARF

PORT CAPTAIN
CUSTOMS
IMMIGRATION

INFO. CENTER

PRODUCE MKT.

MAMAO HOSPITAL

CLINIQUE CARDELLA

THE QUAY

BLVD. POMARE

POST OFFICE

SURETE

BREAKERS

AIRFIELD

17°32'S

17°33'S

149°34'W

149°35'W

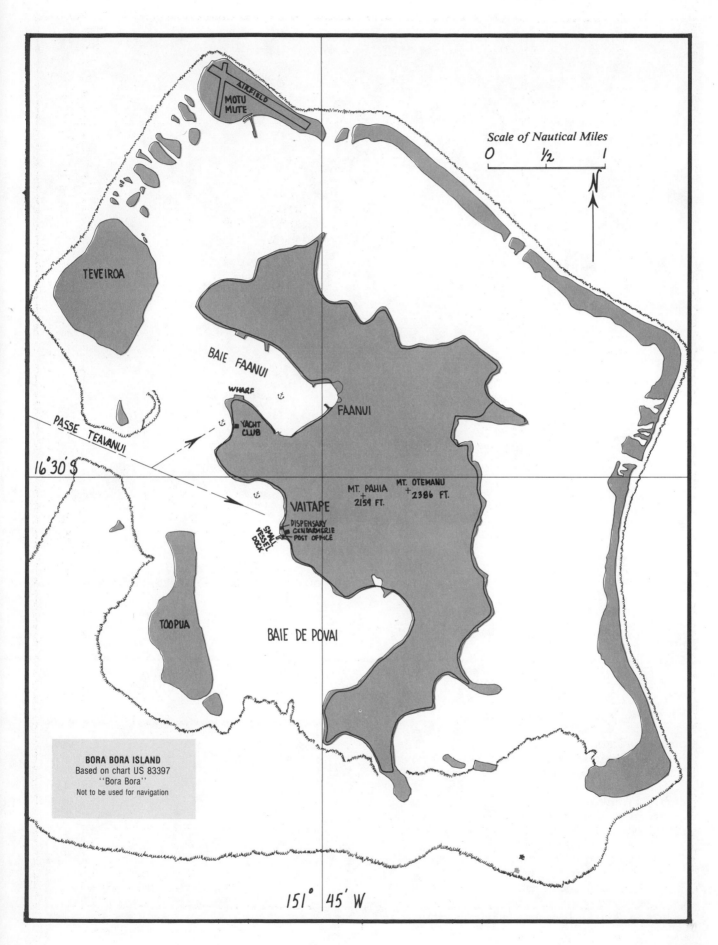

Scale of Nautical Miles

0 ½ 1

N

TEVEIROA

MOTU MUTE

AIRFIELD

BAIE FAANUI

WHARF

YACHT CLUB

FAANUI

PASSE TEAVANUI

16°30'S

VAITAPE

MT. PAHIA
2159 FT.

MT. OTEMANU
2386 FT.

DISPENSARY
GENDARMERIE
POST OFFICE

SMALL VESSEL DOCK

TOOPUA

BAIE DE POVAI

BORA BORA ISLAND
Based on chart US 83397
''Bora Bora''
Not to be used for navigation

151° 45' W

People who know call Bora Bora the most beautiful island on earth. It's massive twin peaks are an ever changing skyline as you sail the calm waters inside the surrounding barrier reef.

to Harbour Captain specifying the date and time of arrival.

Trips around Harbours of Tahiti
—Same as above except no crew list necessary for the immigration office. Once back in Papeete, give a crew list to Harbour Captain.
—No custom manifest necessary for trips between Tahiti and Moorea and around Tahiti.

Trips between Tahiti and Islands of French Polynesia (not including Moorea)

Formalities to fill out:
2 copies of custom manifest and 4 crew lists.

Steps to follow prior departure:
1) Request authorization from Harbour Captain and submit the 4 crew lists of which one will be signed by him.
2) Go to immigration office for visa of the crew lists.
3) Provide custom office with two copies of manifest and a crew list signed by immigration.
4) Submit to Harbour Captain the custom manifest with a copy signed by immigration office.
5) Permit of departure will be provided to you by the agricultural service before your departure.

On your return trip:
—Provide Harbour Captain with a crew list as soon

as possible indicating date and time of arrival.
—For custom office: 2 copies of manifest and a crew list.
—For immigration office: a crew list.

Trips to foreign countries:
—On top of all necessary formalities as mentioned above, request from the Harbour Captain all bills

102

Little-visited Maupiti Island is 20 miles west of Bora Bora and was at one time an independent kingdom. On it is found a jet black basaltic rock which takes an unusually fine polish. Maupiti is probably best known for its cooperative fish drive in which over 300 people take part.

concerning entry and dock fee; bills will be at the treasury building between 0800 to 1030 and 1400 to 1500. If you have some firearms you will pick them up one hour before your departure at the customs office.

Note: The immigration service forbids change of crew.

The same crew arriving will depart on the same boat. Crew list and different formalities will be typed if possible, if not print them properly.

I wish your stay in Tahiti will be a most enjoyable one, any further questions we will be glad to assist you.

Harbour Captain

Practically all services needed to repair or maintain a yacht are available in Papeete. Not all deck and engine supplies are available, however, and those that are come from French sources built to the metric measurement system. If special parts are needed they can be ordered from the United States, New Zealand, or Australia (or most any other country) and shipped by air since Tahiti enjoys excellent air transportation services. If you do order

parts from outside Tahiti, have the sender mark the package "For Yacht _____ in transit". You will not have to pay customs on the parts but you will have to do a lot of paperwork to liberate them from customs.

When you are provisioning for departure from Papeete, visit the Bon Marche market where you can get a discount on supplies. Place your order several days in advance for a 5 percent discount on purchases of $US100 or more with a 10 percent discount on case lots. They will also cut, freeze and wrap meat to order.

103

Radio Communications

Station name and call	Location	Frequency Transmit/Receive	Service hours LMT	Type of service*
Radio Mahina	Mahina	2182/2182 kHz	24 hour watch	International distress frequency
		8780/8230	24 hour watch	Used by ships of Territory
		2620/2704	24 hour watch	Coastal Communications
		8230	0030, 0230, 0640, 1800 and 2100	General call to schooners including weather
		8740	0640 and 2100	Local weather
			0030, 0230, and 1800	Gale warnings added
Radio Papeete		VHF Channel 16	0730-1700	Port Captain
Radio Tahiti (French Region 3)	17°S, 149°W	740 kHz	0600-2130	Commercial service in French language except from 1045 to 1200 when it is Tahitian News in English at 1100 Wednesday
		6135	"	
		9750	"	
		11852	"	
		15170	"	

*In French unless otherwise noted.

Chapter 6-D
AUSTRAL ISLANDS

The Country

The Austral Islands consist of five inhabited and two un-inhabited islands southwest of the Society group arranged in a chain about 800 miles long. This range is an extension of the submerged volcanic elevations that form the Cook Islands to the north. Although classified as high islands, none of the Australs rise more than 1,500 feet above sea level. Economically, the group is unimportant, but some of them, particularly Raivavae, contain many old temples and archeological remains that are of interest to researchers.

The Australs, part of French Polynesia since Pomare II of Tahiti visited there in the early 1820's to convert them to Christianity, have a total area of only 63 square miles which supports a current population of about 4400 persons. The inhabited islands consist of Rurutu, Rimatera, Raivavae, Tubuai and Rapa.

The island of Tubuai is a high volcanic island measuring about five miles long and three miles wide. It is almost oval in shape and rises to a height of 1385 feet. The barrier reef which surrounds it measures nine miles long and six miles wide. The annular lagoon surrounding the island is shallow throughout and not navigable by yachts. The one entrance to the lagoon is on the northwest side and it leads to the principal village of Mataura. There are approximately 1400 persons living on the island.

Tubuai is a very fertile island and coffee, copra, bananas, manioc (arrowroot), and oranges are grown here. The oranges, like most of those throughout the islands of Polynesia, are ripe when the skin is still green, however this does not detract from their delicious flavor.

European eyes first saw Tubuai in 1777 when Captain Cook on his third voyage of exploration visited there just prior to heading north to look for the Northwest Passage above North America. The next Europeans to visit Tubuai were the mutineers from the *Bounty* who landed there in 1789 and attempted to make a settlement. The natives did not look kindly on this invasion and soon violence erupted and 66 natives lost their lives. But it was obvious to the mutineers that this would continue to be an in-hospital island for them so they embarked once more in their quest for a paradise.

In 1882 the first true missionaries arrived in the form of Christianized Tahitians. But Christianity took a severe set-back the following year when an epidemic swept the islands killing hundreds of the islanders. While the Tubuaians blamed it on the anger of their old gods who were being pushed aside, the fact was that the Tubuaians living in isolation for so many years had not developed even the simplest immunity to white man's diseases. This was the start of the decline of the people and culture from which Tubuai never recovered.

Few people have ever heard of Raivavae Island (ry'va-vy) and even fewer have ever visited it. On the chart of the South Pacific it is but a dot located at 27°52′ S latitude and 147°35′ W longitude, 360 miles south southeast of Tahiti. It is a high island of considerable geologic age surrounded by a well-developed barrier reef which is just awash in most places but which also has on it some of the familiar wooded islets known as motus. While the oval barrier reef measures 5 miles N-S and 8 miles E-W, the 1400 foot high volcanic mountains which form the island proper cover an area of only 2 x 5 miles. The intervening annular space is a beautiful lagoon with a coral sand and mud bottom, uncounted coral heads with many rising close to the surface, and a fringing reef along the shoreline making dinghy landing difficult. The blue-green lagoon, the lush green growth of the coastal plains, and the spectacularly eroded mountains give it a beauty rivaling Bora Bora in the Society Islands.

Raivavae today is a quiet, almost subdued island with little of the gaiety and love for pleasure found on the other islands of French Polynesia. But it was not always so. In the 18th and 19th centuries Raivavae was alive with 3000 people in a social order said to rival that of Tahiti. These early people were daring seafarers who not only voyaged to neighboring islands but north to Tahiti and Raiatea and, reputedly, even to the shores of New Zealand. Fishing was then an important part of their daily life although little is done now and, in fact, they no longer

Austral Islands

(Archipielago Tubuai)

Distances between ports in nautical miles:

Between *Tubuai* (23°21′S, 149°30′W) and:

Auckland, New Zealand	2100
Easter Island	2220
Fakarava, Tuamotu Archipelago	480
Papeete, Tahiti	375
Rarotonga, Cook Islands	975

Standard time:

10 hours slow on GMT

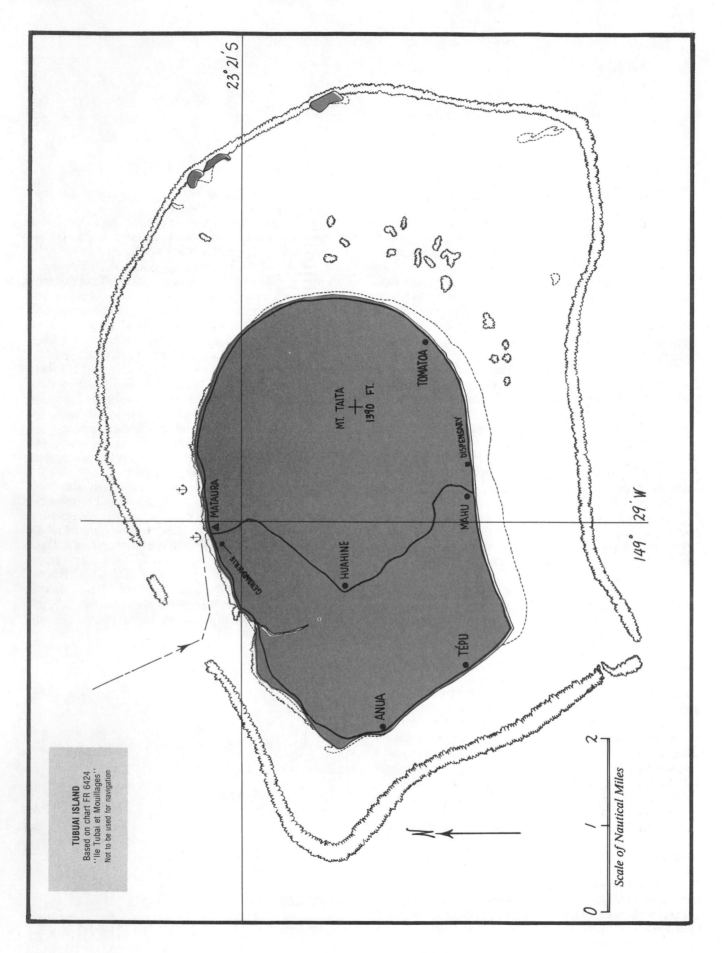

TUBUAI ISLAND
Based on chart FR 6424
"Ile Tubai et Mouillages"
Not to be used for navigation

23° 21′ S

149° 29′ W

MT. TAITA
1390 FT.

TOMATOA

DISPENSARY

MAHU

MATAURA

HUAHINE

GENDARMERIE

ANUA

TÉPU

0   1   2
Scale of Nautical Miles

106

The principal harbor of Raivavae is at Rairua on the leeward side of the island. Although it is well protected from the prevailing southeasterly tradewinds, it is exposed to the north and west. The island-surrounding barrier reef serves to break the force of the seas from those directions but you still have to face the winds.

seem to have an affinity for the sea. Their early civilization developed agriculture to a fine art using terracing techniques for growing taro — the universal food of all Pacific islands. Warfare between the districts of the island was a way of life and the mountainous backbone of the island was in many parts made a fortress. But disaster came to Raivavae in 1826 when a very contagious, malignant fever was brought from the neighboring island of Tubuai. The disease decimated the population, reducing their numbers to an estimated 120 persons. Unable to sustain their culture any longer, it vanished into the underbrush and the Raivavaeans today enjoy no heritage from the past.

The island of Rurutu has a population of about 1500 persons with most of them living in the principal village of Moerai and the second village of Avera. The remaining population inhabits the coastal strip surrounding the island. Rurutu became a French protectorate in 1889 and a possession in 1900.

Remote Bass and Rapa Islands are so far south that they differ from the rest of French Polynesia. They have too moderate a climate for most tropical growth and do not produce copra but concentrate on coffee, taro, and oranges. Bass Island (Morotiri) is actually a cluster of nine islands, eight of which are mere rock pinnacles rising to a maximum height of only 350 feet. They are uninhabited but are visited occasionally by fishermen.

Rapa is a small volcanic island that has an elevation of 2,000 feet. It is populated by approximately 300 people who are believed to have descended from a primitive, pure Polynesian stock. They are darker than most Polynesians but have the sturdy, splendid physique of that ethnic group. Special permission of the French Governor is required to visit Rapa Island.

The Weather

The winds in the area of the main Austral group (ex-

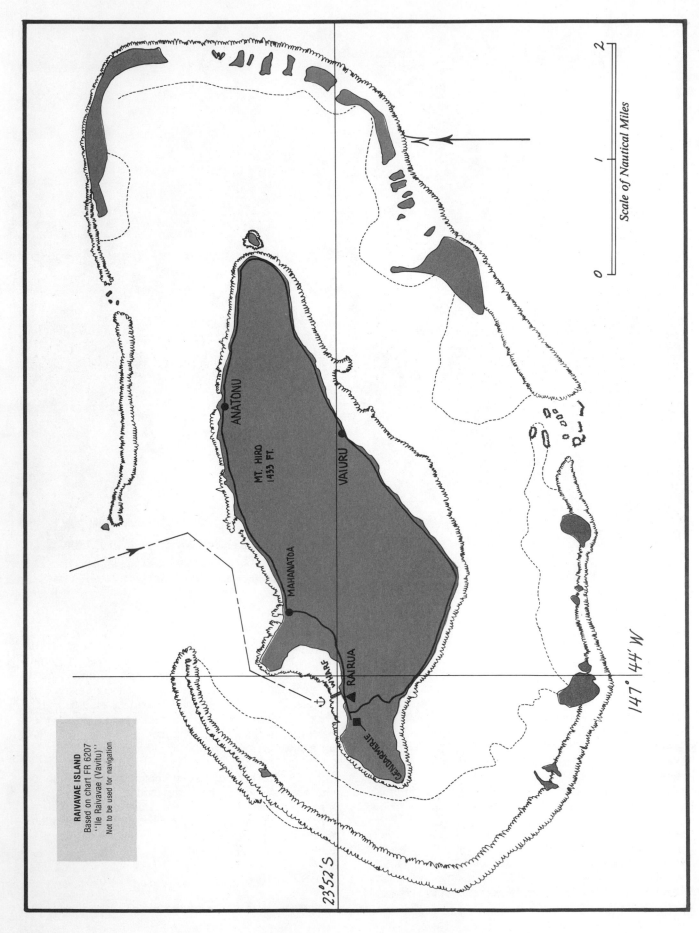

RAIVAVAE ISLAND
Based on chart FR 6207
"Ile Raivavae (Vavitu)"
Not to be used for navigation

Scale of Nautical Miles

ANATONU

MT. HIRO
1433 FT.

VAIURU

MAHANATOA

RAIRUA

GENDARMERIE

WHARF

23°52'S

147°44'W

108

An interisland trading vessel discharges its cargo at the low wharf of Rairua, Raivavae.

cluding Rapa) are similar to those of the windward isles of the Society group. They lie in the tradewind belt and the winds tend to be easterly with southeast winds dominant in June and July. The rest of the year it is equally divided between northeasterlies to southeasterlies.

The climate of these islands is very healthy and the most pleasant months for visiting are September and October. In the southern winter the temperature may drop as low as 52°F.

Yacht Facilities

There are no yacht facilities in the Australs. Some villages have wharfs for the copra boats and these can be used for docking when the copra boats are not present. There are no boat supplies or fuel available but there is water piped to the docks which is untreated but fresh from the mountain streams.

These islands are very fertile and there is an abundance of good fruits available. Vegetables are generally unknown except for taro. The small stores carry a limited variety of canned goods and dried staples.

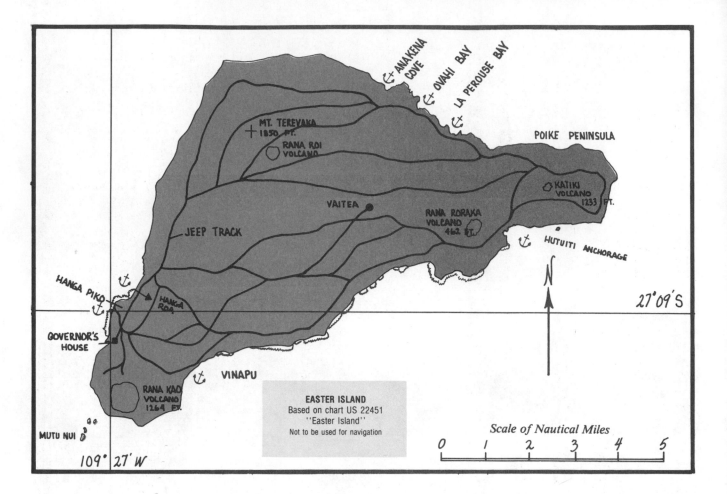

ANAKENA COVE

OVAHI BAY

LA PEROUSE BAY

POIKE PENINSULA

MT. TEREVAKA
1850 FT.

RANA ROI
VOLCANO

KATIKI
VOLCANO
1233 FT.

VAITEA

RANA RORAKA
VOLCANO
462 FT.

JEEP TRACK

HUTUITI ANCHORAGE

N

27°09'S

HANGA PIKO

HANGA
ROA

GOVERNOR'S
HOUSE

VINAPU

RANA KAO
VOLCANO
1264 FT.

EASTER ISLAND
Based on chart US 22451
"Easter Island"
Not to be used for navigation

MUTU NUI

109° 27' W

Scale of Nautical Miles

0   1   2   3   4   5

Chapter 7

EASTER ISLAND
(Isla de Pascua)

The Country

Easter Island is known by a variety of names and has been called the world's loneliest island by Thor Heyerdahl who spent a year there studying the famous brooding statues and other archeological remains of a past civilization. The Chilean administrators call it Isla de Pascua, the islanders refer to it as Rapa Nui (distinguishing it from Rapa Iti which is in the Austral Islands), while the complete Polynesian name for it is Te Pito o Te Henua meaning The Navel (center) of the World.

Whatever you call it, from the water it is a forbidding volcanic rock whose coast is steep-to and rocky with only a few sandy beaches on its total periphery. It measures 14 miles long, 7 miles wide, has a circumference of 34 miles and is roughly triangular in shape. The land is generally high and precipitous in places but the hills are gently rounded and covered to their summits with vegetation. Several extinct volcanoes are on the island. One, Rana Kao, at the southern end of the island rises to 1264 feet and has a small deep lake in its crater which is the largest crater on the island. The highest peak of the island is Cerro Terevaka which reaches 1850 feet.

There are no completely sheltered anchorages on the island but temporary anchorage can be found in many places in the lee of the island. Because of the steep-to sides of this island, anchoring must take place close in to the shoreline and occasional rocky patches present a hazard.

Vegetation consists principally of tall grass that covers most of the island. Few trees exist and most of these are found in the Rana Kao crater. They are known as toro miro trees and are used as the raw material for the wood carvings made by the islanders. All three volcanic craters are marshy and grow reeds. Some eucalyptus will be found which were planted by Europeans in the 20th Century. Cultivated crops include sweet potatoes, yams, bananas, sugar cane, and tobacco. Other than sheep and cattle brought in by the Europeans, there are no animals on Easter Island. Fish abound in the ocean and lobstering along the shoreline is very popular. It is a big lobster without claws which can be speared in waist-deep water.

It is the unwritten history of the island that is so interesting and its vagueness only adds mystery to the presence of almost 900 of the giant stone statues known as moai. Anthropological and archeological evidence suggests that the first colonization of Easter Island took place between 100 BC and 400 AD but nobody really knows from whence they came. Lying midway between South America and Tahiti, it may have been initially settled from either or both directions. This early civilization thrived until sometime between 600 and 1100 AD.

A middle period of settlement and possibly the one that created the statues, began about 1100 AD with an influx of Polynesians led by Hotu Matu'a. They were a slender people known as the Hanau Momoka and often referred to as the short ears. The Hanau Eepe, or long ears, arrived somewhat later from Peru. For the next 500 years there were 4000 inhabitants on this island divided into two tribes. Culture flourished but so did rivalries and around 1600 war broke out between the two factions that all but ended life on Easter Island. The civilization that had created those mystifying stone statues destroyed itself, toppled its moai, and lost to the world the secret of building these 20-ton statues. But worse was yet to follow with the arrival of the first Europeans.

It was Easter Sunday in 1772 when a Dutch navigator named Jacob Roggeveen first sighted the island and

Easter Island
(Isla de Pascua)
A colony of Chile

Port of Entry:

Hanga Roa   27°09'S, 109°27'W

Distances between ports in nautical miles:

Between *Hanga Roa* and:

Acapulco, Mexico	2870
Archipielago de Colon	1950
Honolulu, Hawaii	3910
Islas Juan Fernandez	1630
Lima, Peru	2090
Panama City, Panama	2790
Papeete, Tahiti	2260
Pitcairn Island	1390
San Diego, California	3650
Valparaiso, Chile	1910

Standard Time:

7 hours slow on GMT

named it Easter Island. The name has been retained to this date since Pascua means Easter in the Spanish language. Following Roggeveen came a succession of Spanish, English and French explorers in the late 1700s. That was the second step in the demise of the original inhabitants. They became slaves to foreigners who stopped there to replenish ship's provisions and take advantage of the depressed native population. Many islanders were taken to Peru in 1862 as slaves to work on the coastal sugar plantations. European diseases were brought back to the island and the population was reduced to a mere 111 persons by the year 1870.

Chile annexed the island in 1888 and under more settled conditions the population again started to increase. In 1966 the people of Easter Island became enfranchised Chilean citizens. Today there are 1500 Rapa Nuieans and 500 Chileans on the island with such 20th Century conveniences as telephones and closed circuit television.

Easter Island is administered by an appointed civilian governor with local affairs handled by a mayor and a council of elders. The nationalized sheep farm having about 40,000 sheep, provides a communal income to the island which is used for building materials and equipment. Sources of personal income include wood and shell carv-ings and providing quarters and services for tourists who come in on the twice-a-week jet airplane from Valparaiso and Tahiti.

The island people are devout members of the Roman Catholic Church headed by Father David Reddy, the parish priest. But the past dies slowly and superstition still prevails in many people who believe in the power of guardian spirits or aku aku.

The Weather

There is only one description for the weather at Easter Island and that is unpredictable. Rarely does the wind stay steady from any direction for more than a few days and then it shifts direction in a matter of minutes. A vessel left unattended in a calm leeward anchorage could quickly find itself on a leeshore. While the weather is highly unpredictable, it is never really bad. Easter Island sits at the northwestern edge of the South Pacific high pressure area which accounts for the light variable winds and total absence of fog.

Most of the gales of the great Southern Ocean pass well to the south of Easter Island but their effects are still known. Heavy swells generated by the storms of the Roar-

The brooding statues of Easter Island symbolize the enigma of this remote eastern corner of Polynesia.

ing Forties roll in from the south or southwest making the southern anchorages untenable.

Summer (December, January and February) has the best weather of the year when 60 percent of the winds are between northeast and southeast at speeds of 10 to 12 knots. These are sometimes referred to as the southeast trades. The variable winds which occur are known locally as "Tangariki" and "Anoraru". Gales are virtually nonexistent at this time of the year. The current is flowing from the northeast at about 5 to 15 miles per day and the water is at the annual maximum of 73°F.

In autumn the winds continue their variability but come dominantly from the northwest to northeast at only slightly increased speeds of 10 to 15 knots. Calms are almost nonexistent during this period of the year. There are now a measurable number of gales, averaging about one a month but major storms stay far to the south. The current has shifted to the north but dropped in speed to 0 to 5 miles per day.

Winter (June, July and August) is the period of the westerlies with virtually no northeast or east winds. But all the rest are still variable. The wind speeds have also increased to 15 to 18 knots and gales average less than one per month. Even with the higher winds there are more calms averaging up to five percent of the time. At this time of the year the southern storm tracks have moved their furthest north and Easter Island is barely on the edge of them. The northerly current still exists in its minimal form of 1 to 5 miles per day and water temperatures are at 67°F. The northerly winds which occur during the winter are called "Papakino" and the southwesterly winds of winter are called "Vaitara".

Jetsam and Flotsam

Currency:

Easter Island uses the Chilean peso as its basic unit of monetary exchange. There are 100 centisimos in a peso. At press time the rate of exchange was $US1 = 22 pesos.

Language:

Spanish is the official language of Easter Island but some of the people still speak a Polynesian tongue. French and German are also spoken by a few people as well as English with a Yankee accent.

Electricity:

Chilean electric systems are 200v, 50Hz AC but you may find some 110v, 60 Hz AC supply left over from the former American military base there.

Postal Address:

Mail comes at very irregular intervals and it is recommended that you use other ports of call for mail.

External Affairs:

Chilean embassies and consulates

Information Center:

Agency of National Tourism
Agustinas Street
Santiago, CHILE

Cruising Library:

Aku Aku, Thor Heyerdahl; Rand McNally & Company, New York, USA, 1958.
Easter Island, John Dos Passos; Doubleday & Company, Garden City, New York, USA, 1971.
Island at the Center of the World, Father Sabatian Englert; Charles Scribner's Sons, New York, NY, USA, 1970

In the spring the winds return to the easterly semicircle with virtually no westerlies blowing at all. Gales are nonexistent but calms may occur on at least two days per month. Wind speed averages between 10 and 12 knots. The current is northerly at a speed of 10 to 15 miles per day and the water temperature is at its lowest for the year, 65°F.

Winter is the rainy season although there is some rain every month of the year. The average rainfall is 4 to 5 inches per month with an annual total averaging 53 inches. The months of September and October are the driest.

Although the humidity is surprisingly constant the year around, there is a daily variation ranging from 85 to 87 percent in the morning to 75 to 80 percent in the afternoon.

Temperatures are fairly equable throughout the year with a daily average of 75°F and a daily average low of 63°F. January is the hottest month and August is the coolest month.

Yacht Entry

Entering formalities at Easter Island are simple for the yachtsman. A passport is required but no visa. At Hanga Roa he gets his customs clearance and tourist card from the Chilean governor who resides there. It is wise to also check in with the Port Captain who can advise you on anchorages, landings and the weather. As a matter of courtesy, you should pay your respects to the mayor of Hanga Roa who, next to the island governor, is the most important person on the island. If you have been in ham

radio contact with the island, you will also want to say hello to Father David Reddy, an American from Staten Island, New York, who is a ham radio operator.

Yachtsmen in the past have experienced some theft of items from their boats and you are advised not to tempt the local people. They are not malicious but simply do not understand the rigid property code of a European-type civilization.

Yacht Facilities

There are no safe anchorages at Easter Island and the prudent yachtsman will always leave a capable crewmember aboard who can take appropriate action should the wind suddenly shift and the anchorage develop into a lee shore. A number of small bays and coves indent the rocky coastline and some of them have landing places for dinghies, albeit through the surfline. Four coves in particular may be useable by the cruising boat under different weather conditions. Hanga Roa on the west coast offers a good anchorage from October to April which is the season of the southeast trades. Should a northerly gale set in, the alternative is to duck around the southwest peninsula where the volcano Rana Kao is located, and anchor in Vinapu (Ovnipoo) cove.

During the southern winter Anakena is the preferred anchorage and is probably best all around anchorage on the island for yachts. It is reasonably well protected from all but northerly winds; the sandy beach is quite level and suitable for dinghy landing; and there is little sea or swell that comes into the little cove. (But beware of an errant wave that may make an attempt to upset your

Medical Memo

Immunization requirements:

A vaccination is required for smallpox if arriving from or having transited an infected area within the last 14 days. Typhoid immunization is also recommended.

Local health situation:

There are no reported health problems at this time. Flies are abundant and can be a nuisance.

Health services:

Dispensary type medical care is available on the island. More serious problems would have to be transported by airplane to the parent country of Chile. Expect only emergency dental or optical care on the island. Drug supplies are limited, however, good airplane connections with Chile could bring emergency drugs, if needed.

Water:

You should consider the water suspect and treat it.

dinghy.) Should severe northerly weather develop, the alternate anchorage is around the east end of Poike Peninsula at Hutuite in the sunset shadows of Rana Roraka volcano and the most famous group of stone statues. Dinghy landing here will be much more difficult, and the recommended landing is at the eastern end of the bay on a rock which is actually one of the famous statues at water's edge.

The principal community on Easter Island is at Hanga Roa and, before going ashore elsewhere, you should make an attempt to anchor there for purposes of getting official clearance. Anchorage should be made outside of the six fathom line (about ¼ to ½ mile offshore thereby staying away from numerous rocky hazards and foul grounds. With exceptional care one can come into water one fathom deep just southeast of the ruined pier.

Ships use the harbor at Hanga Piko when offloading supplies on lighters but it appears to have no advantages for small boats and is considerably further from town than Hanga Roa. There is a pier at Hanga Piko which can be used for dinghy landing.

At either Hanga Roa or Hanga Piko you can arrange with local fishermen for shoreboat service at a weekly charge of about $US20, but remembering that you may have to leave an anchorage rather suddenly because of a wind shift, this may not be a good bargain.

There are no boat hardware supplies available on Easter Island and no maintenance services. Water and diesel fuel are available but both have to be carried to your boat via dinghy. A limited stock of canned goods can be found at the Government Store and fresh fruits and some vegetables can be obtained from the local people but they are very expensive. Fresh meat including beef, mutton and poultry are also available.

Although Easter Islanders use the Chilean peso as the medium of exchange, far better bargains can be had through trading in goods not available or priced too high for the people to buy at the Government Store. Items of trade particularly sought by local people are used clothing (especially jeans), shoes, fish hooks, wire, nylon rope, and even canned goods. These can also be bartered for artifacts such as carvings, shells and shell jewelry.

Chapter 8

PITCAIRN ISLAND

The Country

Pitcairn is an isolated island whose base is far below the level of the sea. It is of relatively recent origin since there is no coral reef surrounding it. It measures about two miles long by one mile wide and at its highest point near the west end it rises to a peak of 1000 feet. Approximately one-half of its 1120 acres is cultivated although of that there are only 88 acres of flat land and another 352 acres of rolling land. The shoreline consists of formidable near-vertical cliffs of volcanic rock preventing easy access from the sea all around.

The soil is rich and fertile but very porous being made up primarily of decomposed lava with some rich black earth. All of the island is thickly covered with luxuriant growth right to the cliffs which are skirted with thickly branching evergreen trees. There are no indigenous animals on the island and the indigenous growth includes coconut palms, breadfruit, plantains, yams, taro, pandanus, and paper mulberry for the making of tapa cloth. Water is obtained principally from rain although in the dry season there are intermittent springs in a valley west of the village of Adamstown.

All sea-faring folk know the main element of Pitcairn's history, namely the final settlement of the mutineers from the HMS *Bounty*. This took place on 15 January 1790 following the mutiny off the island of Tofua in the Tonga group on 28 April 1789. Although the mutineers found the island uninhabited, there were signs of earlier dwellers in ruins of huts and some crudely carved images, stone hatchets, fish bones, and burial sites on top of the mountain later called Lookout Ridge.

The first Europeans to sight what is now Pitcairn Island were the crew of the HMS *Swallow*, Capt. Phillip Carteret, commanding, in 1767. It was named after the midshipman, Robert Pitcairn who first sighted it. A description of the island was later published in the 1773 book "Hawkesworth Voyages" which was aboard the *Bounty* and became the inspiration for the mutineers to sail east in their final pursuit of a new home after being driven off the island of Tubuai in the Austral group.

Once settled on Pitcairn the mutineers and their descendants have lived there continuously except for two brief periods when they were removed to other islands for their supposed benefit. The first occasion was in 1831 when the entire population of 87 persons was transferred to Tahiti to begin a new life under Queen Pomare. Unfortunately, disease and the amoral conduct of the Tahitians convinced them that they were better off at Pitcairn. After 24 months away from their home island they were back on Pitcairn, but in the meantime natives from Bora Bora sailing on the French Brig *Courier de Bordeaux* had vandalized their homes and they had to rebuild many of them.

The second migration from Pitcairn took place in 1856 when the entire population, now numbering 187 persons, departed on the ship *Mrayshire* for Norfolk Island 5000 miles to the west. Norfolk Island, a recently-abandoned British penal colony with many facilities built by the prisoners was offered to the Pitcairners as a bigger and better place to live. Unfortunately, the British retained possession of it and the Pitcairners became tenants only. Although it was a larger island and the living was good, many Pitcairners longed for their old home and in 1861 two groups numbering 16 and 26 returned to their home island. From that time on Pitcairners have occupied both islands continuously.

Although under the protection of the British Commonwealth with a governor resident in New Zealand, the Pitcairners essentially rule themselves through an island magistrate and a council. There is also an island court to handle community and civil offences but its last case was tried in 1967.

The population of Pitcairn Island in 1965 was 85 persons of island descent and 10 others. As with so many islands of the Pacific, the population of Pitcairn is dwindl-

Pitcairn Island
A British Dependency

Port of Entry:

Bounty Bay   25°04'S, 130°06'W

Distances between ports in nautical miles:

Between *Bounty Bay* and:

Auckland, New Zealand	3300
Easter Island	1120
Los Angeles, California	3600
Panama City, Panama	4100
Papeete, Tahiti	1350
Rapa Island	810

Standard time:

9 hours slow on GMT

ing as the youth seek opportunities outside.

The economy of Pitcairn is primarily subsistence with bartering the only means of exchange. Money is nonexistent and there are no taxes. Island income is derived from wood carvings, woven baskets and hats sold to tourists who come by ship or small boat. A most profitable source of revenue has been the Pitcairn Island stamps collected by philatelists the world around. The funds so obtained are used for community projects such as the maintenance of the radio station and the landing area at Bounty Bay.

Religion plays an important part in the lives of the Pitcairners ever since 1808 when Alexander Smith, last of the mutineers, seriously took up the Bible. (He had taken the name John Adams in his latter days.) Today the residents follow the teachings of the Seventh-Day Adventists.

Pitcairn Island is the largest and only inhabited island of the Pitcairn District which consists of four islands. The others are Oeno, Ducie, and Henderson atolls.

The Weather

Sitting on the edge of the tropics, Pitcairn enjoys a good climate with moderate winds. There are no regular trade winds and the best weather occurs when the winds are from the southwest. In the southern summer the prevailing winds are mostly from the east southeast. Northerly

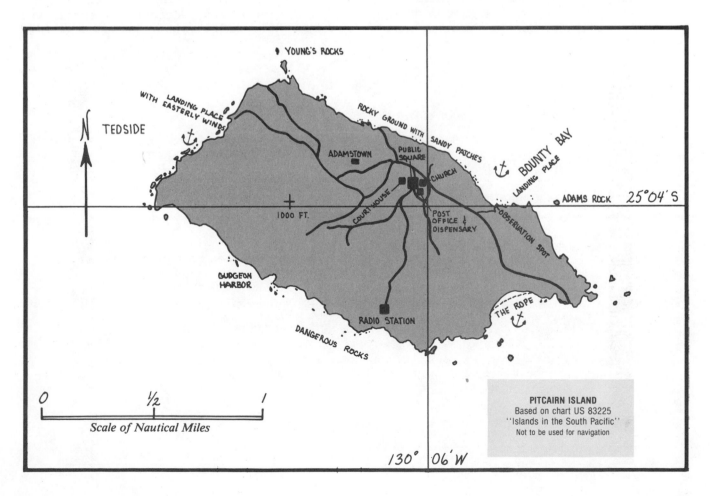

117

winds which are generally light also bring rain and occasionally fog. Following a north wind, the wind will shift to the west which can bring gales. Gales can also come from the southeast. Although out of the normal hurricane belt, hurricanes have been experienced but they are rare.

Maximum temperatures in the summer average about 79°F and in the winter they average about 60°F. Rainfall averages about 78 inches in one year but there have been periods of droughts. There are no pests or endemic diseases.

Yacht Entry and Facilities

Visitors are welcomed to Pitcairn Island with no official formalities. Although these people have developed some immunity to the diseases of civilization, do not plan on landing if there is any illness aboard.

Facilities at Pitcairn for yachts or any other boats are essentially zero. There are two landing places — Bounty Bay on the northeast side of the island and Tedside on the northwest side of the island. Both are open anchorages and you are advised to leave a capable crew-member aboard to handle the boat in case of a sudden wind shift. In Bounty Bay you can anchor in 8 to 10 fathoms of water having a sand bottom with some rock. If the easterly winds pick up then you must go to the Tedside anchorage where you can anchor in 12 fathoms of water. Neither place makes a good anchorage when the wind is northwest to northeast. Then it is necessary to stand off the island until the weather shifts which may be in a day or two. The islanders are known for their local weather predictions and they will advise you of expected changes in the wind necessitating a change in anchorage.

The only suitable anchorage in northwest to northeast winds is the Down Rope bight on the southeast shore. It is so named because there is no way to get up to or down from the plains except by rope.

You do not take your own dinghy ashore at Bounty Bay, the main landing place. Instead, you wait at anchor until one of the island boats comes out to get you. Because of the heavy surf, it takes experienced Pitcairners to negotiate the surf line up to the small pier and landing ramp.

Some provisions can be obtained here, especially fresh fruits, goat meat and poultry. Water may be scarce if it has been a dry year. You should plan on buying handicraft articles because they are not only interesting but it helps support their economy. Stamps are another must at Pitcairn. The people here are very generous and will host you beyond your highest expectations. Reciprocate. See if there is something they need which you have on board and can part with until reaching your next port of call. This does not, however, include alcoholic beverages, ammunition or girlie magazines.

There are no boat parts or services available and no fuels.

Radio communications are made with many countries and ships at sea as well as hams the world over. Principal schedules are maintained with Suva, Fiji, on 21.804 MHz at 0200, 1815, and 2000 GMT daily except Saturdays. Tom Christian, the radio officer, also operates an amateur station, VR6TC, each Tuesday at 0500 and 2100 GMT.

Medical Memo

Immunization requirements:

Pratique is not an official entry requirement but yachties are urged not to land if they have any illness aboard or have recently visited an area having cholera, smallpox or yellow fever.

Local health situation:

No reported medical problems.

Health services:

The Pitcairners have learned to take care of themselves in matters of health and will extend their services to a visiting yachtie in need. Medical officers of the South Pacific Health Service have made visits to the island in past years and some help is received from doctors on ships stopping at the island. Serious illnesses or injuries would have to be attended to elsewhere.

The only drugs available are those that the Pitcairners get from New Zealand for their own use. Use your boat supply first as you will have a better chance of replenishing your stock then they will have of replenishing theirs.

Water:

You should consider the water suspect and treat it.

The landing at Bounty Bay. You do not come in here on your own, anchor offshore and the Pitcairners in their surf boat will come out and get you. The landing jetty, boat shed and canoe houses are visible as is the "Flying Fox" rope running up the hill to the right. In the middle distance is St. Paul Rock.

At the center of Adamstown is the Public Hall and Courthouse. The three doors of the building in the center are (right to left) the Post Office, Library, and Dispensary. A portion of the church entrance is to the left.

Jetsam and Flotsam

Currency:

The New Zealand dollar is the official currency but American, Australian and other currencies can usually be exchanged on the island.

Language:

Most of the people speak English in a dialect that has its roots in the 18th Century. Many also speak Tahitian.

Postal Address:

Mail comes at very irregular periods and it is advised that you use other ports of call for mail.

External Affairs:

New Zealand embassies and consulates

Cruising Library:

The Pitcairners, Robert B. Nicolson; Angus and Robertson Ltd., 89 Castlereagh Street, Sidney, Australia, 1965.
Pitcairn Island, David Silverman; Collins, Williams and World Publishing, Cleveland, OH, USA, 1967.
Pitcairn: Children of Mutiny, Ian M. Ball; Little, Brown & Company, Boston, MA, USA, 1973.
Pitcairn's Island, Charles Nordhoff and James Norman Hall; Little, Brown & Co., Boston, MA, USA, 1934.

Chapter 9

COOK ISLANDS

The Country

The 15 Cook Islands are widely scattered and lie between 8°S and 23°S latitude and 156°W to 167°W longitude. The rectangular area of ocean within which the islands lie amounts to about 800,000 square miles. The Cook Islands fall into two geographic groupings:
(a) Southern group includes Rarotonga, Mangaia, Aitutaki, Mauke, Atiu, Mitiaro, Takutea, and Manuae.
(b) Northern group includes Penrhyn, Manihiki, Rakahanga, Pukapuka, Nassau, Suvarov, and Palmerston.

The southern group of eight islands is made up of three high islands (Rarotonga, Mangaia, and Atiu) while all the rest are on their way to becoming atolls with low, weathered central volcanic cores. Rarotonga and Mangaia are the largest islands at 26 and 20 square miles area, respectively.

Rarotonga is the principal island of the whole Cook group and its rugged volcanic interior rises to a height of 2140 feet. It is surrounded by a fringing reef with very limited boat passages and anchorages. The island has a rich soil on which many vegetables and all types of tropical and subtropical fruits thrive. Most of the islands are covered with thick evergreen bush. Mangaia and Aitutaki are the other two principal islands in the group and they, too, have limited boat passages through the fringing reefs.

The islands of the northern group are mostly dry forested atolls differing only in size. Penrhyn is the most northerly and the largest with a 108 square mile lagoon and three passages of which the biggest, West Passage, has a 21 foot depth and a 40 yard width. The land area of this island is slightly over 2400 acres.

Suvarov is the only other island of the northern group which can be entered by small vessels. The pass depth is 15 feet with only a single suitable anchorage inside. The island has not been inhabited by Cook Islanders for many years but it was the home of the legendary Tom Neale for many years until his death in 1977. Birds abound on the island and it has been proclaimed a bird sanctuary.

All of the other islands of the northern group have small permanent populations limited by water and soil resources.

Early events in the Cook Islands oral history indicate that the Maoris of New Zealand transited through the Cooks on some of their expeditions. However, it is less certain that they ever settled there. The first Polynesians from Tahiti may have arrived about 500 AD. About 1300 AD other Tahitians sailed via the Cooks to New Zealand and return. Hence the Polynesian-Maori culture.

Modern history begins about 1595 when the Spanish explorer, Mendana, saw the first of the 15 islands as he passed by Pukapuka (Danger) Island. His countryman, Quiros, discovered Rakahanga in 1606. Captain Cook is given official credit for discovering the Cook Islands in 1774. The Cook Islands did not escape the *Bounty* mutiny incident. Bligh discovered Aitutaki in 1789 and the mutineers of the *Bounty* called there the same year after seizing the ship in Tonga. It is said that the *Bounty* mutineers brought the first oranges and pumpkin seeds to Rarotonga.

The Rev. John Williams of the London Missionary Society first called at Rarotonga on July 25, 1823. He brought both European and Polynesian missionaries to Rarotonga who soon converted the native population to Christianity and the church gained the dominant role in

Cook Islands

A self-governing country in free association with New Zealand

Port of Entry:

Avatiu, Rarotonga   21°12'S, 159°47'W

Distances between ports in nautical miles:

Between *Avatiu* and:

Apia, Western Samoa	820
Agana, Guam	3890
Auckland, New Zealand	1630
Honolulu, Hawaii	2550
Noumea, New Caledonia	1890
Pago Pago, American Samoa	750
Panama City, Panama	5090
Papeete, Society Islands	620
Ponape, Caroline Islands	3000
Rabaul, New Britain	2990
Suva, Fiji	1260
Tubuai, Austral Islands	980

Standard time:

10 hours, 30 minutes slow on GMT

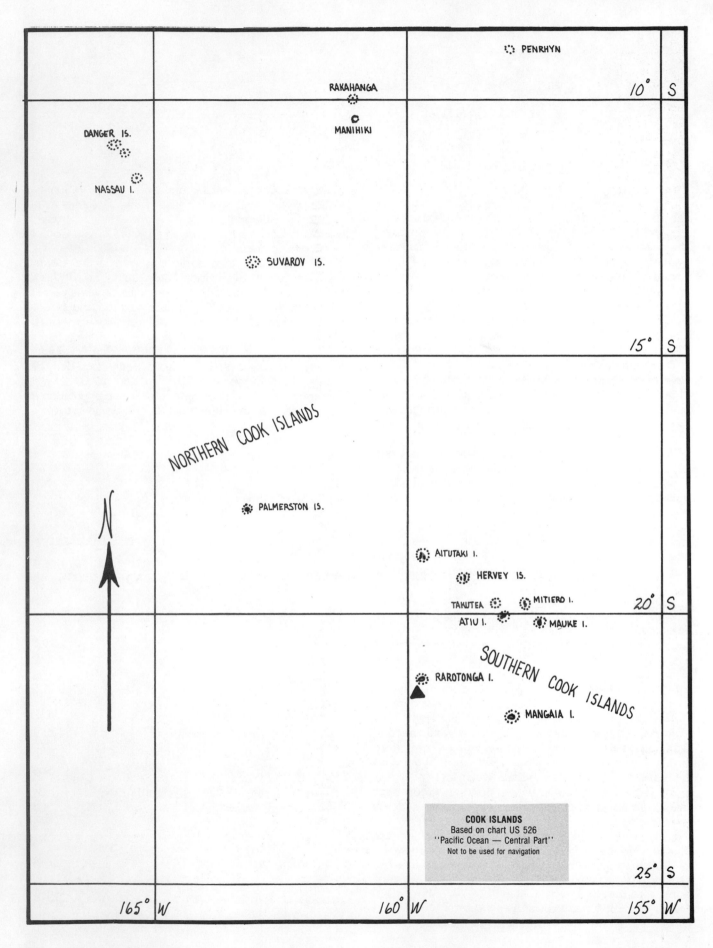

PENRHYN

RAKAHANGA

10° S

DANGER IS.

MANIHIKI

NASSAU I.

SUVAROV IS.

15° S

NORTHERN COOK ISLANDS

N

PALMERSTON IS.

AITUTAKI I.

HERVEY IS.

TAKUTEA   MITIERO I.   20° S

ATIU I.   MAUKE I.

SOUTHERN COOK ISLANDS

RAROTONGA I.

MANGAIA I.

COOK ISLANDS
Based on chart US 526
''Pacific Ocean — Central Part''
Not to be used for navigation

25° S

165° W   160° W   155° W

The northern coast of Rarotonga looking west. Avarua (lower) and Avatiu (upper) harbors are clearly visible as is the airport. Rarotonga has only a fringing reef and there is no protection from northerly winds. This is the Cook Islands only Port of Entry.

Cook Islands affairs. Blue laws were the result but are almost non-existent today. The Cook Islands were put under British protection in 1888 and in 1901 governmental responsibility was taken over by New Zealand.

The people of the Cook Islands are Polynesian Maoris, akin to the people of Tahiti and the Maoris of New Zealand whose traditions and culture they share. The estimated population in 1976 showed a total of 17,326 persons living on the islands with over one-half living on the island of Rarotonga. This was a drop from 21,323 people in 1971. The population growth of the Cooks Islands would be positive but for a steady migration of Maoris to New Zealand amounting to 1000 net migrants per year. It is generally believed that there are now more Cook islanders in Auckland than in Rarotonga.

The basic language of the Cook Islands is a Cook Island Maori, but almost everyone speaks English as a second language.

Cultural development is a major aspect of the Cook Islands government education policy. Among objectives are the creation of an active interest in culture among the Cook Islands children, teachers and the community as a whole, and ensuring the propagation and "keeping alive" of those aspects of Cook Island culture which form the basis of traditional entertainment and festivities. Each island is encouraged to develop its own distinct forms of cultural activity. Religion plays an important part in the lives of the Cook islanders, with approximately 75 percent of them belonging to the Cook Islands Christian Church which was formerly the London Missionary Society. Catholicism claims about 12 percent and the rest are Seventh Day Adventists, Latter Day Saints, Congregational and Anglican. Church services are held in both Maori and the English languages. While the educational system is provided free by the government and is compulsory for children between the ages of six and fifteen years, several church schools are also in being.

The Cook Island economy is primarily agrarian with commercially important crops of oranges, coconuts, and coffee and food crops of taro, yams, manioc (cassava root) and bananas. Only a small number of cattle are raised and fish supply the protein to the islanders diet.

Manufacturing industries with paid employment consist of two plants making pearl shell and other jewelry and two manufacturers of clothing for New Zealand markets. The outstanding business enterprise is the canning of citrus, tomato, and pineapple juices and the label "Raro" is commonly seen in the Pacific Islands. Visiting yachts should take the opportunity to stock up on Raro products when in Rarotonga.

Tipping in the Cook Islands is not customary and can be insulting to these generous Polynesians.

The population of the Cook Islands grew rapidly after World War II expanding from 14,000 in 1945 to 20,000 in 1966. Most of this population lives on the southern islands where they grow copra and fruit for the New Zealand market. But the resources are limited and the Cook Island administration is heavily subsidized from New Zealand.

In 1957 and 1962 steps were taken to grant substantial self-government to the islands. In April 1965 the first general election for the new legislative assembly was held, and in July the islands became self-governing in free association with New Zealand who retained ultimate responsibility for external affairs and defense.

A place was made for the participation of traditional leaders (arikis) in the newly formed House of Arikis, which under the 1965 Constitution was to have an advisory role on questions of Maori land tenure and tradition. This marked a partial return to power of the arikis, who had been the ruling group in the typically stratified Polynesian society before the arrival of the European missionaries in the mid-nineteenth century. The missionaries had changed the society to conform with their Calvinistic ideas, ruling through the chiefs and taking over control of the economic supplies formerly used for traditional purposes, in their search for funds for further mission work. In 1970, the islands still retained strong mission influence in many areas.

The Cook islanders are New Zealand citizens and enjoy unrestricted entry into New Zealand.

Executive Government lies with a cabinet of ministers comprising the premier of the Cook Islands and six other ministers. The premier is elected by the people and the other ministers are appointed.

The Chief Justice of the British Commonwealth is the acting head of state and the Queen's representative. There is also a New Zealand representative on Rarotonga.

The Weather

The southeast tradewinds dominate the vicinity of the Cook Islands. East to southeast winds are the commonest and most dependable throughout the region. In the sea area, 15° to 20°S and 160° to 165°W, they comprise some 50 percent of the annual winds. Northeast winds prevail during September to April, particularly in the northern area, but even in these months they are often equalled by easterly or southeasterly winds. In the northern area northwesterly winds are of some importance in January and February. The average annual wind speed throughout the group is about 11 knots, of which the strongest, 12 to 14 knots, occur in July to September; and the lightest, about 9 to 10 knots, occur usually in January to April. Calms are infrequent.

At Rarotonga, 25 percent each of the winds are east and southeast. South winds are next in frequency with an annual percentage of nine. These south winds are most frequent from May to September. North and northeast winds blow most often in December to February. Calms in the Rarotonga area occur about 13 percent of the time.

All of the Cook Islands lie within the hurricane belt of the Southwest Pacific, thus all islands of the group in the past have suffered from tropical cyclones. Occurrences are infrequent in this area, only about one every ten years. Mangaia, Palmerston, Rakahanga, and Pukapuka have all suffered severe hurricane damage in past years. While the main hurricane season extends between December and April, significant occurrences are known as early as November and as late as June. Only the islands of Penrhyn and Suvarov provide anchorages with any degree of safety during the hurricane season. In February 1978 a hurricane hit Rarotonga causing severe damage in the harbor. The atolls of Palmerston, Aitutaki, Mitiaro, Mauke, and Atiu were also damaged.

Hurricanes come from the northwest in the direction of the Samoa Islands. Gales at sea have occurred at times from May to September.

The climate is warm and humid tempered by the tradewinds. Temperatures range between 48° and 92°F with the cooler months being from May to October. These are also the drier months.

Rarotonga has an average annual rainfall of 83 inches of which 30 inches fall in January to March and 19 inches fall in June to September. At sea, ship reports indicate most frequent rainfall in November to February, and least frequent fall in June to October. Thunderstorms are most

Jetsam and Flotsam

Currency:

The Cook Islands use New Zealand currency. For the approximate exchange rates see New Zealand.

Language:

The indigenous language of the Cook Islands is known as Cook Islands Maori, a Polynesian dialect. English is a second language understood by everyone.

Electricity:

Where electricity is available, it is 240v, 50Hz AC

Postal address:

Yacht (   )
Poste Restante
Rarotonga, COOK ISLANDS

External Affairs Representative:

New Zealand consulates or embassies

Information Center:

Cook Islands Tourist Authority
P.O. Box 14
Rarotonga, COOK ISLANDS

Cruising Library:

Land Tenure in the Cook Islands, R.G. Crocombe; Oxford University Press, New York, NY, USA
The Book of Pukapuka, Robert Dean Frisbee; John Murray, Publisher, London, 1929

Rarotonga's principal harbor, Avatiu, is man-made by blasting out the coral of the fringing reef. This is not a good harbor during the months of December through March because of the frequency of northerly gales which may force you to put to sea even at night.

common from February to April and are rare from May to September.

Yacht Entry

Rarotonga is the only Port of Entry for the Cook Islands and no vessel, except one in distress, may call at any other island of the group before calling at Rarotonga. Since Rarotonga is to windward of the majority of the islands, this poses no problem to the cruising yacht. Yachts should enter at Avatiu Harbor flying the Q flag and wait for clearance at anchor. Subsequently, when visiting any other Cook Island, yacht captains should personally call on the Resident Agent at the island. Only Takutea, Manuae, Suvarov, and Nassau Islands do not have Resident Agents. Prior to departing Rarotonga for the other Cook Islands, yachts need to obtain visiting permission from the Director of Works and Communications.

Yachtsmen visiting the Cook Islands will need passports and the WHO yellow immunization card. Temporary visitors permits for 14 days stay can be obtained. For longer stays, applications must be made at Rarotonga and there is a charge of $5.00 per passport involved for the application papers. There is another charge of $7.00 upon issuance of the extension.

Because of the Cook Islands extensive citrus industry, the agriculture inspectors will confiscate all citrus fruits aboard your boat on entering. Liquor in reasonable amounts can be brought in and retained.

The importation of firearms is expressly forbidden.

Because Rarotonga is still free from the voracious rhinoceros beetle you will be subjected to a very thorough agricultural search for the horned black monster and, possibly, a fumigation if you have arrived from an infected area. Uninfected ports are: Cook Islands, Futuna, Bismarck Archipelago, Palau Islands, Indonesia and Philippine Islands.

The famous Dutch priest, Father George Kester, who was the yachtsman's chaplain for so long at Rarotonga, has been transfered to the island of Aitutaki. His yacht register containing the colorful entries of hundreds of visiting yachts over the years is destined for future publication in Australia.

Yacht Facilities

At Rarotonga yachts stay at Avatiu Harbor which is small and open to northerly weather. Yachts generally anchor Tahiti-style at the quay, but due to the small size of the harbor, they must frequently shift positions to help accommodate additional yachts or to make room for the supply ships. There are now port charges levied as follows:

Boat length	Daily charges
23 to 45 feet	$NZ1.75 plus a $NZ2.00 surcharge
over 45 feet	$NZ2.50 plus a $NZ2.00 surcharge

The Immigration Department handles the docking fees and will collect them at departure before a clearance is granted.

Potable water is available from faucets at the wharf. A shower is at the end of the wharf in the Harbor Master's building. It costs 5 cents NZ.

Haulouts can be made on the slipways of the Fisheries Department at a cost of $NZ2.75 per foot. Some help can be obtained from local sources but mostly you are on your own for work and supplies.

Medical Memo

Immunization requirements:

Vaccinations for smallpox, cholera and yellow fever are required if you have transited or visited within the last six days (smallpox 14 days) an area currently infected.

Local health situation:

The climate of the Cook Islands is healthy and there are none of the common tropical diseases. You will find mosquitoes but no dengue fever or malaria. Inhabitants of Rarotonga occasionally suffer from a bad form of diarrhea and this "Raro bug" is also known to have attacked visitors. Filariasis (and the subsequent development of elephantiasis) still occurs but is being successfully treated in the clinics. Visitors should take simple precautions such as wearing sandals in inhabited and common walking areas. Leprosy and pulmonary tuberculosis are still persistently present in the native population although to a small degree.

Health services:

A new 100-bed hospital serves Rarotonga and there is a 40 bed hospital at Aitutaki which will provide medical care at a low cost. In the other islands with populations of 700 or more, there are cottage hospitals with Fiji-trained medical officers and locally-trained nurses. Radio advisory service from Rarotonga is available to these facilities. The less populated outer islands have dispensaries with trained attendants. Government schools in Rarotonga have dental clinics and mobile dental clinics are used elsewhere. Medical and dental service (mostly for the school children) is free for Cook Islanders but available also to visitors who have emergency problems . There is one private practitioner in the island group.

Drugs are available at both hospitals or the chemist in downtown Avarua. The cost is minimal.

Water:

Tap water at Rarotonga is reported to be safe. Water in the outlying areas should be considered suspect and treated.

Oversea's yachts moor Tahiti-style in Avatiu harbor to enjoy Polynesia at its best. The harbor is small and yachts may occasionally have to shift positions to make room for commercial traffic.

Public correspondence radio telephone and telegraph are maintained at Avarua which connect to New Zealand and thence to the rest of the world. Airline connections are maintained to New Zealand with jet aircraft and to the local islands with small nine passenger aircraft. Commercial transport to all islands is provided by interisland trading vessels — the familiar copra boats.

Not all the Cook Islands have harbors suitable for yachts. In fact, Atiu, Mauke, and Mangaia have no lagoons at all and you must anchor off the reef to visit them. (Plan to leave someone on-board if you do this, since a dragging anchor could either put you on the reef or let your home float out to sea.) The large atoll of Palmerston does not have a pass over four feet deep.

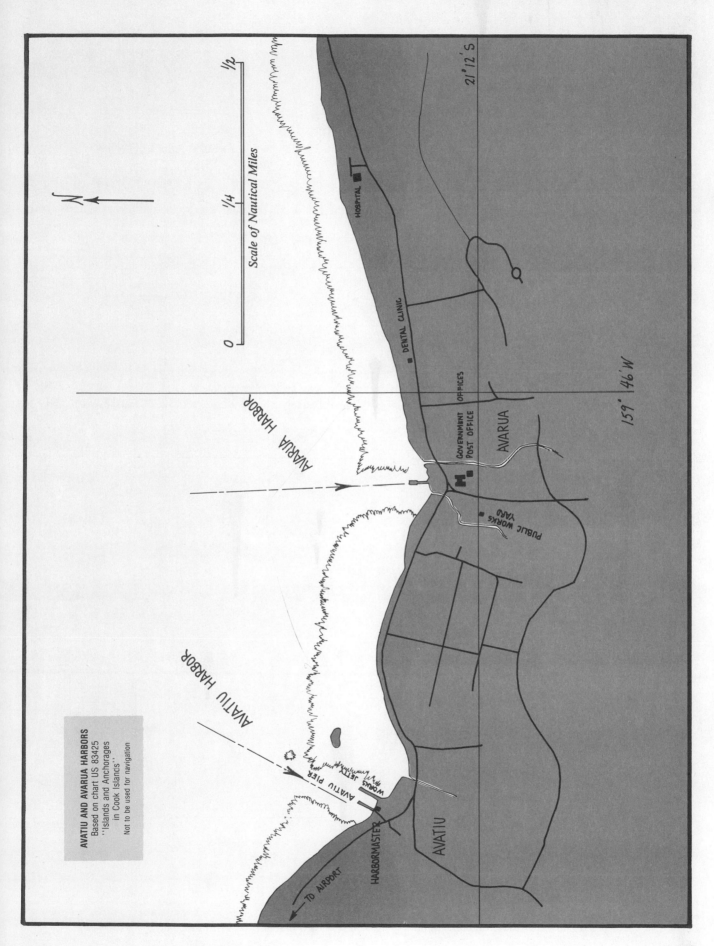

AVATIU AND AVARUA HARBORS
Based on chart US 83425
"Islands and Anchorages
in Cook Islands"
Not to be used for navigation

N

Scale of Nautical Miles

0   ¼   ½

AVARUA HARBOR

AVATIU HARBOR

HOSPITAL

DENTAL CLINIC

GOVERNMENT OFFICES

GOVERNMENT POST OFFICE

AVARUA

PUBLIC WORKS YARD

21° 12' S

159° 46' W

WORKS JETTY

AVATIU PIER

HARBORMASTER

AVATIU

TO AIRPORT

Radio Communications

Station name and call	Location	Frequency Transmit/Receive	Service hours LMT	Type of service
Radio Cook Islands (ZK1ZC)	21°07'S 159°29'W	600 kHz	Mon-Sat 0530-1500 1730-2200 Sunday- 0630-1500 1730-2200	Commercial broadcast
Harbor Master: Rarotonga Radio (ZKR)		500 kHz 2182 kHz 2206 kHz 8748.1 kHz	0700-0200 " " "	CW watch Voice watch " " " "

Chapter 10

SAMOA ISLANDS
(Navigator Islands)

The Country

Historians tell us that the Dutchman, Roggeveen, in 1772 sighted a new group of islands in mid-Pacific on his way west to Java but having calculated their position incorrectly, they continued unknown for another 46 years. In 1768 the French navigator, Bougainville, refound Roggeveen's islands. He saw natives paddling outrigger canoes far from shore and, thinking they were far-ranging sailors (navigators), called the island group the Navigator Islands. But his assumption turned out wrong as these sailors using specially designed fast outrigger canoes were actually chasing schools of ocean bonito returning every night to their villages. Since his basis for the name Navigator Islands was erroneous, the islands eventually became known to the Europeans by their native name, Samoa. Following many years of political struggles between Germany, Britain, and the U.S., the islands were partitioned into Western (German) Samoa and Eastern (American) Samoa. The British withdrew their claims in return for rights in the Tonga Islands to the south.

Although the Samoas are really populated by only one people, they are politically divided between Western Samoa, now an independent country, and American Samoa, a U.S. territory. Family members live in both Samoas and they travel freely (if not free) between the islands. Both Samoas are dedicated to "fa'a Samoa" which means the preservation of the Samoan way of life. Don't think that this hasn't given the foreign rulers a real headache in trying to Westernize the islands. It has also resulted in the Samoan reputedly being the purest surviving Polynesian stock.

Traditions and customs of the Samoans are particularly strong and all visitors should defer to them in order to enjoy their visit. The influence of missionaries is obvious in the Samoan's manner of dress which is a contradiction to the weather. Men wear long pants or lava-lavas with shirts. Women wear almost floor-length skirts and sleeved blouses. Body coverup in public is "fa'a Samoa" and visitors are advised to dress accordingly. Sunday is strictly a day of rest and worship.

There are other customs which should be followed to get along better with the Samoans such as:
— Don't eat while walking along the street in a village
— Don't drive a vehicle, ride a horse, or carry packages when passing in front of a *fale* where the chiefs are meeting
— Do not enter a *fale* if the family is in the act of praying
— When visiting, do not take or do anything without first asking permission of the chief

The Weather

The sea which embraces the Samoa Islands is dominated by east to southeast winds during 57 percent of the annual observations. The easterly winds, however, exceed the southeasterly in the ratio of 2 to 1, and during June to September more than half of all the winds are from that direction. Northeast winds exceed the southeast only during January to March, but the percentages of occurrence of both are comparatively low. From December to March a monsoon current from west to northwest is rather frequent, and in February the west wind is dominant. Calms are observed on about 20 percent of the days in the southern summer months.

At Apia the southeast winds are infrequent, being exceeded by those from the northeast. More than half of the winds are easterly. In the southern summer season there is a noticeable monsoon current, which is here mostly deflected into the northwest. Calms are frequent, particularly in December, February, and March.

The average annual wind speed both at Apia and at sea is about 8 knots. The higher speeds at sea, some 10 to 11 knots, occur in August and September, and the lower speeds some 2 to 7 knots, occur from November to April.

Gales are occasional at sea during most months. At Apia most or all are due to the presence of hurricanes in the vicinity of Samoa. Most of these storms occur in December to April and there is an annual average of five days during these months in which the weather at this station is more or less affected by tropical cyclones.

The islands lie within the hurricane belt of the Western Pacific. Hurricanes occur especially from January to March, and occasionally up to the middle of April. The

islands experience occasional earthquakes, but they have not in the past caused much damage.

Since the islands in the Samoa group are, as a whole, in close proximity to each other, the climate conditions affecting all of them will be similar. The climate on the islands is mild, equable, and healthy. Although not far from the equator, it is pleasant, even at sea level. The climate varies but little from year to year because of the great area of water surrounding the group. December is the hottest month, with an average temperature only 2 degrees over the mean temperature for July, the coldest month.

With regard to rainfall, the year divides itself distinctly, but not sharply, into a dry season. May to October, and a wet season, November to April. There is a wide variation in monthly rainfall from year to year. The wettest month, January, has a range between 5 inches to 65 inches. The annual rainfall has varied in the past 21 years from 130 inches to 284 inches.

Rainfall is frequent in all localities, more particularly during the southern summer season, and at sea, extending even into July. The annual rainfall at Apia is over 100 inches, while that at Pago Pago is nearly 200 inches. The local differences are due to the considerably varying exposures among the islands. Thunderstorms are most frequent during December to March.

The climate in Pago Pago is tropical and very wet all the year around with temperatures ranging from around 75° to as high as 90°F.

The heaviest rainfall occurs from December to March. During the cooler months from April to November, the trade winds make living more pleasant and comfortable.

The climate in Apia is tropical with temperatures ranging between 72° and 86°F. The cooler months are May through November and the rainy season extends from December through April.

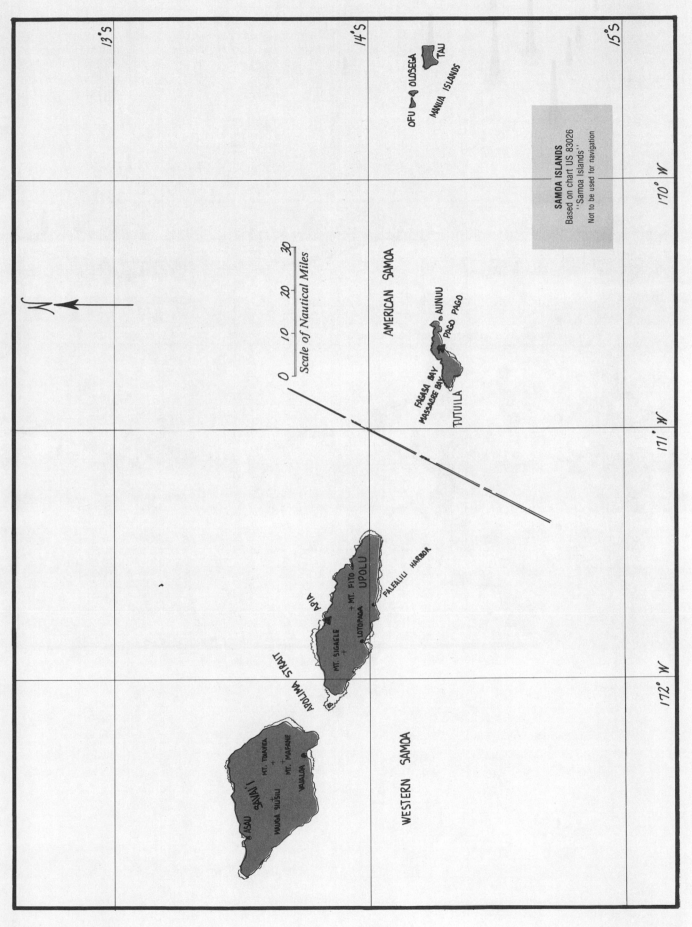

N

Scale of Nautical Miles
0   10   20   30

SAMOA ISLANDS
Based on chart US 83026
"Samoa Islands"
Not to be used for navigation

13°S

14°S

15°S

OFU — OLOSEGA
TAU
MANUA ISLANDS

AMERICAN SAMOA

AUNUU
PAGO PAGO
FAGASA BAY
MASSACRE BAY
TUTUILA

170° W

171° W

172° W

UPOLU
APIA
MT. FITO
LOTOPAGA
MT. SIGAELE
PALEALILI HARBOR

APOLIMA STRAIT

SAVAI'I
ASAU
MT. TUMANA
MT. MAFANE
MAUGA SILISILI
VAIALOA

WESTERN SAMOA

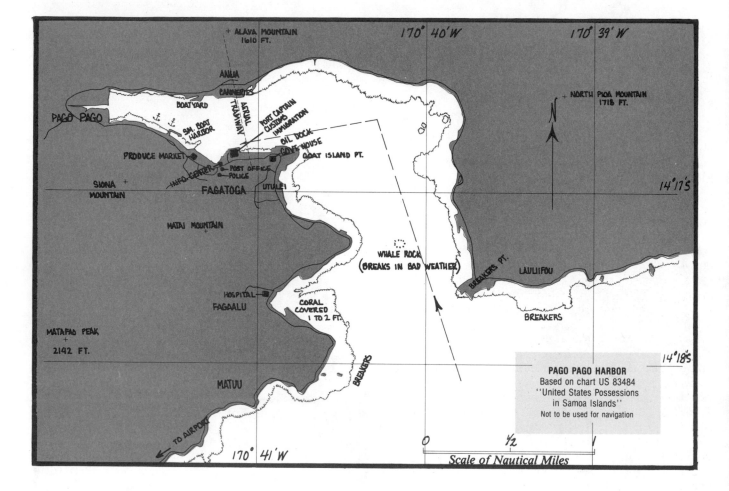

Scale of Nautical Miles

PAGO PAGO HARBOR
Based on chart US 83484
"United States Possessions
in Samoa Islands"
Not to be used for navigation

Chapter 10-A

AMERICAN SAMOA

The Country

The Territory of American Samoa is an insular possession of the United States, administered by the Department of the Interior. Comprising the eastern islands of the Samoa group, it is located south of the equator at 14° south latitude and at about 170° west longitude.

American Samoa is composed of seven tropical islands and is the only United States soil south of the equator. The islands lie some 2,300 miles southwest of Hawaii and about 1,600 miles northeast of New Zealand.

The total land area of all seven American Samoa islands is only 76.2 square miles. A very small amount of the land is owned in fee simple by individuals, but over 96 percent is owned communally and is regulated as to occupancy and use by traditional Samoan custom.

The main island of Tutuila runs east and west with a spiny, jungle-covered mountain range running from one end to the other. Tutuila is almost bisected by famed Pago Pago Bay, which is recognized as one of the best harbors in the South Pacific. Governmental operations and a great portion of the commercial activities are located in the bay area.

Aunu'u is a small island off the southeastern shore of Tutuila. The Manu'a group, composed of Tau, Olosega and Ofu, lie about 60 miles east of Tutuila. The Manu'a population is below 4,000. Swains Island, a small privately-owned coral atoll, is about 280 miles north of Tutuila and has a population of about 70 people. Rose Island, a small island 250 miles to the east of Tutuila and the seventh in the American Samoa group, is a tiny uninhabited atoll.

United States exploration of what is now American Samoa came 61 years before formal relations were established between the powerful nation of the northern hemisphere and the group of tiny islands in the South Pacific.

American interest in the islands of Samoa began with a report made by the United States exploring expedition which visited the islands under the leadership of Lt. Charles Wilkes in 1839. It was not until some 30 years later, however, that a formal relationship was entered into with the people of Samoa by a representative of the United States. Primarily as a result of commercial interest in obtaining harbor facilities and rights for a coaling station on the shores of Pago Pago Harbor, the U.S.S. Narragansett visited Tutuila in 1872 and Comdr. Richard Meade entered into an agreement entitled "Commercial Regulations, etc." with High Chief Mauga, the high chief of Pago Pago. While this treaty was never ratified by the

U.S. Senate, it served effectively to prevent foreign influence from asserting any strong claim to the harbor.

In January of 1878, a further treaty of friendship and commerce was negotiated with the leaders of the villages adjacent to Pago Pago and this treaty was ratified later in the same year. It was proclaimed jointly by the United States and "the Government of American Samoan Islands." This treaty remained in force for more than 20 years until it was superseded.

As a result of international rivalry between Great Britain

American Samoa

A territory of the United States

Port of Entry:

Pago Pago, Tutuila   14°17'S, 170°41'W

Distances between ports in nautical miles:

Between *Pago Pago* and:

Apia, Western Samoa	80
Agana, Guam	3100
Auckland, New Zealand	1570
Avatiu, Cook Islands	750
Butaritari, Kiribati	1450
Christmas Island	1260
Honolulu, Hawaii	2260
Jaluit, Marshall Islands	1700
Noumea, New Caledonia	1420
Nuku'alofa, Tonga	490
Panama City, Panama	5660
Papeete, Society Islands	1240
Ponape, Caroline Islands	2270
San Diego, California	4180
Suva, Fiji	690
Truk, Caroline Islands	2600
Vancouver, Canada	4640

Standard time:

11 hours slow on GMT

and Germany and because of warfare between various factions of the Samoan population, the United States, Germany and Great Britain entered into a general act on June 14, 1889, for the purpose of providing for "the security of life, property, and trade of the citizens and subjects of the respective governments who were residing in or having commercial relations with the islands of Samoa." This act also had as its aim the desire "to avoid all occasions of dissensions between their respective governments and the people of Samoa" while at the same time "promoting as far as possible the peaceful and orderly civilization of the people."

Under this tripartite agreement a form of government for the islands was brought into being. However, after a trial of some 10 years, it proved to be ineffective and destructive of the ends for which it was created and was superseded by the convention of 1899.

A major provision of the convention was the renunciation by Great Britain and Germany of any claims to the islands of the Samoa group east of longitude 171° west of Greenwich. Reciprocally, the United States renounced in favor of Germany all rights and claims in respect to the islands of Upolu and Savaii and all other islands west of 171° longitude west of Greenwich. This treaty was proclaimed, after ratification on February 16, 1900, and on February 19 of the same year, President McKinley directed the Secretary of the Navy to "take such steps as might be necessary to establish the authority of the United States" on the island of Tutuila and other islands of the Samoa group east of longitude 171° west of Greenwich.

The Secretary of the Navy established a naval station at Pago Pago. In April of 1900, deeds of cession were negotiated with the leading chiefs and orators of Tutuila and Aunu'u, and on April 17 the United States flag was raised for the first time over these islands. On June 14, 1904, High Chief Tuimanu'a, the King of Manu'a and the chiefs of Manu'a agreed also to cede their lands to the United States.

Swains Island was settled in 1856 by American trader Eli Jennings and his Samoan wife. Although it had been linked historically to the Tokelau Islands chain, Jennings' citizenship linked it to American Samoa. The Jennings family still own Swains and its people still produce copra as their only crop, along with handicraft. Government personnel of American Samoa on Swains include an agent who teaches school, a public health nurse who staffs the dispensary, and a radio operator who maintains the island's communication station.

Rose Island is still uninhabited and is today a natural wildlife refuge for birds and marine life. It is periodically inspected by a team sent out from American Samoa to insure that no persons are destroying natural properties of the atoll.

The islands remained under naval administration with Pago Pago as an active naval base from 1900 to June 30, 1951. During this time considerable progress was made in the establishment of public works and medical and educational facilities. Little, however, was done to disturb the traditional village life of the Samoan people.

The people of American Samoa are closely related to the Hawaiians, Tahitians, Tongans, and New Zealand Maoris. They are friendly, generous and totally dedicated to ceremonial and mythological practices which are centuries old.

The Samoans are among the last remaining true Polynesians, and they cling steadfastly to their Samoan culture and traditions. The Interior Department and the United States Naval government before it have strongly supported the people in their desire to preserve their culture, while encouraging them to advance in the areas of health and education.

The Samoan social structure is built around the *aiga*, an extended family which may take in as many as several thousand relatives. At the head of the *aiga* are *matais* (chiefs) who guide the communal economy, which still exists to a great degree. The *matai* is responsible for control of the family lands and property, and it is also his responsibility to care for the well-being of the *aiga* and to represent it in the county and district councils.

The Governor and Lieutenant Governor are appointed by the Secretary of the Interior, and the territory's affairs, within all branches of the United States Government, are handled through a Deputy Assistant Secretary for Territorial Affairs.

The 28,000 American Samoans are not United States citizens but are classed as nationals and have free access of entry to the United States.

Under the terms of the deeds of cession, the United States agreed that the chiefs of the villages would be permitted to retain their individual control over their separate villages, providing that their control was in accordance with the laws of the United States pertaining to Samoa and provided that such control was not obstructive to the peace of the people and the advancement of civilization. The United States also agreed to respect and protect the individual rights of the people, especially in respect to

Looking south out of the entrance to Pago Pago Harbor from the Governor's house. The village of Utulei is at the near right and the Lyndon B. Johnson Tropical Medicine Center is at the far right.

their lands and other property. As a result of this commitment, no large tracts of Samoan communally-owned land have been alienated during the years that the United States has had administrative responsibility of these islands.

On June 28, 1951, the President of the United States by means of Executive Order 10264 transferred the administration of American Samoa from the Secretary of the Navy to the Secretary of the Interior, effective July 1, 1951.

Since that time there have been great advances in the social welfare of the people of American Samoa, as well as political advancement towards internal self-government.

Yacht Entry

A yacht entering American Samoa must clear at Pago Pago. Fly the Q flag and tie up at the main dock. Wait for either the Harbor Master or Customs officer to arrive and start proceedings. Do not leave your boat since you are in quarantine until cleared. If you arrive on a weekend or holiday, anchor out in the harbor and stay on your boat until you can clear at the dock.

A passport or visa is not required for U.S. citizens to en-

ter American Samoa. A birth certificate, drivers license or other valid identification is sufficient. All other persons must have a valid passport.

You may visit American Samoa for a period of up to 30 days without getting special permission from the Department of Immigration. All visitors must have a return or onward ticket or a cash landing bond. A boat is considered valid transportation for those whose names appear on the entry crew list and have sufficient funds for 30 days.

If you wish to stay for a period longer than 30 days, you must apply for a permit through the Department of Immigration.

Visitors are required by law to make a written customs declaration. Firearms, ammunition, and explosives of any kind are prohibited.

Yacht Facilities in American Samoa
Tutuila

This is the main and largest island and the Port of Entry. Pago Pago Harbor is the finest natural harbor in the South Pacific and probably the best hurricane hole also. Surrounded by steep mountains over 1000 feet high and with an L-shaped, reef-bordered entrance, it offers about as much protection as possible from heavy winds and high seas.

There are eight mooring buoys in the channel which are on a first come first serve basis, otherwise anchoring is good at the west end of the harbor in deep water. A small boat harbor has been built but opens to the east into the prevailing winds and is generally too rough to use for dinghy landing. Instead it is recommended that you land your dinghy on the lee side of this harbor and climb up the rocks. There is a mooring fee whether you use the moorings or not. The charge is $US12.50 per month.

Pago Pago Harbor has a shipyard with slipways suitable for yachts and repair shops where practically all maintenance work can be done at reasonable prices. You will not find yacht-type hardware here because the yard is set up to service fishing boats and small interisland freighters.

However, any special needs you may have can be easily and quickly satisfied by air freight from the United States or New Zealand. Fuel, fresh water, and all necessary provisions can be obtained in the Pago Pago harbor area. This is probably the best resupply and maintenance port between Hawaii and New Zealand.

It is also worth noting that for airlines and mail, American Samoa is considered a domestic destination thereby enjoying low domestic airline rates to the United States as well as all first class mail by air.

American Samoa is becoming an increasingly popular port of call for yachts as shown by the numbers of visiting yachts:

1971	38
1972	55
1976	85

Jetsam and Flotsam

Currency:

American Samoa uses United States currency. See Hawaii for description.

Language:

The indigenous language of American Samoa is Samoan but 85 percent of the population can speak English.

Electricity:

Tutuila is well electrified with 110v, 60 Hz AC

Postal Address:

Yacht ( )
General Delivery
American Samoa 96779, USA

External Affairs Representative:

United States consulates or embassies

Information Center:

Director of Tourism
Government of American Samoa
P.O. Box 1147
Pago Pago, American Samoa 96799, USA

Cruising Library:

Samoa, A Photographic Essay, Frederick Koehler; The University of Hawaii Press, Honolulu, HI 96814, USA
Amerika Samoa, Captain J.A.C. Gray; U.S. Naval Institute, Annapolis, MD, USA.
Samoa in Color, James Siers; A.H. & A.W. Reed Publishers, Wellington, New Zealand, 1970

Manu'a Islands

Ofu is a small island with a population of 415 persons but does have a small harbor suitable for yachts.

Olosaga is the sister island to Ofu and is separated only by a narrow, shallow strait. You can walk across the strait at low tide.

Tau is the largest of the Manu'a Islands with a population of 1300 persons. There are no docks at any of the Manu'a Islands, so you will have to anchor and go ashore in your dinghy.

Rose Island

This island is located about 125 miles east of Tutuila and is the only uninhabited island in American Samoa. It does not have enough water to support human life. Rose Island is a National Wildlife Refuge and entry is forbidden except by permit issued by the Refuge Manager, U.S. Fish and Wildlife Service, 337 Ululnu Street, Kailua, Oahu, HI 96734, USA. The restriction applies equally to all persons and civilian and military agencies.

Swains Island

Swains Island is just over 200 miles north of Tutuila and is the northernmost island in American Samoa. Historically, it is part of the Tokelau Group. The island is privately owned by descendents of the Jennings family. Population is about 75 persons who engage primarily in the harvest of copra. There is a small anchorage for boats north of the village of Tauloga on the western part of the island. Although the island has a lagoon, it is not accessible from the sea.

Medical Memo

Immunization requirements:

All incoming visitors must possess an International Certificate of Health (yellow WHO card) showing a smallpox vaccination within the last three years. Vaccinations for cholera and yellow fever are required if you have transited or visited within the last six days an area currently infected.

Local health situation:

You will find mosquitoes a nuisance in American Samoa but there is no dengue fever or malaria. Visitors are advised, however, to have typhoid shots. In the water the crown of thorns starfish and the stonefish should be avoided for their sting is painful and debilitating.

Health services:

There is no private medical practice in American Samoa, the LBJ Tropical Medicine Center provides both a hospital and doctors, most of the doctors are from the United States. Both dental and optical services are available at the LBJ Center. Medications are dispensed at the LBJ Center or the one pharmacy in town. A doctor's prescription will be required for certain drugs.

IAMAT Center:

Pago Pago: Lyndon B. Johnson Tropical Medicine Center
Medical Director: Peter F. Beales, MB, CHB, MRCS, LRCP, DTM&H, AIST, MFCM
Deputy Medical Director: J.P. Turner, MD

Water:

The tap water at Pago Pago is reported to be questionable and should be treated as should water taken at any other American Samoa stop.

The inner bay of Pago Pago Harbor showing commercial docks in the foreground with the villages of Fagatogo to the left and Pago Pago at the far end of the harbor. The fish canneries are at the far right. A cable car is in transit up to Mt. Alava on the right side of the harbor. This is the Port of Entry for American Samoa and a reasonable hurricane hole.

The small boat harbor and anchorage is located off of Fagatogo. The anchorage is in fairly deep water and the small boat harbor is too shoal for keel boats to use. Winds sweep the length of this harbor and rain is plentiful coming off Mt. Pioa (Rainmaker Mountain) to the east. Pago Pago is one of the most beautiful harbor settings in the world.

Radio Communications

Station name and call	Location	Frequency Transmit/Receive	Service hours LMT	Type of service
Tutuila Radio	Pago Pago	2845/2182 kHz	24 hours	Port operations
WVUV	14°21'S 170°47'W	1120 kHz	24 hours	Commercial broadcast ½ time Samoan, ½ time English

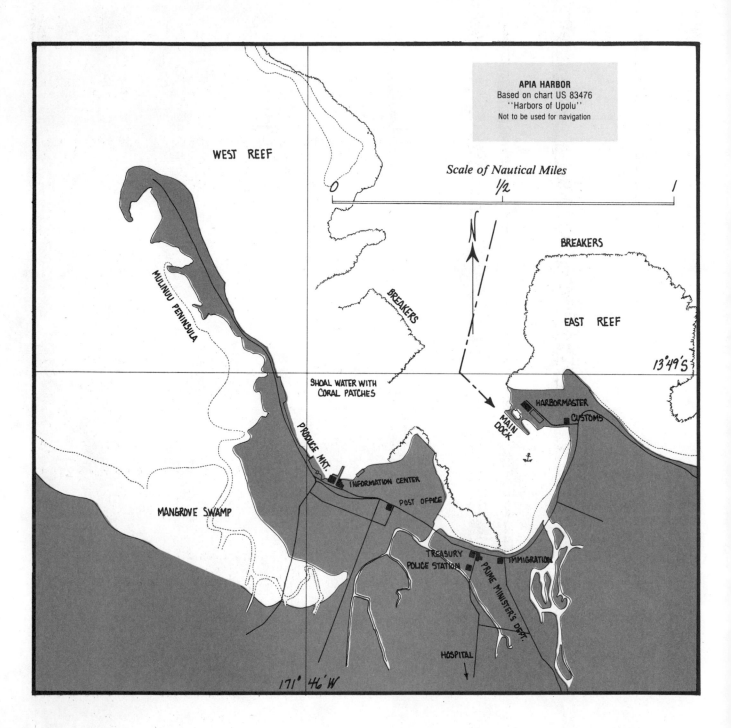

WEST REEF

APIA HARBOR
Based on chart US 83476
''Harbors of Upolu''
Not to be used for navigation

Scale of Nautical Miles

0   1/2   1

BREAKERS

MULINUU PENINSULA

BREAKERS

EAST REEF

13°49'S

SHOAL WATER WITH
CORAL PATCHES

HARBORMASTER

CUSTOMS

MAIN DOCK

PRODUCE MKT.

INFORMATION CENTER

MANGROVE SWAMP

POST OFFICE

TREASURY

IMMIGRATION

POLICE STATION

PRIME MINISTER'S DEPT.

HOSPITAL

171° 46' W

Chapter 10-B
WESTERN SAMOA

The Country

Western Samoa lies in the Pacific Ocean 1,600 miles northeast of Auckland, New Zealand. The main islands are formed from ranges of extinct volcanoes which rise to 6,094 feet on Savai'i and 3,608 feet on Upolu. Volcanic activity last occurred in 1911. The climate is tropical, with wet and dry seasons.

Archeological evidence suggests that Western Samoa was inhabited as early as 1000 B.C., but Polynesian oral histories and traditions do not go back beyond A.D. 1250.

Samoan contact with Europe began with the visit by Dutch navigator Jacob Roggeveen, but not until 1830, following the arrival of English missionaries under John Williams, did contacts become intensive.

Between 1847 and 1861, the United Kingdom, the United States, and Germany established consular representation at Apia. Intrigues and jealousies among these representatives and the Samoan royal families reached a climax in 1889, when the signing of the Final Act of the Berlin Conference on Samoan Affairs brought Samoan independence and neutrality. Malietoa Laupapa was recognized as King.

After the death of the King in 1898, a dispute over succession to the throne led to adoption in 1900 of a series of conventions, whereby the United States annexed Eastern Samoa and Germany took Western Samoa. The United Kingdom withdrew in return for recognition of its rights in other Pacific islands.

In 1914, following the outbreak of war in Europe, New Zealand's armed forces occupied Western Samoa. In 1919 New Zealand was granted a League of Nations mandate over the territory. By the Samoa Act of 1921, New Zealand made provisions for a civil administration, and progress was made in education, health, and economic development.

However, some of the New Zealand government's measures were unpopular with the conservative Samoans and a resistance movement based on civil disobedience lasted until 1936. Steps taken by New Zealand toward a more effectively representative Samoan administration were interrupted by World War II.

In December 1946 Western Samoa was placed under a U.N. trusteeship with New Zealand as administering authority. The Samoans asked that they be granted self-government but this was not accepted by the United Nations at the time.

From 1947 to 1961 a series of constitutional advances, assisted by visits from U.N. missions, brought Western Samoa from dependent status to self-government and finally to independence. In 1947 a Legislative Assembly was established in Western Samoa. In March 1953 New Zealand proposed a quickened pace of political and economic development, and a Constitutional Convention, representing all sections of the Samoan community, met in 1954 to study proposals for political development. Most of its recommendations were adopted by New Zealand and governed the territory's evolution toward cabinet government.

In January 1959 a Working Committee of Self-Government empowered to work out a draft constitution was established with New Zealand's approval. Cabinet government was inaugurated in October 1959, and Fiame Mataafa. F.M. II, became the first prime minister.

Western Samoa
An independent parliamentary democracy

Port of Entry:

Apia, Upolu   13°50'S, 171°55'W

Distances between ports in nautical miles:

Between *Apia* and:

Agana, Guam	3080
Avatiu, Cook Islands	820
Funafuti, Tuvalu	630
Honolulu, Hawaii	2260
Malakal, Palau Islands	3450
Noumea, New Caledonia	1370
Nuku'alofa, Tonga	510
Pago Pago, American Samoa	80
Papeete, Society Islands	1300
Ponape, Caroline Islands	2190
Rabaul, New Britain	2230
Raoul, Kermadec Islands	1010
Selwyn Bay, Solomon Islands	1580
Suva, Fiji	650
Taiohae, Marquesas Islands	1890
Yap, Caroline Islands	3300

Standard time:

11 hours slow on GMT

At the request of the United Nations, a plebiscite was held in May 1961, and an overwhelming majority of the Samoan people voted for independence. In November 1961 the U.N. General Assembly voted unanimously to end the Trusteeship Agreement, and the New Zealand parliament passed the Independent State of Western Samoa Act, formally ending New Zealand's powers over the country on January 1, 1962.

More than 2,000 years ago waves of Polynesians migrated from Southeast Asia to the Samoan Islands. Samoans are the second largest Polynesian group (after the Maoris of New Zealand) and speak a Polynesian dialect.

Samoans have tended to retain their traditional ways despite exposure to European influence for more than 150 years. Most Samoans live within the traditional social system based on the *aiga*, or extended family group, headed by a *matai*, or chief. The title of *matai* is conferred upon any eligible member of the group, including women, with the common consent of the *aiga*. In addition to representing the *aiga* in village and district *fono* (councils), the *matai* is responsible for the general welfare of the *aiga* and directs the use of family lands and other assets.

Apart from Apia, the capital and commercial center, Western Samoa has no major towns. Most people live in some 400 coastal villages, whose populations range from 100 to over 2,000. Approximately 2,500 Europeans live in Western Samoa.

Western Samoans are Christians, with 55 percent of the population belonging to the Congregational church and with 40 percent equally divided between the Roman Catholic and Methodist churches.

Education is free but not compulsory. In 1967, 95 percent of the children of primary school age went to school.

On a hillside above Apia is the homestead of Robert Louis Stevenson. Stevenson endeared himself to the Samoan people who called him Tusitala - teller of tales. This beautiful Victorian house is called Vailima and is now the residence of the head of state of Western Samoa.

In addition, about 180 Samoans are enrolled in secondary or technical schools and universities abroad.

The 1960 Constitution of Western Samoa is based on the British pattern of parliamentary democracy, modified to take Samoan customs into account.

The present head of state, the scion of a traditional royal line, does not hold his position for life. Future heads of state will be elected by the Legislative Assembly for 5 year terms. The head of state appoints the prime minister (head of government). He also appoints, with the advice of the prime minister, the members of the Cabinet. Cabinet ministers hold office as long as they command the confidence of the Legislative Assembly.

The Parliament consists of the Legislative Assembly together with the head of state. The Legislative Assembly has 47 members, of which 45 are elected by *matai* suffrage on a territorial basis. Two other members, usually European with Western Samoan citizenship, are elected by universal adult suffrage. All terms of office are three years.

The Supreme Court is the superior court of record and has full jurisdiction in civil, criminal, and constitutional matters. Its Chief Justice is appointed by the head of state on the recommendation of the prime minister.

Jetsam and Flotsam

Currency:

The Western Samoa dollar is called a tala and it is equal to 100 sene. Coins are issued in 1, 2, 3, 10, 20 and 50 sene. At press time the rate of exchange was $US1= 83 sene.

Language:

The official language of Western Samoa is Samoan but English is widely used and understood by most Samoans.

Electricity:

Where electricity is available it is 250 v, 50 Hz AC.

Postal Address:

Yacht (   )
Poste Restante
Apia, WESTERN SAMOA

External Affairs Representatives:

New Zealand or British consulates or embassies.

Information Office:

Department of Economic Development
Government of Western Samoa
Apia, WESTERN SAMOA

Cruising Library:

My Samoan Chief, Fay G. Calkins; University of Hawaii Press, Honolulu, HI, USA 1971
Samoa, The Polynesian Paradise, Kipeni Su'apa'ia; Exposition Press, New York, NY, USA, 1962
No Kava for Johnny, John O'Grady; Ure Smith Ltd., Sidney, Australia, 1961
Western Samoa, James W. Fox and Kenneth B. Cumberland; (Whitcomb & Tombs) Tri-Ocean Books, San Francisco, CA, USA

The commercial wharf at Apia Harbor, Upolu Island, can be used long enough to get your clearance into Western Samoa. Afterwards, anchor your boat in the harbor to the right. The harbor opens through the reef directly to the north (left) offering little protection from northerly gales and it is not a safe anchorage during the hurricane months of January through March.

Medical Memo

Immunization requirements:

Vaccinations for smallpox, cholera and yellow fever are required if you have transited or visited within the last six days (smallpox 14 days) an area currently infected.

Local health situation:

You will find mosquitoes a nuisance in Western Samoa and they have at times carried dengue fever. There is no malaria.

Health Services:

These can be had at the Apia General Hospital and district hospitals in the outlying areas. There is no private service. Dental and optical care is also available at these hospitals. Drugs are available from the Apia General Hospital or the private chemists in Apia. Prescriptions are not needed and the prices are extremely low.

Water:

Tap water at the Apia dock has been reported safe but water in the outlying areas should be considered suspect and treated.

Western Samoa is divided into districts for purposes of government service in health, education, police, and agriculture. The only district officer is the administrator on Savai'i.

Yacht Entry

There is only one Port of Entry for Western Samoa and that is Apia. Yachts arriving in Apia should proceed to the main dock and lay alongside until boarded by the Harbor Master who will call other appropriate government officials. Do not leave your yacht until clearance is given by Immigration and Health officers. If Customs does not come to the boat, you will have to go to them at the main entrance to the harbor property.

Passports are required of all foreigners but no permit or visa is needed for a visit of less than three days. Since three days is too short a time to see this country, you must apply for a permit to stay longer. Visas will be granted for periods of 30 days and extensions may be applied for to the Immigration Officer, Prime Minister's Department. Normally, yachts may obtain entry permits for two week visits on arrival.

If you wish to visit other harbors with your boat while in Western Samoa you will need to obtain permission from the prime minister's office. The prime minister's office will prepare a letter of permission in five copies, one for each department involved, and you will have to go to each of the departments to get their endorsement. If you plan on departing Western Samoa from one of the other ports, be certain that your letter of permission clearly states which one.

Yacht Facilities

The harbor at Apia is normally safe from May to November but is exposed to gales during the wet season of December to April. It is advised that yachts proceed to Pago Pago during the hurricane season.

There are no dockside-type facilities at Apia. The commercial dock may be used temporarily for loading and unloading but not for overnight tieup. Yachts generally anchor inshore where there is good holding ground. Security of unattended yachts has been questioned in past years so it is best to inquire of the Harbor Master on the state of affairs when you arrive. Your dinghy can be tied-off inside the main dock but stay clear of the harbor tugs which may have to make a departure while you are gone. There are no harbor charges.

While it is recommended that all repairs and maintenance of your yacht be undertaken at Pago Pago because of better facilities and more adequate supplies, you can get a haulout at Apia on slips used for small boat maintenance. The facilities are quite rustic, however, and skilled labor hard to find.

Potable water and diesel fuel are available at the dock and the town of Apia has a good variety of canned and dried foods and much fresh fruit at reasonable prices.

There is another harbor with wharf at Asau on the island of Savai'i but it is not a Port of Entry so can be used only for interisland visits.

The colorful waterfront at Apia still has all of the charm of its British Colonial heritage. The town extends along the waterfront and most points of interest and necessity can be reached by walking the tree-lined street.

Radio Communications

Station name and call	Location	Frequency Transmit/Receive	Service hours LMT	Type of service
Apia Radio	Apia	2182	24 hours	RT - marine operations
Voice of Western Samoa 2AP	13°56'S 171°47'W	1050 kHz 1420 kHz	Weekdays 1700-2300 Mon. - Sat. 0600-2300 Sunday 0900-1500 and 1800-2200	Commercial broadcast (English language) " " Commercial broadcast (bilingual)

Chapter 11
TOKELAU ISLANDS
(Union Group)

The Country

The Tokelau group is a New Zealand dependency composed of three small atolls lying about 250 miles north of Samoa. The atolls do not lie in close proximity to each other, Fakaofo and Nukunonu are 40 miles apart and Nukunonu and Atafu are 50 miles apart. Each atoll is composed of a number of coral islets surrounding a central lagoon into which there are no passages. These islets vary in size from 100 yards to four miles long and none are wider than 400 yards. The number of islets encircling each lagoon is: Fakaofo — 61, Nukunonu — 30, and Atafu — 19. Their maximum elevation is 10 to 15 feet above sea level. The land area of each atoll is: Fakaofo — 650 acres, Nukunonu — 1350 acres, and Atafu — 500 acres.

There is little farming in the accepted sense. The coarse

Canoe Making

rubbly sand is devoid of humus and can support little vegetation other than the pandanus, casuarina, and coconut palms. One islet of each atoll is reserved for growing the tauanave, a short stubby tree which yields the only locally grown timber for the construction of canoes and utensils. The only food plants are a few breadfruit trees, bananas, and papaya grown in compost pits. These are supplemented by fish, fowl and pigs and imported staples from New Zealand.

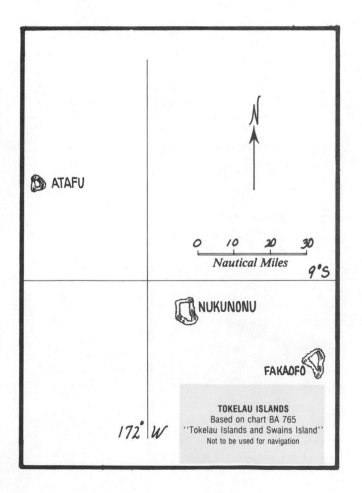

ATAFU

0   10   20   30
Nautical Miles

9°S

NUKUNONU

FAKAOFO

TOKELAU ISLANDS
Based on chart BA 765
"Tokelau Islands and Swains Island"
Not to be used for navigation

172° W

Tokelau Islands

(Union Group)

A New Zealand dependency

Port of Entry:

Nukunonu (the central island)   9°10'S, 171°50'W

Distances between ports in nautical miles:

Between *Nukunonu* and:

Apia, Western Samoa	280
Funafuti, Tuvalu	530
Honolulu, Hawaii	2050
Howland Island	650
Rarotonga, Cook Islands	1050
Suva, Fiji	800

Standard time:

11 hours slow on GMT

Jetsam and Flotsam

Currency:

Western Samoa currency is used in the Tokelau Islands. New Zealand currency will also be accepted.

Language:

The official language of Tokelau is English.

Electricity:

None except an occasional home generator.

Postal Address:

You would do better to use Apia, Western Samoa, or your next enroute port of call.

Information Center:

Office for Tokelau Affairs
P.O. Box 865
Apia, WESTERN SAMOA

External Affairs Representative:

New Zealand embassies or consulates.

Nukunonu was the first of the Tokelaus to be discovered, this by Captain Edwards in the *Pandora* in 1791. They were put under the protection of Great Britain in 1877 and formally annexed in 1916. In 1925 the New Zealand government agreed to administer the islands and in 1948 they were included in the boundaries of New Zealand. Tokelauans are British subjects and New Zealand citizens.

Village affairs are managed by the Council of Elders or *Fono*, comprising representatives of the families, and this body also exerts influence over the "*aumaga*" or village labor force. In this way the traditional form of *patriarchal* authority has been preserved to operate in parallel with the public government officials such as the *Fapule and Pulenuku*. Local government is carried out on each atoll by an elected *Faipule* who is also magistrate. He is assisted by a village mayor, a village clerk, and other lesser officials.

The group lies in a border area between Polynesia and Micronesia. The indigenous inhabitants are Polynesians similar to the Samoans in physical appearance and cultural life. A 1973 census showed that there were 1600 persons on the islands. Because of the very restricted economic and social future in the atolls, the islanders agreed in 1965 to resettle the majority in New Zealand. By 1975 there were 500 Tokelauans in New Zealand.

Schools are staffed by both trained native teachers and New Zealand teachers.

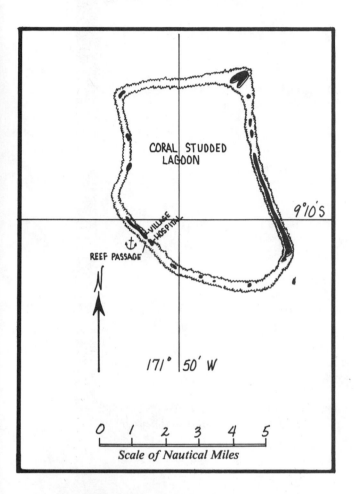

Communications with other islands is made via radio-telephone on each island. Trading vessels operate between Tokelau and Western Samoa on regular schedules. The economy of Tokelau is primarily based on copra with minor income from handicrafts and postage stamps for collectors.

The Weather

The Tokelau group lies in the zone of the southeast trades but the northeast and north winds are common and predominate during the period of November to February.

The islands lie at the north edge of the South Pacific hurricane region and rarely have severe tropical storms. But it can and did happen in January 1914 when a hurricane and two great sea waves washed over the island of Atafu demolishing the church and most of the houses. Another hit the islands in January 1966.

The temperature of the air is an almost constant 82°F the year around varying only slightly throughout the day and night. There is no natural fresh water source on the atolls so they depend on rainfall. Drinking water is collected from roofs of buildings and stored in concrete rain tanks for the villagers use. The average annual rain-

Medical Memo

Immunization requirements:

Pratique is not a formal process in Tokelau but yachties are urged not to land if they have any illness aboard or if they have recently visited an area having cholera, smallpox or yellow fever.

Local health situation:

The incidence of disease in the islands is comparatively slight.

Health services:

A Fiji-trained Tokelauan medical practitioner is stationed on each of the islands and he has a staff of assistants trained in Apia, Western Samoa. Serious illnesses or major injuries would have to be taken care of elsewhere, probably at Apia, Western Samoa.

The only medical drugs available are what the Tokelauan dispensaries receive from New Zealand for their own purposes.

There are no dental or optical services available.

Water:

You should consider the water suspect and treat it.

---

fall is 115 inches with the highest recorded being 177 inches and the lowest 87 inches.

Yacht Entry and Facilities

There are no official formalities to visiting any one of the three atolls comprising Tokelau. Common sense tells you to check in with the resident New Zealand administrator and the mayor *(Faipule)* of each atoll. Showing deference to their officials is certain to make your stay in the atolls a more interesting experience.

Yacht facilities in these atolls are virtually zero with the result that they are little visited by cruising yachts. This is bound to change as the yachties become less enchanted with the crowded harbors along the beaten path and seek unspoiled South Seas islands. Tokelau is just such a group waiting to be discovered by the yachtsman.

A word of caution in anchoring off any of the atolls (there are no passages into them). Leave a crew member on board in case your anchor doesn't hold. Their economy is not capable of accepting more mouths to feed

on an emergency basis.

Except for coconuts and fish, do not expect to get any supplies or provisions from these atolls. In a dry year even water may be a scarce commodity. You are only a two-day sail from Samoa if you are in desperate need of anything.

Chapter 12

TONGA
(Friendly Islands)

The Country

Tonga is a kingdom of some 200 islands and 87,400 people that became an independent state in mid-1970. It is the sole remaining Polynesian kingdom and has successfully retained the family-subsistence basis of its ancient culture. The people speak a Polynesian variant called Tongan and are closely related to the inhabitants of Samoa.

The islands are mixed as to type, and the combination of high volcanic and low coral forms gives the group a physical character all its own. The islands are dispersed in three indentifiable groups — a northern or Vava'u group, a central or Ha'apai group, and a southern or Tongatapu group. The kingdom is bordered on the east by the deep Tonga Trench, indicating that it lies at the eastern extremity of the continental shelf. It is an area of great structural instability and vulcanism, some of whose islands are little more than active or extinct volcanic cones. One, Falcon Island, in the Vava'u group has a unique up-and-down character. It is a submerged active volcano that erupts periodically. When it is active, lava and ash rise above sea level, forming a clearly visible island. When the eruption is over the unconsolidated pile is destroyed by wave action, and the island disappears until the next period of eruption.

Yachties should be aware of a new and uncharted island in the group. It is called Lateiki and lies on the Metis shoal about midway between Late and Kao. In July of 1979 the island measured 1060 feet long and 400 feet wide rising to a height of 50 feet. The island is composed of volcanic ash, pumice and loose lava rock. This island is expected to disappear after a few years as volcanic activity ceases and the seas erode away the loose rock.

The Vava'u group consists of thirty-four islands having a total land area of forty-five square miles and a population estimated at 13,000, about two-thirds of whom are on Vava'u, the largest island in the group. Fourteen of the other islands are uninhabited.

The Ha'apai group is a cluster of thirty-six islands of mixed form, only twenty of which are permanently inhabited. The largest of this group is Tofua, an active volcano whose crater contains a steaming lake. A few miles north of Tofua is Kao, an extinct volcano with a perfect conical peak rising to 3,400 feet. Most of the group's 10,000 people live on low coral islands in the eastern chain.

The Tongatapu group contains seven major islands, the largest of which is Tongatapu, a wholly coralline island on which Nuku'alofa, the capital city is located. Roughly one-half of the kingdom's entire population reside on it. Other major islands in the group include Eua, Ata, Atata Euaki, Kala'au, and Kenatea. Ata is an ancient volcano 1165 ft. high; Euaki, Kala'au and Kenatea are uninhabited.

Archeological evidence indicates that the islands of Tonga have been settled since at least 500 B.C., and local traditions have carefully preserved the names of the Tongan sovereigns for about 1,000 years. At its height in the 13th century, the power of the Tongan monarch extended as far as Hawaii.

In about the 14th century the King of Tonga delegated much of his temporal power to a brother while keeping himself the spiritual authority. Sometime later this process was repeated by the second line, thus resulting in three distinct lines: the Tui Tonga with spiritual authority (which

Tonga
(Friendly Islands)
A constitutional monarchy

Ports of Entry:

Nuku'alofa, Tongatapu	21°08'S, 175°12'W
Neiafu, Vava'u	18°39'S, 173°59'W

Distances between ports in nautical miles:

Between *Nuku'alofa* and:

Apia, Western Samoa	500
Agana, Guam	3200
Auckland, New Zealand	1100
Honolulu, Hawaii	2750
Los Angeles, California	4630
Noumea, New Caledonia	1060
Pago Pago, American Samoa	490
Panama City, Panama	5950
Papeete, Society Islands	1470
Suva, Fiji	420

Standard time:

13 hours fast on GMT

(Tonga's motto is: Where time begins)

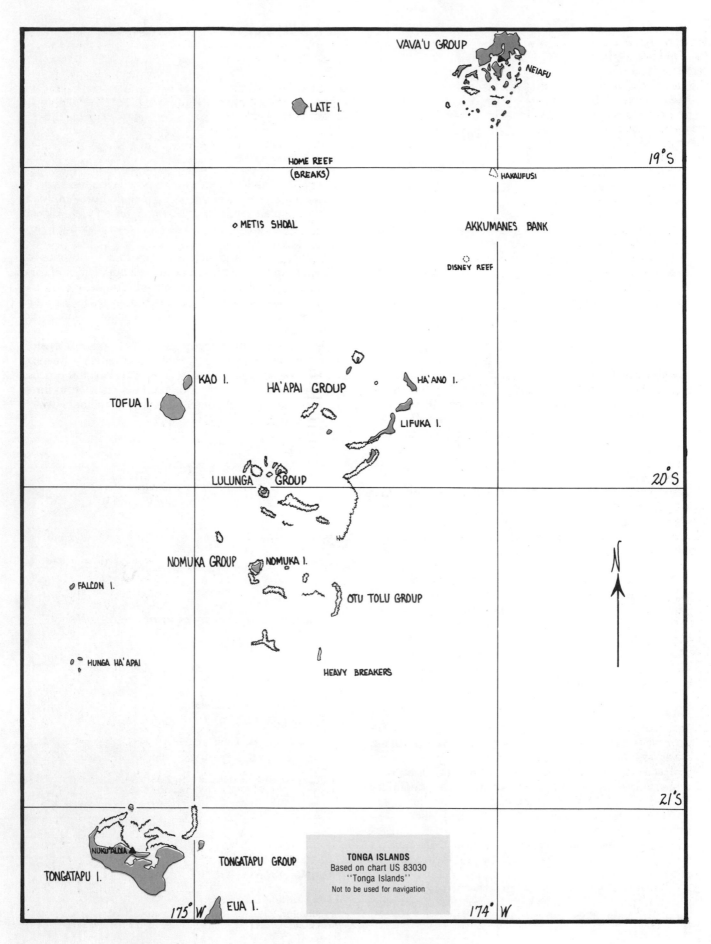

VAVA'U GROUP

LATE I.

NEIAFU

HOME REEF
(BREAKS)

HAKAUFUSI

METIS SHOAL

AKKUMANES BANK

DISNEY REEF

KAO I.

HA'APAI GROUP

HA'ANO I.

TOFUA I.

LIFUKA I.

LULUNGA GROUP

NOMUKA GROUP

NOMUKA I.

FALCON I.

OTU TOLU GROUP

HUNGA HA'APAI

HEAVY BREAKERS

N

NUKU'ALOFA

TONGATAPU GROUP

TONGA ISLANDS
Based on chart US 83030
''Tonga Islands''
Not to be used for navigation

TONGATAPU I.

EUA I.

175° W

174° W

19°S

20°S

21°S

is believed to have extended over much of Polynesia) and the Tui Ha'atakalaua and the Tui Kanokupolu, both with temporal authority responsible for carrying out much of the day-to-day administration of the Kingdom.

The first Europeans to sight the Tongan archipelago were Dutch navigators in 1616. The main island of Tongatapu was first visited by the Dutch explorer, Abel Tasman, in 1643. However, continual contact with Europeans did not begin until more than 125 years later. Captain James Cook visited the islands in 1773 and 1777 and gave the archipelago the name "the Friendly Islands" because of the gentle nature of the Tongans he encountered. In 1789 the famous mutiny on the British ship *Bounty* took place in the waters of the Ha'apai group between the islands of Nomuka and Tofua.

The peaceful conditions in Tonga changed shortly after Captain Cook's last visit. The islands were torn by civil strife and warfare as the three lines of kings each sought dominance over the others. This was the state of affairs

when the first missionaries, attached to the London Missionary Society, arrived in 1797. A second missionary group arrived in 1822, led by Walter Lawry of the Wesleyan Missionary Society. They converted Taufa'ahau, one of the claimants to the Tui Kanokupolu line, and Christianity began to spread throughout the islands.

At the time of his conversion, Taufa'ahau took the name of Siaosi (George) and his consort assumed the name Salote (Charlotte), in honor of King George III and Queen Charlotte of England. In the following years he united all of the Tongan islands for the first time in recorded history and in 1845 founded the present royal dynasty when he was formally proclaimed King George Tupou I. He gave his country a constitution and representative parliamentary government based in some respects on the British model. In 1862 he abolished the system of semiserfdom, which had previously existed, and established an entirely alien system of land tenure whereby

The Royal Palace at Nuku'alofa is a majestic symbol of Victorian architecture. It is located on the waterfront and is surrounded by stately Norfolk pines brought from the island of Norfolk near Australia.

Nuku'alofa, the capitol of Tonga, is situated on the northern edge of Tongatapu island with little shelter from northerly winds. The approach to Nuku'alofa is made by winding your way through the many coral patches seen here. This is a Port of Entry.

every male Tongan, upon reaching the age of 16, was entitled to rent for life and at a nominal fee a plot of bush land *(api)* of 8¼ acres, plus a village allotment of about three-eighths of an acre for his home.

Under a Treaty of Friendship and Protection, concluded with the United Kingdom on May 18, 1900, Tonga came under British protection. Tonga retained its independence and autonomy, while the U.K. agreed to handle its foreign affairs and protect it from external attack.

During World War II Tonga, in close collaboration with New Zealand, formed a local defense force of about 2,000 men which saw action in the Solomon Islands. Additionally, New Zealand and United States troops were stationed on Tongatapu, which became a staging point for shipping.

A new treaty of Friendship and Protection with the United Kingdom was signed in 1958 and ratified in May 1959. It provided for a British Commissioner and Consul in Tonga who were responsible to the governor of Fiji in

his capacity as British Chief commissioner for Tonga. In mid-1965 the British commissioner and Consul became directly responsible to the United Kingdom Secretary of State for Colonial Affairs. Tonga became a fully independent country on June 4, 1970, an event officially designated by the King as Tonga's "reentry into the comity of nations.

You can believe whom you would — Captain Cook who named the Tonga Islands the Friendly Islands, or Captain Bligh who on the Tonga island of Tofua suffered his only casualty in his remarkable 3,620 mile trip in an open launch after the mutiny on the *Bounty*. The Tonga Islands are beautiful, the customs and climate in contradiction, and the economy poor; but these are a proud and independent people.

Tongans, a Polynesian group with a very small mixture of Melanesian, represent more than 98 percent of the inhabitants. The rest are European, mixed European, and other Pacific islanders.

Tonga with a 90,000 person population is a constitutional monarchy — the last in Polynesia. As a point of royal interest, the present king's mother, Queen Salote, attended the London coronation of England's Queen Elizabeth in 1953 and reportedly almost stole the show because of her regal bearing and warm personality. We are told that this event did more to make Tonga known to the world than any political maneuvering could have accomplished.

This monarchy is closely interwoven with religion and the constitution specifically sets aside the Sabbath as a day of religious observance in the following words: "the Sabbath Day shall be sacred in Tonga for ever and it shall not be lawful to do work or play games or trade on the Sabbath. And any agreement made or documents witnessed on this day shall be counted void and not recognized by the government". While in principal this guides the people to appropriate Sunday observance, in practice it is not working out well. There is simply too much communication with the outside world and hotels, restaurants, transportation, police and fire services find a growing need to operate on Sunday. Like the rest of the modern world, expediency whittles away at principal and now Tonga's Sunday law is being legally challenged in their court system. The motto of the Tongan people is "God and Tonga are my heritage", this appears on the King's coat of arms.

Naturally churches abound and church schools are common. The early missionaries influence has not only hung on in the church but in their conservative way of dress. Except for the kids, body exposure of any kind in public places by either sex is *tapu* (forbidden). Long sleeve blouses and long skirts *(valas)* for women and *lava-lavas* or pants for men.

A well-dressed Tongan also wears a unique wrap-

around-the-waist mat called a *ta'ovala* which in western world formal dress is called a cummerbund. It is most often a mat woven of pandanus fronds but sometimes a more ornamental one is made of yarn or plastic. The common *ta'ovala* is 12-16 inches high, but some reach the ground. The long *ta'ovalas* are mats about the size of

a sleeping mat! These *ta'ovalas* seem to be traditional and not religious. None of the other Polynesian peoples wear them.

The Tongan people while very similar in physical appearance to the heavy set Samoans, displayed a more congenial disposition. like the Tahitians. In the market place one hears light-hearted laughter as bargaining takes place between buyer and seller. These patient people with their wide, deep brown eyes have a great love for both their children and their country.

Tonga is also noted for its postage stamps — probably the most unusual and beautiful in the world. The stamps have irregular shapes outlining the particular subject being honored (a banana is one!). They also have self-sticking backs to eliminate licking. The banana stamp is small enough to get on a postcard but most stamps are so large that they overrun the address space. Furthermore, the Tongan postal clerks take great delight in giving you the maximum number of small denomination stamps meeting the postal requirement so that your mailings will look like a Tongan public relations billboard.

Primary education between the ages of 6 and 14 is compulsory and free in the state schools. Mission schools provide about one-third of the primary and 9/10ths of the secondary-level education. Additionally, there is a 2-year state teachers' training college and one private liberal arts college.

Tonga's constitution, promulgated at the time of independence, is based on the one granted in 1875 and provides for a constitutional monarchy.

The executive branch includes the Monarch and the Cabinet, which becomes the Privy Council when presided over by the Monarch. In intervals between legislative sessions, the Privy Council makes ordinances which become law if confirmed by the legislature.

The unicameral Legislative Assembly consists of seven nobles who are elected by the 33 hereditary nobles of Tonga and seven people's representatives elected by universal adult suffrage for 3-year terms. In addition, there are seven Cabinet Ministers appointed by the Monarch who hold office until they reach retirement age. The governors of Ha'apai and Vava'u are appointed to their offices and serve as ex officio members of the Cabinet. The Legislative Assembly sits for 4 or 5 months a year.

The court system in Tonga consists of the King-in-Council, the Supreme Court, the Magistrates Court, and the Lands Court. Judges are appointed by the Monarch.

The only form of local government is through town and district officials. The town official represents the central government in the villages; the district official has authority over a group of villages. These officials have been popularly elected since 1965.

There are no political parties in Tonga. The people's representatives in the Legislative Assembly are elected as independents — three from the Tongatapu island group and two each from the Ha'apai and Vava'u groups.

For most of the 20th century Tonga has been quiet, inward-looking, and somewhat isolated from developments elsewhere in the world. The Tongans as a whole continue to cling to many of their old traditions, including a respect for the nobility. However, the people are begin-

A village road in Neiafu. It is along roads like this that you will see the Tongans making their famous tapa cloth out of the bark of the paper mulberry tree.

ning to face the problem of preserving their cultural identity and traditions in the wake of the increasing impact of Western technology and culture. Educational opportunities for young commoners have advanced, and their increasing political awareness has stimulated some dissent against the nobility system. In addition, the rapidly increasing population is already too great to provide the constitutional 8¼ acre *api* for each adult male. The pressures to move to the Kingdom's only urban center or to emigrate are, therefore, considerable.

The Weather

Nearly 60 percent of the annual sea winds among the Tonga Islands and vicinity are from southeast to east. During May to August when the southeast winds are in their ascendency, the easterly wind components are in con-

siderable part replaced by the southerly component, and at Nuku'alofa, by southwesterly to northwesterly winds as well. About 24 percent of the annual winds are from the northeast and south, about equally divided between the two directions. The average wind speed at sea is 12 knots while at Nuku'alofa it is 9 knots. The December wind speed at Nuku'alofa is 10 knots and in May to July, about 7 knots. At sea the range is between 13 and 11 knots during the corresponding period.

From May to November the strongest winds are generally experienced from south-southeast to east-southeast, usually accompanied by rain from these quarters lasting up to three days. On the wind shifting to the northward of east, fine and settled weather may be expected for a time.

After September strong northwesterly winds with thick dirty weather and heavy rains may occasionally be ex-

Jetsam and Flotsam

Currency:

The Tongan dollar is called a pa'anga and equals 100 seniti. Coins are issued in denominations of 1, 2, 5, 10, 20, and 50 seniti and also 1 and 2 pa'anga. At press time the rate of exchange was $US1 = 87 seniti.

Language:

Tongan, a Polynesian dialect, is the indigenous language but most people also speak English.

Electricity:

240 volt, 50 Hz AC

Postal address:

Mail to the outlying islands is slow, so it is recommended that all your mail be sent to the capital city:

Yacht ( )
Poste Restante
Nuku'alofa, TONGA

External Affairs Representative:

British embassies or consulates

Information center:

Tonga Visitors Bureau
P.O. Box 35
Nuku'alofa, TONGA

Cruising Library:

Minerva Reef, Olaf Ruhen; Little, Brown and Co., Boston, MA, USA, 1964.
Harpoon in My Hand, Olaf Ruhen; Tri-Ocean Books, San Francisco, CA, USA, 1966
The Friendly Islanders: The Story of Queen Salote and Her People, Kenneth Bain; Hodder and Stoughton, London, England, 1967
Shirley Baker and the King of Tonga, Noel Rutherford; Oxford University Press, Melbourne, Australia, 1971
Gentle People, Donna Gerstle; Tofua Press, San Diego, CA, USA, 1973
Friendly Island, Patricia Ledyard; Pacific Publications Ltd., Sidney, NSW, Australia, 1974
Tonga Pictorial — A Tapestry of Pride, Donna Gerstle and Helen Raitt; Tofua Press, San Diego, CA, USA, 1975

pected, but the wind does not appear to remain longer than 12 hours in that quarter, and will probably shift to the southward and clear up.

From December to April the winds are generally easterly, but sudden and violent westerly and north-westerly squalls are common. An average year brings about three days of gales.

Tropical cyclones occur in the Tonga Islands at the rate of about two annually. They are most frequent in January and March. The hurricane season begins in November and usually ends in April. However, one such storm has been known to occur in May.

Tongan climate has less rain and is slightly cooler than the other tropical areas. From May to December, the dry season, the weather is as good as any found in the tropics. Maximum temperatures average 80°F with moderate humidity. During the rainy season from December to April, the maximum average temperature climbs to 90°F with high humidity. People from the temperate climes usually find this weather oppressive.

The annual rainfall at Nuku'alofa is 58 inches with as much as 10 inches falling in the month of April and as little as one inch falling in the months of May and July. Records from ships show a considerable variation in the rainy periods, but with greatest precipitation frequencies, some 10 to 20 percent, occuring in April, July and September to January. Two to four percent of the days each month have thunderstorms with the greatest frequency in December to February. There is a measurable rainfall on about 130 days of the year. Vava'u is the wettest part of the Tongan group. Nearly 20 inches of rain fell there in one month.

Yacht Entry

There are two ports of entry for yachts into Tonga — Nuku'alofa, Tongatapu; and Neiafu, Vava'u. At Nuku-'alofa it is necessary to fly the Q signal and come alongside the Queen Salote wharf, there to await the arrival of officials. At Vava'u you will anchor in the harbor at Neiafu while flying the Q signal and wait to be boarded by Tongan officials.

Pangai, Lifuku, in the Ha'apai Group also has a Customs officer but because this area is free from the rhinoceros beetle, you have to get special agricultural clearance at either Neiafu or Nuku'alofa to visit there. The rhinoceros beetle is a devastating enemy of the coconut tree and yachtsmen are urged to cooperate in the control of it.

Passports are required of all persons on the crew. Onward tickets are not required for persons listed as crew members who are expected to depart the islands on the yacht. Proof of adequate funds will be required.

A visa is not required for a stay under 30 days in length. If you wish to stay longer, then permission must be requested from the principal Immigration officer. Extended stays up to six months are possible.

Cruising within Tongan waters is strictly controlled. In past years renegade yachtsmen have trafficked in marijuana which has resulted in the current yacht restrictions. After clearing in at Nuku'alofa or Neiafu, you can request permission from customs to cruise specific areas of the group for one week periods. Remember that you are in a foreign country and abide by their laws.

Medical Memo

Immunization requirements:

Vaccinations are required for smallpox, cholera and yellow fever if you have transited or visited within the last six days (smallpox 14 days) an area currently infected.

Local health situation:

Insect bites can be irritating and you should have medications on board for them. Infectious hepatitis is endemic to the islands but not a great risk if you avoid contaminated food and water.

Health services:

There are private hospitals at Nuku'alofa, Tongatapu; Neiafu, Vava'u; and Pangai, Lifuka. Private practitioners are also available at Nuku'alofa and the costs are reported to be moderate.

Maintenance dental services are available at all three of the hospitals but optical service is available only at the Vaiola Hospital in Nuku'alofa.

There are no private pharmacies (chemists) in Tonga. Drugs must be obtained through the hospitals.

IAMAT Center:

Nuku'alofa: Vaiola Hospital
        Medical Director: Alo Eva, MD
        Administrative Director: Supileo Foliaki, MD

Water:

Tap water from the public supplies at Neiafu and Nuku'alofa is reported to be good. Water from other sources should be considered suspect and treated.

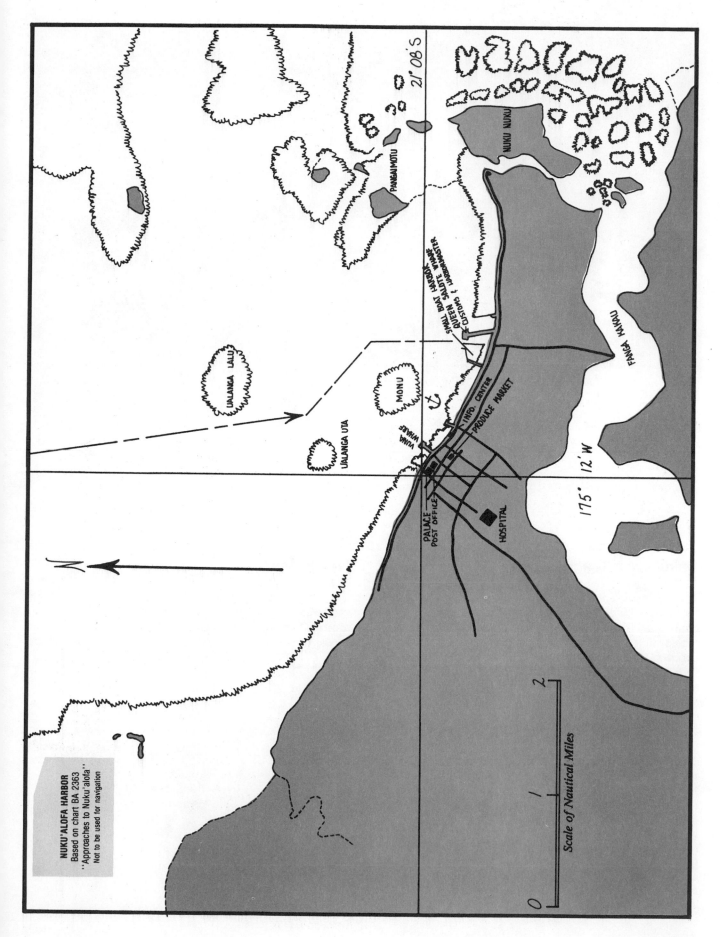

NUKU'ALOFA HARBOR
Based on chart BA 2363
"Approaches to Nuku'alofa"
Not to be used for navigation

21' 08' S

175° 12' W

PANGAI MOTU

NUKU NUKU

FANGA KAKAU

UALANGA LALU

MONU

UALANGA UTA

SMALL BOAT HARBOR
QUEEN SALOTE WHARF
CUSTOMS & HARBORMASTER

VUNA WHARF

INFO. CENTER

PRODUCE MARKET

PALACE
POST OFFICE

HOSPITAL

N

Scale of Nautical Miles

0   1   2

The small boat harbor close to the Queen Salote wharf at Nuku'alofa, is used by the fishing boats and out island sailing workboats. There is usually room enough for visiting yachts of less than six feet draft.

Yacht Facilities
Nuku'alofa, Tongatapu

There is a small boat harbor which can handle boats to 70 feet long with a maximum draft of six feet. There is no charge in this harbor where you tie stern-to the breakwater. It also has a small slipway suitable for boats to about 60 feet. There are virtually no repair and maintenance facilities for boats but shops servicing automobiles may provide some help. Hardware supplies are limited to those which the Tongans would use in their own workboats and these are scarce.

Diesel fuel and gasoline are available in limited quantities although diesel fuel has been reported as somewhat dirty. Potable water is available at the wharfs and a hotel across the street from the small boat harbor. Fresh provisions can be obtained from the central market and other provisions from the large trading stores in the downtown area. Nuku'alofa, although small, is surprisingly modern in its merchandising.

If you do not desire to moor in the small boat harbor or it is full, you can anchor any place along the town shoreline and dinghy ashore. There is a fringing reef so be careful of it. There is also little protection from northerly winds so beware of a wind shift.

Neiafu, Vava'u

The Vava'u group is composed of high islands reaching moderate heights of 700 feet. The islands are compactly arranged so that your passage into the harbor at Neiafu takes you for eight miles between the islands. Cruise ships

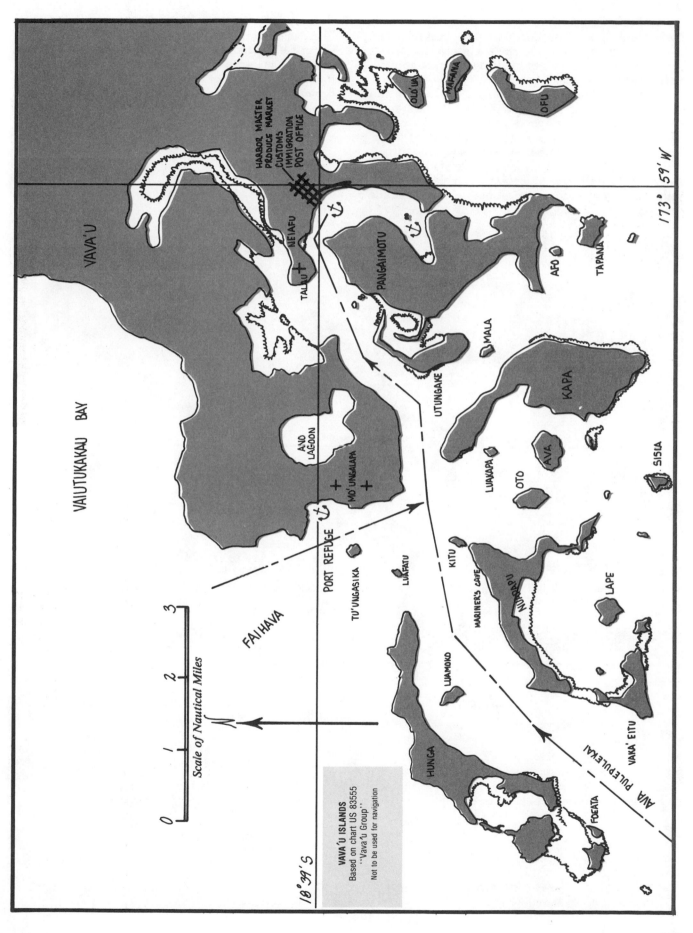

VAIUTUKAKAU BAY

VAVA'U

HARBOR MASTER
PRODUCE MARKET
CUSTOMS
IMMIGRATION
POST OFFICE

NEIAFU

TALAU +

PANGAIMOTU

AND
LAGOON

MO'UNGALAPA

PORT REFUGE

FAIHAVA

UTUNGAKE

MALA

KAPA

AVA

OTO

LUAKAPA

KITU

MARINER'S CAVE

NUAPAPU

LAPE

AFO

TAPANA

SISIA

VAKA'EITU

AVA PULEPULEKAI

FOEATA

HUNGA

LUAMOKO

LUAFATU

TU'UNGASIKA

OLO'UA

MAFANA

OFU

173° 59' W

18° 39' S

Scale of Nautical Miles

0   1   2   3

N

VAVA'U ISLANDS
Based on chart US 83555
"Vava'u Group"
Not to be used for navigation

163

are able to transit the first seven of these. All along this channel are attractive anchorages but the best anchorage is at Neiafu itself. There you can anchor to a coral sand bottom in 2 to 3 fathoms of sparkling water. Surrounded by hills 400 to 600 feet high with a narrow reach to its south (closed) end, small boats can find haven there from the tropical cyclones which generate between November and April. While not as good a hurricane hole as Pago Pago, it appears adequate and, in fact, it is the only hurricane hole between Samoa and New Zealand.

Fuel supplies are not available at Neiafu but potable water is. No deck provisions are available. Foodstuffs, both staples and fresh, are available in limited but adequate quantities.

A unique phenomenon of Neiafu is the bumboat. These are local persons who will approach your boat to sell or barter foodstuffs, handicrafts, or services at prices which are in excess of those found ashore. It is recommended that you not do business with them until you have reconnoitered the situation ashore. Further, do not allow them on board until you have established the validity of their friendly ways.

Pangai, Ha'apai

There are absolutely no yacht facilities here making it a truly South Seas island.

A cruise ship approaches the wharf at Neiafu, Vava'u, which is also a Port of Entry to Tonga. Yachts generally anchor further down the channel to the right and dinghy back to the wharf. When a cruise ship comes into any small island for the day, it inundates the local facilities and that is a good time to go shelling out on the reef.

Radio Communications

Station name and call	Location	Frequency Transmit/Receive	Service hours LMT	Type of Service
Nuku'alofa Radio	Nuku'alofa	2182/2182 kHz	0640-2240	Calling and distress watch
		2080/2080	0640-2240	Marine traffic
Radio Tonga ZCO "Call of the Friendly Islands"	21°09'S 175°10'W	1020 kHz	Sunday 1900-2200 Daily 0700-1000 1200-1400 1830-2300	Commercial broadcast

Chapter 13

TUVALU
(Ellice Islands)

The Country

Tuvalu became an independent country on 1 October 1978 having formerly been part of the Gilbert and Ellice Island group administered by Great Britain. Tuvalu lies between 5° and 11° south latitude and 176° east longitude and the 180° meridian. It extends for a distance of 360 miles in a northwesterly-southeasterly direction and is composed of nine islands with a land area of 11 square miles. The national waters of Tuvalu encompass approximately ½ million square miles of the Pacific Ocean. The islands are all low atolls with coconut palms reaching 60 to 80 feet at the highest points. An estimated 9000 persons inhabit the islands.

There is very little known of the settlement of Tuvalu. The people and their language are definitely Polynesian with strong strains of Samoan and Tongan dialects.

The island group was first seen in March 1819 by the American ship, *Rebecca,* under the command of Captain De Peyster. The first charting of the area was done by Lieut. Wilkes, USN, as part of the 1840 United States Exploration Expedition.

The capital of the group is located at Funafuti which is an atoll consisting of 30 islets on a reef surrounding a lagoon 13 miles long with a maximum width of 10 miles. The islet of Funafuti has a population of about 700 persons and its principal village is Fongafale. The people are Christian with great influence being wielded by the London Missionary Society.

The thin sandy soils of the atolls support only a narrow range of vegetation of which coconut and pandanus are the dominate forms. Taro is grown in artificial pits and there are some banana trees. Otherwise the basic foodstuffs are obtained from the sea and lagoon.

The Weather

The climate of Tuvalu is moderate with temperatures averaging about 80°F. Extremes are reported to be between 72° and 92°F. The average rainfall for a year is about 180 inches with the wettest season between December and March. The driest months are between September and October. Occasional squalls are experienced in the afternoon but they are of short duration. Except in those squalls, the visibility is good.

Prevailing winds are easterly with a northerly component between May and October. East to southeast winds are steadier but east to northeast winds are the more common. Average wind speeds are from 10 to 13 knots. The strongest winds occur in the season from November to

April. In 1942 and 1943 storms with wind speeds of 30 and 40 knots were experienced. These storms came from north through west and the water inside the lagoons became rough with waves of 5 to 6 feet. The islands are out of the belt of normal hurricane activity. Waterspouts however, are frequently seen in the area.

Yacht Entry and Facilities

Funafuti is the only Port of Entry and yachts should check in there. Customs, immigration, health and agriculture formalities must be observed.

Primary entrance to the Funafuti Lagoon is made through Te Ava Fuagea Pass and the preferred anchorage is off the village of Fongafale but beware of sunken small craft and pontoons left over from the war. There is one small jetty at the government station for ship-

Tuvalu

(Ellice Islands)
An independent nation within
the British Commonwealth

Port of Entry:

Funafuti   8°31'S, 179°12'E

Distances between ports in nautical miles:

Between *Funafuti* and:

Agana, Guam	2455
Apia, Western Samoa	630
Honiara, Solomon Islands	1150
Honolulu, Hawaii	2250
Jaluit, Marshall Islands	1040
Noumea, New Caledonia	1130
Papeete, Society Islands	1910
Suva, Fiji	710
Tarawa, Gilbert Islands	690
Vila, New Hebrides	860

Standard Time:

12 hours fast on GMT

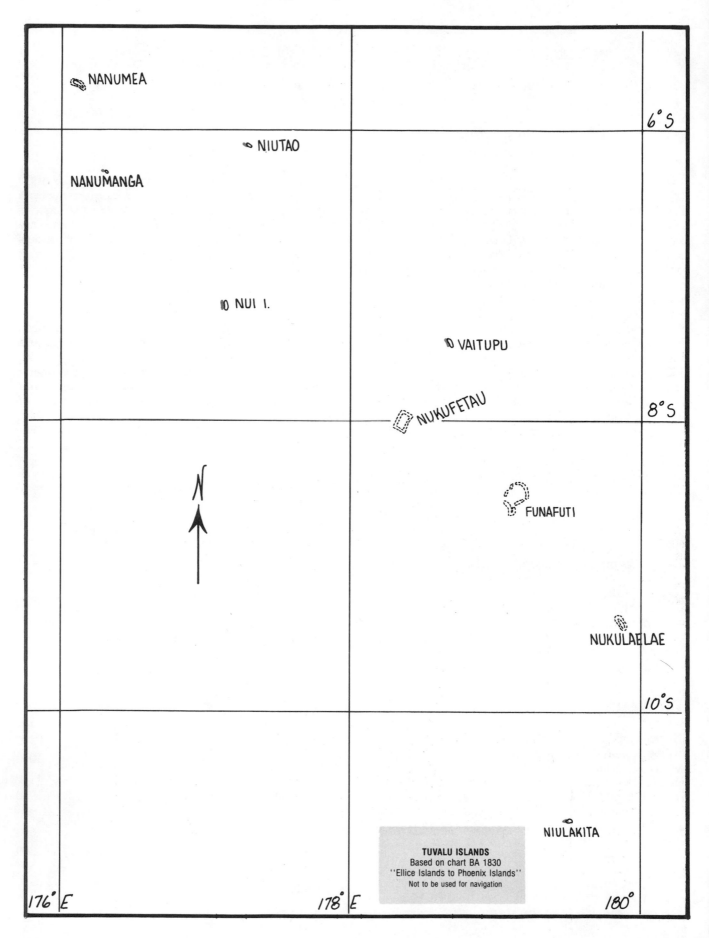

NANUMEA

6°S

NIUTAO

NANUMANGA

NUI I.

VAITUPU

NUKUFETAU 8°S

N

FUNAFUTI

NUKULAELAE

10°S

NIULAKITA

TUVALU ISLANDS
Based on chart BA 1830
''Ellice Islands to Phoenix Islands''
Not to be used for navigation

176° E

178° E

180°

Jetsam and Flotsam

Currency:

Tuvalu uses Australian currency. At press time the rate of exchange was $US1 = $A.85.

Language:

The native language of Tuvalu is fairly closely related to modern Samoan with a sprinkling of words from the Tongan and Nuiean languages. English is spoken by many of the people.

Electricity:

If you find any electricity on these islands, it will be of 240 volt, 50 Hz AC.

Postal Address:

Yacht (   ).
Poste Restante
Funafuti, TUVALU

External Affairs Representative:

British or Australian embassies or consulates.

---

ping and a small wharf for mail and passengers which can also be used by yachts on a temporary basis.

The anchorage off the village of Fongafale is well protected from the prevailing east and southeast winds making it safe during the months of May through September. After October the summer westerlies set in and the anchorage can become untenable.

Provisions are scarce and there is only a limited amount of rain water available for drinking. A government hospital is located on the southwestern part of the island.

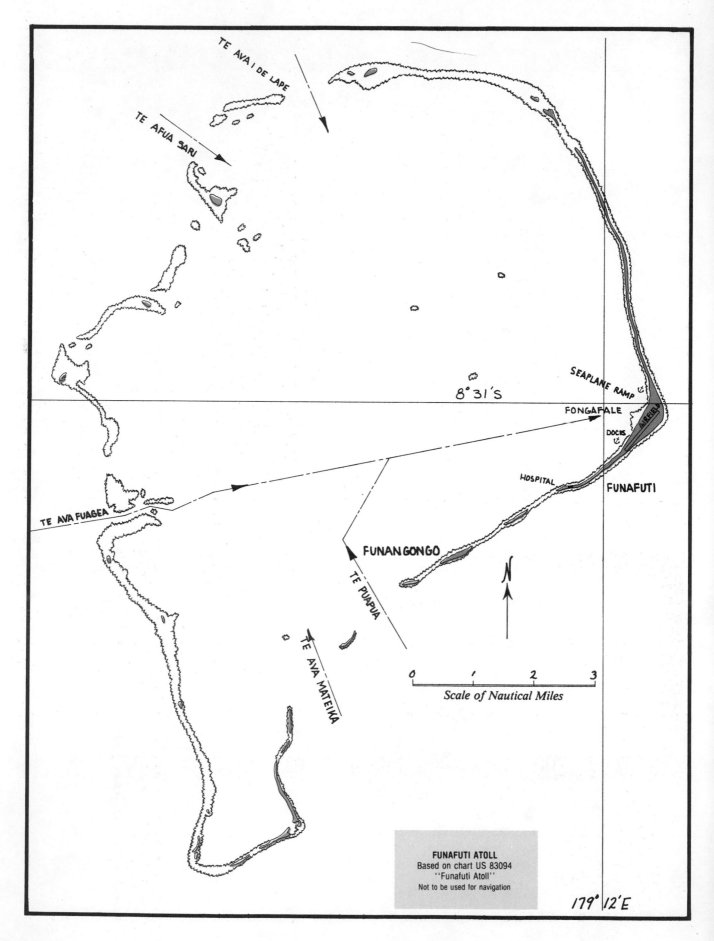

TE AVA I DE LAPE

TE AFUA SARI

TE AVA FUAGEA

8° 31'S

SEAPLANE RAMP

FONGAFALE

MIREILA

DOCKS

HOSPITAL

FUNAFUTI

FUNANGONGO

TE PUAPUA

TE AVA MATEIKA

N

0   1   2   3

Scale of Nautical Miles

FUNAFUTI ATOLL
Based on chart US 83094
''Funafuti Atoll''
Not to be used for navigation

179° 12'E

Medical Memo

Immunization requirements:

A smallpox vaccination is required and also cholera and yellow fever vaccinations if you are arriving 14 days after visiting or transiting an infected area.

Local health situation:

There were cases of cholera reported in 1977 but no other medical problems.

Health Services:

There is a government hospital on Funafuti and drugs are available only at the hospital. There are no dental or optical services.

Water:

Water from all sources should be considered suspect and treated.

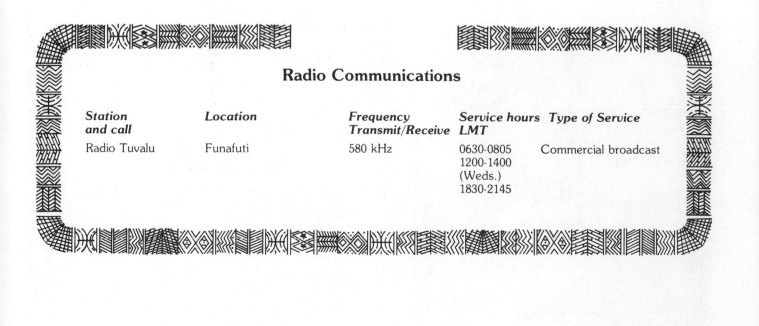

Radio Communications

Station and call	Location	Frequency Transmit/Receive	Service hours LMT	Type of Service
Radio Tuvalu	Funafuti	580 kHz	0630-0805 1200-1400 (Weds.) 1830-2145	Commercial broadcast

Chapter 14
NIUE

The Country

Niue Island, discovered by Captain Cook in 1774, became part of New Zealand in 1901, when the boundaries of New Zealand were extended to include the Cook Islands. The island is situated approximately 300 miles east of Tonga, 350 miles southwest of Samoa, and 580 miles west of Rarotonga. The island, which has an area of 64,900 acres, is an elevated coral outcrop with a fringing coral reef around a precipitous and broken coastline. The central saucer-shape plateau, rising to a height of 220 feet, is encircled by a narrow terrace about 90 feet above the water. The soil, though fertile, is not plentiful, and this feature combined with the rocky and broken nature of the country, makes cultivation difficult. The Niueans live mostly along the coastline in 12 villages which are connected by crushed coral roads.

Niue was probably settled over a thousand years ago by migrations from Samoa and Tonga. Their descendants even today are found in the northern and southern villages, respectively. It was Captain Cook, in his 1774 visits that named the island the Savage Island because of the hostility of the natives. History has proven the name to be ill advised and resented by the Niueans.

The London Missionary Society attempted to land teachers on the island in 1830 but, they, too, were repulsed. In 1849, Niuean and Samoan teachers were landed and established the first mission. The first European missionary arrived to stay in 1861.

Niue started as early as 1887 to try to become a member of the British Empire but it did not happen until 1900 when it was declared a British Protectorate. The next year it was annexed to New Zealand.

On 19 October 1974 (Constitution Day), Niue became self-governing in free association with New Zealand. The leader of government became the Premier of Niue and the Executive Committee became the Cabinet. Under the Constitution the Niue Assembly consists of 20 members elected by the universal suffrage, 14 members each representing a village constituency and six members elected on a common roll.

It is written into the Niue Constitution Act of 1974 that

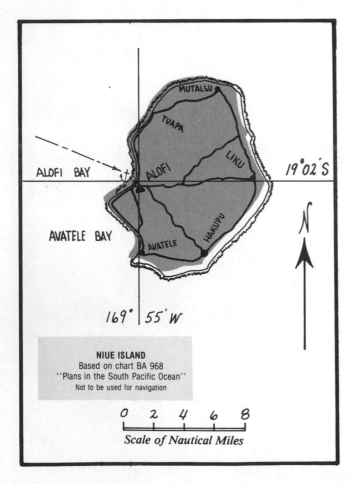

NIUE ISLAND
Based on chart BA 968
"Plans in the South Pacific Ocean"
Not to be used for navigation

0 2 4 6 8
Scale of Nautical Miles

Niue

A self-governing country in
free association with New Zealand

Port of Entry:

Alofi   19°02′S, 169°5′W

Distances between ports in nautical miles:

Between *Alofi* and:

Auckland, New Zealand	1500
Nuku'alofa, Tonga	340
Pago Pago, American Samoa	275
Papeete, Tahiti	1200
Raoul, Kermadec Islands	750
Rarotonga, Cook Islands	580

Standard time:

11 hours slow on GMT

New Zealand will continue to be responsible for the external affairs and defense of Niue and for providing necessary economic and administrative assistance. Niueans are British subjects and New Zealand citizens.

The population at 31 December 1973 was estimated to be 4,142 persons. There has been a steady decline in recent years as Niueans emigrate to New Zealand in search of economic opportunity.

The only substantial employer of labor is the government which employs Niueans in the education, police, public works, health, agriculture, and other departments and in the loading and discharge of vessels. A large number of unskilled workers are employed on public works. The basic government wage rate as of 31 December 1974 was 52½ NZ¢ per hour. Most workers who do not work for wages work in their family planations.

The principal agricultural exports are passion fruit, honey, copra, and limes. Of the total area of the island of 64,900 acres, approximately 50,900 acres are available for agriculture, while some 13,600 acres are in forest. The remaining 400 acres are in buildings and roads.

The forests are in the interior of the island and are made up of mahogany, miro (rosewood), and sandlewood. Although there is much timber on the island, it is not used for exporting but in building houses and other buildings. Some cattle are now being raised on the island to supplement the imported frozen mutton from New Zealand.

The Weather

The climate of Niue is mild and equable with an average mean temperature in July of 76°F and in January of 81°F. December to March is the wettest season (and also the hottest) although the rainfall is well distributed throughout the year. The average annual rainfall is 79 inches with the highest recorded of 133 inches and the lowest of 32 inches.

The prevailing wind is from the east southeast. Winds of high speed occur during the summer months of November to April. Niue is on the edge of the hurricane belt but hurricane force winds are rare. Hurricanes did visit the island in 1959 and 1960.

Yacht Entry

Passports are required of all foreign visitors to Niue. A visa is not required for stays of 30 days or less but sufficient funds and an onward airline ticket or the equivalent are required.

Check in with the Harbor Master on arrival since Niue is free of the rhinoceros beetle and yachts from infected areas must be fumigated.

Yacht Facilities

The port of Alofi is an open roadstead on the west side of the island and yachts must anchor close in because of the very deep water. There is a mooring buoy available and this is preferable to anchoring. Dinghies can be taken in to the shoreline through a natural passage in the reef which is also used by lighters when unloading ships. If you land at the jetty in Alofi Bay, it is wise to lift your dinghy onto the jetty to avoid pounding. There are landings but really no safe anchorages at Tuapa and Avatele. However lacking in moorage, Niue makes up for it in hospitality to the yachtsmen at the Niue Island Blue Water Yacht Club.

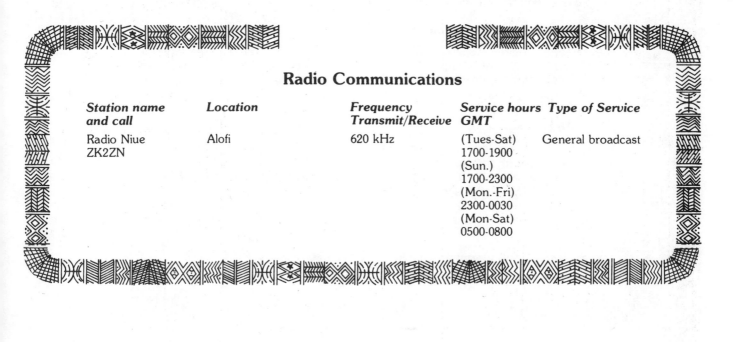

Radio Communications

Station name and call	Location	Frequency Transmit/Receive	Service hours GMT	Type of Service
Radio Niue ZK2ZN	Alofi	620 kHz	(Tues-Sat) 1700-1900 (Sun.) 1700-2300 (Mon.-Fri) 2300-0030 (Mon-Sat) 0500-0800	General broadcast

Jetsam and Flotsam

Currency:

Niue uses New Zealand currency. For the approximate rate of exchange see New Zealand.

Language:

The indigenous language is a Polynesian dialect peculiar to the island, but closely related to that of Tonga and Samoa with some elements from eastern Polynesia. English is the official language.

Electricity:

Where electricity is available it is 240 volt, 50 Hz AC.

Postal address:

Mail comes so infrequently to Niue that it is recommended that yachts use Tonga, Samoa, Rarotonga, or New Zealand for mail drops.

External Affairs Representative:

New Zealand consulates or embassies.

Medical Memo

Immunization requirements:

Smallpox vaccinations are required unless arriving from neighboring islands. Yellow fever and cholera vaccinations are required if arriving within six days after leaving or transiting an infected area.

Local health situation:

Niue, although situated in the Tropics, is largely free from diseases prevalent in tropical countries. There are no significant endemic diseases on the island although cutaneous disease and ophthalmia are common. Insects, in general, are few but flies can be a nuisance.

Health services:

All medical treatment including hospital service is provided by the government through grants from New Zealand. There is a government hospital X-ray unit, laboratory, dispensary, and out-patient department. Dental and optical services are available at the hospital. Drugs are available only at the hospital.

Water:

Water from all sources should be considered suspect and treated.

Chapter 15

NEW ZEALAND
(Aotearoa — The Long White Cloud)

The Country

New Zealand has two main islands, the North, 44,200 square miles, and the South, 58,200 square miles. The two islands are long and narrow, 1,100 miles separating the extremity of the south from the slim tip of the north. No point is farther than 68 miles from the sea. It lies at latitudes south of the equator, similar to California's position north of the equator and, hence, has a similar climate.

The country is predominantly mountainous. Alps run almost the length of the South Island with New Zealand's highest peak, Mount Cook (12,349 feet), midway along the chain. There are 16 mountains of more than 9,840 feet. In keeping with this great alpine system is a network of glaciers, some of which reach the forests of the west coast.

As huge and permanent as the mountains seem, New Zealand has changed its shape many times, for it is in a region where the earth's crust has long been changing. This is particularly true of the volcanic and thermal area which stretches in a line from just south of Lake Taupo in the center of the North Island to White Island, off the Bay of Plenty. It begins, in the central plateau, with three great volcanic peaks, Ruapehu (9,175 feet), and Ngauruhoe, which have both, from time to time, emitted steam and ash, and Tongariro. The remarkable thermal activity of this belt is most spectacular at Rotorua, where geysers spout and mud pools bubble and plop like boiling porridge.

New Zealand's deeply folded landscape has many lakes and rivers. The rivers vary from short and torrential, along the west coast of the South Island, to the long, braided, glacier-fed waters of its eastern plains and the impressively deep-flowing Wanganui and Waikato rivers that drain the volcanic plateau of the North Island.

Of the many lakes, Taupo (234 square miles), is the largest. In the south, Te Anau, Wakatipu, Wanaka, and Manapouri lie still and deep, creating classically beautiful scenery in valleys left by glaciers.

Although over three-quarters of New Zealand is more than 650 feet above sea level, there are large expanses of easier country. The most extensive are the Canterbury Plains which spread across 4,800 square miles of the South Island's east coast. The North Island has the rich grasslands of the Wairarapa, Manawatu, the Waikato, and Taranaki and the green valleys of the Auckland province.

Geologically speaking, New Zealand as it exists today is only about 5 million years old. It's hills and mountains are still jagged and conversion by erosion has not pro-

gressed very far. Other than the Canterbury plains of the South Island, there is little level land in this country and, consequently, crop farming has not developed. On the other hand, the hillsides of both islands covered with lush grass interspersed between the valleys of inpenetrable bush make it ideal grazing grounds for sheep and cattle.

The north end of North Island is subtropical enabling the growing of citrus fruits while the south end of South Island has cold and snowy winters. South Island on its

New Zealand
(Aotearoa - The Long White Cloud)
A fully independent member of the
British Commonwealth of Nations

Ports of Entry:
(Partial)

Auckland	36°50'S, 174°46'E
Opua (Bay of Islands)	35°19'S, 174°07'E
Tauranga	37°39'S, 176°11'E
Wellington	41°18'S, 174°47'E
Whangarei	35°44'S, 174°20'E

Distances between ports in nautical miles:

Between *Auckland* and:

Apia, Western Samoa	1580
Agana, Guam	3500
Avatiu, Cook Islands	1630
Honolulu, Hawaii	3820
Jaluit, Marshall Islands	2590
Noumea, New Caledonia	1000
Nuku'alofa, Tonga	1010
Pago Pago, American Samoa	1570
Panama City, Panama	6510
Papeete, Tahiti	2210
Pitcairn Island	2890
Ponape, Caroline Islands	1820
Rabaul, New Britain	2340
Raoul, Kermadec Islands	600
San Diego, California	5660
Suva, Fiji	1150

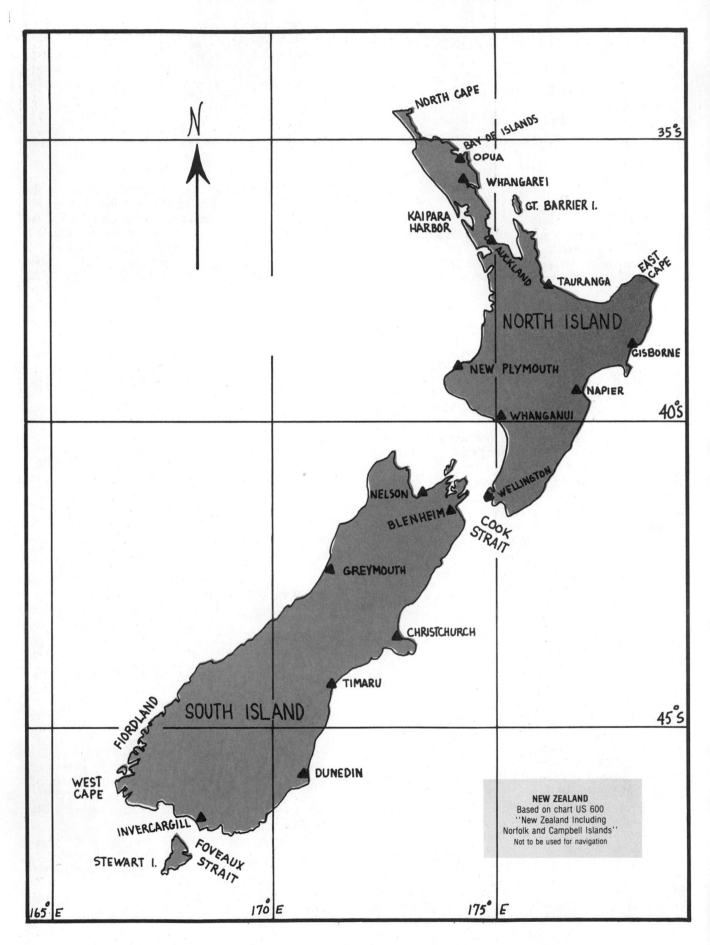

NORTH CAPE

35°S

BAY OF ISLANDS

OPUA

WHANGAREI

GT. BARRIER I.

KAIPARA HARBOR

AUCKLAND

TAURANGA

EAST CAPE

NORTH ISLAND

GISBORNE

NEW PLYMOUTH

NAPIER

40°S

WHANGANUI

WELLINGTON

NELSON

BLENHEIM

COOK STRAIT

GREYMOUTH

CHRISTCHURCH

TIMARU

FIORDLAND

SOUTH ISLAND

45°S

WEST CAPE

DUNEDIN

INVERCARGILL

FOVEAUX STRAIT

STEWART I.

165° E

170° E

175° E

NEW ZEALAND
Based on chart US 600
''New Zealand Including
Norfolk and Campbell Islands''
Not to be used for navigation

| Talomako, New Hebrides | 1420 |
| Truk, Caroline Islands | 3000 |

Between *Auckland* and:

Bluff, New Zealand	950
Lyttleton	675
Russell (Bay of Islands)	130
Tauranga	145
Wellington	550
Whangarei	84

Standard time:

12 hours fast on GMT

rugged southwestern rim has spectacular fjords and glaciers. It is this jagged and indented coastline that gives New Zealand a coastline length which approximates that of the contiguous 48 United States. Westerly winds are the rule and rain, while seasonal, is well spread over the two islands giving lush natural pastures, "bush" that is impenetrable in spots, and trees of magnificent stature.

Besides good summer weather the yachtsman is attracted to its highly indented coastline which provides innumerable harbors for exploration, isolation, or a sanctuary from a local storm. In particular, the northeast coast of North Island is favored by the Kiwi yachtsman and has also become the overwhelming favorite of overseas yachts. South of East Cape to Bluff there are only a handful of snug harbors while even fewer exist along the entire west coast of both islands facing the Tasman Sea. Separating the two islands is Cook Strait which is noted for its violent winds. Here the prevailing westerlies are funneled between mountain ranges forming the strait and the resultant winds and currents make the Alenuihaha Channel of Hawaii look like a millpond.

The flora and fauna of New Zealand are uniquely described by their abundance—much of the flora and little of the fauna. This is the land of the giant kauri tree although they are also found in limited numbers on islands to the north and west as far away as Malaysia. A slow growing tree living over 1,000 years, the kauri reaches heights of over 150 feet with the lowest limbs often 60 feet above the ground and the trunk has a girth of up to 50 feet. In once great stands, it started to disappear rapidly after the arrival of the Europeans—first for masts for English warships, then settler's buildings and export to Australia. Now it is protected and its uses limited to those applications requiring its fine wood qualities such as boat building. Kauri gum for varnish was a much sought by-product in the 1880's and "gum diggers" scoured North Island for buried chunks of fossilized resin left from ancient stands of the trees. To help save the remaining kauris, faster growing pines are now farmed to supply New Zealand's timber needs and for export.

There are some other unusual trees in this unusual country such as the "punga" which is a tree fern reaching heights of 50 feet and the cabbage palm similar to the pandanus palm of tropical islands. But a favorite of many is the pohutukawa tree—a massive, gnarled, many-limbed tree as big as the largest oak or Brazilian pepper tree. It grows in the most improbable spots on steep hills, rocky bluffs, and at the ocean's edge. Covered most of the year with conservative gray-green leaves, it bursts forth in summer (December and January) with brilliant crimson powder puff flowers. The pohutukawa trees form dramatic red splotches in the "bush" covering much of the hilly land.

New Zealand has few native land animals, but a great diversity of birds—some 250 species in all.

There is the flightless kiwi, shy and nocturnal, and the fat and comical weka, also wingless. More common are the bellbird and tui, the fantail, the kaka and kea (forest and mountain parrots, respectively). The pukeko, or swamp hen, and the morepork, or native owl. The kotuku, or white heron, is a rare bird of great beauty, though rarest of all is the takhe, a large flightless type of rail, believed to be extinct and rediscovered some years ago in the remote areas of southwest Fjordland..

The only indigenous land animals are two species of bats and a rare Maori rat. Among reptiles, the lizard-like tuatara is described as a living fossil and is now found only on some offshore islands.

There is some evidence that the first New Zealand natives were lost Polynesians who arrived there by accident and not intent. Possibly they were out fishing or in small canoes voyaging between the islands far to the north and east and had been blown south to ultimately land on these islands. The time of arrival of these first inhabitants was about 500 AD and they found the islands to have little vegetable growth to sustain their lives so they turned to hunting the giant flightless and now extinct moa bird. Their nomadic, isolated existence lasted until about the year 1100 AD when adventuresome Polynesians from Hawaiiki (believed to be Raiatea Island in the Society group) started migrating throughout the vast triangular area of the Pacific formed by Easter Island, Hawaii, and New Zealand. These later Polynesian arrivals—now called Maoris—eventually eliminated the earlier race of moa hunters and established their own society based on independent tribes but having a common culture.

The Maoris were the most fierce of all Polynesians engaging constantly in warfare in which the loser would expect to be eaten. While wars were usually fought for the purpose of conquering neighbor tribes or for revenge, it was also a sport with chivalrous periods. Halts in battle were frequently called to return the wounded. After the arrival of the European guns, battles were sometimes extended by one side giving additional ammunition to the other side. It was the guns in the hands of warring tribes together with disease which reduced the Maori population from an estimated 200 to 400 thousand in 1780 to a low of 42,000 in 1896. Today they number about 250,000 persons.

The first European explorers to see these islands were the Dutch under Abel Tasman in 1642 and, subsequently, the islands were named after a Dutch province—Sea Land. It was, however, the English explorer, Captain Cook, who in 1769-77 thoroughly explored and charted New Zealand for the first time.

The most northerly Port of Entry for New Zealand is Opua in the Bay of Islands. Yachts are cleared at the inner side of the wharf by officials who on call drive up from Whangarei.

Following closely on the heels of the explorers were the exploiters of the period—sealers, whalers, and traders. Sealers managed to virtually exterminate the seal population found principally off the South Island by 1830 and then turned to whaling. It was the humpback whale which became the new hunting target. These whales migrated south along the New Zealand coast in October-November to spend the summer months in the Antarctic and returned north in June-July to winter in the tropics. Their shoreline migration at slow speeds (4 knots) and their huge bulk (40 to 50 tons) was their undoing.

Beautiful, isolated Whangamumu Harbor on the North Island was one of the last whaling stations and along its shoreline lie ruins of a mechanized whaling station which operated from 1905 to 1931. The station is at the open end of a wooded valley which supplied their fresh water and wood for steam power and to fire their blubber rendering boilers. The utilization of the whale was complete in this process—blubber was turned into oil, meat was canned for export to Pacific islands, and bones and other residuals were converted to stock feed and fertilizer.

New Zealand whaling reached its peak in 1838. Whalers sought their R&R (resupply and ribaldry!) in a little Bay of Islands settlement called Kororareka* which could boast of 30 grog shops. At one time in 1836 there were 36 whaling ships from around the world anchored at Kororareka. While whaling greatly diminished in these waters in the following years, the town of Kororareka survived. Today it has but one pub and carries the respectable name of Russell.

Serious colonization of New Zealand began after the Treaty of Waitangi was signed in 1840 between the Maoris and British. Traders, missionaries, and farmers from England flocked to the islands which proved to be fertile grounds for the work of all three. While many settlements happened, some were deliberately planned like the bit of Scotland developed on South Island's Otago Harbor now known as Dunedin. It is New Zealand's 4th largest city with a population of 110,000. Or Christchurch on the Canterbury plain of the South Island which was a planned Church of England settlement.It is more familiar in today's world activities as the jumping-off place for the Antarctic expeditions. Wellington, New Zealand's capitol, was sited by the New Zealand Company on the north side of Cook Strait separating the North and South Islands. The land for Wellington was bought by the New Zealand Company in 1839 from a Maori tribe who supposedly owned it.

But the true ownership of land in New Zealand is very confused and poses a problem for land courts even today.

New Zealand was declared a Dominion by a royal pro-

*Kororareka is a Maori word meaning "tasty blue penguin".

clamation effective September 26, 1907 (Dominion Day). It achieved full internal and external autonomy by the Statute of Westminster Adoption Act in 1947, although this only formalized a situation which had existed for many years.

New Zealand has a parliamentary system of government closely patterned on that of the United Kingdom and is a fully independent member of the British Commonwealth of Nations. It has no written constitution. Queen Elizabeth II is the sovereign and Chief of State, represented in New Zealand by a Governor General.

The leader of the political party or coalition of parties that wins the majority of seats in parliamentary elections is named Prime Minister (Head of Government). Executive authority is vested in the 16-member Cabinet, led by the Prime Minister. All Cabinet Ministers must be members of Parliament and are collectively responsible to it.

The unicameral Parliament, called the House of Representatives, consists of 87 members, four of whom must be Maoris and are elected on a separate roll. Representatives are elected by universal adult suffrage to a term of 3 years.

New Zealand's judiciary consists of the Court of Appeal, the Supreme Court, and the Magistrates' Courts. The law applied in the courts has three principal sources—the common law of England, certain statutes of the British Parliament enacted before 1947, and statutes of the New Zealand Parliament. In interpreting the common law, the courts have been concerned to preserve uniformity with the common law as interpreted in the United Kingdom. This unity is ensured not only by the existence of the Privy Council as the final court of appeal but also by the practice of the judges of following English decisions, even though they are, in theory, not bound by them.

Local government in New Zealand is based on the county, borough, and town district. The 112 counties

The little town of Russell is a focal point for all types of boating activities and a popular holiday resort. The wharf has fuel and is the terminus for ferry service across the Bay of Islands to Paihia.

A favorite anchorage and meeting place for overseas yachts is Matauwhi Bay in the Bay of Islands. The waters are shoal and the bottom is mud but it is a quiet place with good access to Russell via the dinghy dock at the Russell Boat Club shown to the right in this picture.

make provision for the primary needs of the more widely scattered population of the rural areas. The requirements of the larger urban areas are looked after by the 142 borough organizations. The town districts are an intermediate form between the counties and boroughs. Local governments are headed by mayors.

The kiwi is a flightless, nocturnal bird standing about 10 inches high and found only in New Zealand. It is said to have lost its flight capability long ago because food was plentiful on the ground and there were no predators from which it had to flee. Today's New Zealander is appropriately named a "kiwi" because he, too, lives in a land of plenty and has no reason to leave.

The estimated population in 1972 totalled 2.9 million persons and the annual growth rate was 1.7 percent. Of the total population, 234,400 are indigenous Maoris of Polynesian stock; the remainder are predominantly British in origin. The 3 million persons living in this beautiful country are fiercely holding to old traditions, both Maori and European, but taking advantage of 20th century opportunities.

While other more populace countries may envy New Zealand's capacity to spread its population to an average of only 28 people to the square mile, New Zealanders, despite their heavy dependence on agriculture, are predominantly urban dwellers. More than 70 percent of the population is on the North Island and about 40 percent live in the four main centers of Auckland, Wellington, Christchurch, and Dunedin. The milder climate of the North Island, the expansion of the forest industries there, more specialized farming, and the building of factories near the larger local markets are factors which have helped lead to the uneven distribution of population.

New Zealand over the years has had political ties with many of the island countries giving their citizens free right of access to New Zealand. The result has been a steady migration of island peoples to New Zealand, particularly Auckland, in hopes of getting jobs in local industries. As

of 1976, New Zealand's Polynesian population (excluding the indigenous Maoris) was reported to be 61,360 persons made up of:

Western Samoans	27,880
Cook Islanders	18,610
Niueans	5,690
Tongans	3,980
Tokelauans	1,740
Others	3,460

New Zealand children receive compulsory education from the ages of 6 to 15, although virtually all start at age 5. New Zealand has six universities and a Central Institute of Technology plus adult education and university extension.

Although there is no officially established church or state religion, non-Christian sects are few. About 80 percent of the people belong to four denominations—Anglican, Presbyterian, Roman Catholic, and Methodist. Church schools receive government assistance as do other private schools and follow curricula prescribed by the Department of Education.

The official language of the country is English although Maori (a Polynesian language) is still spoken by the Maori majority. The literacy rate is 98 percent.

New Zealand is a strong welfare state and interwoven into the social security network is a full range of health services for its citizens. Public hospital treatment and medicine prescribed by doctors is all free. The state pays a portion of all doctors' bills amounting to almost half. Private hospital bills are paid in part by the state and some private health plans exist.

State benefits also apply in one instance to visitors. Accident compensation exists for all visitors to the country. It's automatic and for the visitor it is free except for a motor vehicle levy if you have your own car. Upon disembarkation on your arrival, coverage for personal injury by accident extends to you for 24 hours per day. Full information is available from the state insurance office.

Jetsam and Flotsam

Currency:

The unit of currency is the New Zealand dollar. There are 100 cents in the dollar and coins are issued in amounts of 1, 2, 5, 10 and 50 cents. At press time the exchange rate was $US1 = $NZ.92.

Language:

English is the national language and understood by everybody. In addition, Maori, a Polynesian dialect is spoken by most of the indigenous Maoris.

Electricity:

New Zealand is fully electrified and the current is 230 volt, 50 Hz AC.

Postal address:

New Zealand has an extensive postal system and you can receive your mail General Delivery at any town you choose. Since there is more than one post office in some towns, it is wise to have it sent to the main post office. A typical address would, therefore, read:
Yacht   (   )
General Delivery
General Post Office
Whangarei, NEW ZEALAND

External Affairs Representative:

New Zealand has embassies and consulates in the principal countries of the world. Should you be in an area where there is none, you can get assistance from any British consulate.

Information center:

New Zealand Government Tourist Office
P.O. Box 95
Wellington, NEW ZEALAND

Cruising Library:

Coastal Cruising Handbook, The Royal Akarana Yacht Club
New Zealand Chart Catalog & Index, Hydrographic Office, Royal New Zealand Navy.
New Zealand Nautical Almanac and Tide Tables, Marine Division, Ministry of Transport.
Pickmere Atlas of Northland's East Coast
The Shell Guide to New Zealand

Note:

All of the above references plus New Zealand navigation charts can be obtained from:
Thomson Marine
P.O. Box 25-120
St. Heliers
Auckland 5, NEW ZEALAND
        or
Trans Pacific Marine Ltd.
29-31 Fort Street
Auckland, NEW ZEALAND

The Weather

The mean atmospheric pressure tends to be greater at the northern than at the southern end of New Zealand and, therefore, the general direction of the wind over New Zealand should be westerly; but it is deflected by the high mountain chains, and consequently the wind often blows up or down the coast, and almost invariably through Cook Strait either from northwest or southeast. When, however, at a sufficient distance from the coast to be free from local influences, the winds generally commence at east, and veer through north and west, etc., showing that they are mainly caused by depressions passing southward of New Zealand.

The high pressure cells (anti-cyclones) generated over Australia march with regularity across the North Island every 6 to 10 days, normally moving eastwards at a speed of 300 to 400 miles per day. When the high pressure (1020-1025 millibars on the barometer) is over the North Island, weather is fine. But between the successive high pressure cells are troughs of low pressure (1000-1010 mb) usually containing a cold front from the south and with some rain. A typical weather pattern is shown in the illustration.

Owing to these peculiarities and, as the temperature in the north is higher than that in the south, the wind and weather over the islands vary greatly between different sections of the country. Only the northern end of the North Island, which is of primary interest to yachtsmen, is covered here.

Between North Cape and Mercury Bay during summer (October to March), a northeasterly or regular sea breeze is constant; it starts in the morning and gradually dies away toward sunset when it is succeeded by a westerly or land breeze. Should the sea breeze, however, continue after sunset and the sky become cloudy, it will generally increase to a fresh gale accompanied by heavy rain lasting for several hours when the wind will suddenly shift to the westward and the weather clear.

These regular land and sea breezes cannot be depended on during winter when northwest to southwest winds prevail. A north wind with cloudy weather usually terminates in a gale of short duration, but accompanied by rain.

A northwesterly wind is generally strong with heavy rains, and seldom lasts more than 24 hours, the general shift being counter-clockwise. With westerly wind the weather is unsettled and squally, but immediately it veers to west-southwest and southwest, which it almost invariably does, fine settled weather sets in and usually continues for several days.

A strong easterly or southeasterly gale generally occurs about once in six weeks, usually about the time of the full moon or change. It is accompanied by rain and thick weather, lasting from two to three days. This wind is preceded by a high barometer and generally shifts through north to southwest.

There is also an exceedingly cold southeast wind, with a clear sky and fine settled weather, which frequently continues for several days, terminating in a calm, or shifting to southwest. Westerly gales generally die away at

sunset within a short distance of the land, their continuance is indicated by a sensible fall in the barometer.

Between Mercury Bay and East Cape, and in the Bay of Plenty, westerly breezes prevail, freshening during the day almost to a gale at times, and moderating at sunset. Northwesterly gales are frequent and sometimes last three days bringing a heavy sea into the Bay of Plenty. With strong westerly winds the weather is generally fine and clear, but in fine weather with light winds there can be a haze over the land. Northeasterly and northerly gales are indicated by a swell from the north rolling into the Bay of Plenty a day or two before.

Southeasterly winds are infrequent, but they generally blow freshly for a few hours, and bring rain. Northeasterly gales in winter always work round through north to southwest.

During summer southeasterly winds are most common in the vicinity of Cape Runaway. Strong westerly winds are frequently met with 5 miles offshore, while it is quite calm at Cape Runaway.

Gales accompanied by heavy rain are experienced, both during winter and summer. These gales are generally preceded by a high barometer (1025 mb) and with the wind from southward and eastward. As the barometer falls the wind increases for 12 to 18 hours followed by a sudden shift to the westward and southwestward. The weather rapidly clears and the barometer rises quickly. During the intervals between these gales, which occur about once a month, winds between northwest and southwest prevail, calms being uncommon.

Southeast winds are common near East Cape, sometimes lasting for several days, and are often very strong. A strong southwest gale, which is dangerous in the roadsteads between Cape Runaway and East Cape, sometimes occurs; it is preceded by rollers and unsteady flows of wind.

Typical New Zealand summer weather pattern.

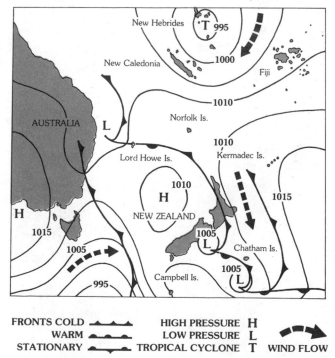

FRONTS COLD ▲▲▲   HIGH PRESSURE H
WARM ●●●   LOW PRESSURE L
STATIONARY ▲●▲●   TROPICAL CYCLONE T   WIND FLOW

One of the many natural harbors along the shore of North Island is Tutukaka. It is actually three harbors in one with the left leading to a small modern marina and a village where some provisions can be obtained. The gnarled tree in the foregound is the pahutakawa which blossoms with flaming red flowers in the Christmas season.

When in sight of White Island the weather can be forecasted by the appearance of the condensed steam from its volcano; with westerly winds this steam is low and there is a quantity of it; southeasterly winds are said to smother the steam.

Cyclones (low pressure cells) traveling eastward most frequently pass southward of Stewart Island, and are most severe over the South Island, but sometimes their influence is felt over all New Zealand. The wind begins at northeast or north, with a falling barometer, it veers to northwest and blows hard; as the center of the storm passes eastward the barometer rises, and the wind shifts (usually suddenly with heavy rain, hail, thunder, and lightning, the temperature falling several degrees) to southwest in a strong gale; fine weather returns as the wind veers through south to southeast or east. If, however, the wind backs through west to north or northeast, it is a sure indication that another similar storm is approaching. These changes frequently take place with considerable rapidity, and succeed each other for weeks at a time. The barometer rises and falls quickly, and the weather is very unsettled.

The western South Pacific hurricane season occurs during the southern hemisphere summer months of November through March. An average year, if such can be meaningful, generates 11 tropical storms with winds from 35 to 64 knots and four hurricanes (called cyclones in this area) with winds in excess of 64 knots. While most of these storms originate and move well north and west of New Zealand, a few each year move east posing threats to Fiji, Tonga, Samoa, and the sailing routes to New Zealand. For this reason the prudent yachtsman intending to summer in New Zealand starts his passage south at least by the first of November.

The climate is temperate without marked extremes but with sharp regional contrasts caused by the high relief of the country. It is warmest in the subtropical Northland to the north of Auckland and gets increasingly colder to the south. Rainfall is heavy in most areas, especially on the west coasts, which are exposed to the prevailing winds.

The extremes of daily temperature in New Zealand only vary throughout the year by an average of 20°F. The mean annual temperature of North Island is 57°F and that of the South Island is 52°F. The temperature on the west coast of both islands is more equable than that on the east.

The abundance and frequency of the rainfall are the leading features in the climate of New Zealand as a whole, and very rarely, indeed, is there a month without rain in any part of the islands. On the other hand, on very few occasions is there rainfall every day of the month. The rainfall is usually more intense and frequent at night than in the daytime.

In the Auckland area winter rains bring about 4 inches per month while summer rains bring about 3 inches per month. Long term averages show an annual rainfall of 44 inches. North of Auckland in the section known as the Northland around Whangarei, the average annual rainfall is greater ranging between 60 and 100 inches per year.

The contrast between the rainfall on the east and west coasts is most striking in the South Island, where the lofty Southern Alps lie broadside to the prevailing westerly winds, and on their windward slopes are condensed the vapors which have been swept by the breezes over vast stretches of ocean. Over North Island the rain bands are more irregular in form and show that the rainfall itself is more regular over the country. Here, again, the control of the mountains and plains on precipitation is apparent.

Thunderstorms are comparatively rare in the coastal districts except in the southwestern part of the South Island. In summer the thunderstorms usually occur in the afternoon, and in the winter with low pressure, at night.

Fog is rare, excepting at the south end of New Zealand. In the Bay of Islands and in Hokianga there is sometimes a morning fog in September, October, and November, which generally clears by mid-morning. Dense fog occurs occasionally during winter. In the Bay of Plenty fog has continued for three days in October, but this duration is unusual.

Yacht Entry

There are approximately 20 Ports of Entry to New Zealand, all of which can be used by cruising boats but because of geography most boats enter at Auckland, Whangarei or Opua in the Bay of Islands. Yachts should not make any subports before checking in at a controlling Port of Entry. Specific locations and actions for these three ports are as follows:

Auckland:

Overseas yachts or yachts returning to New Zealand from abroad should call Mount Victoria Signal Station by radio on 2182 kHz for instructions. The officer in charge

The city of Auckland is a modern urban area and can provide the yachtie with any necessary service besides having a wide variety of places to see. Princess Wharf is the passenger ship terminal and the wharf to the left is Queen's Wharf. Queen Street, the main street of Auckland, runs from the foot of Queen's Wharf. This is New Zealand's largest city and its principal Port of Entry.

will advise where to meet the Port Doctor. It is correct to fly the yellow Q flag from the spreaders. Yachts without radio should fly the Q flag and anchor off Compass Dolphin where they will be observed from Mount Victoria Signal Station. Arrivals at night may be advised to anchor for the night off Compass Dolphin. In unpleasant conditions with strong west or east winds, yachts may call Mount Victoria and request an alternative anchorage for the night.

After the doctor has cleared the vessel, Customs will either come aboard or direct the vessel to proceed to the Admiralty Steps, between Queen's Wharf and Captain Cook Wharf. Before being cleared by the doctor and Customs, no person can visit nor anyone leave the yacht. It is the skipper's responsibility to see that this regulation is adhered to. (Coastal Cruising Handbook, Royal Akarana Yacht Club).

Whangarei:

Town Wharf—call Customs locally and wait aboard your boat.

Opua:

Opua Wharf—call Whangarei Customs and the inspectors will drive up to Opua to clear you. There is no charge for inbound clearance but there is a charge for outbound clearance ($NZ12.00). If you anchor at Russell on your way in, the Town Constable will come out to your boat to welcome you and direct you to Opua. He will notify Customs of your moving to Opua.

Before arriving at New Zealand it is most important to obtain visas for the entire crew. New Zealand is very sticky about this and they have been known to send boats away into hurricane weather when their visitors permits expired. If you come to New Zealand without a visa you can get a thirty day non-renewable visitors permit only. By all means get your visas before you arrive in New Zealand. Extensions of time can only be granted if the vessel is in serious need of repairs which are being done at a legitimate shipyard.

You can write for visa application forms to the Department of Labour, Wellington, New Zealand, and it may be

Another popular Port of Entry for yachties is Whangarei. Here you can dock at the City Wharf, no longer used commercially, and you are right in the center of town. Practically all supplies and services needed for your boat are obtainable within walking distance.

possible to get a one-year visa plus a six months extension. Otherwise apply for visas through any New Zealand consulate or British consulate. Enroute this can be done at Rarotonga, Cook Islands; Suva, Fiji; Nuku'alofa, Tonga; and other locations. Canadian and Common Market nationals do not need a visa for stays up to six months.

Your application for a visa made in a foreign country must document financial responsibility in the amount of $NZ250 per month per person. Foreign nationals are prohibited from taking employment in New Zealand except by special work permit so your visa when granted will carry the notation "Employment Prohibited."

Customs can be just as sticky as Immigration so mind the rules carefully. Foreign yachts cannot move freely about the waters of New Zealand. You need a cruising license if you are from a country that grants reciprocal privileges to New Zealand yachts. The United States and members of the British Commonwealth all fall in that category. Other nationalities should check on arrival. The cruising license reads:

"I (   ) hereby declare that I have arrived in New Zealand for a temporary visit of 12 months and will sail the yacht from New Zealand within that time.

The yacht will not be sold or otherwise disposed of without the permission of the Collector of Customs.

I further declare that the Collector of Customs (of chosen Port of Entry) will be advised of the yacht's movement and of my current postal address."

All members of the crew must show financial responsibility to the tune of $NZ250 per month of stay. In addition, all members must have outward fares and this includes the owners in the event that the yacht becomes damaged in New Zealand beyond the owner's ability or willingness to pay for repairs.

You can enter normal stores and equipment associated with the yacht without paying duty. You can bring in foreign money but not New Zealand money.

Agricultural inspection on entry is very vigorous because New Zealand is singularly free from most of the major animal and plant diseases and they intend to keep it that way. There is a long list of prohibited imports including: eggs and egg crates, fruits and vegetables, skins or raw wool, wooden crates, meat of any kind (uncanned meat will be destroyed, canned meat must not be opened), seeds, and potted plants.

Medical Memo

Immunization requirements:

No additional immunizations are required for persons from Canada, Australia, United States and most South Pacific islands who have not been outside those areas for the prior 14 days. Smallpox vaccinations are required if you have come from an infected area.

Local health situation:

New Zealand is a very healthy country and there are no significant medical problems to be concerned about. Occasional cases of hepatitis and cholera are reported but it is not endemic. There are mosquitoes but no malaria.

Health services:

There are hospitals and registered medical practitioners in all of the cities and larger towns. The St. Johns Ambulance Service can advise on emergency medical help and also provides free ambulance service. The quality of medical service is on a par with any country of the world.

Both optical and dental services are available in every city and most towns. Drugs are available from chemists in most towns.

IAMAT Center:

Auckland: Iamat Center — Byron Chambers
           Takapuna
           Coordinator: Peter James Dowsett MD

Water:

Tap water is safe to drink thoughout New Zealand.

Sailing further into Auckland's Waitemata Harbor you come to West Haven Marina, New Zealand's largest and most modern marina. It is fully occupied and usually difficult to get room for an extended stay.

Cars, motorcycles or bicycles owned by crew members which are to be used in New Zealand must be cleared to the satisfaction of an authorized officer of the Ministry of Agriculture and Fisheries.

If there are any ship's pets (including birds, reptiles and fish) you are required to post a $NZ500 bond for their safe custody on board the boat while in New Zealand waters. They are not allowed ashore under any condition. An agricultural inspector will visit your boat at different intervals to determine that the pet is on board. You must give notice 48 hours in advance if you intend to change ports. This quarantine lasts for one year.

Pratique is granted if there is no sickness on board and if all crew members have valid smallpox vaccinations.

Leaving New Zealand is somewhat easier but there are still formalities to be taken care of. You will need to do the following:
— Declare that you are not taking any money out of New Zealand that you didn't bring in.
— Fill out a "10-minute form" which is really a float plan.
— Have your duty free stores brought aboard by the merchant (liquor and tobacco).
— Get your certificate of clearance from the Customs of-

ficer on board your boat just prior to departure, once you have that, you cannot reenter without going through the whole entry procedure again.

Yacht Facilities

New Zealand is a haven for yachting probably unlike any place in the world. Its citizens are descendants of seafarers from one hemisphere or the other and Aucklanders claim to have more boats per capita than any other city in the world. New Zealand lies in one of the greatest cruising areas of the world. Within easy grasp of a three-month cruise are Samoa, Tonga, Fiji, New Hebrides, and Solomon Islands in various combinations. For six months you can throw in French Polynesia and the Cook Islands. More than one overseas yacht has made New Zealand its base for seasonal cruising in the South Pacific.

Besides its location it is blessed with good yachting weather and a geography that enhances cruising. The coast of North Island has a length of nearly 1,500 miles indented on the east side with numerous bays suitable for anchoring and seeking shelter from the easterlies. Many

The capitol of New Zealand is Wellington at the southern tip of New Zealand's North Island. It is located on magnificent Lambton Harbour but its higher latitude and prevailing blustery winds make it less attractive to the yachtie who is used to moderate tropical weather.

harbors exist in the 200 miles distance between North Cape and Cape Colville but they become fewer from there south. The harbors on the west coast of North Island all have shifting sand bars at their entrances for which local knowledge is necessary.

There are good harbors to the south such as Tauranga, Gisborne, Napier and Wellington on the North Island and Port Lyttleton, Timaru, Dunedin, and Bluff on the South Island. In addition the South Island has numerous deep and extensive sounds which provide good anchorages and scenery beyond description but few facilities.

Tides around New Zealand are significant and must be considered in navigating the interesting shallow waters along the coast. Tidal ranges of 10 to 14 feet are common producing in many places strong tidal currents. If you want to explore the shallow waters of the coast line, you should procure a copy of the current New Zealand Nautical Almanac and Tide Tables.

New Zealand goes on Daylight Saving Time the last Sunday in October until the First Sunday in March. Dur-

ing this period New Zealand time is 13 hours fast on GMT.

The country is almost fully converted to the metric system and all navigation publications use it except in the instance of the nautical mile which still measures one minute of arc at the equator. Water depths and heights of objects are shown on charts in meters and tenths of a meter. All liquids are measured in liters and weights in kilograms. The currency is in the decimal system which replaced pounds-shillings-pence in the 1960's.

Sea waves resulting from earthquakes in the Pacific (tsunamis) can have a serious effect on boats in harbors or anchorages along the coast. Tsunami waves are not dangerous to vessels at sea because the wave crests are far apart and the wave heights fairly small. In shallow waters, though, the crests move closer together and the height of the wave increases significantly. Changes in surface heights of water can range as high as 35 to 50 feet. In the event of the possibility of a sea wave approaching New Zealand, the Civil Defense Organization will notify harbor masters who will spread the word to vessels in the harbor. In major harbors the signal is five prolonged blasts on a siren. Auckland, Wellington, and Whangarei have such a warning system. At the Bay of Islands and other smaller harbors, the signal is passed by vehicle-mounted loudspeakers.

The primary source of weather information for small craft operating off the coasts of New Zealand are the post office radio stations, however, local conditions are broadcast by regional radio stations. The best stations to listen to for weather broadcasts are:

Post Office Radio
Auckland (ZLD) . . . . 2207 kHz
Wellington (ZLW) . . 2153 kHz

Regional
1ZN Northland . . . . . 970 kHz
1ZK Kaitaia . . . . 1440 kHz
1ZE Kaikohe . . . . . . 1220 kHz
1ZB Auckland . . . . . 1070 kHz
1ZD Tauranga . . . . . 1000 kHz
2ZB Wellington . . . . . 980 kHz

Warnings, situations and coastal forecasts are given from the post office stations at the following times with announcement made first on 2182 kHz:
ZLD (Auckland): . . 0318, 0918, 1518, 2118 NZST
ZLW (Wellington): . 0303, 0903, 1503, 2103 NZST
Weather forecasts and announcements are made from the regional stations on schedules mixed in with their regular programming.

New Zealand being in the southern hemisphere has its summer in the Christmas-New Years season. The country takes a holiday for the summer starting on Boxing Day, the day after Christmas, and it continues for up to six weeks. From a yachtie's standpoint it is both good and bad. The bad part is that many shops and stores close or go on limited hours preventing work getting done on your boat. The good part is that if you are doing the work yourself, you can get bargain haulout and yard rates during the holiday season when the kiwis are busy doing their own yachting. Although the kiwis will tell you that small craft harbors and anchorages become crowded during the holiday season, it is only relative. They have so many waterways that it is virtually impossible to saturate them to the extent known on the west coast of the United States, for instance.

Yacht Facilities at Main Ports of Entry

Opua and the Bay of Islands: Most cruising yachts coming from the tropics make the Bay of Islands their first landfall. Besides being the most northerly Port of Entry, it is a yachtsman's paradise. There are over 50 smaller bays or inlets having good holding ground and providing good weather protection. In addition, the 100 or more islands provide a variety of scenery, good beaches, and many more sheltered coves for anchoring. Several rivers, some navigable at high tide like the famous Kerikeri River, flow into the bay.

The Northland Harbor Board has set aside the following areas as protected anchorages for yachts:
Russell: On the northern and southern sides of Russell Wharf.
Matauwhi: In Matauwhi Bay about a quarter mile southeast of Russell Wharf.
Opua: In the bay about 200 feet southwest of Opua Wharf.
Paihia: Within and southwest of a line joining Motu Maire and Motu Arahi.
Waitangi: On the northern side of the Waitangi River mouth on both sides of the bridge.
The town of Russell is located at the head of Kororareka Bay and was an important whaling center in the early nineteenth century. It is sheltered from the north to southeast and has 14 feet of water abreast at the end of the wharf. The bottom is black shingle and not very good holding ground in a blow. The wharf is used mainly by sport fishing boats and the ferries to Paihia but yachts can tie alongside for the purpose of taking on supplies. This small town which burgeons with people during the holiday season has small but good food stores, some hardware and lots of tourist shops. Fuel and water can be obtained at the wharf. Laundry can be done at the local campground facilities.

In Matauwhi Bay there is good anchoring in water depths of six feet or more well sheltered from most winds. The Russell Boat Club provides a dinghy dock and a pair of grids for bottom work at low tide.

The commercial wharf and a ferry slipway at Opua enclose a yacht anchorage suitable for shoal draft vessels only. There are many moorings here but all are used by local yachts. There is a cleaning grid near the ferry landing for vessels drawing up to six feet. There are two boatbuilders with slipways in the immediate vicinity. Fresh water is available at the wharf but no fuels. Limited shopping can be done at the small store in Opua. Yachts using the Opua wharf should tie along the inner side and, if you are there for clearance purposes, tie up near a ladder marked for Customs use.

Paihia is a very popular holiday resort and historic spot for New Zealand. It is a terminus for ferry service from Russell as well as a sport fishing center. Holding ground is very indifferent on a shingle bottom. The area is exposed to north and east winds with little protection from the offshore islands. There are many good general stores for personal and food shopping but no marine hardware. Fuel and fresh water can be obtained at the wharf.

At Waitangi there are pile moorings in the river for transient yachts. Fresh water is available on the Waitangi wharf and liquor supplies can be purchased from the Waitangi Tourist Hotel. The Bay of Islands Yacht Club is located at the foot of the wharf and has a haulout area and facilities for boats up to 35 feet for do-it-yourself work.

Whangarei: Whangarei is an inland city of 35,000 inhabitants connected with the ocean by tidal waters which snake for 12 miles across mud flats and sand banks to eventually meet the outflow of the Hatea River at the city center. Along the way are many pleasant anchorages such as Urquhart Bay, Parua Bay and the "Nook", and

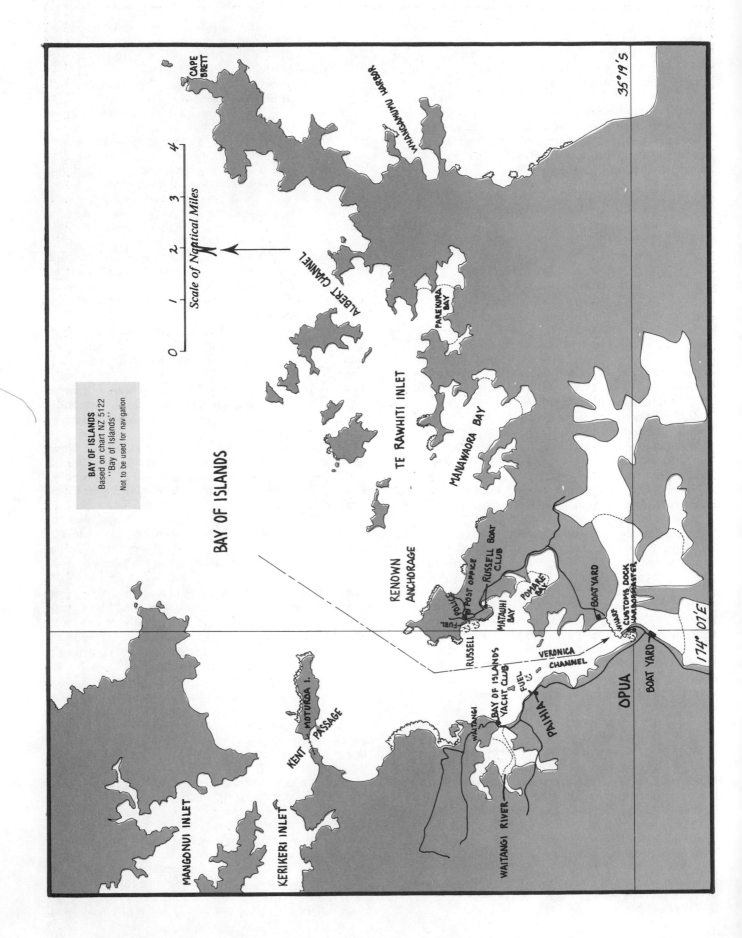

BAY OF ISLANDS
Based on chart NZ 5122
"Bay of Islands"
Not to be used for navigation

Scale of Nautical Miles

0 1 2 3 4

35°19'S

174° 01'E

CAPE BRETT

WHANGAMUMU HARBOR

ALBERT CHANNEL

PAREKURA BAY

TE RAWHITI INLET

MANAWAORA BAY

BAY OF ISLANDS

RENOWN ANCHORAGE

POST OFFICE

RUSSELL BOAT CLUB

POLICE

FUEL

RUSSELL

MATAUHI BAY

POMARE BAY

BOATYARD

WHARF

CUSTOMS DOCK
HARBORMASTER

OPUA

BOAT YARD

VERONICA CHANNEL

PAIHIA

FUEL

BAY OF ISLANDS YACHT CLUB

WAITANGI

WAITANGI RIVER

MANGONUI INLET

KERIKERI INLET

KENT PASSAGE

MOTUROA I.

188

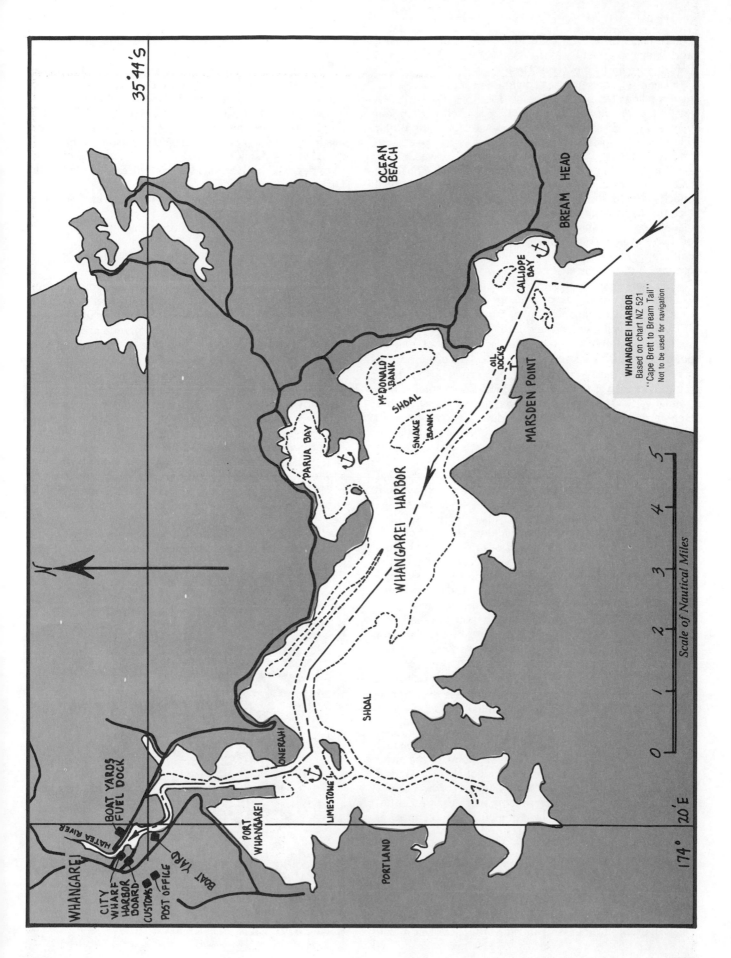

WHANGAREI HARBOR
Based on chart NZ 521
"Cape Brett to Bream Tail"
Not to be used for navigation

Scale of Nautical Miles

0 1 2 3 4 5

35°44'S

174° 20'E

BREAM HEAD

OCEAN BEACH

CALLIOPE BAY

McDONALD BANK

SHOAL

SNAKE BANK

OIL DOCKS

MARSDEN POINT

PARUA BAY

WHANGAREI HARBOR

SHOAL

ONERAHI

LIMESTONE I.

PORT WHANGAREI

PORTLAND

WHANGAREI

CITY WHARF
HARBOR BOARD
CUSTOMS
POST OFFICE
BOAT YARD

BOAT YARDS
FUEL DOCK

HATEA RIVER

Onerahi. You also pass the Marsden Point oil refinery and later the general cargo wharves at Port Whangarei before coming to the Town Basin.

Resident yachts in the Town Basin are moored between pilings for which they pay $NZ55 per year. A few jetty side ties are available at $NZ85 per year. Transient yachts raft up alongside the now unused City Wharf where the charge is $NZ5 per week for water, electricity, and hot showers. Laundry facilities are also available.

When arriving at the City Wharf and after you have cleared customs and the rest of the officials, you must check in with the Northland Harbour Board which is located just across the street from the City Wharf. They will allow you to stay at the wharf for a maximum period of two weeks. After leaving for at least one night you can reapply for another three weeks stay which is usually granted if space permits.

The only marina available and it is very crowded, is Oram's. Your chances of staying there are almost nil unless it is in conjunction with significant maintenance work which will involve their yard.

Whangarei has three boatyards capable of hauling boats up to 100 tons and a complete line of supporting services from sailmaking to engine overhaul to electronic repair. Largest of these is Whangarei Engineering Company—WECO, which also builds steel vessels. Oram's Boatyard has facilities for building in ferro-cement, fiberglass or wood with good maintenance facilities. Smith's Boatyard builds fiberglass boats and also does maintenance work.

Haulouts are made on conventional marine railways ("slipping") and the owner can do his own work without limit. Most kiwis and some cruising boats take advantage of the 10 foot tidal range, resting their boat's keel on a water's edge timber grid which allows several hours of work to be done while the tide is out. Boats up to about 40 feet can be hoisted out of the water and placed on the "hard" at Oram's for extended work or dry storage. There are two good marine chandleries and innumerable repair shops for boat and equipment maintenance.

The Town Basin is almost at the center of Whangarei making it possible to walk to all parts of the town for shopping. Immigration and customs offices are also within walking distance. All necessary provisions can be purchased here and it is possible to buy in case lots to reduce costs. On leaving you can purchase duty free liquor and tobacco. Fuel can be obtained at Oram's pier.

Auckland: Auckland Harbor is a large landlocked estuary at the head of the Hauraki Gulf and one of the most secure and commodious harbors in all of New Zealand. It has a total area of 73 sq. mi. and a water frontage of 194 miles. It is completely sheltered from all gales by an outlying chain of islands and the peninsula at the entrance. Anchorage in the inner harbor is good in 5 to 12 fathoms of water. The tidal range is 5 to 14 feet.

West to south winds prevail at Auckland throughout the year. Gales from these directions blow hard in winter (June to October), commencing in the northeast and shifting suddenly to northwest, accompanied by heavy rain. Westerly gales occasionally continue for over a week. During summer land and sea breezes prevail in fine weather, the wind being northeasterly during the day and southwesterly at night.

Visiting yachts can tie up alongside Marsden Wharf which at night is distinguishable by three fixed lights—red, orange, orange arranged vertically with the red being the highest. These are located at the head of the wharf. There are no charges at the wharf and both electricity and water are available. Marsden Wharf is in the center of Auckland convenient to all forms of shopping needs. The Harbor Master's office is located at the Queens Wharf.

Other yacht mooring areas in Auckland Harbor are as follows:

Devonport	St. Mary's Bay
Bayswater	Okahu Bay
Northcote	Karaka Bay-Glendowie
Little Shoal Bay	Panmure

Westhaven Marina in St. Mary's Bay is the premier mooring near the south end of the Harbor bridge. It is usually very crowded. There are several yacht clubs located along a breakwater fill enclosing the marina area. Visiting yachts should apply for space at the custodian's office in the northwest corner of the harbor. A road behind the hauling out area leads to the slipways and sailmakers on the east side and thence to the commercial center of downtown Auckland. Groceries and marine equipment can be purchased along the breakwater fill and water and fuel can be obtained on the jetties.

Throughout the Auckland Harbor area are numerous chandleries, repair shops, slipways and other businesses supporting the yachting community. Since New Zealand builds yachts of all types and in all materials, they are fully capable of doing any repairs necessary on visiting yachts. Labor costs are moderate but materials are quite expensive because all raw materials must be imported. For this very reason there has developed a good service industry which can repair most anything you have in place of throwing it away.

2/-
MAORI ROCK DRAWING
NEW ZEALAND

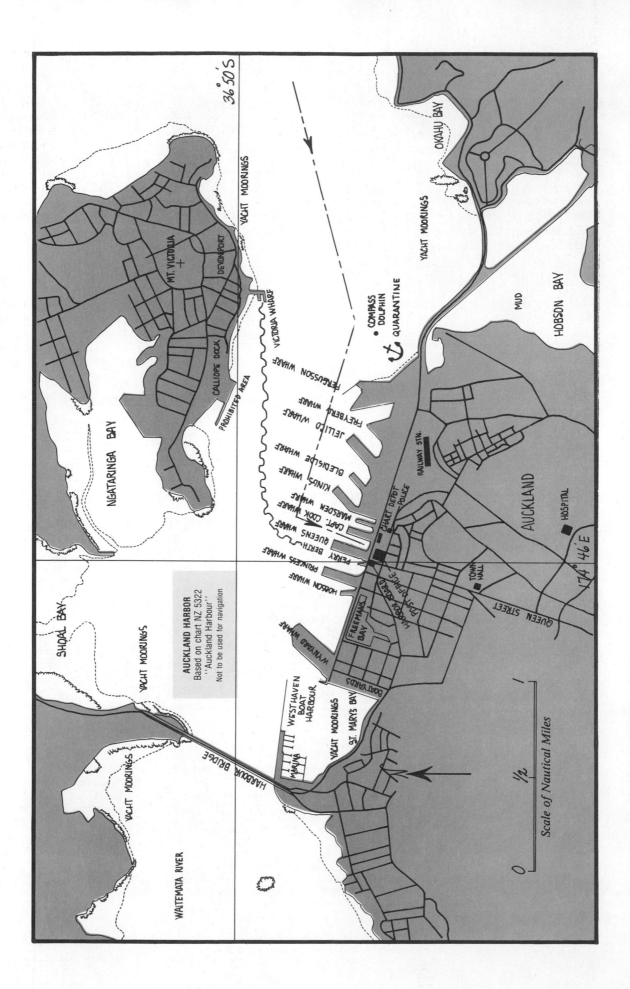

AUCKLAND HARBOR
Based on chart NZ 5322
"Auckland Harbour"
Not to be used for navigation

36° 50' S

174° 46' E

Scale of Nautical Miles
0   ½

WAITEMATA RIVER

SHOAL BAY

YACHT MOORINGS

YACHT MOORINGS

HARBOUR BRIDGE

MARINA

WESTHAVEN BOAT HARBOUR

YACHT MOORINGS

ST. MARY'S BAY

WYNYARD WHARF

BOAT YARDS

HOBSON WHARF

FREEMANS BAY

HARBOUR ROAD

PRINCESS WHARF

FERRY BERTH

QUEENS WHARF

CAPT. COOK WHARF

MARSDEN WHARF

KINGS WHARF

BLEDISLOE WHARF

JELICO WHARF

FREYBERG WHARF

FERGUSSON WHARF

VICTORIA WHARF

PROHIBITED AREA

CALLIOPE DOCK

DEVONPORT

MT. VICTORIA

NGATARINGA BAY

YACHT MOORINGS

COMPASS DOLPHIN

QUARANTINE

OKAHU BAY

YACHT MOORINGS

MUD

HOBSON BAY

RAILWAY STN.

CHART DEPOT
POLICE

POST OFFICE

TOWN HALL

AUCKLAND

HOSPITAL

QUEEN STREET

191

Radio Communications

Station name and call	Location	Frequency Transmit/Receive	Service hours GMT	Type of Service
Opua Harbor Master (ZLUP)	Opua	2012/2182 kHz	By arrangement only	Harbor operations
Marsden Point	Whangarei	2162/2182 2012/2182 2045/2182 VHF channel 16	Continuous " " "	Harbor operations " " "
Mount Victoria Signal Station (ZLKW)	Auckland	2012/2182	Continuous	Harbor operations
Auckland Port Control	Auckland	VHF channel 16	Continuous	Harbor operations

National Radio Communications

Station name and call	Location	Frequency Transmit/Receive	Service hours GMT	Type of Service
Radio New Zealand	41°03'S 174°30'E	1160 kHz 15130 17710 11705 11780	1800-2215 1800-0730 2230/0250 0300/0530 0545/1030	Overseas national program, beamed 30° for Pacific service
Kaitaia - 1YK		1010	Continuous	Regional station
1ZK		1440	1700-1205	Network programs
Kaikohe - 1YE		1050	Continuous	Regional station
Whangarei - 1YX		830	Continuous	Regional station
1ZN		970	1700-1205	Network programs
Auckland - 1YA		760	Continuous	Regional station
1YC		880	1800-2230	Concert programs
1ZB		1070	1700-1205	Network programs
1ZM		1250	1800-1200	Network programs

The author's yacht "Horizon" on the grid at Orams Boatyard, Whangarei.

The harbor at Picton, South Island, provides good facilities for yachts and is also the terminus of the Cook Strait ferry from Wellington.

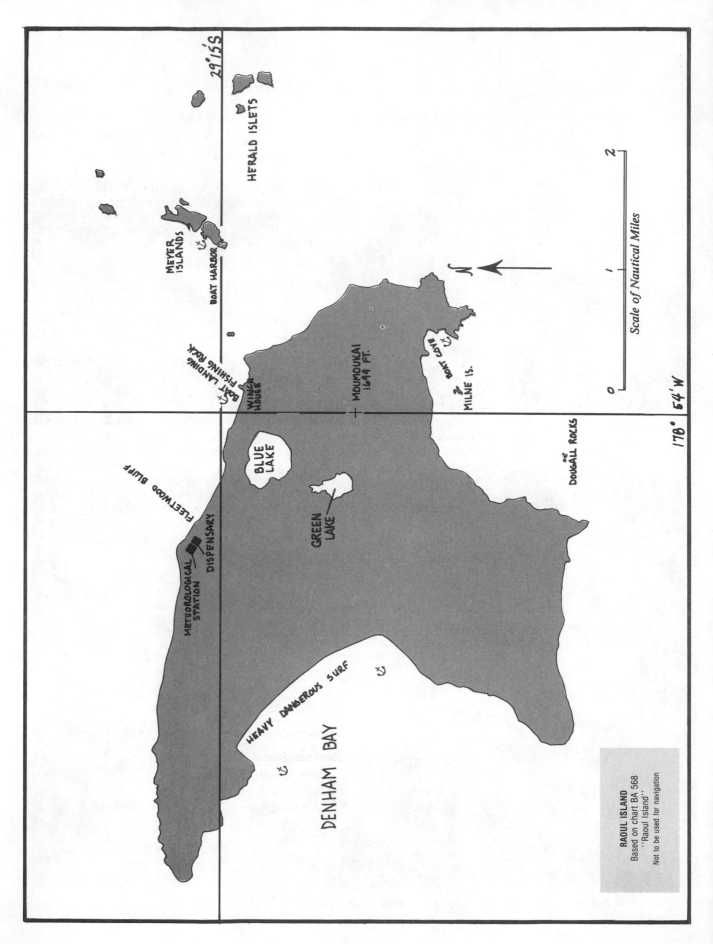

29°15'S

HERALD ISLETS

MEYER
ISLANDS

BOAT HARBOR

BOAT LANDING
FISHING ROCK

WINCH
HOUSE

MOUMOUKAI
1494 FT.

BOAT COVE

MILNE IS.

DOUGALL ROCKS

FLEETWOOD BLUFF

METEOROLOGICAL
STATION

DISPENSARY

BLUE
LAKE

GREEN
LAKE

HEAVY DANGEROUS SURF

DENHAM BAY

N

Scale of Nautical Miles

0   1   2

176° 54'W

RAOUL ISLAND
Based on chart BA 568
"Raoul Island"
Not to be used for navigation

Chapter 16

KERMADEC ISLANDS

The Country

The Kermadec Islands are a group of rocky islands lying 600 miles north of Auckland. The principal islands are:

Raoul (Sunday Island)   7200 acres
Macauley Island   760 acres
Herald Group   85 acres

The islands are all volcanic and in Raoul and Curtis islands signs of activity are still visible. Earthquakes occur at times and in 1870-1872 a small island was upheaved in Denham Bay, Raoul Island, which gave some shelter to vessels at anchor. Unfortunately, it disappeared again in 1877.

Raoul Island is thickly wooded and rises toward one end to a height of 1700 feet. The ground is very fertile and can support many forms of tropical and sub-tropical fruits. Wild cats, rats, and goats, however, prevent much extended growth. Fresh water is sometimes scarce but rainwater is collected in three lakes near the center of the island and, being volcanic, steam sometimes issues from them.

There is no indigenous population but about 10 persons live and work on the island manning a weather station for the New Zealand Government.

The Weather

The climate is mild, equable, and slightly warmer than that in the northern part of New Zealand. Extreme temperatures range between 48 and 82 degrees F. There is no frost and rainfall is plentiful but not excessive. It averages about 57 inches annually. Southwesterly and westerly winds prevail in the winter and northeasterly and easterly in the summer. There are strong gales in the winter. Hurricanes commencing in the southeast and backing to northeast have been experienced in January and February but they are rare.

Yacht Entry and Facilities

Visiting Raoul Island is an adventure in itself. There are no entry formalities other than to meet the personnel stationed there who are happy to see visitors. There are no boat landings so you anchor out and try your luck in two locations. Boat Cove at the southwest extremity of the island can be used in good weather but there is considerable surge in the cove.

The best landing is at Fishing Rock on the north side of the island where there is a crane to lift personnel from the water up onto the landing. You will need the cooperation of Raoul personnel to effect a landing. If the wind is from the north forget this landing. There is a depth of 13 feet in this area with good fine-sand holding ground but you are advised to leave a crewman aboard for safety.

Kermadec Islands

A dependency of New Zealand

Port of Entry:

Raoul Island   29°15′S, 177°54′W

Distances between ports in nautical miles:

Between *Raoul* and:

Apia, Western Samoa	1010
Agana, Guam	3370
Auckland, New Zealand	600
Noumea, New Caledonia	960
Papeete, Society Islands	1710
Suva, Fiji	700

Standard Time:

12 hours fast on GMT

Part II - Islands of Melanesia

•**Fiji**
•**Wallis and Futuna Group**
•**Papua New Guinea**
•**Solomon Islands**
•**New Caledonia**
•**New Hebrides**

Melanesia is far smaller than Polynesia in global area covered but it has as large a population and land area. It is made up of predominantly high islands, some even with active or threatening volcanoes. The islands are mountainous and generally very rugged. Rainfall is quite heavy over the area supporting heavy vegetation and in some places dense jungles. Some of the islands have large rivers and extensive swamps and in the past malaria has been a serious problem. While malaria is still present, it is no longer the serious problem that it was.

The climate of Melanesia varies from distinct seasonal changes in the south where the trade winds predominate, to hot and humid equatorial areas in New Guinea which have mostly monsoon winds. Because several of the islands are quite large, there are distinct differences in local climates ranging from snow-capped mountains to high plateaus to temperate coastal plains.

The Melanesian people are descendants of wandering Malaysians and Australoids both of which had the Negroid element rendering the heavy dark features of today's Melanesians. It is suspected that their arrival in Melanesia took place about 8000 years ago and they traveled as far to the east as Fiji. They were not navigators such as the Polynesians and they maintained strong independent tribal structures even on single islands. This has resulted in no semblance of a common language for Melanesia. Instead, there are hundreds of native dialects plus new languages brought in from the Orient and Europe. Except for New Caledonia, English seems to be the only one common language. As many of the countries forming Melanesia become independent, they legislate a national tongue.

197

Island Groups
of Melanesia

Island Group	No. of islands	Land area sq. mi.	Population (1967/71)	Government
Fiji	332	7,055	524,500	An independent nation within the British Commonwealth
Wallis & Futuna	3	93	8,500	French Overseas territory
New Caledonia (incl. Loyalty Islands)	6	7,000	115,000	French Overseas territory
New Hebrides	83	5,700	86,000	Great Britain and France condominium
Solomon Islands	10	11,500	175,000	An independent nation within the British Commonwealth
Papua New Guinea	Mainland	69,700	1,470,000	A parliamentary democracy
Mandated New Britain	1	14,600	153,700	Under mandate to Papua New Guinea
New Ireland	1	3,800	50,600	
Bouganville	1	41,000	78,000	
Admiralty Group	22	800	22,000	
Lesser islands	600			

Chapter 17

FIJI
(Fidgee)

The Country

Fiji is a group of 332 islands and islets centered along the 180th meridian and 15 degrees south latitude. The island of Rotuma some 240 miles north-northwest of the main group, although not geologically related, is also considered to be part of the area. The main group rises from two platforms in the submerged mountain chain of the continental shelf. Most of the larger islands are ancient volcanic peaks, many others are upthrust limestone sometimes pierced by volcanic cones, and still others are coral formations that cap elevations remaining below the surface. Excluding the outlying island of Rotuma, The Dominion of Fiji covers about 274,000 square miles of area of which 97% is ocean.

The western platform is the broadest, and from it rise Viti Levi and Vanua Levu (the two largest, highest, and most populous islands in the group) and the smaller Yasawa and Lomaitivi groups. The eastern platform forms the base of the Lau island group, a 400-mile long chain of some fifty islands composed mainly of raised limestone but also containing a few atolls and some that are predominantly volcanic in composition. The combined land area of the group is 7,055 square miles, and the population in 1970 was estimated to be 502,956.

About one half the area of the high islands is covered by tropical rain forest on their windward sides. Much of the forest has been destroyed by slash-and-burn agricultural methods and is now replaced by secondary bamboo, reed, and scrub growth. On leeward sides the rain forest gives way to more open areas, called *talasiga* (sunburned land), that is dry and contains only sparse low vegetation.

Coastal areas of the high islands are usually broad and are fringed along their seaward extremities by impenetrable mangrove swamps and the usual strand vegetation. Further inland they are covered by great stretches of sugar cane, which is the country's main money crop. The low coral islands are given over to coconut plantations, which provide relief from the low casuarina, pandanus and other strand vegetation.

The big islands of Viti Levu and Vanua Levu contain numerous rivers that are unusually large for the size of the island masses in which they occur. Some of these, such as the broad Rewa in Viti Levu, are navigable by small boats and launches as far as 100 miles upstream. These rivers usually enter the sea through broad, fertile flatlands on which most of the sugar plantations are located.

Despite evidence that Fiji has been inhabited for over 2,500 years, little is known of the history of Fiji before the coming of the Europeans. The early reputation of the Fi-

jian tribes as fierce maneaters, which earned the group a place on the map as the "Cannibal Islands" is belied by the friendly and open manner of today's population.

The first known European to sight the Fiji islands was a Dutchman; Abel Tasman, in 1643. Eurpean missionaries, whalers, traders, and deserters settled during the first half of the 19th century. Their corrupting in-

Fiji
(Fidgee)
An independent nation within
the British Commonwealth

Ports of Entry:

Suva, Viti Levu	18°08'S, 178°26'E
Lautoka, Viti Levu	17°36'S, 177°27'E
Levuka, Ovalau	17°41'S, 178°51'E

Distances between ports in nautical miles:

Between *Suva* and:

Apia, Western Samoa	650
Agana, Guam	2750
Auckland, New Zealand	1150
Avatiu, Cook Islands	1260
Butaritari, Kiribati	1460
Honolulu, Hawaii	2780
Malakal, Palau Islands	3040
Noumea, New Caledonia	730
Nuku'alofa, Tonga	420
Ocean Island	1210
Pago Pago, American Samoa	690
Papeete, Society Islands	1840
Raoul, Kermadec Islands	700
Truk, Caroline Islands	2230
Wake Island	2500
Wotje, Marshall Islands	1880
Yap, Caroline Islands	2940

Standard time:

12 hours fast on GMT

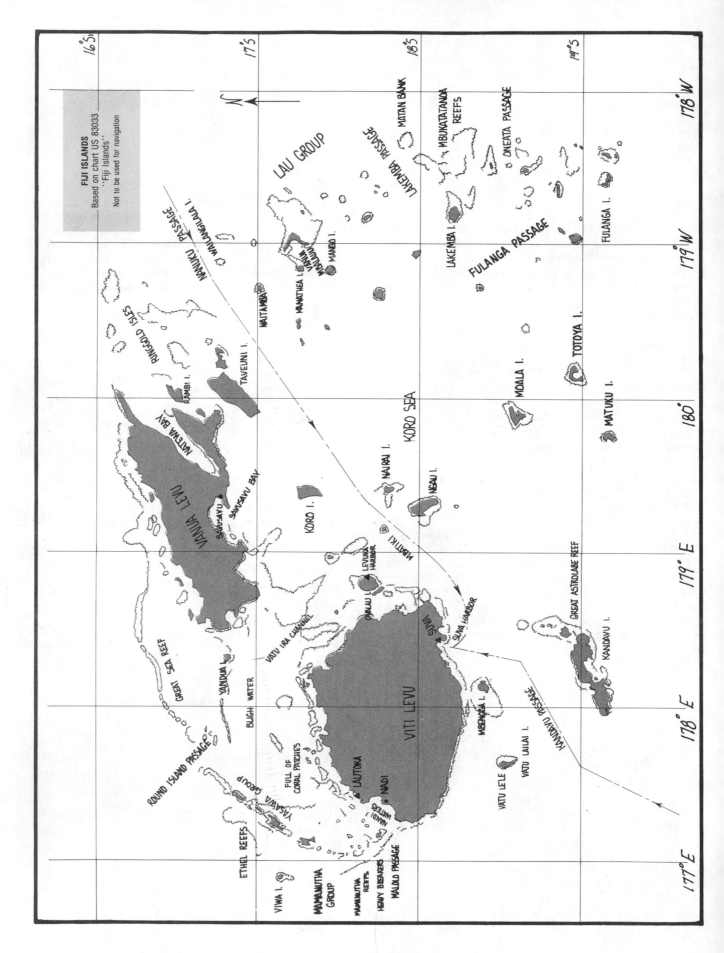

LAU GROUP

MATAN BANK

MBUKATATANDA REEFS

LAKEMBA PASSAGE

ONEATA PASSAGE

LAKEMBA I.

FULANGA PASSAGE

FULANGA I.

MANGO I.

MARAMBO I.
KANATHEA I.
VANUA MBALAVU

MAITAMBA

TOTOYA I.

MOALA I.

MATUKU I.

KORO SEA

MANUKU (KUINI) PASSAGE

MATANGLALALA I.

RINGGOLD ISLES

RAMBI I.

TAVEUNI I.

NATEWA BAY

VANUA LEVU

SAVUSAVU

SAVUSAVU BAY

NAIRAI I.

NGAU I.

KORO I.

MBATIKI

LEVUKA HARBOR
OVALU I.

SUVA
SUVA HARBOR

GREAT ASTROLABE REEF

KANDAVU I.

VATU IRA CHANNEL

GREAT SEA REEF

VANDUA

BLIGH WATER

FULL OF CORAL PATCHES

VITI LEVU

LAUTOKA

NADI

NANDI WATERS

MBENGA I.

VATU LEFE
VATU LAILAI I.

KANDAVU PASSAGE

ROUND ISLAND PASSAGE

YASAWA GROUP

ETHEL REEFS

VIWA I.

MAMANUTHA GROUP

MAMANUTHA REEFS

HEAVY BREAKERS

MALOLO PASSAGE

200

fluence caused increasingly serious wars to flare among the native Fijian confederacies. In 1871 the Europeans in Fiji (about 2,000) established an administration under Ratu Serv Cakobau, who had become Paramount Chief of Eastern Viti Levu some years before. A chaotic period followed until 1874, when on October 10 a convention of chiefs ceded Fiji unconditionally to Great Britain.

The pattern of colonialism during the following century was similar to that in other British possessions: the pacification of the countryside, the spread of plantation agriculture, and the introduction of Indian indentured labor. Many traditional institutions, including the system of communal land ownership, were maintained.

Fijian soldiers fought for Great Britain during both World Wars. The United States maintained military forces and installations in Fiji during World War II, but on the whole the war did not seriously affect the country.

In April, 1970, at London, a constitutional conference agreed tht Fiji should become a fully sovereign and independent nation with Dominion status in the British Commonwealth on October 10, 1970.

Close to 80 percent of the population lives on Viti Levu. The urban centers have been swollen by a steady migration from the villages and now account for nearly half of the population. Most people live in metropolitan Suva, in the area between Nandi and Mba, and in coastal towns and villages. The interior is sparsely populated because of its rough terrain.

Indigenous Fijians are a mixture of Polynesian and Melanesian resulting from the original migrations to the South Pacific many centuries ago. The Indian population has grown rapidly from an original nucleus of about 60,000 indentured laborers who were brought from India between 1879 and 1916 to work in the sugarcane fields. Unlike the native Fijians who live throughout the country, the Indians reside primarily near the urban centers and in the cane-producing areas of the two main islands.

Virtually all native Fijians are Christian—about 85 percent Methodist and 12 percent Roman Catholic. About 70 percent of the Fijian Indians are Hindu and about 25

The public yacht anchorage off downtown Suva. Princess Landing, used by the interisland trading vessels, is to the left. Most services and supplies can be obtained within walking distance and where you have to go farther, good public transportation is available.

The Royal Suva Yacht Club plays host to many overseas yachts and it is a good place to get acquainted with the local yachting scene and learn where to find the things you need. The Quarantine Anchorage for yachts is just offshore from the Club.

Fiji is an independent nation within the British Commonwealth. The Governor General, appointed by Elizabeth II, in turn appoints as Prime Minister the leader of the majority party in the House of Representatives. On the recommendation of the Prime Minister the Governor General also appoints the Cabinet, composed of the Attorney General and 12 Ministers.

Twenty-two Senators are appointed for 6-year terms; half are appointed every 3 years. Eight are nominated by the Council of Chiefs, 7 by the Prime Minister, 6 by the leader of the opposition, and one by the council of Rotuma (the small northern island peopled by Polynesians).

Under the Constitution, the House of Representatives has 12 Fijians, 12 Indians and 3 general members elected on communal rolls; and 10 Fijians, 10 Indians, and 5 general members elected on national rolls. The general communal roll consists of electors who are not eligible on the Fijian and Indian rolls, mainly Europeans and Chinese. On the national roll members of all races vote together.

The independent judiciary includes a Court of Appeals and a Supreme Court presided over by a Chief Justice appointed by the Governor General. An ombudsman investigates complaints concerning the actions of governmental authorities. A Commissioner appointed by the Prime Minister heads each of Fiji's four divisions.

percent are Muslim; the remainder are of other sects, including Christian. English is the official languge; however, the Bauen dialect of the indigenous Fijian language is spoken by most Fijians. Hindustani, a locally developed form of Hindi, is spoken by most Indians.

The pomp and ceremony of former British colonial days is carried over to the present by the guards at Government House.

Jetsam and Flotsam

Currency:

Fiji issues its own currency in the form of Fiji dollars. There are 100 cents in a dollar and coins are issued in values of 1, 2, 5, 10, and 20 cents. At press time the rate of exchange was $US1 = $F.80

Language:

Fijian is the indigenous language of the ethnic Fijian people. Hindi is the language of the Indians in the Fiji Islands. English is the official language of the islands and is understood by just about everybody.

Electricity:

Where electricity is available, it is 240v, 50 Hz AC

Postal Address:

Yacht ( )
Poste Restante
General Post Office
Suva, FIJI

Yacht (,)
c/o Tradewinds Hotel
P.O. Box 1354
Suva, FIJI

External Affairs Representative:

Australian consulates or embassies

Information Center:

Fiji Visitors Bureau
P.O. Box 92
Suva, FIJI

Cruising Library:

Handbook of Fiji, Judy Tudor; Pacific Publications, Box 3408, GPO Sidney, NSW 2001, Australia, 1972.
Pickmere's Yasawa Charts, available from Transpacific Marine, P.O. Box 3269, Auckland, New Zealand
Pocket Almanac and Tide Tables (for current year); Marine Department, Government of Fiji, P.O. Box 326, Suva, Fiji.
The Story of Fiji, G.K. Roth; Oxford University Press
Fiji: Islands of the Dawn, Leonard Wibberly; Ives Washburn Press
A Gift of Islands, June Knox-Mawer; Trans-Atlantic Arts
With Hook, Line and Snorkel in the South Pacific, Rob Wright; Pacific Publications (Aust.) Pty. Ltd., Technipress House, Sydney, NSW 2000, Australia

Suva's Tradewinds Hotel is the gathering place for overseas yachts after they have obtained their clearance. You can anchor out or moor Tahiti-style along the shoreline. A fuel dock is at the left of the picture.

The Weather

The Fijis and vicinity are under the major influence of easterly and southeasterly winds, which combined, blow about 65 percent of the time on the open sea, and about 50 percent of the time at Suva. The southeasterly trades blow most persistently during the period June to October, varying to easterlies in February and March.

Northeast winds blow about 14 percent of the time over the area as a whole, but only in March are they more frequent than those from the southeast. The mean annual wind velocity at Suva is about 5 knots and on the open sea about 11 knots. Little month-to-month variation in strength occurs at sea and the lowest average velocity is 8 to 9 knots in February and March and 10 to

12 knots during the remainder of the year. Calms are rather frequent at Suva but are rare at sea. Among the islands off the west and northwest coasts of Viti Levu, the southeast winds, interrupted by the lofty hills, are deflected irregularly into south to northeast winds.

Gales are occasional in all months, but are most frequent from December to March during the height of the hurricane season, but they occasionally occur also in November and April. These tropical cyclones affect the Fijis on the average about twice yearly, moving in from north or northeast. An occasional hurricane moves slowly among the islands for several days, accompanied by gales, heavy blinding rains, and dangerous storm tides which most severely affect the northerly slopes of the islands. These hurricanes usually originate near or west of the Samoa Islands, and mostly south of the 10th parallel, but a few are known to have originated to the northward of 10° South. After leaving the vicinity of the Fijis, most hurricanes curve into the southeast and cross into extratropical waters. The course of these storms is erratic, however, and it may be years before a destructive one strikes any particular location.

Fiji's climate is typically oceanic and tropical. Temperatures are high with maximums averaging about 84°F from January through June, dropping to about 82°F from July through December. These high levels are tempered and made quite pleasant especially in the higher altitudes, by unfailing breezes from the sea. The southeast tradewinds prevail during most of the year but are replaced by the northwest monsoon in the hot summer months. Both bring abundant rain which, never-

Suva's Civic Center is another attractive bit of architecture from the days of the Colonial administration. Automobiles are quite common but all have engine sizes under two liters displacement.

theless, varies in the windward/leeward pattern characteristic of Oceania.

Rainfall varies in different parts of the islands. On the southeastern coasts it is about 120 inches; inland it reaches 200 inches; on the northwest, lee side, it drops to from 60 to 80 inches. Rainfall at Suva varies from 75 inches to 170 inches, with an average of 120 inches. The dry season, June to October, is not as apparent in Suva as it is on the lee coast.

There is an average of about 20 days per month with precipitation, with the greatest monthly amounts falling from December to May. Thunderstorms in the open sea are most frequent, as a rule, during the foregoing months.

The interiors of the larger islands, which rise over 5,000 feet in places are often drenched with as much as 300 inches of rainfall per year. The low islands, over which the winds blow without losing any of their moisture, are often so dry that drinking water is scarce. This condition is somewhat alleviated by the location of the group within the hurricane belt, where severe cyclonic, tropical storms are likely to develop, bringing water to high and low islands alike.

Overall the Fiji Islands enjoy a healthy climate presenting two seasons—December through April when it is hot and humid and May through November when it is cool, dry and exceptionally pleasant.

Yacht Entry

Entry to the Dominion of Fiji must be made at one of the three designated Ports of Entry—Suva, Lautoka, or Levuka. Passports are required and they must be valid for a period six months beyond the date of entry. A visa is not required for a stay up to 30 days which may be extended to a maximum duration of six months. You are required to have "sufficient" funds to support yourself while in the Dominion. Crew members other than bona fide owners of the boat are required to have an onward

ticket with documentation to enter another country or a return ticket to the country of their origin.

Yachts may visit Fiji under the following conditions of temporary entry:

1. Visiting yachts may enter and be kept temporarily in Fiji without payment of customs duty provided the condi-

205

tions of the Customs Tariff Concession Code are complied with. The conditions of the Code are:

That the vessel is the property of, or has been hired by, the Tourist or temporary resident and is imported solely for this personal use for a period not exceeding 12 months and will not be used commercially.

2. You must report your yacht inwards at a Customs Port on arrival in Fiji and must clear your yacht outwards at a Customs Port before leaving Fiji. You must report your yacht inwards at, and clear outwards from, any Customs Port at which you call while you are in Fiji waters.

3. Set out hereunder is a summary of other conditions relating to your yacht while it is in Fiji waters. You will be asked to sign a copy of this Notice saying that you understand and accept the conditions. Please ask the Customs Officer attending you if you do not fully understand the Notice. This is important as failure to comply with any of the conditions may render you liable to penalties under the Customs Laws.

4. Yachts and other vessels are liable to duty and tax on importation into Fiji. These charges are payable on your yacht if it is disposed of in Fiji, or if it is put to commercial use whilst in Fiji water, or if it is not exported

within 12 months of the date of its arrival in Fiji.

5. On first arrival you are required to make Customs Entry of your yacht and you must sign a declaration thereon that your yacht will not be used for any commercial purpose whilst in Fiji. The Customs Officer will assist you with this requirement.

6. If you wish to cruise within Fiji waters, in addition to

Medical Memo

Immunization requirements:

Vaccinations for smallpox, cholera and yellow fever are required if you have transited or visited within the last six days (smallpox 14 days) an area currently infected.

Local health situation:

There are no significant medical problems in Fiji. Mosquitoes can be a nuisance but they are not the malaria-carrying variety. Infectious hepatitis is occasionally reported.

Medical services:

Government hospitals and health care centers are located in all of the larger towns and in most outlying districts. There are private practitioners in the larger towns for those that can afford them. Dental and optical services are also available in the larger towns.

Drugs can be purchased from the chemists in the larger towns. Many United States drug products are stocked.

IAMAT Center:

Suva: 3 Victoria Parade
        Coordinator: J.T. Cassidy, MD, FRCPI, MRACP

Water:

Tap water in the principal populated areas is treated and reported to be safe. Water from all other sources should be considered suspect and always treated.

the Customs clearance you must obtain a clearance at any port whether a Customs Port or not, from the Coconut Pests and Diseases Board. Certain islands and places in Fiji are free of Rhinoceros Beetle and you may be proceeding from a "dirty" area to an uninfected area.

7.   No live animals, reptiles or birds of any kind, or fresh meat, fruit and vegetables on aboard the yacht may be landed or taken ashore. Some restriction whether such goods will be permitted to remain on board after your first arrival at a Customs Port may be enforced by officers of the Department of Agriculture.

The old clock tower at Levuka regulates the activities of the community.

8.   On arrival, all arms and ammunition must be cleared and surrendered to the Customs Officer for safe keeping by the Fiji Police. These may, by timely arrangement with the Police (48 hours at least), be collected before leaving Fiji.

9.   No high duty goods such as liquor, beer, tobacco and cigarettes or other bonded or drawback goods may be shipped duty free, as stores for yachts of less than 100 net tons.

10.   Yachtsmen require permits from an Immigration Officer before they disembark in Fiji, and if an Immigra-

tion Officer does not meet the yacht on its arrival, a message should be sent via the Customs Officer to the Immigration Office, or a telephone call made to that office (312-622) requesting the attendance of an Immigration Officer. He will need to be provided by the person in charge of the yacht with two copies of a manifest listing all persons aboard, and will need to see every person, every such person's passport, and receive from all concerned, a correctly completed passenger arrival card. In addition he may require the production of onward tickets or security bonds from any person or persons aboard. Before leaving Fiji, all such persons should report to the Immigration Office with their passport, for outward Immigration clearance, specifying their date, time and means of departure, and next port of call and E.T.A.

Check list for visiting Fijian waters:

First Port of Entry

Customs Clearance*
   Declare all Animals
   Declare all Firearms
   Declare all Dutiable Goods
   Sign Customs Declaration sheet

Immigration
   Two copies of Manifest
   Passports and Crew Identification
   Visas where necessary
   Passenger Arrival Cards
   Bond or Onward Arrangements for Crew
   Financial Status Statement

Health
   Clearance from Port Health Officer

Cruising Fiji Waters

Fijian Affairs
   Permission to cruise Lau Group

Customs*
   Customs Clearance Outwards From "Port of Entry"
   Customs Clearance Inwards To "Port of Entry"

Departing Fiji

Customs*
   Customs Clearance Outwards

Immigration
   Departure Cards All Crew
   Two Lists of Crew
   Details Next Destination
   ETA Next Destination

*You must report entry and exit to Customs at each Port of Entry that you visit.

Ovalau, Levuka, was chosen as the early capitol of Fiji for seafaring reasons. It has a barrier reef three-quarters mile offshore giving protection from the Pacific swells and two fortuitously-placed passes allowed their huge sailing canoes to sail in and out of the harbor. Today Levuka is a quiet, unspoiled Port of Entry inviting yachties to enjoy a touch of Fijian history.

When entering Fiji, anchor in a quarantine area and fly the Q flag requesting pratique. At Suva, the quarantine buoy is near the Royal Suva Yacht Club. Health officials will give the first clearance and nobody is to go ashore until it has been obtained. Pets are not welcome on shore and a bond of $100 will have to be posted if you have one on board. Liquor import duties may be paid or the liquor may be bonded. Guns will be impounded. If you take a motorbike ashore, it will have to be licensed and you will need to obtain insurance on it.

Yacht Facilities

Suva: Upon arrival anchor near or tie up to the quarantine buoy to await the arrival of a Health Officer. After pratique has been granted, proceed to Kings Wharf for customs and immigration clearance. Liquor and tobacco will be placed in bond and your firearms must be surrendered to the police.

Anchorage may then be taken in any part of Suva Harbor but the Royal Suva Yacht Club area at Korovou is a favored area. The yacht club charges $F2.00 per week per person or $F10.00 per boat for the use of their facilities.

After properly clearing into Fiji at Suva and paying your respects to the Royal Suva Yacht Club, you may want to spend some time at the Tradewinds Marina in the Bay of Islands. It is a favorite gathering place for overseas yachts and the Tradewinds Hotel provides some welcome facilities such as showers and toilets (which you must use in this small bay), a swimming pool, restaurant, trash disposal, and fuel and water. The shower and head facilities cost $F1.50 per person per week and dock space moored Tahitian style is $F7.50 per week. There is, however, plenty of good anchoring space in the bay over a mud bottom.

If you plan on spending the hurricane season at Suva

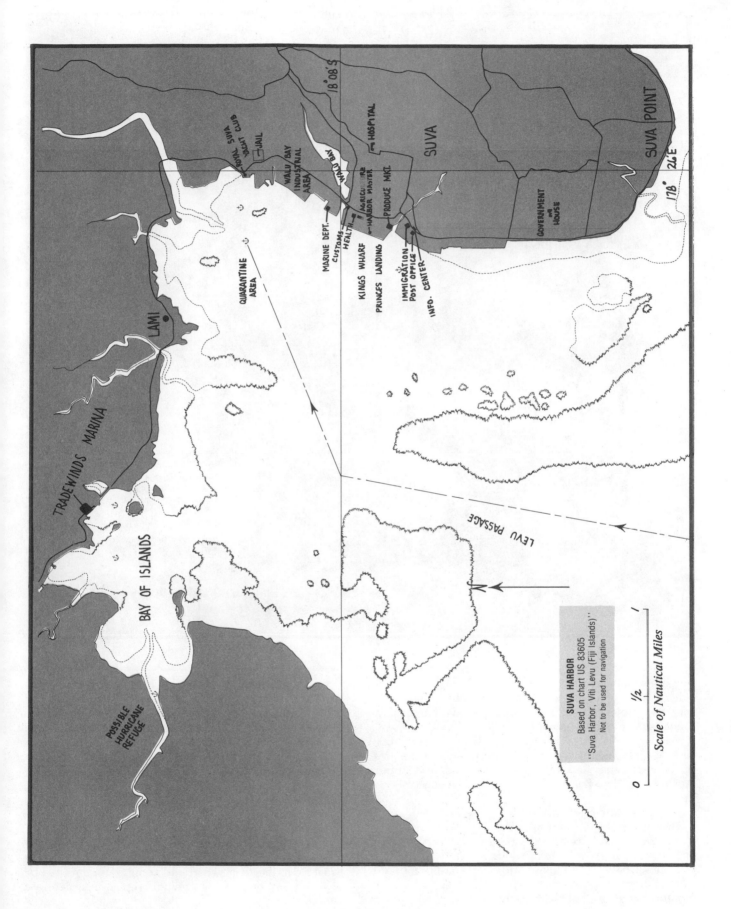

18° 08' S

ROYAL SUVA YACHT CLUB

JAIL

WALU BAY INDUSTRIAL AREA

WALU BAY

HOSPITAL

SUVA

SUVA POINT

AGRICULTURE
HARBOR MASTER

PRODUCE MKT.

178° E

177° E

MARINE DEPT.

CUSTOMS

HEALTH

KINGS WHARF

PRINCES LANDING

IMMIGRATION

POST OFFICE

INFO. CENTER

GOVERNMENT
HOUSE

QUARANTINE
AREA

LAMI

TRADEWINDS MARINA

BAY OF ISLANDS

POSSIBLE
HURRICANE
REFUGE

LEVU PASSAGE

N

SUVA HARBOR
Based on chart US 83605
"Suva Harbor, Viti Levu (Fiji Islands)"
Not to be used for navigation

Scale of Nautical Miles

0   ½   1

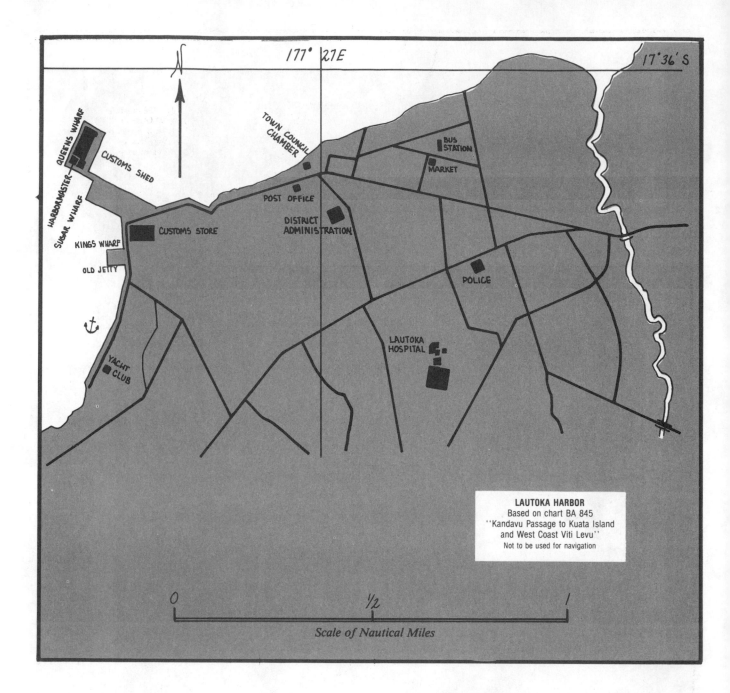

LAUTOKA HARBOR
Based on chart BA 845
"Kandavu Passage to Kuata Island
and West Coast Viti Levu"
Not to be used for navigation

Scale of Nautical Miles

you may want to check out Kumbuna Creek on the west side of the Bay of Islands as a hurricane refuge. It may offer some protection although in a full blown hurricane it would still be questionable.

Slipways and workshops are available in Suva Harbor to help with yacht repairs but hardware and mechanical items are scarce and may have to be ordered from Australia or New Zealand. Principal maintenance shops are:

Williams Marine (engines)
Bish Engineering (mechanical)
Amalgamated Wireless (electronics)
International Aeradio (electroncs)
Millers Boat Yard (haulout and mechanical)

These shops are set up mostly to handle ships and workboats but can help with yacht repairs.

Fuel and water are obtainable at King's Wharf. If you lay along the wharf for other than taking on fuel and water, you will have to pay wharf fees which amount to $F1.00 per 12 hour period. Provisions of just about all types can be obtained in Suva.

Lautoka: This is Fiji's second largest port with plenty of anchoring room for yachts inside Vio Island. Water is available and some provisions but only limited repair facilities exist.

Levuka: There is good anchorage in the harbor protected by a reef ¾ miles offshore. Water and diesel fuel are available at the main wharf and some provisions can be obtained ashore. Only limited repair facilities are available.

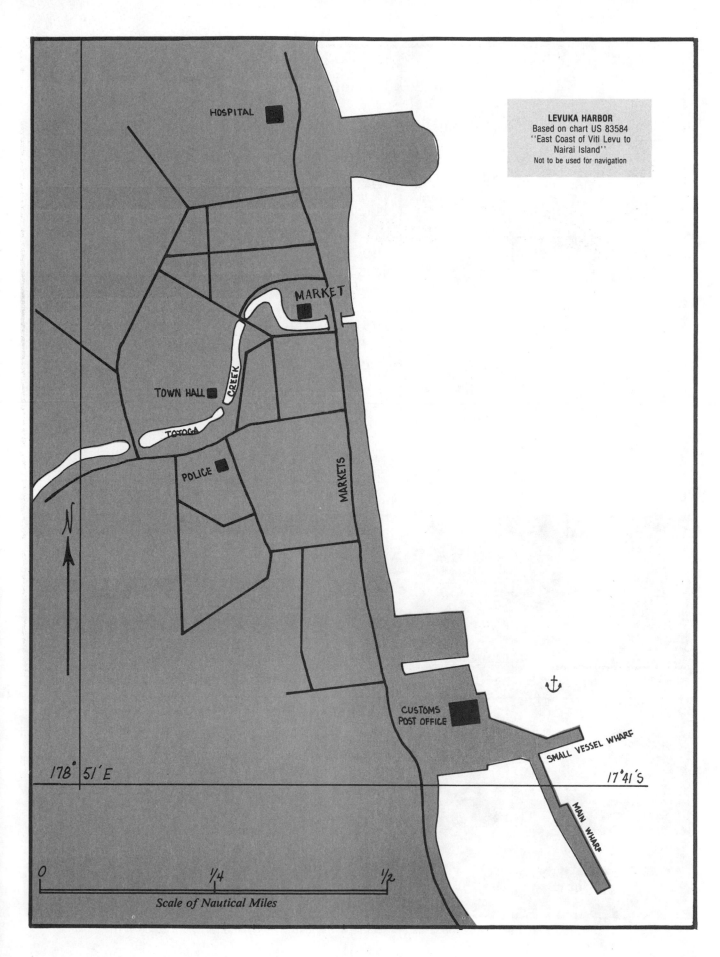

LEVUKA HARBOR
Based on chart US 83584
"East Coast of Viti Levu to
Nairai Island"
Not to be used for navigation

HOSPITAL

MARKET

TOWN HALL

CREEK

TOTOGA

POLICE

MARKETS

N

CUSTOMS
POST OFFICE

SMALL VESSEL WHARF

178° 51′ E

17° 41′ S

MAIN WHARF

0   1/4   1/2

Scale of Nautical Miles

211

Radio Communications

Station name and call	Location		Frequency Transmit/Receive	Service hours LMT	Type of service
Suva Radio (3DP)	18°07'06"S 178°26'34"E		500 kHz	24 hours	CW-marine operations
			2182 kHz - calling	24 hours	RT - marine operations
		Working	2162/2111 kHz 4078.8/4377.4 kHz 8262/8796 kHz		
			6204	24 hours	RT - South Pacific Safety Frequency
Harbor Master (Suva)			Channel 16	24 hours	
Radio Fiji (Suva)	18°04'12"S 178°32'06"E		560 kHz	Sun-Fri 0555-2300 Sat. 0555-2400	Commercial broadcast (Radio Fiji 1)
			710 kHz (also 90.6 MHz)		(Radio Fiji 2)
Radio Fiji (Lautoka)	17°36'45"S 177°27'51"E		640 kHz	0500Sun-Fri 0555-2300 Sat. 055-2400	(Radio Fiji 1)
			890 kHz (also 94.5 MHz)		(Radio Fiji 2)

Supplies of fresh native foods are transported to the market by traditional poling canoe.

Chapter 18

WALLIS & FUTUNA ISLANDS

The Country

The Wallis and Futuna Islands consist of two sections, both of which are French Overseas Territories located just north of the Fiji group. They are groups of small volcanic and coral islands that have a combined land area of 93 square miles and a total population of about 8,500. Although geographically located in Melanesia, the people are Polynesians who originally came from Tonga.

The Wallis group consists of the main island of Uvea and twenty-two outlying islets enclosed within a single barrier reef that classifies the unit as an almost-atoll. Uvea is seven by four miles in extent and rises to a maximum height of 479 feet. Its population of roughly 5,700 once was engaged in a flourishing copra business. Most of the palms, however, were wiped out by the rhinoceros beetle and in 1970 the people had reverted to subsistence farming. The soil is rich and grows virtually every type of tropical fruit in abundance, including oranges and pineapples. Uvea's encircling islets are mostly uninhabited but are used occasionally for minor agricultural and fishing pursuits.

The Futuna (sometimes called Hoorn) group consists of two volcanic high islands, Alofi and Futuna. These islands are higher than Uvea, rising to 2,629 and 1,310 feet, respectively. Both are well watered and densely wooded, containing valuable stands of timber that are extensively exploited as a source of cash income. The two islands have an area of about thirty-five square miles and a total population of about 3,000.

Wallis and Futuna were the only French territories in the Pacific to continue under a Vichy administration until after Pearl Harbor. The Wallis and Futuna Islands were until 1959 under the jurisdiction of the administration of New Caledonia. Local government, however, had been headed by indigenous sovereigns since the time of the French-established protectorate in the late 1880s.

The Polynesian population, thought to have migrated from Tonga originally, was less than 5,000 in the 1920s. Most of the people lived on Wallis. In 1959 they chose by referendum to become a territory of overseas France, as were New Caledonia and French Polynesia. After the referendum, in which 94 percent of the voters concurred, Wallis and Futuna were removed from the jurisdiction of New Caledonia and were more closely integrated into the metropolitan political structure. French citizenship was given to the islanders.

In 1970, as formerly, subsistence farming and fishing were supplemented by copra production. The traditional law and customs of the islanders were retained under the

administration of the traditional rulers. Population pressure on these small and poor islands led to migration of laborers to the New Hebrides, New Caledonia, and Fiji.

The Weather

The Wallis and Futuna islands are located only 130 miles

Wallis and Futuna Islands
French Overseas Territory

Port of Entry:

Mata Utu, Wallis Islands   13°17′S, 176°08′W

Distances between ports in nautical miles:

Between *Mata Utu* and:

Apia, Western Samoa	130
Funafuti, Tuvalu	330
Futuna Island	130
Nuku'alofa, Tonga	480
Santo, New Hebrides	1500
Suva, Fiji	445

Standard time:

12 hours fast on GMT

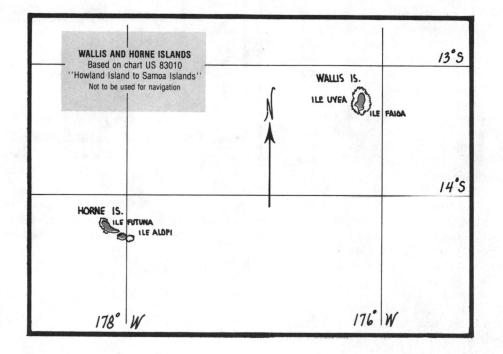

west of Apia, Western Samoa, hence its weather patterns are similar to those described for the Samoas. The only difference is that the group is farther into the South Pacific hurricane zone and could be expected to experience more of the seasonal tropical storms.

Yacht Entry and Facilities

The official Port of Entry of the Wallis and Futuna islands is at Mata Uta, Uvea, in the Wallis group. There a French Administrator will process customs and immigration papers and ascertain the health of the crew. A deputy administrator resides at Sigave Bay, Futuna Island, and visits to that island group should be preceded by a visit to the deputy administrator. Passports and papers showing boat ownership are all that is required.

As with all atolls care should be used in entering the lagoon surrounding Uvea. Enter at slack low water to avoid high currents in the main pass, Honikulu. Once inside, there are three bays in a row affording good anchorage with varying degrees of protection. The first bay is Mua and it offers protection from the southeast trades in the lee of Faioa Island and from the northerlies by Uvea, itself. Unfortunately, it is away from all the action. Just off Mua Bay, the next in line going north, is the small village of Gahi. It has a pier and some provisions are available. The third bay is Matu Utu with an anchorage

WALLIS ET FUTUNA 60F RF
FIJI 72
POSTE AERIENNE
FESTIVAL DES ARTS DU PACIFIQUE SUD

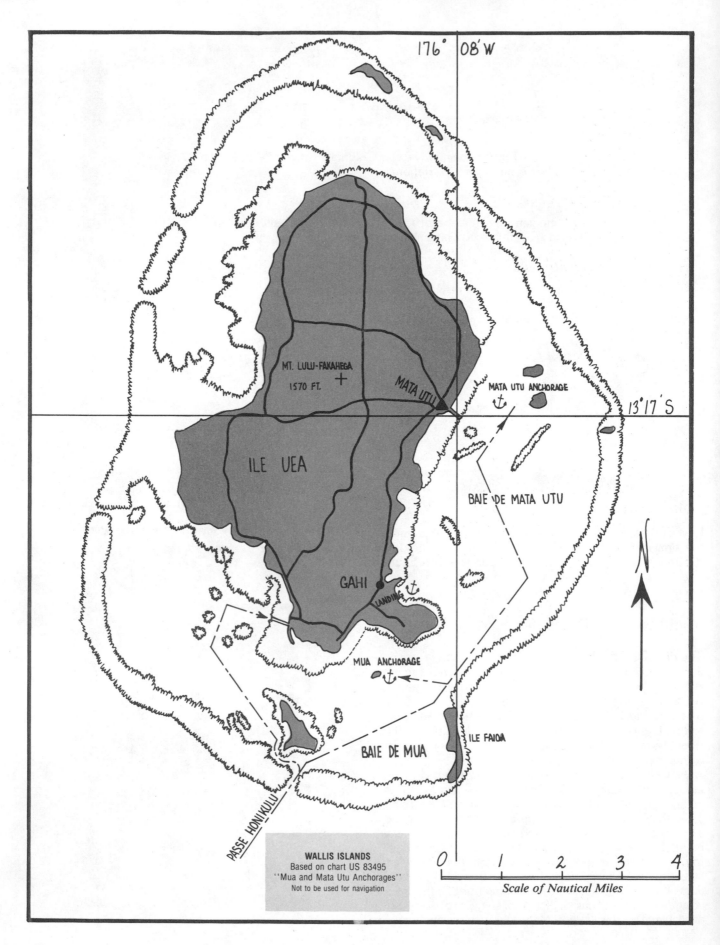

176° 08' W

13° 17' S

MT. LULU-FAKAHEGA

1570 FT. +

MATA UTU

MATA UTU ANCHORAGE ⚓

BAIE DE MATA UTU

ILE UEA

GAHI ●

⚓

LANDING

MUA ANCHORAGE ⚓

BAIE DE MUA

ILE FAIOA

PASSE HONIKULU

N

WALLIS ISLANDS
Based on chart US 83495
"Mua and Mata Utu Anchorages"
Not to be used for navigation

0   1   2   3   4

Scale of Nautical Miles

Medical Memo

Immunization requirements:

No official statement but yachties are urged not to land if they have any illness on board or have recently visited an area having cholera, smallpox or yellow fever.

Local health situation:

The native population suffers from filariasis and there is still some leprosy being treated in the leprosy hospital. There are no reported medical problems with visitors.

Health services;

There is a hospital at Mata-Utu staffed by a French army doctor. In addition, there are two clinics, one of which is at Futuna. Serious illnesses or major injuries would have to be taken elsewhere. There are no dental or optical services available in this group. Drugs are available only through the hospital and clinics.

Water:

You should consider the water suspect and treat it.

just off the fringing reef at the village of the same name. You must visit here to check in with the Administrator but the anchorage is totally exposed to the east and gets rough in stormy tradewind weather.

The rhinoceros beetle has almost totally destroyed the coconut crop so the islanders subsist mostly on indigenous fruits and vegetables like manioc. Fishing is also done for subsistence. There is fresh water available.

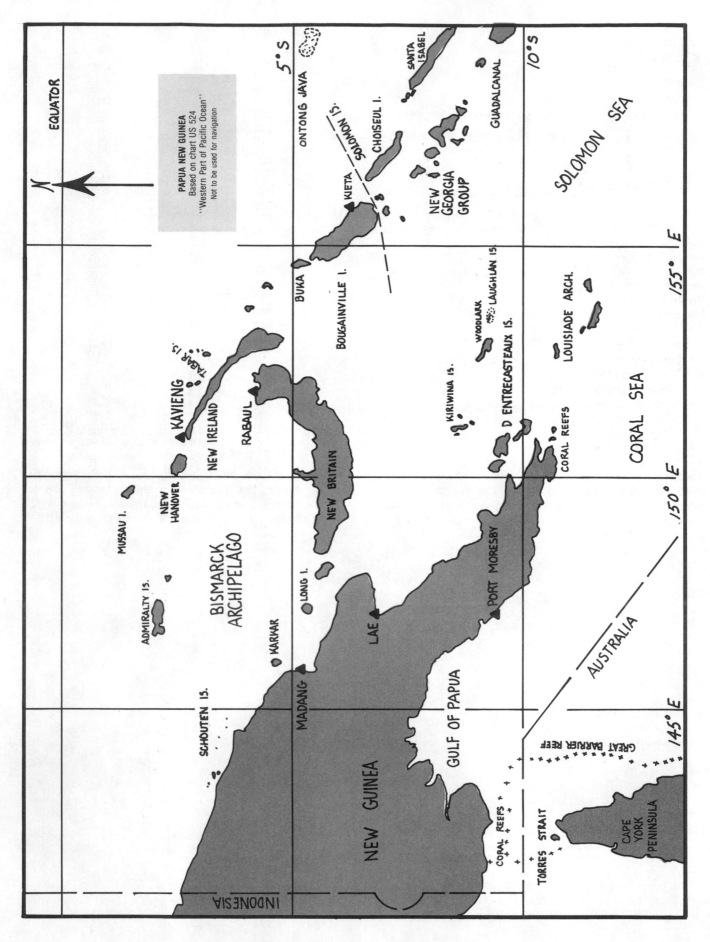

PAPUA NEW GUINEA
Based on chart US 524
"Western Part of Pacific Ocean"
Not to be used for navigation

EQUATOR

5°S

10°S

ONTONG JAVA

SANTA ISABEL

GUADALCANAL

SOLOMON IS.

CHOISEUL I.

KIETA

NEW GEORGIA GROUP

SOLOMON SEA

BUKA

BOUGAINVILLE I.

WOODLARK

LAUGHLAN IS.

KIRIWINA IS.

D ENTRECASTEAUX IS.

LOUISIADE ARCH.

155°E

KAVIENG

TABAR IS.

NEW IRELAND

RABAUL

NEW HANOVER

MUSSAU I.

ADMIRALTY IS.

BISMARCK ARCHIPELAGO

NEW BRITAIN

LONG I.

KARKAR

SCHOUTEN IS.

MADANG

LAE

PORT MORESBY

CORAL REEFS

CORAL SEA

150°E

AUSTRALIA

NEW GUINEA

GULF OF PAPUA

GREAT BARRIER REEF

145°E

CORAL REEFS

TORRES STRAIT

CAPE YORK PENINSULA

INDONESIA

Chapter 19
PAPUA NEW GUINEA
(Tanna Papua)

The Country

Papua New Guinea lies in the southwest Pacific about 100 miles northeast of Australia. It includes the eastern half of the island of New Guinea; the Bismarck Archipelago of which New Britain, New Ireland, and Manus are the largest islands; Bougainville and Buka islands in the Western Solomons; and the Trobriand, Woodlark, D'Entrecasteaux, and Louisiade island groups to the east of the New Guinea mainland.

The main island has about 85 percent of the land area. A complex system of mountains extends from the eastern end of the island to the western boundary with Indonesian Irian Jaya. Precipitous slopes, knife-sharp ridges, great outcroppings of mountains to heights of almost 15,000 feet, and broad upland valleys at altitudes of 5,000 to 10,000 feet characterize this area. Large rivers flow to the south, north, and east; few are navigable except by small boats in the lower reaches. The largest of them, the Fly, rises in the mountains of western Papua, flows over 700 miles through the southwestern plains, and can be navigated for nearly 500 miles by shallow draft vessels drawing less than 8 feet. The same is true of the Sepik which rises in the central cordillera but first flows northward and then east into the Bismarck Sea. Between the northern and the central range of mountains is the Central Depression which includes the valleys of the Sepik, Ramu, and Markham rivers. On the smaller islands, mountains cover much of the area; many of them are active or dormant volcanoes and some reach peaks of 8,500 feet.

Along most of the coasts are lowlands and rolling foothills of varying widths. Swamps cover large areas of the country, and on the southwest littoral of the mainland the great delta plain of the Daru coast forms one of the most extensive swamps in the world. The Sepik and Ramu rivers also flow for hundreds of miles through large riverine swamps of sago, bamboo, and other forest land.

The luxuriant rain forest which covers most of Papua New Guinea gives a misleading impression of widespread highly fertile soils. In fact many of the inland soils are shallow, heavily leached, and relatively infertile. Notable exceptions are the broad lowland valleys of the Markham and Ramu rivers and many highland valley systems where alluvial loams or soils of volcanic origin can be very productive. The greatest soil fertility problem is the leaching which results from heavy rainfall. This has already degraded the soils of the Sepik and Daru plains.

As a consequence of these geographical and climatic conditions, establishing adequate transport and communications facilities is difficult and expensive. These conditions inhibit the development of some of the interior areas and impact upon the entire process of social, political, and economic integration and development.

Little is known about the pre-history of Papua New Guinea, but it is now established that man was in New Guinea highlands at least by 8,000 B.C., and the probable first arrival of man in the area may have been as early as 50,000 B.C. There appears to have been several migrations from Asia by way of Indonesia over a great

Papua New Guinea
(Tanna Papua)
A parliamentary democracy

Ports of Entry:

Port Moresby, New Guinea	9°29'S, 147°08'E
Lae, New Guinea	6°44'S, 146°59'E
Madang, New Guinea	5°12'S, 145°49'E
Rabaul, New Britain	4°13'S, 152°12'E
Kavieng, New Ireland	2°35'S, 150°48'E
Kieta, Bouganville	6°13'S, 155°38'E

Distances between ports in nautical miles:

Between *Rabaul* and:

Apia, Western Samoa	2230
Agana, Guam	1190
Auckland, New Zealand	2350
Avatiu, Cook Islands	2990
Honolulu, Hawaii	3360
Lae, New Guinea	450
Levuka, Fiji	1840
Noumea, New Caledonia	1380
Omura, Bonin Islands	2010
Papeete, Society Islands	3530
Ponape, Caroline Islands	850
Selwyn Bay, Solomon Islands	690
Talomako, New Hebrides	1100
Yap, Caroline Islands	1200

Between *Lae* and:

Agana, Guam	1315

Noumea, New Caledonia	1520
Rabaul, New Britain	450

Standard time:

10 hours fast on GMT

length of time, and the earliest migrants were evidently hunters, not agriculturalists, who used bone and stone tools and weapons. Later migrations introduced agriculture and plants such as yams, taro, sugar cane, bananas, and green vegetables and animals such as pigs and dogs. There was no central government during the early history. Each community was virtually its own government, often with little or no contact with other areas or groups.

The first Europeans to sight New Guinea were probably the Portuguese and Spanish navigators sailing in the South Pacific in the early part of the 16th century. Don Jorge de Meneses in 1526-27 accidentally came upon the principal island and is credited with naming it Papua. The term "New Guinea" was applied to the island in 1545 by a Spaniard, Ynigo Ortis de Retez because of some fancied resemblance between the island inhabitants and those found on the African Guinea coast. Although European nagivators visited the islands and explored their coastlines for the next 170 years, little was known of the inhabitants until the late 19th century.

On November 6, 1884, a British protectorate was proclaimed over the southern coast of New Guinea (the area called Papua) and its adjacent islands. The protectorate, called British New Guinea, was annexed outright on September 4, 1888. The possession was placed under the authority of the commonwealth of Australia in 1902.

As a consequence of Europe's growing need for coconut oil, Godeffroy's of Hamburg, the largest trading firm in the Pacific, began trading for copra in the New Guinea islands. In 1884 Germany formally took possession of what later came to be called the Trust Territory of New Guinea and put its administration in the hands of a chartered company. In 1899 The German Imperial Government assumed direct control of German New Guinea. In 1914 Australian troops occupied German New Guinea, and it remained under Australian military control until 1921. The British Government, on behalf of the Commonwealth of Australia, assumed a mandate

Port Moresby, the capitol of Papua New Guinea, is on a peninsula between the harbor shown here and beautiful Ela Beach off the bottom right of the picture. It has most of the amenities of the modern world including the growing pains of suburbia. Although situated in the Tropics, it does not have the luxuriant growth associated with tropical areas.

from the League of Nations for governing the Territory of New Guinea in 1920. It was administered under this mandate until the Japanese invasion in December 1941 brought about the suspension of Australian civil administration. Following the surrender of the Japanese in 1945 civil administration of both Papua and New Guinea was restored, and under the Papua New Guinea Provisional Administration Act, 1945-46, both Papua and New Guinea were combined as an administrative union.

The Papua and New Guinea Act of 1949 formally approved the placing of New Guinea under the International Trusteeship system and confirmed the administrative union of New Guinea and Papua under the title of "The Territory of Papua and New Guinea." Elections in 1972 resulted in the formation of a Ministry headed by Chief Minister Michael Somare who pledged to lead the country to self-government and then to independence prior to the next scheduled elections in 1976. Self government was achieved on December 1, 1973. Since that date Papua New Guinea has moved rapidly toward full independence, and the political and administrative responsibilities of government have been progressively transferred from the Australian government to that of Papua New Guinea.

The Constitution provides for a national government with legislative, executive, and judicial branches. The parliament is a single-chamber legislature based on a modified Westminster system consisting of not less than 81 nor more than 87 elected open members, not less than 18 elected regional members, and not more than 3 nominated members. The term of office for elected members normally is for a 5-year period. Members of Parliament (other than the nominated members) are elected under a system of universal, adult, citizen suffrage.

The Constitution considers Her Majesty Queen Elizabeth II of the United Kingdom as Head of State. She is represented in Papua New Guinea by a Governor General and makes this appointment on the advice of the Papua New Guinea National Executive Council (Cabinet) following parliament's decision on the nominations. The selection of a Governor General is limited to Papua New Guinea citizens and the appointee acts under the advice of the National Executive Council. Executive power is vested in the Cabinet led by the Prime Minister—the leader of the majority party of coalition in the National Legislature. The Cabinet is chosen by the Prime Minister from among the members of parliament.

The Papua New Guinea legal system is largely based on that of the Commonwealth of Australia. The National Judicial System consists of the Supreme Court, the National Court, and such other courts as may be established. The Supreme Court is the final court of appeals; it has inherent powers to review all acts of the National Court and has original jurisdiction in constitutional matters. The Constitution provides a human rights chapter which is similar to that found in Western democratic systems.

The indigenous population is one of the most heterogeneous in the Pacific. Papua New Guinea has hundreds of separate communities, most with only a few hundred people. Divided by language, customs, and tradition,

some of these communities have engaged in tribal warfare with their neighbors for centuries. Some groups, until recently, have been unaware of the existence of neighboring groups a few miles away. About 700 separate languages are spoken, and a significant number of them are wholly different from any other. Only a small number of them are spoken by more than a few thousand persons, while Melanesian Pidgin and Hiri Motu serve as lingua franca, neither language is universally spoken. English is spoken by the relatively small group of educated people.

About 722,000 people live in Papua and the rest in New Guinea. Although the overall population density is low, it is unevenly distributed with pockets of overpopulation. The Western District of Papua, covering 40,000 square miles or nearly 22 percent of the country, has only about 4 percent of the population. By contrast the Eastern Highlands District with less than 4 percent of land area has about 11 percent of the population. Within this

district and in the Chimbu District are small areas exceeding 500 persons per square mile. The greatest concentration is in the highlands area on the New Guinea mainland where there are now an estimated 950,000 people or nearly 40 percent of the entire population.

A considerable urban drift has occurred in the past 10 years, and the urban growth rate for 1966-71 has been calculated at 14 percent. The cities of Lae and Port Moresby have shown the biggest increases and in the past few years have grown about 10 percent per year. The indigenous and non-indigenous populations of major cities and towns, according to 1971 census figures are:

	Indigenous	Non-indigenous	Total
Port Moresby	59,563	16,944	76,507
Rabaul	33,093	4,226	37,319
Lae	32,077	6,630	38,707
Wewak	13,837	1,178	15,015
Madang	14,695	2,170	16,865

Estimates of populations in 1979 for Port Moresby (107,000), Lae (45,000), and Madang (20,000) indicate a continuing high urban attraction.

Over half of the population are nominally Christian. Of these over 490,000 are Catholic, more than 320,000 Lutheran, and the balance are members of other Protes-

The town of Lae was built in response to a need for an airfield to serve the nearby goldmining activities. It is now the third largest shipping port in Papua New Guinea and a Port of Entry.

tant sects. The non-Christian half of the indigenous population adheres to magico-religious beliefs and practices that are an integral part of their traditional cultures. They are numerous and diverse in character and are largely based on ancestor and spirit worship.

The chief characteristics of the traditional Papua New Guinea social structure are; (1) the practice of subsistence economy; (2) the recognition of bonds of kinship with obligations extending beyond the immediate family group, (3) generally egalitarian relationships with an em-

phasis on acquired, rather than inherited, status; and (4) a strong attachment of the people to land. Most Papua New Guineans are still deeply associated with this traditional social structure, which finds its roots in village life.

Papua New Guinea's economy is solidly based on both the exploitation of mineral resources and on traditional tropical crops. It has undergone rapid change over the past half dozen years. The country had a typical South Pacific plantation-oriented economy until the mid-1960's when the first major copper mines were discovered at

A short distance from Port Moresby is the village of Hanuabada with its distinctive houses built on stilts over the water.

Panguan on Bougainville Island.

The majority of the indigenous inhabitants are subsistence farmers, but education and foreign investment are increasing the acreage of commercial crops for export. On the coast, near centers like Lae, Madang, Rabaul and Port Moresby, there are large plantations growing coconuts, cocoa and rubber. In the highland area of Goroka and Mt. Hagen, coffee and tea are grown. At Bulolo, one of the largest plywood mills in the world is supplying all of the country's needs in this field plus a surplus for export.

Expatriate-owned plantations, which account for under one percent of the arable land, are slowly being sold back to Papua New Guinea nationals—usually groups of individuals laying claim to the land, on the basis that it was theirs before it was alienated, or individuals organized into cooperatives. The return of land is expected to continue for several years until foreign ownership is phased out.

Jetsam and Flotsam

Currency:

The Papua New Guinea dollar is called a kina and equals 100 toea. Coins are issued in values of 1, 2, 5, 10, 20, and 50 toea and 1 kina. At press time the rate of exchange was $US1 = 80 toea.

Langauge:

There are over 700 different languages used by the various tribes of Papua New Guinea. English is the official language of business and government and Pidgin and Hiri Motu are used as lingua francas.

Electricity:

240 volt, 50 Hz AC

Postal Address:

Postal service is nominally good to the Ports of Entry. An example address is:
Yacht (   )
Poste Restante
General Post Office
Port Moresby, New Guinea
PAPUA NEW GUINEA

External Affairs Representative:

Australian embassies or consulates

Information Center:

Papua New Guinea Office of Tourism
P.O. Box 773
Port Moresby,
PAPUA NEW GUINEA

Cruising Library:

Papua New Guinea Handbook, Pacific Publications, Ltd., Box 3408, General Post Office, Sydney, NSW 2001 Australia

The Weather

The most noticeable feature of the climate is the seasonal change in the direction of the winds. The East Indies lie along and just south of the equator, between the two trade-wind systems. In the summer of the Northern Hemisphere low barometric pressure prevails on the continent of Asia, causing an indraft of air from the western Pacific. At that time the southeast trades extend northward, resulting in an air stream which crosses the East Indies from the southeast to northwest, and is drawn further northwestward into the low-pressure system over Asia. This movement is strengthened by the relatively high pressure prevailing over Australia at that time.

In the northern winter, pressure is high over Asia and relatively low over and to the immediate northward of Australia. This distribution of pressure causes outflowing winds from Asia, which combine with the northeast trades, and extend southeastward across the equator and over practically all of the East Indies.

The cause of these pressure differences is found in large annual range of temperatures over the continents of Australia and Asia, as compared with the slight temperature changes over the adjacent ocean surfaces. As a result of the air circulation thus produced, in combination with the trades, there are pronounced seasonal changes in the winds, which are known as monsoons.

At the height of the monsoon season in the East Indies region, the winds blow with much constancy from one quarter. There is, however, considerable variation in wind direction during the transitional periods between monsoons.

To a considerable extent the character of the weather depends upon the direction of the prevailing monsoon, the east or "good" monsoon is relative drier, though its moisture content increases as it progresses. Its direction of movement is from the east and southeast, and it blows with greatest constancy in August. Much haziness characterizes this monsoon, especially in the southern part of the archipelago.

The west or so-called "bad" monsoon blows from the west and northwest, and reaches its height in January. Its moisture content is high, especially in the south, so that it is quite depressing as compared with the east monsoon. In the vicinity of the equator there is not much difference, so far as humidity is concerned, between the two monsoons.

While these winds are known as east and west monsoons, their directions are not the same in all parts of the archipelago. In some northwestern sections, for example, the winds are northerly in the northern winter and southerly in summer. Nevertheless they are termed

The Koki Market at Port Moresby offers fruits and vegetables fresh from the fields.

Water is still a primary means of transport as native peoples come in outrigger canoes to make their purchases at the Madang market.

"east" and "west" monsoons, and the terms are so used here.

The transitional periods occur as an average in April and in October or November. In the northern part of the archipelago the "west" monsoon prevails for a longer period than it does in the southern part while the east monsoon prevails longer in the south than in the north. Hence the transitional periods vary somewhat with latitude. There is also some variation from year to year in the general direction, duration, and force of the monsoons.

In the extreme southeastern part of the region covering Papua New Guinea, including the Louisiade Archipelago and the northern portion of the Coral Sea, the southeast trade wind prevails nearly all the year. The winds tend to be light and variable from January to March, but in other months they blow from the east-southeast and southeast much of the time. From May to September they are strong and of great constancy, occasionally at all seasons the winds of this area rise to gale force.

Westward of New Guinea, between 5° and 10° south latitude, the east monsoon blows with great constancy from May to September.

The average velocity of the west monsoon in January

in the open sea is about 10 knots, except in the area northwest of New Guinea, where it averages about 6 knots. The velocity of the west monsoon gradually diminishes until April, when the average velocity for the region as a whole is 6 to 8 knots.

The east monsoon sets in during May and reaches its greatest speed in August, when it averages about 13 knots with the greatest wind strength (15 knots) over the Coral Sea. The east monsoon then gradually diminishes until November and December, when the average speed for the open sea in the region as a whole is about 8 knots.

Owing to the unequal heating and cooling of islands and adjacent seas, land and sea breezes are developed in the harbors and along the coasts of the islands. In some situations these local interchanges between land and sea are not strong enough to reverse the prevailing monsoon, but serve to produce diurnal changes in wind velocity. In general, the monsoon becomes stronger in the daytime on coasts facing into the wind, and is weaker at night. On lee shores the opposite is true. If an island affords a good protection against the monsoon, the land and sea breezes are likely to be the dominant winds on lee shores.

Where the monsoon blows more or less along the coast, the local effect is a daily variation in the direction of the winds, but this variation is not nearly so pronounced as the changes attending full development of land and sea breezes.

The land breeze begins to be felt some time after sundown, usually toward midnight, and continues until after daylight. The sea breeze begins about mid-morning. Very strong land winds blow locally in harbors and along shores in places where the mountains are near the sea.

The strongest regular winds of the region are found locally where the monsoons blow through narrow straits bordered by elevated land.

The extreme southern part of the area including the Louisade Archipelago, lies within the influence of the southeast trades. The west monsoon does not reach this area with any dependability, even in January and February, and easterly and northeasterly winds continue to blow frequently in these months. In March the winds are variable, mostly easterly. From April to November the southeast trades, reinforced by the east monsoon, are felt

with much constancy and force. The average speed is 12 to 15 knots and it rises to gale force frequently during the prevalence of the east monsoon. The prevailing wind in December is from the east.

The region covered is infrequently affected by tropical cyclones. Typhoons are fairly common in the Philippine area and a few of them move on tracks which lie far enough to the southward to affect the section immediately to the south of Mindanao. Occasionally, when passing to the northward of New Guinea, they cause strong winds and sometimes heavy rains on the north coast. It is extremely rare that a typhoon center actually passes south of Mindanao, however. When they do occur there, they come from the east and continue on a westerly or north-westerly course into the China Sea.

Tropical cyclones are rather common in the waters bordering Australia and among the islands to the eastward. Those which pass over or close to Australia appear to originate in the region between Australia and the East Indies. One type moves south-westward across western Australia, or along the west coast and recurves to the southward. These originate chiefly in the waters near and to the eastward of Timor. Storms of the other type cross eastern Australia or skirt the eastern coast of the continent. They originate chiefly in the Coral Sea.

At least two of these storms have been recorded in the sea immediately to the southward of the eastern portion of New Guinea, between 145° and 150° east longitude. Both of them occurred in December.

The usual track of both of these types is such as to carry them away from the East Indies into higher latitudes.

Tropical cyclones occur infrequently within 6° to 8° of the equator, hence much of the region is free of danger from such storms. Cyclones forming or passing in neighboring higher latitudes cause heavy sea swells and sometimes strong winds and rain in the archipelago.

During the west monsoon there is much rain along the coast and squalls are frequent. The west ("wet") monsoon weakens in April and the east ("dry") monsoon becomes established in May, although the winds are variable in both months. The seasonal distribution of rainfall also depends on the topography, but as a rule the wet season extends from December to March and the dry season reaches its height in August and September. Overall, the best months for seeing New Guinea are April through September.

Average annual rainfall is high, ranging from 80 to 100 inches for most districts. Many areas receive more than 200 inches but a few, like Port Moresby, lie in a rain shadow and record figures as low as 40 inches or less annually.

In general, there is less rainfall in the southern part of the archipelago because the rains occur chiefly with the east monsoon, which contains less moisture there than the west monsoon. However, topographic effects result in very great differences in the distribution of rainfall.

Although wet/dry seasons exist in many zones, this term is relative since even in the so-called dry season, precipitation ranges from 2 to 4 inches a month in most areas.

While there are no systematic records of rainfall in the open sea in this region, the rainfall records at coast stations during periods when the winds blow from the sea, indicate that the rains at sea are much more regularly distributed through the day and the year than on the larger islands.

In the interior of the larger islands, rainfall occurs largely in the afternoon hours; this is also true along coasts when the wind blows from the interior. During the part of the year when the wind blows from the sea, the rains are distributed about equally throughout the 24 hours.

Thunderstorms occur frequently, especially during the transitional periods.

The mean annual temperature is 80°F throughout this region and the annual range of temperature is small. In the southeastern part of the area the highest temperatures occur, as a rule, in October and November, while in the northwestern part the period of highest temperatures is in April and May. Their warm periods coincide with the turning of the monsoons. On the smaller islands, and in the open sea, the difference in temperature between the warmest and coolest months is only about 2°F.

The daily range of temperatures is small at sea and in low areas near the sea. Day temperatures are, therefore, not excessively high, averaging for the year about 86°F as a daily maximum on the smaller islands and on the coasts of the larger islands. Night temperatures stay relatively high. For the region covered by this chapter the daily minimum at places near the sea is about 75°F as an average for the year.

Lowland humidity is uniformly high at about 80 percent, with very little seasonal variation. Fluctuations are much greater in the highlands, where temperatures are lower.

The barometer, on an average the year round, stands at about 1010 mbs at sea level. It is slightly higher in August and September (about 1012 mbs) and slightly lower in January (about 1000 mbs). The almost complete absence of traveling cyclones accounts for the fact that there are seldom any noteworthy changes in the barometer except the daily variations, with maxima at about 0900, and 2100, and minima at about 0300 and 1500. The daily range averages approximately 4 mbs.

Yacht Entry

The Ports of Entry for Papua New Guinea are Port Moresby (capital), Lae, and Madang on the island of New Guinea; Rabaul, New Britain, and Kavieng, New Ireland, both in the Bismarck Archipelago; and Kieta, Bouganville, which is geographically in the Solomon Islands group but politically is part of Papua New Guinea.

Visas are required for visits to Papua and must be obtained before arrival from PNG consulates such as at Suva and Wellington or from Australian consulates such as at New Caledonia. A passport is required for all crew members. Onward tickets must be in the possession of all crew members except the documented owners of the boat who must have ownership papers in their possession. The visas will require two passport-type photos but there is no charge. For stays longer than two months, you

The town of Rabaul and adjacent Simpson Bay look peaceful enough today but 1500 years ago a volcanic holocaust split open a mountain to form this topography. Rabaul is a Port of Entry and Papua New Guinea's third largest city.

must apply in person upon arrival for registration.

Papua New Guinea will issue a cruising permit for the yacht for a period of two months to coincide with the visas.

Yacht Facilities at Ports of Entry

Port Moresby: Yachts entering Port Moresby should anchor near the Papua Yacht Club and notify the customs officials of their presence by telephone. It is also possible to tie up to the Harbor Board's concrete jetty which is used as a landing place for small craft. The four small piers between the Government wharf and the L-head pier are privately owned and used for coastal shipping.

The Papua Yacht Club at Port Moresby has showers,

bar, lunch and dinner service. It is a socially active club and short-term membership can be obtained. There is a grid at the club and sufficient tidal range for doing bottom work on most boats.

There are two commercial shipyards with slipways which could haul out small boats and give repair services but there is little in the way of good small boat hardware available. Diesel fuel and gasoline are both available as is water.

Port Moresby is a town of about 100,000 persons and, being the capital of Papua New Guinea, it is the best place to resupply and reprovision in their country. Duty free stores to be used after leaving the country can be obtained here.

There are both Indonesian and Australian Consuls in

Medical Memo

Immunization requirements:

Smallpox and cholera vaccinations are required of all new arrivals. Also, a yellow fever vaccination is required if you have transited within the last six days an infected area.

Local health situation:

The hot, humid climate of Papua New Guinea and a still-primitive way of life away from the towns is a cause for concern of personal health. Native diseases are ringworm and the New Guinea sore. There is some dengue fever. the risk of malaria exists the year around in all parts of the country including the urban areas. It is recommended that crews take malaria drugs before arrival, during their stay, and after departure from the country. It is also recommended that crews be innoculated against typhoid and tetanus.

Health services:

The major hospitals are at Port Moresby, Goroka, Lae, and Nonga. Besides these, there are 15 provincial hospitals and many government health centers and aid posts. Private doctors practice in the main cities and native medical treatments still prevail in many of the outlying rural areas.

Dental care is available at Port Moresby and the main cities. An ophthalmologist practices at Port Moresby and an optometrist visits various parts of the country.

Drugs are available from several pharmacies in the larger towns and also at the hospitals and health centers.

IAMAT Center:

Port Moresby: Okari Street
              Coordinator: George Chong Wah, MD

Water:

Tap water in Port Moresby is reportedly good but it is recommended that all water be considered suspect and treated.

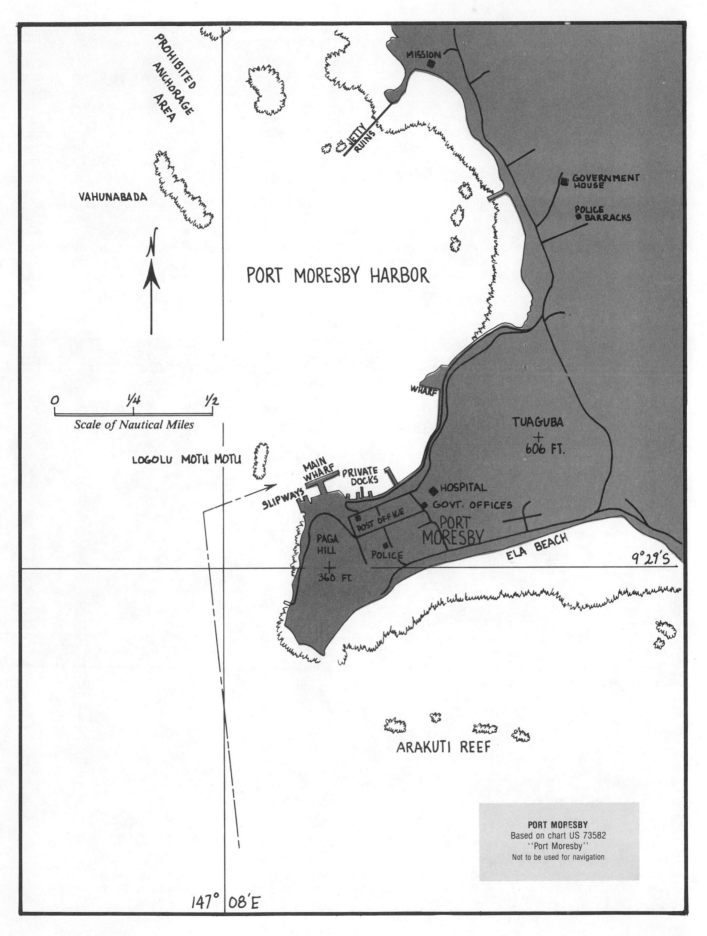

PROHIBITED ANCHORAGE AREA

VAHUNABADA

N

PORT MORESBY HARBOR

MISSION

JETTY RUINS

GOVERNMENT HOUSE

POLICE BARRACKS

0   ¼   ½
Scale of Nautical Miles

WHARF

TUAGUBA
+
606 FT.

LOGOLU MOTU MOTU

MAIN WHARF

PRIVATE DOCKS

SLIPWAYS

HOSPITAL

GOVT. OFFICES

POST OFFICE

PORT MORESBY

PAGA HILL
+
360 FT.

POLICE

ELA BEACH

9°29′S

ARAKUTI REEF

147° 08′E

PORT MORESBY
Based on chart US 73582
''Port Moresby''
Not to be used for navigation

Port Moresby so you can apply for visas there to visit those countries. When applying for visas also ask about a cruising permit for your boat.

Lae: The harbor at Lae is an open roadstead fairly well sheltered but open to the southeast. Small craft can tie up alongside the jetty with a steel pontoon head which has 8 feet of water alongside. The Customhouse is located nearby and you can either call them or walk over to announce your arrival.

Fuel and water are available at the main wharf but the water should be treated before use. Boat supplies and repair facilities are very limited here but provisions can be obtained from local stores and there is a bank.

Madang: The harbor at Madang is landlocked, therefore well sheltered and provides good anchoring. It is a small town of only 20,000 persons so facilities and supplies are limited. There is one slipway run by the Rabaul

Stevedore and Steamship Company which can handle small craft. Charges are reported to be 20 kina up and 20 kina down with a daily rate of 12 kina while on the ways. Local workshops can do minor engine and general repairs.

Diesel fuel is available in drums at the wharf.

Visitors can get a one month membership in the private Madang Club for a fee of 5 kina. There you can enjoy bar and meal service as well as TV and movie entertainment. The club can arrange for laundry service.

Rabaul: Simpson Harbor at Rabaul is a deep, completely sheltered harbor that is believed to be a large volcanic crater that was breached by the ocean to form an entry. It is considered to be one of the best harbors in the world. Proceed to the main wharf at the west end of Simpson Harbor to contact customs and port officials. There is ample anchoring area around the periphery of this one mile square harbor after you have checked in.

A short distance from Goroko in the Eastern Highlands is the village of the Asaro Mudmen. Legend has it that they were going to attack a Highlands village but first had to cross a rain-swollen river having heavy mud banks. Emerging from the river, they were covered with mud and in their crouched stance going into battle they terrified the defenders who quickly fled.

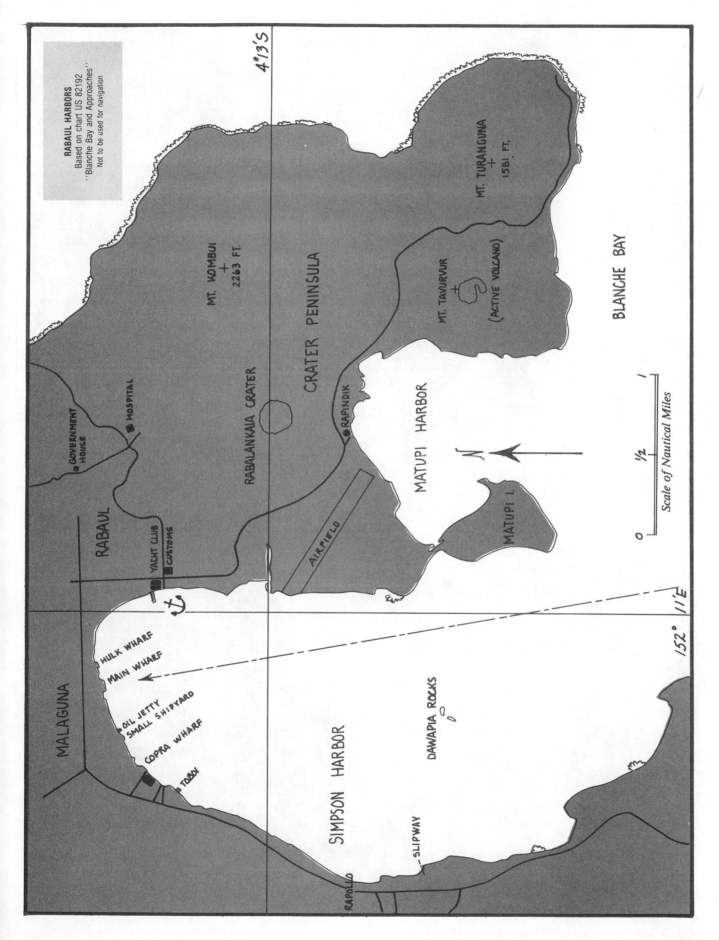

RABAUL HARBORS
Based on chart US 82192
"Blanche Bay and Approaches"
Not to be used for navigation

4°13'S

MT. TURANGUNA
+ 1581 FT.

MT. KOMBIU
+ 2263 FT.

CRATER PENINSULA

BLANCHE BAY

RABALANKAIA CRATER

MT. TAVURVUR
+ (ACTIVE VOLCANO)

GOVERNMENT HOUSE
HOSPITAL

RAPINDIK

RABAUL

MATUPI HARBOR

YACHT CLUB
CUSTOMS

AIRFIELD

MATUPI I.

N

Scale of Nautical Miles
0   ½   1

MALAGUNA

HULK WHARF
MAIN WHARF

OIL JETTY
SMALL SHIPYARD
COPRA WHARF
TOBOI

SIMPSON HARBOR

DAWAPIA ROCKS

SLIPWAY

RAPOLO

152° 11'E

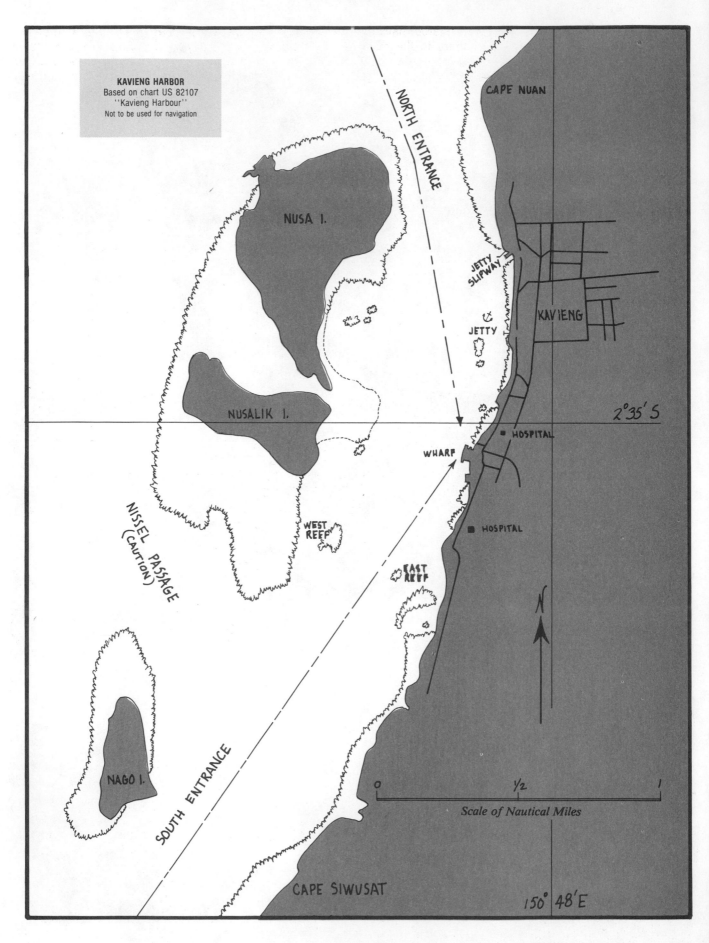

KAVIENG HARBOR
Based on chart US 82107
"Kavieng Harbour"
Not to be used for navigation

NORTH ENTRANCE

CAPE NUAN

NUSA I.

JETTY
SLIPWAY

JETTY

KAVIENG

NUSALIK I.

2°35' S

WHARF

HOSPITAL

WEST
REEF

HOSPITAL

NISSEL PASSAGE (CAUTION)

EAST
REEF

N

SOUTH ENTRANCE

NAGO I.

0   ½   1

Scale of Nautical Miles

CAPE SIWUSAT

150° 48' E

There have been reports on Simpson Harbor having a poor holding bottom but that is contrary to the many yachties who stay there during the hurricane season. A good anchorage is reported on the east side of the bay just south of the yacht club pier.

There are slipways available adequate to handle any size cruising boat. Most needed repairs can be effected here with the help of the local repair shops. Yacht type hardware is virtually non-existent. Batteries, starters and alternators can be rebuilt and diesel engine injectors serviced. Water is availble at most of the docks but it should be filtered and treated before use. Diesel fuel and gasoline are available at John Tay's dock across from the yacht club and also at the Toboi Wharf and Blanche Street Wharf.

Rabaul is a town of over 60,000 persons so most essential provisions and supplies can be obtained here.

Through the courtesy of the yacht club your mail drop for Rabaul should be:

c/o Rabaul Yacht Club
P.O. Box 106
Rabaul, New Britain
PAPUA NEW GUINEA

Kavieng: Kavieng Harbor is formed by three islands at the northern tip of New Ireland and it is practically landlocked offering good shelter. It is the principal port for the island and the residence of the District Officer. Check-in can be made at the small jetties about a ¼ mile north of the Government Wharf.

A marine railway located near the north jetty can handle small craft for repair. Repair services and hardware are limited. Petroleum products are available by drum or tank truck. Water is piped onto the main wharf but it should be treated before use. Small quantities of fresh meat and vegetables are available in the town.

Kieta: This is probably the best harbor on Bougainville Island. The town of Kieta is located at the southwest end of the bay and there is good anchoring 200 yards off the coastal reef. There is a small pier at the town which should be used for check-in with customs and other officials before proceeding to anchor.

Minor repairs can be made here but there is no marine hardware available. Water needs to be carried to the boat and engine fuels are available by tank truck. Limited provisons are available.

Radio Communications

Station name and call	Location	Frequency Transmit/Receive	Service hours LMT	Type of service
Radio Lae	Lae, New Guinea	670 kHz	0550-2400	National* commercial
Radio Wewak	Wewak, New Guinea	670	0550-2400	programs in English,
Radio Rabaul	Rabaul, New Britain	810	0550-2400	Pidgin, Hiri Motu,
Radio Madang	Madang, New Guinea	860	0550-2400	and Kuanua.
Radio Goroka	Goroka, New Guinea	900	0550-2400	"
Radio Port Moresby	Port Moresby, New Guinea	1250	0550-2400	"
P2K3	"	3925	0550-0830 1930-2400	"
P2T4	"	4890		"
P2K4	"	4890	0830-1730	"
P2T9	"	9520	0700-1800	"

*There are also a number of District radio stations of low power which broadcast only in Pidgin.

Port Moresby, Radio	Port Moresby, New Guinea	6280 kHz	24 hours	Port and coastal operations
Rabaul Radio	Rabaul, New Britain	2201 & 4407	24 hours	SSB & AM - weather at 0703 and 1403
		6204		Port and coastal operations

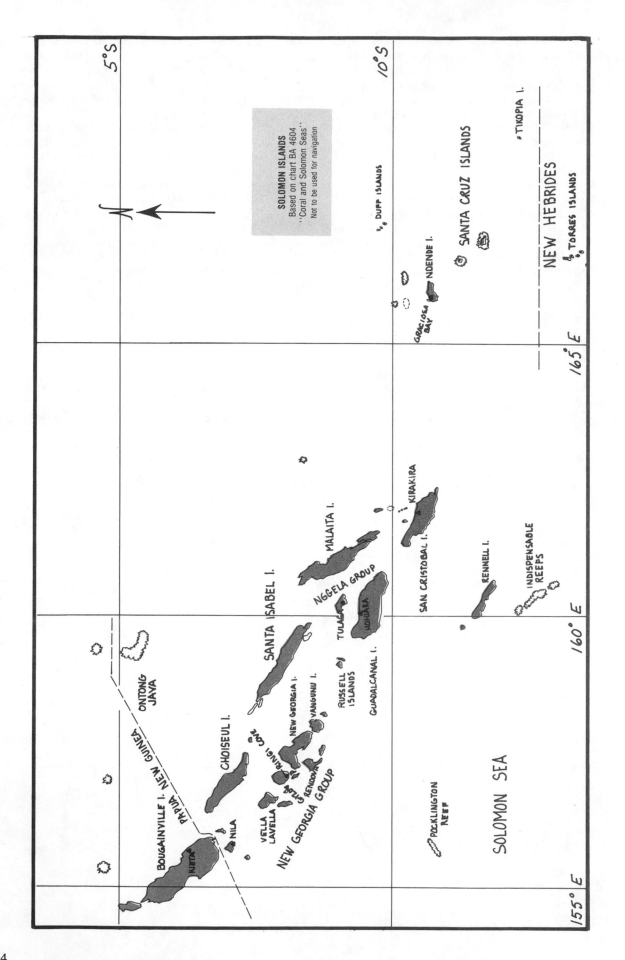

SOLOMON ISLANDS
Based on chart BA 4604
"Coral and Solomon Seas".
Not to be used for navigation

5°S

10°S

TIKOPIA I.

SANTA CRUZ ISLANDS

DUFF ISLANDS

NDENDE I.

GRACIOSA BAY

NEW HEBRIDES

TORRES ISLANDS

165° E

MALAITA I.

KIRAKIRA

SANTA ISABEL I.

NGGELA GROUP

TULAGI

HONIARA

SAN CRISTOBAL I.

RENNELL I.

INDISPENSABLE REEFS

160° E

ONTONG JAVA

CHOISEUL I.

KOLO

RENDI

NEW GEORGIA I.

VANGUNU I.

RUSSELL ISLANDS

GUADALCANAL I.

POCKLINGTON REEF

SOLOMON SEA

BOUGAINVILLE I.

PAPUA NEW GUINEA

NILA

VELLA LAVELLA

KOLOMBANGARA

RENDOVA

NEW GEORGIA GROUP

KIETA

155° E

234

Chapter 20
SOLOMON ISLANDS
(Yslas de Salamon)

The Country

The Solomon Islands group, located between 5° and 10° south latitude and 157° and 162° east longitude consists of a double row of high, continental islands formed from the exposed peaks of the submerged mountain range that extends from New Guinea to New Zealand. The group, excluding Buka and Bougainville which are part of Papua New Guinea, are augmented by the Ontong Java atolls north of the group, the Santa Cruz islands to the east, and the raised atolls of Rennell and Bellona to the south. These make up the new country of the Solomon Islands, formerly the British Solomon Islands.

The country has a combined land area of 12,000 square miles and a total population of about 215,000 persons. The people are predominantly dark-skinned Melanesians. Other ethnic groups totaling less than 10,000 persons are Polynesian, Micronesian, European, and Chinese.

The double row of islands of the main group are the largest of the entire country and they are as follows;

Island	Size (sq. mi.)	Population (persons)
Choisuel	980	8,000
Guadalcanal	2500	45,000
Malaita	1750	54,000
New Georgia	1600	13,500
San Cristobal	1350	12,000
Santa Isabel	1500	9,000

All of these are volcanic, covered with steaming jungle and have climates that are continuously hot, humid and generally unattractive. Some small amounts of gold have been found in them but major economic activity is concerned with the production of copra and coconut oil and logging the many hardwoods found in the jungle areas.

The Ontong Java group of low atolls is small and only sparsely populated. Its few hundred people form one of the occasional pockets of Polynesians found in Melanesia. These tall, light-skinned inhabitants are engaged mainly in subsistence agriculture, but some collect trochus shells from the reefs for the export market.

The Santa Cruz group consists of three main high islands and a host of smaller outliers that are mostly coral atolls. The inhabitants of the high islands are Melanesians while those of the outliers are Polynesian. Many of the smaller outliers are totally uninhabited.

Rennell and Bellona are both low islands of the makatea type containing deposits of phosphate. Little extrac-
tion has been done, however, and both are primarily given over to coconut palm and subsistence food agriculture. Bauxite has been mined on Rennell in an on-again, off-again operation by a Japanese company. The population of both islands is small and composed of mixed Polynesian and Melanesian types.

The land mammals of the Solomons include both wild and domesticated pigs and dogs plus bush rats and bats. The reptilian dwellers include snakes, crocodiles, lizards, geckoes and turtles. Out in the waters, surrounding the islands are found whales, blackfish and porpoise. Insects are a particular nuisance in these islands and among

Solomon Islands

(Yslas de Salamon)
An independent nation within
the British Commonwealth

Ports of Entry:

Honiara, Guadalcanal	9°25'S, 159°58'E
Gizo, Gizo Island	8°06'S, 156°50'E
Graciosa Bay, Ndenda Island	10°46'S, 165°50'E
Kira Kira, San Cristobal Island	10°28'S, 162°05'E
Nila, Shortland Island	7°05'S, 155°54'E
Ringi Cove, Kolombangara	8°07'S, 157°06'E

Distances between ports in nautical miles:

Between *Honiara* and:

Apia, Western Samoa	1710
Agana, Guam	1640
Honolulu, Hawaii	3050
Levuka, Fiji	1280
Nauru Island	680
Noumea, New Caledonia	980
Ponape, Caroline Islands	1020
Port Moresby, Papua New Guinea	760
Rabaul, New Britain	570
Vila, New Hebrides	690

Standard Time:

11 hours fast on GMT

them are found white ants, flies and mosquitoes. Bird life consists of cockatoos, parrots, lorries, kingfishers, ducks, eagles, hawks, hornbills, crows and pigeons.

The first European to see the Solomon Islands was Alvaro de Mendana de Neyra, a Spanish navigator, who sighted them in 1568 and it was he who named the island of Santa Ysabel after his wife. He also sighted and named Guadalcanal and San Cristobal. He later attempted to colonize the islands but died in the attempt and the colonizing party later went to the Phillipines.

Nothing much happened for the next two hundred years and then a succession of European explorers arrived including Quiros, Le Maire and Schouten, Carteret, Bougainville, D'Urville, and La Perouse. By 1830 the islands were well known to the Europeans and routine calls became commonplace.

Next followed a period of mission founding by the French and New Zealand missionaries but these were in general unsuccessful because of the resistance of the natives to outsiders. Murder was the most convincing resistance and the missions had difficulty getting established.

The practice of "blackbirding" was conducted in the Solomons as it was in so many of the Pacific islands. This was a system of recruiting persons for work on plantations or guano or phosphate diggings on other islands—many went to Australia and some as far away as South America. It was nothing better than slavery and the native resentment was such as to end up in murder of many Europeans in the islands. The practice was stopped in 1903 and at least the natives who had been sent to Australia were repatriated.

In 1893 the British established a protectorate over the southern islands to protect the Europeans who were now coming in increasing numbers as traders. By 1900 all of the present Solomon Islands were placed under the protectorate. With greater security for the Europeans, large scale plantations were developed and the South Sea trading firms of Burns, Philp and W.R. Carpenter were established.

Between 1930 and 1940 the Solomons were neglected and remained in a coconut economy. But this all changed very fast when the Japanese started World War II in the Pacific. Japan occupied the islands in 1942 and it was turned into a battleground of furious proportions until mid-1943. During this time the Solomon Islanders distinguished themselves in aiding the Australian and British coastwatchers who reported on enemy movements and assisted in the recovery of Allied fliers.

The native capitol of the Solomons had been located at Tulagi in the Florida group before the war. During the war it was totally destroyed so when the war was over the government took up quarters in the former military buildings on Guadalcanal near what is now Honiara. In spite of not having a good harbor, the capital has stayed at Honiara and new buildings have been built to replace the wartime structures.

The Solomon Islands took their independence from British rule on July 7, 1978 at which time they became an independent nation within the British Commonwealth. The national government is a Parliamentary Legislature with the Chief Minister being selected from the majority party of the Legislative Assembly. District governments handle local affairs and there are four of these districts: Western headquartered in Gizo; Central headquartered in Honiara; Malaita headquartered in Auki; and the Eastern headquartered in Kira Kira.

The indigenous peoples of the Solomons are dark-skinned and heavily built. Those living near the Bougainville Straits are very black but in the southern areas they are somewhat lighter. There are also some Gilbertese in the Gizo area who were settled there by the British when conditions on their islands in the Gilberts group became too crowded. These latecomers have not been assimilated too well into the social structure of the Solomon Islands.

There is no single native language for the Solomons but about 60 dialects are spoken in the various villages and islands. Because of the long occupancy of the group by the British and the presence of large numbers of Americans during World War II, English has become the main langugage of the islands.

Much of the responsibility for the moral, mental, and physical welfare of the indigenous peoples of the islands has been undertaken by the missionary groups promoted and led by various Christian churches. Missionary stations are found on many of the inhabited islands within the country.

The Anglican church, with headquarters at Honiara, Guadalcanal, has missions in the British Solomon Islands.

The Roman Catholic church with headquarters at Chabal, Buka Passage, has missions on Bougainville, Buka and Choiseul. Vicariate Apostolic of the Southern Solomon Islands, has missions on the main islands of San Cristobal, Guadalcanal, Santa Isabel, Malaita, Florida, New Georgia, and the Russell group. Headquarters are at Honiara, Guadalcanal.

The Methodist church of New Zealand, with headquarters at Auckland, New Zealand, has missions on Roviana, Buka, Banga, Choiseul, Vella Lavella, Bougainville and Honiara.

The South Sea Evangelical Mission, with headquarters at Sydney, New South Wales, carries on work mainly on the islands of Malaita, Guadalcanal and San Cristobal.

The Bismarck-Solomons Union Mission of the Seventh Day Adventist Missions, with headquarters at Rabaul, has missions on New Britian, Guadalcanal, New Ireland, Gizo, Kambubu, Bougainville and Kolombangara.

The missions have had the major responsibility for education in past years. Not until 1957 did the government take part in education and then through the development of a secondary school program and a teachers college. Children generally live away from home when attending school. Advanced schooling takes place overseas for both government-sponsored and mission-sponsored students. Many of the government-sponsored students attend the University of Papua New Guinea near Port Moresby. Medical training is given the Solomon Islanders at the Fiji School of Medicine. There is a modest public library at Honiara.

Agriculture is the mainstay of the islands, although there is no means for measuring accurately its importance to the economy of the land and its people. The two most valuable exports, copra and timber, are principal products of the land; cocoa also is exported. Agriculture and forestry accounted for about 23 percent of registered employment, more than any other sector except government. In 1967 total registered employment was 12,090 persons.

Ownership and use of land also indicates the importance of agriculture, both subsistence and commercial. In 1965 it was estimated that about 96 percent of the land total, which is 12,000 square miles, was held by native people, and the land was classified according to use as bush, garden, and village land. Bushlands produce wild crops that are gathered by local residents, who also hunt animals for food in those same areas.

The major crops grown for domestic food consumption are sweet potatoes, yams, taro, and green vegetables of various kinds. The demand for these crops is increasing because of the growth of urban areas where any surplus can be marketed. Tobacco and peanuts also enjoy a local market.

Coconuts, as the source of copra, are the most valuable commercial crop, coconut plantations were initiated near the end of the nineteenth century by European traders who had been obtaining coconuts from native growers. Early enterprises were small in size, but after 1900 operations increased in scale and in the

The anchorage at Honiara, Guadalcanal, is in an open roadstead. Some protection is offered by Point Cruz from the east or west depending on where you anchor. Honiara is a new city built on the site of the World War II Allied Operations Base. It is the capitol of the Solomon Islands and a Port of Entry.

A few miles to the east of Honiara is the picturesque Matanikau River.

amount of investment required. In 1904 Lever Pacific Plantations entered the Solomon Islands, and in 1908 the Burns-Philp Company initiated operations. Both firms built up large-scale plantations and enterprises for growing coconuts and processing them into copra.

Production of livestock is mostly on a small scale, carried on more to keep weeds down on plantations than to produce beef for consumption. In 1967, however, the Guadalcanal Plains Enterprise, which was engaged in rice growing, became interested in beef production as well and established a herd of good stock on a ranch near Honiara.

Small-size commercial fishing operations are conducted near the major population centers, Honiara, Guadalcanal; Auki, Malaita; and Gizo in the New Georgia islands; otherwise, fishing is on a subsistence basis. Marine products, including shells and green snails, are exported and provide welcome foreign exchange.

Since World War II, forests have been recognized as an important resource, although no survey of their potential was undertaken until 1956. Timber had been cut and exported as round logs from Gizo, Santa Isabel, and the Shortlands.

The Weather

The weather of the Solomon Islands is dominated by the southeast tradewinds during the period of April through October. During this period 75 percent of the winds are easterly and 60 percent of those are east to southeast. These trades tend to be steadier and stronger over the south part of the group particularly in the Santa Cruz islands region.

November through March the winds blow predominantly between northeast and northwest but with considerble variability including significant east and south winds. In the vicinity of the larger islands the winds are affected by daily land and sea breezes.

Winds of storm force are practically unknown. Very few tropical cyclones have visited this area. When they do the area may experience a northerly gale due to the formation of the tropical cyclone not far to the southward or westward of the group.

May to October is the drier season of the year with rainfall averaging about five inches per month. During the rest of the year it averages 9 to 12 inches with March being the wettest at over 14 inches of rainfall. What it lacks

Medical Memo

Immunization requirements:

Vaccinations for smallpox, cholera and yellow fever are required if you have transited or visited within the last six days (smallpox 14 days) an area currently infected.

Local health situation:

This is a humid, tropical country and malaria, although being eradicated, is still present and anti-malarial treatment should be taken before arriving, while there and for a period after leaving. Tuberculosis among the natives is still a problem.

Health services:

The main government hospital is Central Hospital at Honiara with district hospitals at Auki, Gizo, Kira Kira, and Santa Cruz. These facilities are staffed by Fiji-trained medical officers. There are also small clinics throughout the country with mission doctors present at Munda and Atoifi.

The few dentists in the Solomon Islands are completely absorbed in helping the native population. There are no optical services.

Drugs can be obtained from the hospitals and there is a pharmacy in Honiara.

Water:

Tap water at Honiara is supposedly good but it is recommended that all water be considered suspect and treated.

From the harbor at Gizo, a Port of Entry, one can look across the waters to 5000 foot high Kolombangara. This is an extinct volcano with the crater partially broken away and the sides of the mountain are densely wooded.

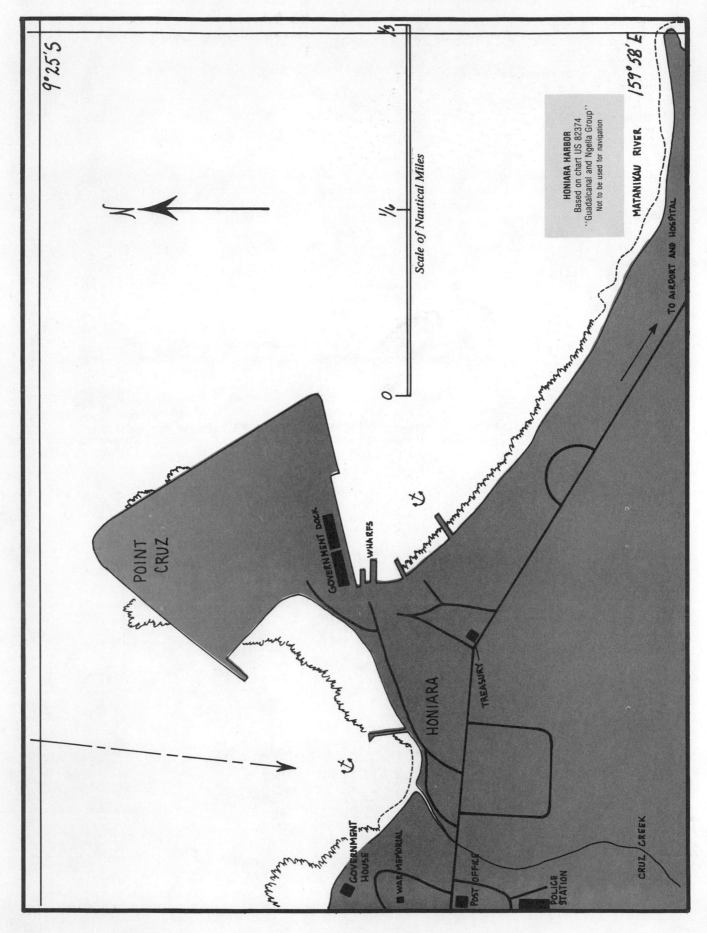

9°25'S

N

Scale of Nautical Miles

0   ⅙   ⅓

HONIARA HARBOR
Based on chart US 82374
"Guadalcanal and Ngella Group"
Not to be used for navigation

159°58'E

POINT
CRUZ

GOVERNMENT DOCK

WHARFS

HONIARA

TREASURY

MATANIKAU RIVER

TO AIRPORT AND HOSPITAL

GOVERNMENT
HOUSE

WAR MEMORIAL

POST OFFICE

POLICE
STATION

CRUZ CREEK

Jetsam and Flotsam

Currency:

The Solomon Islands use Australian currency. At press time the rate of exchange was $US1 = $A.85.

Language:

English is the official language of the Solomon Islands. Pidgin is commonly heard and there are over 60 dialects in the group.

Electricity:

Where electricity is available it is 240v, 50 Hz AC.

Postal Address:

Yacht   (   )
Poste Restante
Honiara, SOLOMON ISLANDS
   Post offices are also located at Yandina, Gizo, Auki, and Kira Kira

External Affairs Representative:

British embassies or consulates

Information Center:

Solomon Islands Tourist Authority
P.O. Box 321
Honiara, SOLOMON ISLANDS

Cruising Library:

Headhunting in the Solomon Islands, Caroline Mytinger; Macmillan, New York, USA, 1942
The Solomon Islands, Janet Kent; Stackpole Books, Harrisburg, PA, USA, 1972

---

in rainfall, however, it makes up for in humidity. July to September the humidity is about 73 percent rising to a maximum in March of 80 percent.

Average temperature the year around is between 79°F and 80°F making it one of the most consistent climates the year around.

Yacht Entry to the Solomon Islands

The principal Port of Entry to the Solomon Islands is Honiara, Guadalcanal, which is the seat of government and also headquarters for the Central District. The Port of Entry for the Western District is at Gizo on Gizo island. Auki Harbor on Malaita is the headquarters of the Malaita District but is not designated a Port of Entry. The Port of Entry for the Eastern District is Graciosa Bay on Ndende island in the Santa Cruz group. Other Ports of Entry are Nila in the Shortland Islands, Kira Kira on San Cristobal and Ringi Cove on Kolombangara island.

Passports are required of all entering visitors. Visitor's visas can be applied for on entry and are good for three months. An onward airline ticket is required for non-owner crew members.

You should be aware that the Solomon Islands impresses "light dues" on all vessels including yachts. It is $A120 minimum plus 5 cents per ton. This is ostensibly a user tax which may be reasonable for a commercial ship but is excessive for a pleasure yacht and can only end up being damaging to their tourist trade. Nevertheless, it is there and will be collected by Customs, especially at Honiara.

While it is recommended that a yacht enter an island group at a designated Port of Entry, the Solomon Islands cover such a vast area that you may have to put into a nearer port for reasons of safety or provisions. If so, you can get a temporary permit from the local administrator, but you must clear at a Port of Entry within seven days.

If you are carrying firearms, be aware that they will be

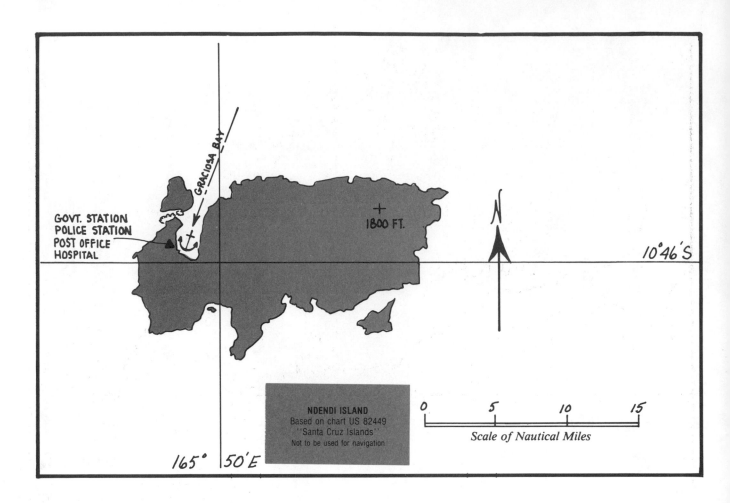

GRACIOSA BAY

GOVT. STATION
POLICE STATION
POST OFFICE
HOSPITAL

1800 FT.

N

10°46′S

NDENDI ISLAND
Based on chart US 82449
"Santa Cruz Islands"
Not to be used for navigation

165° 50′E

0   5   10   15

Scale of Nautical Miles

impounded when you check into the group and will be returned on departure. All liquor will be bonded on entry.

Yacht Facilities at Principal Ports of Entry

Honiara: Small craft with local knowledge can anchor on either side of Point Cruz depending on the wind. The principal anchorage, however, is on the west side near the Point Cruz Yacht Club. There you can anchor in about 50 ft. of water close to shore with stern lines tied ashore or to the sunken barge near the club.

The Point Cruz Yacht Club extends a warm welcome to all visiting yachts. For short stays the club extends temporary honorary membership. If an extended stay is envisaged, then yachtsmen are requested to arrange for some form of membership. On arrival, visiting yachtsmen are requested to enter themselves in the register kept in the club house. The club has a well-stocked bar, showers, and toilet facilities, potable water supply, and a lively calendar of social events which visitors are encouraged to enjoy. To assist the club committee, visiting yachtsmen are requested to make themselves known to a club officer who will then be able to give them any further information required.

The secretary of the Point Cruz Yacht Club has furnished the following information regarding membership:

1. People who are members of another recognized yacht club and show membership papers will be given a one month's membership with full rights to use all club facilities. After one month they will be charged $A1 per week for each adult.

2. People who are not members of another yacht club will be required to pay $A5 per adult per week. A Country Membership in the Point Cruz Yacht Club can be taken out by all for a $A10 joining fee and a $A9 annual fee.

Although Honiara is a small town, about 12,000 persons, you will be able to secure most needed provisions. Potable water and fuel can be obtained at the wharf on the east side of Point Cruz. There are no local boat repair facilities but some help can be obtained from local garages and workshops. Fairly comprehensive ship slip and repair facilities exist at Tulagi in the Nggela group of islands. Some are private and some belong to the Marine Department. The Marine Department also has some local charts for sale.

Gizo: Gizo has a population of only about 1,000 persons and is the copra and cocoa receiving port for the Western District. Limited supplies of dry provisions are available as is potable water and some diesel fuel. Deck and engine stores are in limited supply. There are only limited haulout and repair facilities for vessels to 40 feet long at Gizo.

Graciosa Bay: Small boats can anchor in the bay with

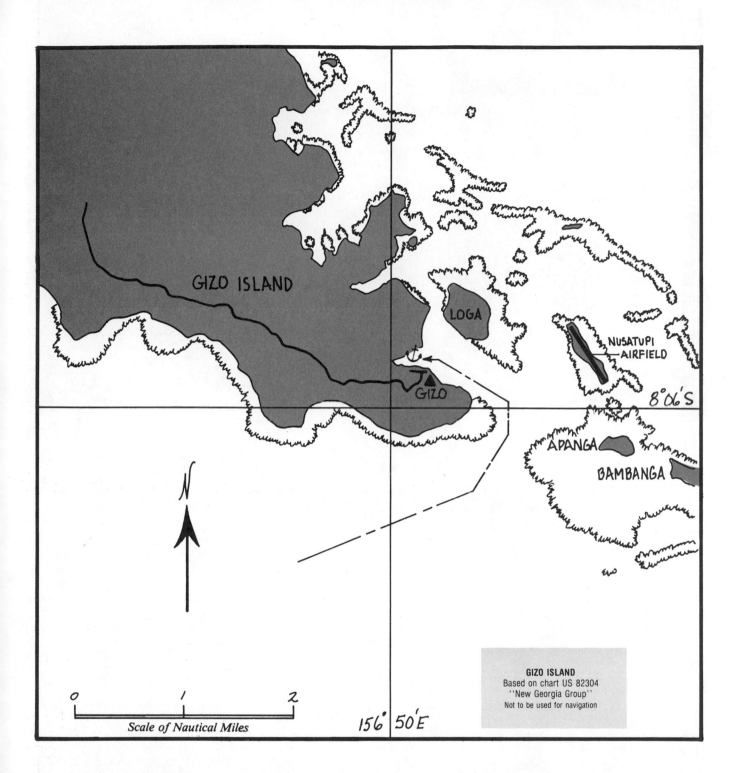

GIZO ISLAND

GIZO ISLAND
Based on chart US 82304
''New Georgia Group''
Not to be used for navigation

LOGA

NUSATUPI
AIRFIELD

GIZO

8°06'S

APANGA

BAMBANGA

N

0   1   2
Scale of Nautical Miles

156° 50'E

good holding ground and there are ship berths in the southeastern part of the bay. Water is available but few other supplies. There is a Government Station, post office, police station, and hospital on the western side of the bay.

Kira Kira: The island of San Cristobal is about 76 miles long by 23 miles wide and had a total population of about 11,000 persons in 1970. Kira Kira is the headquarters of the Eastern District and is located on the north coast. The main anchorage in the bay at Kira Kira is reported to be unsafe in northwest winds. It has been recommended that small boats anchor off the concrete pier in a coral sand bottom with a sprinkling of rocks. Both customs and immigration clearance can be made here and there is a charge of $A.05 per net ton of the craft.

243

Radio Communications

Station name and call	Location	Frequency Transmit/Receive	Service hours LMT	Type of Service
Honiara Radio	Honiara	6215.5/6221.6 kHz	24 hours	RT - Marine operations
				Small ships call schedule (LT): 0833, 1033, 1503, 1633, 0203. Note that a silence period of three minutes is observed on the hour and half-hour 24 hours per day. This is for emergency use and there are to be no transmissions except emergencies.
		6204	24 hours	RT-South Pacific Safety Frequency — will give weather on call
Solomons Radio (Honiara)	9°15′S 160°02′E			
VQO		1030 kHz	0530-2300	Commercial broadcast
VQO5		5020	0530-2300	″ ″
VQO9		9545	0930-1630	″ ″

Chapter 21
NEW CALEDONIA
(Nouvelle Caledonie)

The Country

The Overseas Territory of New Caledonia consists of the main island of New Caledonia and its dependencies made up of the Loyalty Group, to the east, and the Isle of Pines and Ile Ouen to the south. New Caledonia is the largest island as shown in the following:

New Caledonia (250 mi. long by
25 mi. wide) . . . . 6,530 sq.mi.
Loyalty Islands . . . . 756 sq.mi.
Isle of Pines . . . . 52 sq.mi.
Ouen Islands . . . . dots

New Caledonia is the fourth largest island in the Pacific being exceeded in size only by New Guinea, and the North and South Islands of New Zealand. It is mountainous rising to an altitude of almost 5,400 ft. (Humboldt Peak). The mountain ranges run almost the full length of the island but they are discontinuous with steep northeast slopes and more gentle southwest slopes. A barrier reef lies offshore and is the longest insular coral reef in existence.

New Caledonia occupies one of the most southerly portions of Melanesia and, therefore, has a climate that, although tropical, is neither excessively hot nor damp. The eastern, or windward side of the island has a heavy rainfall and is well forested. The western side in the rain shadow is drier, and the coastline is fringed erratically by tidal flats and mangrove swamps. Vegetation in the western lowlands is often meager although at higher elevations remnants of old stands of araucaria pine can be found.

The first impression of the navigator who has been accustomed to the luxuriant vegetation of most of the Pacific islands is that New Caledonia is bare and arid. The prevailing growth is a small, drab tree the niaouli, similar in appearance to the common eucalyptus scrubs of Australia. But that is only in some places. The coconut palm grows on the coast and a great many valleys are filled with a luxuriant growth of the magnificent kauri pine.

There is very little animal or bird life on New Caledonia. There are many varieties of bright plumaged small birds and several kinds of pigeons along with hawks.

The French explorer Bougainville discovered New Caledonia in 1768 but it was Captain Cook who named it six years later. To Cook the pine-clad ridges bore a resemblance to Scotland. From that time to 1840 when the missionaries arrived, the island was visited by explorers, traders and ship deserters. New Caledonia became a French colony in 1853 and was used as a penal settlement starting in 1864. Some 40,000 prisoners were sent there before it was closed as a penal colony about 1897. However, many of the prisoners and their dependents stayed on to populate the island.

The French did little to develop the island beyond its use as a penal colony. The native population was in an almost continuous state of rebellion up to 1917. During both World Wars, New Caledonia fought on the side of the Allies.

During World War II New Caledonia was a major strategic base for the United States and New Zealand after having been a prime military target of the Japanese

New Caledonia
(Nouvelle Caledonie)
An Overseas Territory of France

Port of Entry:

Noumea, New Caledonia   22°16′S, 166°26′E

Distances between ports in nautical miles:

Between Noumea and:

Apia, Western Samoa	1370
Agana, Guam	2530
Auckland, New Zealand	1000
Avatiu, Cook Islands	1890
Funafuti, Tuvalu	1130
Lae, New Guinea	1520
Malakal, Palau Islands	2610
Nuku'alofa, Tonga	1060
Pago Pago, American Samoa	1420
Ponape, Caroline Islands	1890
Rabaul, New Britain	1380
Raoul, Kermadec Islands	960
Selwyn Bay, Solomon Islands	850
Suva, Fuji	730
Truk, Caroline Islands	2070
Wotje, Marshall Islands	1970
Yap, Caroline Islands	2570

Standard time:

11 hours fast on GMT

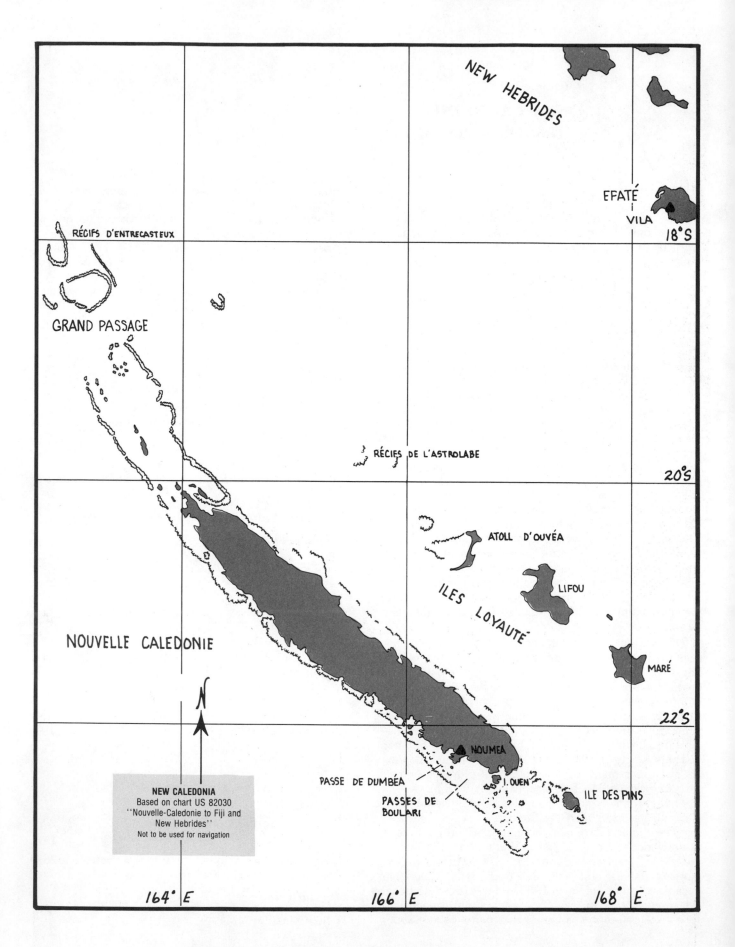

RÉCIFS D'ENTRECASTEUX

GRAND PASSAGE

RÉCIFS DE L'ASTROLABE

NOUVELLE CALEDONIE

NEW HEBRIDES

EFATÉ
VILA
18°S

20°S

ATOLL D'OUVÉA

ILES LOYAUTÉ

LIFOU

MARÉ

22°S

N

NOUMEA

PASSE DE DUMBÉA

PASSES DE
BOULARI

I. OUEN

ILE DES PINS

NEW CALEDONIA
Based on chart US 82030
''Nouvelle-Caledonie to Fiji and
New Hebrides''
Not to be used for navigation

164° E

166° E

168° E

Rue de L'Alma is one of Noumea's main streets leading away from the harbor.

expansion campaign. After the fall of France to Germany in 1940, New Caledonia followed the Free French under De Gaulle.

The wartime need of the Allies for strategic minerals, such as nickel and chrome, led to the government unilaterally extending the contracts of indentured workers from Java and Indo China. Many of these Indonesians

and Vietnamese stayed on after the war to open up small businesses replacing the prewar Japanese trading concerns. Many workers for New Caledonia came from Indonesia and were supplemented by Wallis Islanders and Tahitians for non-mining work.

The inhabitants of the New Caledonia Overseas Territory are considered to be French citizens. The Territory is represented in the French National Assembly, and French Senate, and on the French Economic and Social Council.

New Caledonia is administered by an appointed governor who exercises effective control of the administration. The governor of New Caledonia is also the French High Commissioner for the New Hebrides Condominium and formerly supervised the administration of the Wallis and Futuna group. A Council of Governments assists the governor.

A Territorial Assembly elected by the people handles questions of economics and general administration and may be consulted by the governor on questions of administrative organization, education, and other aspects of local needs. Within the system of local tariffs, it can im-

Away from the frantic pace of the commercial harbor, yachts can find anchorage in Baie de L'Orphelinat or, possibly, a slip at the Club Nautique de Caledonie in Baie des Pecheurs.

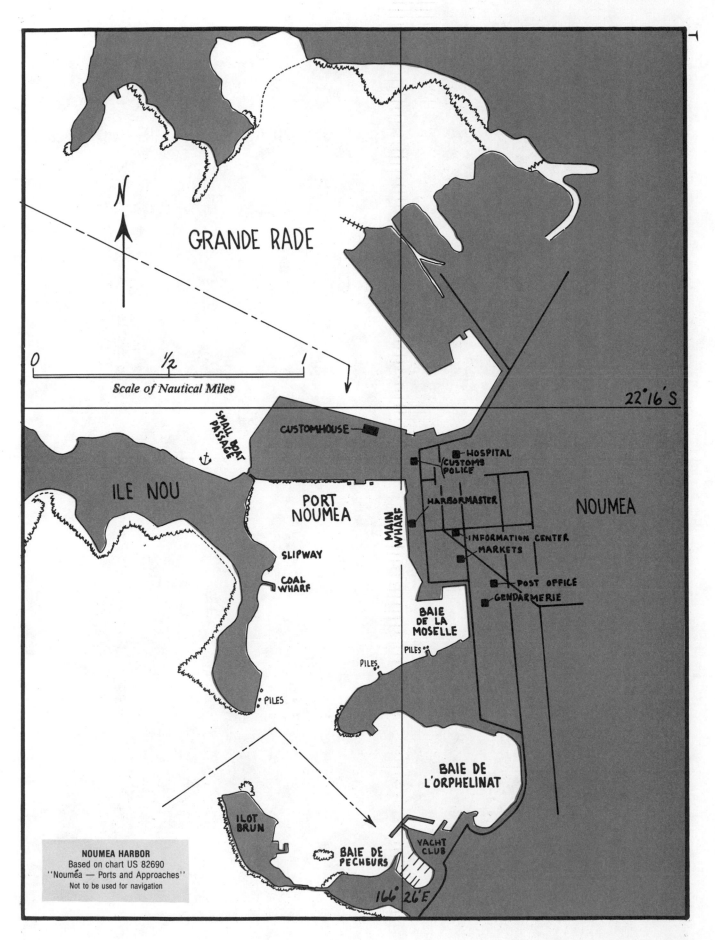

GRANDE RADE

N

0   ½   1
Scale of Nautical Miles

22°16'S

SMALL BOAT PASSAGE

CUSTOMHOUSE

ILE NOU

PORT NOUMEA

HOSPITAL
CUSTOMS POLICE

HARBORMASTER

NOUMEA

MAIN WHARF

INFORMATION CENTER
MARKETS

SLIPWAY

POST OFFICE

COAL WHARF

GENDARMERIE

BAIE DE LA MOSELLE

PILES

PILES

PILES

BAIE DE L'ORPHELINAT

ILOT BRUN

BAIE DE PECHEURS

YACHT CLUB

166°26'E

NOUMEA HARBOR
Based on chart US 82690
''Nouméa — Ports and Approaches''
Not to be used for navigation

249

The city of Noumea bears little resemblance to a South Seas port of call. It is, in fact, a very modern city and is sometimes called the Riviera of the South Pacific. For yachties it is the Port of Entry to New Caledonia.

Modern slip facilities and boats are in evidence at the Club Nautique de Caledonie.

A corner of the Isle of Pines south of the "mainland" of New Caledonia

pose import and export duties and develop a budget for the expenditure of those funds.

The basic laws of New Caledonia are those of France made applicable as the occasion demands. The principal officers of the court are appointed by France.

Noumea, the capitol of New Caledonia and virtually the only town in the territory, is the seat of all administrative and political activity. The town has a mayor and 12 municipal councilors who are elected for six years by universal suffrage. The mayor is responsible for law enforcement, publishing local decrees, maintaining the electoral rolls, and conducting elections.

Other centers of population are locally administered by municipal commissions. The commissioner's powers and functions are subject to financial control and supervision by the central government.

The island group had a total population in 1974 of 131,600 persons composed of 53,800 Melanesians, 51,600 Europeans, and the remaining distributed between Wallis Islanders, Tahitians, Indonesians, and Vietnamese. Most of the indigenous population lives on the east coast of New Caledonia and on the Loyalty Islands. They live in villages on native reserves and in the towns. Their houses are made of earthen or cement walls with thatched roofs which have replaced the traditional beehive shaped quarters of earlier days. Many Europeans live on small coffee plantations and ranches. About 15,000 Melanesians live in the Loyalty islands.

As elsewhere, there has been a trend of the population to the big city. Noumea has a population of about 60,000 persons of which Europeans constitute over 55 percent.

The principal religions are Roman Catholic and Protestant. Masses are sung weekly in Wallisian, Melanesian, and Tahitian and are very colorful.

The island of New Caledonia is unique among all island groups of the Pacific in that it has an abundance of mineral resources. These include large deposits of nickel, iron, chrome, manganese and cobalt with sizeable quantities of mercury, lead, silver and gold. There is also some coal present. In 1967 New Caledonia was the third largest producer of nickel in the world.

In addition to the minerals, crops, forests, livestock and fisheries contribute significantly to the economy. Land is held by the state and leased for farming and mining. Land is reserved for native use. Among the subsistence crops grown by the natives are yams, taro, mangoes, corn, sweet potatoes, rice, bananas, and other fruit. Coffee and coconuts are the main commercial crops.

Forests cover about 15 percent of the land and produce several varieties of trees of commercial value. The New Caledonian pine is found no other place in the world.

Livestock is of considerable importance and include large herds of cattle, some pigs and sheep, and modern poultry farms near Noumea. Dairy farming is limited.

Abundant saltwater fish of good quality exist in the nearby waters but there is proper concern for the future due to the high contamination of the shoreline by mining and smelting operations. Commercial fishing supplies only the local market and no fish processing plants for export had been established by 1967.

Unlike Papeete, Noumea is high profile French, with numerous white apartment buildings, chic shops, and restaurants to rival those in Paris. Fortunately, the Parisian hauteur is absent and the Noumeans are warm and friendly.

Loyalty Islands

The Loyalty Islands are a French possession and a dependency of New Caledonia. They were discovered in 1800 or 1803 (not certain) by the British, but it was the French hydrographer, Dumont d'Urville who first really explored them. Surveying of these islands is not completed to this date.

The Loyalty group is east of New Caledonia and is composed of three large islands—Mare, Lifu, and Uvea plus a larger number of islets, rocks and islands. The Northern and Southern Pleiadies Islands are among them. The island chain stretches northwest to southeast parallel to new Caledonia. The maximum elevation of the islands is only 330 feet and the island of Uvea does not exeed 100 feet elevation. The coasts which are exposed to the prevailing southeast winds are generally steep cliffs. Other parts of the coastline have wooded cliffs which descend to the sea in gentle slopes. Low lying areas abound with coconut trees.

The population of the group was about 14,000 persons in 1956. They are of Polynesian origin with a language similar to Fijian. The Loyalty Islands grow food crops and fish for subsistence. They also produce about 75 percent of the copra for the New Caledonia area.

The administrative headquarters for the Loyalties is at Shepenehe on the west side of Lifu island. Uvea island is the most popular stop for yachts after checking in at Noumea. There are no supplies available here but some foodstuffs can be bought.

The Weather

The winds in the New Caledonia area are dominated by the southeast trade but they vary in strength and steadiness throughout the various seasons. The trades are most dependable between November and May when about 60 percent of the winds are between east and southeast. The remaining part of the year, which is the southern hemisphere's winter, sees an increase in the southerly components of the wind although east and southeast winds still prevail and the average wind strength is greater. The westen side of the island frequently experiences offshore breezes but the east side of

Located two miles inside the northern passage to Noumea, Amadee Island provides not only range markers for safe navigation but it is a popular picnic spot for Noumeans. The lighthouse is called in French Phare Amadee.

the island does not because of the dominant trade wind.

New Caledonia lies in the southwest Pacific hurricane belt. Tropical cyclones in this area generally move south--southeastward but occasionally cross from northeast to southwest. Strong gales from a northerly direction occur with these storms. The main season for tropical cyclones is December to March.

Noumea has a very pleasant climate with temperatures ranging between 68°F in the winter months and 80°F in the summer months. The relative humidity hovers about 70 percent the year around.

February through April are the wettest months of the year with a monthly average rainfall of about five inches at Noumea. Total annual rainfall measures 40 to 45 in-ches at Noumea. Because the mountain chains of the island lie athwart the prevailing winds, the eastern slopes get an abundance of rainfall while the western slopes get only half as much. This rain distribution results in the eastern slopes being well forested with kauri, pines and hardwood above the 1,200 foot level. The interior of the island as well as the dry western slopes are covered with savanna and a eucalyptus-like scrub called niaouli. Mangroves are common along the coasts.

Ships report thunderstorms to be common in this area in February and March and infrequent between June and October.

Although New Caledonia is sometimes referred to as the Island of Eternal Spring, spring as everywhere has its

Jetsam and Flotsam

Currency:

New Caledonia uses the Coloniale Franc Pacifique (CFP) which is issued in coinage of 1, 5, 10, 20 and 50 francs and notes of 100, 500, 1000 and 5000 francs. At press time the rate of exchange was $US1 = 83 francs.

Language:

Like Tahiti, New Caledonia's official language is French. A multiplicity of other languages are occasionally heard including some indigenous Melanesian dialects, Vietnamese, and some Polynesian dialects.

Electricity:

In the city of Noumea there is 220v, 50 Hz AC electricity.

Postal Address:

Yacht   (   )
Poste Restante
Noumea, NEW CALEDONIA

or, if you are staying at the yacht club:

Yacht   (   )
c/o Club Nautique de Caledonia
 B.P. 235
Noumea, NEW CALEDONIA

External Affairs Representative:

French consulates and embassies

Information Center:

Office du Tourisme
P.O. Box 688
Noumea, NEW CALEDONIA

Cruising Library:

The Loyalty Islands, K.R. Howe; University of Hawaii Press, Honolulu, HI 96822, USA, 1977

drawbacks and new Caledonia has an abundance of mosquitos.

Yacht Entry at Noumea

There is only one Port of Entry for New Caledonia and the Loyalty islands and that is Noumea. All yachts should make their entry there before proceeding elsewhere. Yachts arriving in Port Noumea can check in at either the main docks or the Club Nautique de Caledonie. The Customhouse is located near the center of the main wharf and the yacht skipper should proceed there after securing his yacht at the wharf and announce his arrival to the authorities. As in all new ports, the crew should remain on board until clearance has been granted. If you elect to go to the yacht club, you can call the customs officials from there and they will come over to affect clearance.

A visa is not required for a stay of 30 days or less. For longer periods you will need to obtain a visa which can be done on arrival. Four photographs and $US2.45 will be required for each person. Obviously you will need your passport and health record. In addition, all crew members will need an onward or return air ticket or

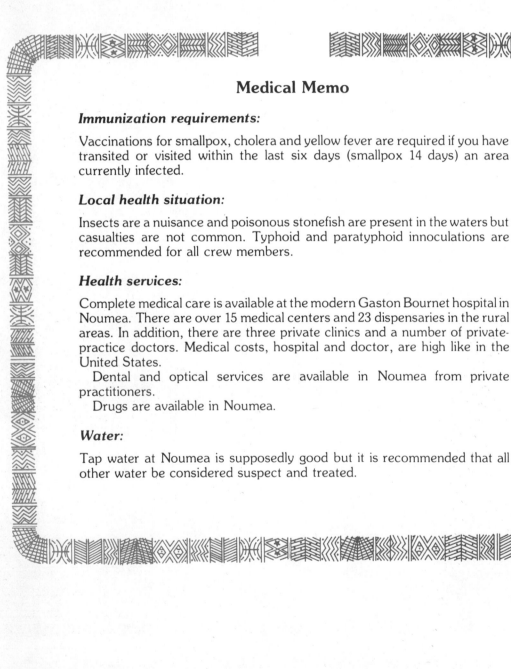

Medical Memo

Immunization requirements:

Vaccinations for smallpox, cholera and yellow fever are required if you have transited or visited within the last six days (smallpox 14 days) an area currently infected.

Local health situation:

Insects are a nuisance and poisonous stonefish are present in the waters but casualties are not common. Typhoid and paratyphoid innoculations are recommended for all crew members.

Health services:

Complete medical care is available at the modern Gaston Bournet hospital in Noumea. There are over 15 medical centers and 23 dispensaries in the rural areas. In addition, there are three private clinics and a number of private-practice doctors. Medical costs, hospital and doctor, are high like in the United States.

Dental and optical services are available in Noumea from private practitioners.

Drugs are available in Noumea.

Water:

Tap water at Noumea is supposedly good but it is recommended that all other water be considered suspect and treated.

equivalent funds. Bona fide owners of the boat will need to present proper boat ownership documents.

Yacht Facilities at Noumea

The harbor at Noumea is very good providing extensive anchorage in 3 to 7 fathoms of water with basically a coral bottom but with some silt and sand to hold vessels with little dragging. While the harbor is virtually land locked there is some question how good a hurricane hole it really is. Yachts can anchor at a small boat anchorage southwest of the main docks. There is a dinghy dock nearby and it is convenient to the center of town. (Progress is changing the coastline of this harbor and recently the Baie de la Moselle has been filled in for a parking lot.)

Fuel and potable water are readily available. Provisions of all kinds including fresh fruits and vegetables are available in the city but are high priced. A modest amount of marine hardware is available also but keep in mind that like Tahiti, it will be designed to the metric system. There is a good marine railway for haulout purposes and adequate shops available for repair of any yacht equipment.

The Club Nautique de Caledonie is located a short distance south from town in the Baie de Pecheurs. It has a large permanent contingent of 200 or so yachts and there are guest slips available. The CNC will grant two weeks free use of their facilities but there is a charge of $US1.00 per day after that.

Radio Communications

Station name and call	Location	Frequency Transmit/Receive	Service hours LMT	Type of service
Noumea Radio (FJP)	22°16'S 166°28'E	2182/2182 kHz	Continuous	Distress freq. watch
		4386.2/4100	0800-0830 1030-1100 1430-1500 1630-1700	Marine operations
		8776/8200	1000-1030 1500-1530	Marine operations
	Noumea Port	VHF Channels 12, 14, 16	Mon.-Fri. 0715-1115 1330-1730	Port operations
Radio Noumea	22°10'S 166°16'E	670 kHz 3355 7170 9510 11710	0600-2200	Broadcast in French language

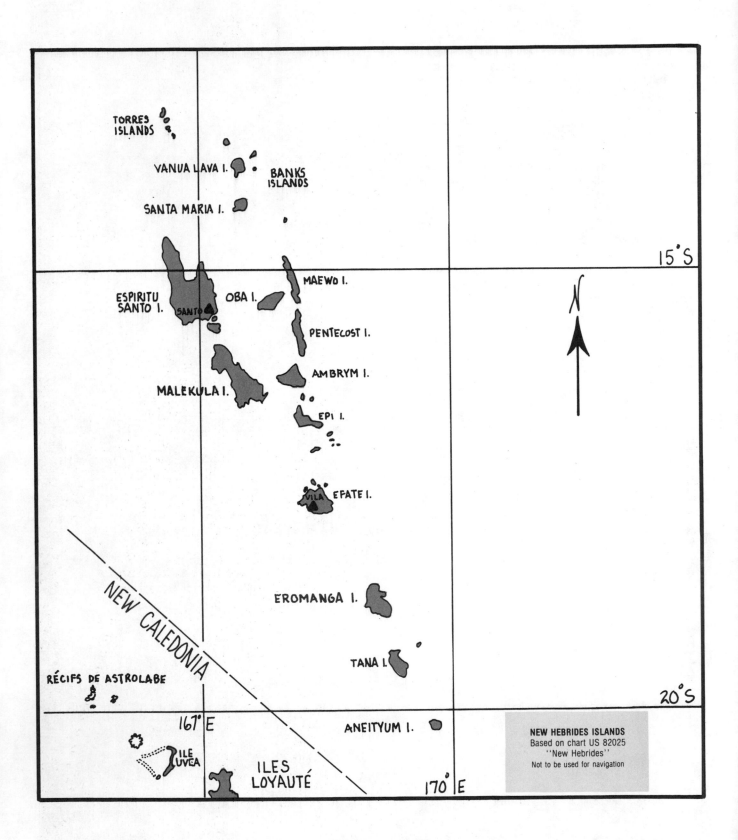

TORRES ISLANDS

VANUA LAVA I.

BANKS ISLANDS

SANTA MARIA I.

ESPIRITU SANTO I.

SANTO

OBA I.

MAEWO I.

PENTECOST I.

AMBRYM I.

MALEKULA I.

EPI I.

EFATE I.

VILA

NEW CALEDONIA

EROMANGA I.

TANA I.

RÉCIFS DE ASTROLABE

167° E

ANEITYUM I.

ILE UVEA

ILES LOYAUTÉ

170° E

15° S

20° S

N

NEW HEBRIDES ISLANDS
Based on chart US 82025
''New Hebrides''
Not to be used for navigation

Chapter 22

NEW HEBRIDES
(Austrialia del Espiritu Santo)

The Country

The New Hebrides group is a chain of 13 large and about 70 small islands laying between 13° and 21° south latitude and 166° and 171° east longitude. The group is composed of three sections forming a "Y" whose open end is in the north. Banks Islands and Torres Islands form the northern legs. The central section contains the largest islands of the group, Espiritu Santo and Malekula, and a number of other islands of considerable size. The southernmost of the central section is Efate, the seat of colonial administration. The southern section consists of Eromanga, Tana, and Aeityum together with a few smaller ones.

The total land area of the group is approximately 5,700 square miles of which Espiritu Santo makes up 1,400 miles. The islands are mountainous with Mt. Talwesamana on Santo reaching 6,170 feet and neighboring Santo peak reaching 5,500 feet. The northern islands in general are quite mountainous with several active volcanoes. Earthquakes are not uncommon. The islands are the crest of a submarine ridge. Many are raised coral plateaus with cultivable coastal strips.

The islands are well wooded and have numerous fertile valleys. They are well watered and covered by extensive rain forests containing valuable stands of kauri and sandlewood. Some of the mountain areas have small deposits of manganese but their exploitation has not been developed.

In accordance with a convention signed in 1906 the government of the islands is vested jointly in England and France, each country being represented by a Resident High Commissioner. The British High Commissioner, who is also the High Commissioner for British interests throughout the Pacific, is resident at Honiara, Solomon Islands. The French High Commissioner, who is also the High Commissioner for French interests in the Pacific and the governor of New Caledonia is resident at Noumea, New Caledonia. Both High Commissioners have assigned administrative responsibility to their respective commissioners resident in Vila, Efate island. There are three sets of laws, three currencies (British, Australian, and French) and two kinds of weights and measurements. French and English are both official languages and in addition there is a pidgin English commonly used.

There are approximately 113,000 (1979) persons in the islands. About 100,000 are native New Hebrideans, who are part of the Melanesian race. The rest are French or English who live in the area either as administrators of the jointly operated condominium government or as entrepeneurs. The more populated islands are Malekula,

Tana, Espiritu Santo, Loba, and Efate. Although about half of the persons live near the sea, the other half lives well inland in the hills because of the prevalence of malaria near sea level.

The economy is mainly agrarian. yams, taro, manioc, and bananas are grown for local consumption. They also export copra, frozen fish, cocoa, coffee and sandlewood. Manganese ore is mined in limited quantities for export. The New Hebrides are underdeveloped with a population density of only 11 persons per square mile and being very fertile they have good possibilities for the future.

New Hebrides

(Austrialia del Espiritu Santo)

A Condominium administered jointly by
Great Britain and France

Ports of Entry:

Vila, Efate	17°45'S, 168°18'E
Santo, Luganville Bay, Espiritu Santo	15°36'S, 167°12'E

Distances between ports in nautical miles:

Between *Vila* and:

Agana, Guam	2360
Apia, Western Samoa	1210
Auckland, New Zealand	1240
Funafuti, Tuvalu	850
Honiara, Solomon Islands	720
Honolulu, Hawaii	3020
Noumea, New Caledonia	330
Nuku'alofa, Tonga	1020
Rabaul, New Britain	1280
Suva, Fiji	620

Standard time:

11 hours fast on GMT

The Weather

The southeast trades dominate the New Hebrides area from May to October. More than 80 percent of the winds then blow between the east and south with westerly winds being almost unknown. During the remainder of the year east to southeast winds still predominate but the directions are much more variable. At Erroman island in the south, the annual mean wind speed is 7 knots with a total of 3.4 days per year of gale force winds.

From January to March the northern part of the region experiences considerable northwest winds and many calms. In these months tropical cyclones arise in or cross the New Hebrides area, usually traveling southward. This type of storm is quite rare in the northern islands but not uncommon in the southern islands of the group.

The average annual rainfall ranges from 90 inches in the south to 150 inches in the north. Torrential rainfalls occur during the passages of tropical storms. The least rainy months are June through August.

The climate of the group is quite hot and humid, although the southeast trades have some tempering effect. Average temperatures at Vila range between 72°F and 82°F while the average humidity ranges between 85 and 91 percent. The most pleasant time of the year is May through October.

Yacht Entry

There are two ports of entry to the New Hebrides islands —Vila, Efate; and Santo, Luganville Bay, Espiritu Santo. Visas will be required and they can be obtained at an Australian consulate in another country or obtained on arrival at Vila. Citizens of the United Kingdom apply for their visas at the British Headquarters while those of French origin apply to the French Headquarters. Other nationalities may elect to apply at either headquarters but recent experience indicates that more favorable treatment is afforded by the French administration. The British allow one month but extensions can be granted up to three months. An onward airfare to country of passport is required or a bond of $A200 per person must be posted.

All South Pacific islands including Australia and New Zealand are free of rabies and they are very concerned about the possible introduction of the animal disease. New Hebrides will impose stiff fines and even confiscation

Native New Hebridean culture still flourishes on most of the islands. Besides traditional dances, Pentecost Island is the home of the famous land-divers. Divers leap headfirst from rickety wood towers 80 feet high and are brought up short of a skull-cracking impact by vines tied to their ankles.

of the vessel for entering their waters with pets aboard. They do not have rabies and they do not want them. Vaccinations are not considered reliable and you could easily lose your pet, money, or boat by violating this entry regulation.

If you are an artifact collector, be advised that the Government prohibits the exporting of any artifacts more than 20 years old.

The condominium government poses an unusual situation relative to flag protocol. It is proper to fly the courtesy ensigns of both Britain and France at the same time but they must be flown at the same height.

Yacht Facilities at Ports of Entry

Vila: Vila Harbor is a well-protected inlet on the eastern side of Meli Bay affording excellent shelter from westerly winds. While the harbor is mostly free of dangers, there are fringing coral reefs which extend out from the shores and must be avoided.

When entering Vila Harbor for clearance, proceed to the quarantine area first. After formalities, you can anchor Tahiti-style off the quay. It is reported that showers can be arranged at the Rossi Hotel for a nominal charge.

The condominium governments are located in the

Jetsam and Flotsam

Currency:

There are three different currencies in use in the New Hebrides - Australian, British and French. At press time the rates of exchange were:
Australian: $US1 = $A.85
British: $US1 = £.52
New Hebrides franc: $US1 = 76 fr

Language:

Both English and French are official languages depending on which government you are dealing with. There are also New Caledonian and Fiji dialects in use. A form of Pidgin involving French and Bichelamar is the lingua franca. Names for islands and towns will be found in both English and French.

Electricity:

Where electricity is available it is 240v, 50 Hz AC.

Postal Addresses:

Yacht ( )
Poste Restante
Vila, NEW HEBRIDES
Other towns useful for mail drop in a descending order of preference are Santo, Forari, and Tanna.

External Affairs Representatives:

Both British and French consulates and embassies can be of use in official contacts.

Information Center:

New Hebrides Tourist Information Bureau
P.O. Box 209
Vila, NEW HEBRIDES

Cruising Library:

Journey to the End of the World, Charlene Gourguechon; Charles Scribner's Sons, New York, USA 1978.

town of Vila as is the French Resident commissioner. The British Resident commissioner resides on Iriki Island.

Provisions and deck supplies can be obtained at Vila but prices are higher than in Fiji and, being a smaller town, the selection is less than in Suva. While Vila is a duty-free port as far as purchases are concerned, there will be duty charges applied to incoming supplies such as parts which you may have shipped there for your boat. Diesel fuel, lube oil, and fresh water are available.

It is permissible to leave a yacht in Vila for a season but it should be securely anchored and left in someone's care. If your boat is here during the hurricane season you might find helpful shelter in Erakor Lagoon

Santo, Luganville Bay: This is the main shipping harbor of the New Hebrides since the larger share of the population lives on the big islands in this area. It is a deep bay with good holding in a bottom of mud and sand.

Yachts requiring pratique should proceed to Quarantine Anchorage and anchor flying the Q flag. For clearance best advice is to arrive at Main Wharf, West End, and proceed from there. Customs hours are 0730-1130 and 1330-1630 weekdays. Customs requirements on entry are:

Medical Memo

Immunization requirements:

Smallpox vaccinations are required of all persons. In addition cholera and yellow fever vaccinations are required if you have transited or visited within the last six days an area currently infected.

Local health situation:

There are malaria-carrying mosquitoes in the New Hebrides and you would do well to take anti-malaria drugs before, during and after your visit. Amoebic dysentery is also common so water taken aboard should be treated with a strong disinfectant. Local people have been infected with hepatitis. Some marine life like the stonefish and the poisonous dart cone shells should be avoided. Coral cuts should be disinfected immediately to avoid complications resulting in fever and inflammation. The hot, humid climate requires that all cuts and abrasions be tended to quickly to prevent possible infection. During the rainy season of November to April, flies can be a nuisance.

Health services:

There are French and British hospitals in Vila and Santo supervised by medical officers of the two countries. There are smaller hospitals and dispensaries throughout the islands. Except for one private doctor at Vila, all medical personnel are government workers or members of the mission staffs. Medical costs are moderate.

There are dentists in Vila and Santo and an optometrist from overseas that makes occasional calls throughout the islands.

Drugs from both France and the United Kingdom are available. There is one pharmacy in Santo and two in Vila. In addition, supermarkets sell proprietary brands of medicine.

IAMAT Center:

Santo: Aore Seventh Day Adventist Hospital
             Medical Director: Joeli Taoi, DSM

Water:

Tap water from public supplies in Santo and Vila are supposedly safe. However, it would probably be wisest to treat all water from whatever source.

The town of Santo on Luganville Bay is the second largest in all New Hebrides. It is sometimes erroneously called Luganville. The whole island of Espiritu Santo is often simply called Santo adding to the confusion.

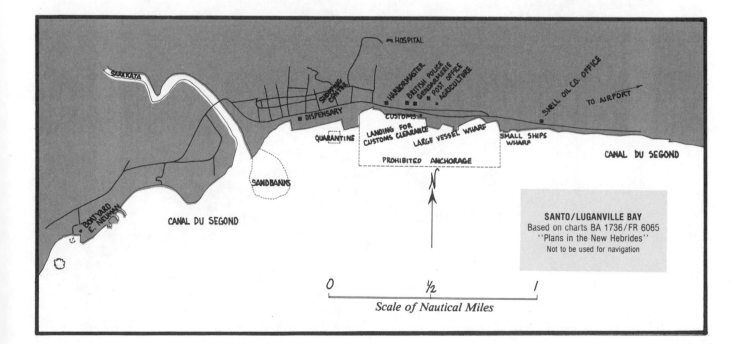

HOSPITAL

SARAKATA

SHOPPING CENTER

HARBORMASTER
BRITISH POLICE
GENDARMERIE
POST OFFICE
AGRICULTURE

SHELL OIL CO. OFFICE

TO AIRPORT

DISPENSARY

CUSTOMS

QUARANTINE

LANDING FOR
CUSTOMS CLEARANCE

LARGE VESSEL WHARF

SMALL SHIPS
WHARF

CANAL DU SEGOND

SANDBANKS

PROHIBITED ANCHORAGE

N

BOATYARD
E. NEUMAN

CANAL DU SEGOND

SANTO/LUGANVILLE BAY
Based on charts BA 1736/FR 6065
"Plans in the New Hebrides"
Not to be used for navigation

0   ½   1

Scale of Nautical Miles

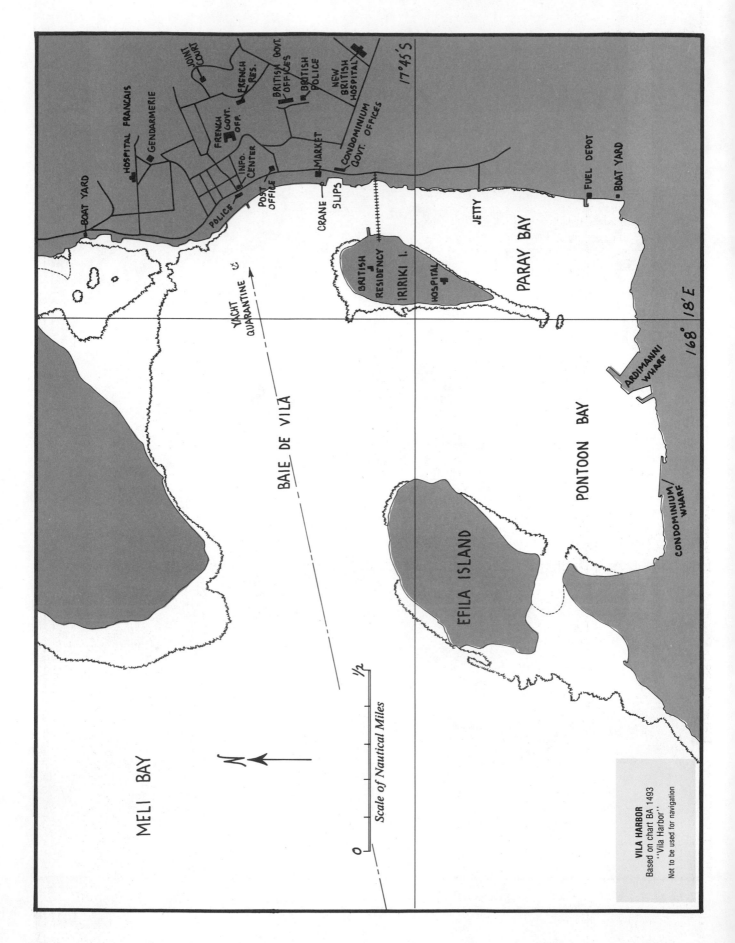

MELI BAY

MELI BAY

BAIE DE VILA

N

Scale of Nautical Miles

0   ½

YACHT
QUARANTINE

BOAT YARD

HOSPITAL FRANCAIS

GENDARMERIE

JOINT COURT

FRENCH RES.

BRITISH GOVT. OFFICES

BRITISH POLICE

NEW BRITISH HOSPITAL

FRENCH GOVT. OFF.

INFO. CENTER

POLICE

POST OFFICE

MARKET

CONDOMINIUM GOVT. OFFICES

CRANE

SLIPS

BRITISH RESIDENCY

IRIRIKI I.

HOSPITAL

17°45'S

168° 18'E

JETTY

PARAY BAY

FUEL DEPOT

BOAT YARD

PONTOON BAY

ARDIMANNI WHARF

CONDOMINIUM WHARF

EFILA ISLAND

VILA HARBOR
Based on chart BA 1493
"Vila Harbor"

Not to be used for navigation

2 Crew Lists
2 Animal Lists
2 Bonded Stores Lists

The Master will also be required to fill out a form regarding the amount and type of safety equipment on board.

This port is generally not regarded as a good port for cruising boats due to the lack of well-protected anchorages. This is because of the depth of the canal and the port's exposure to the southeasterlies. A prudent yachtsman should arrive by daylight in the canal only and proceed either to the quarantine anchorage or to customs and immigration and then contact the Harbor Master. The berthing of large vessels at this port requires plenty of room in both directions and thus the prohibited anchorage. In addition, the port does not have a tug to assist the ships.

The main wharf is not considered entirely suitable for yachts, expecially along the main face. A current up to 1½ knots flows past it. Flood runs to the west and ebb runs to the east. Vessels approaching the the Main Wharf should use extreme caution. During the cool season, April to October, the southeast wind is strong and blows onto the wharf. At times there is a heavy swell in the canal. Vessels are prohibited from lying at the wharfs for extended periods without permission of the Harbor Master.

Slip facilities are available at Palikula, 8 miles to the east and E. Neuman's Boatyard is at the west end of the harbor. Water is available at the Main Wharf and the Small Ships Wharf. Fuel may be delivered in bulk at wharves after arrangement with Shell Oil Co. Most food supplies are available at the shopping center.

Iriki Island in Vila Harbor, Efate Island, is the residency of the British Commissioner for the New Hebrides Condominium Government. Vila is the capital of the New Hebrides and a Port of Entry.

Radio Communications

Station name and call	Location	Frequency Transmit/Receive	Service hours LMT	Type of Service
Vila Radio	Vila	4396 kHz	0930-1000	Weather report
		2182	Mon-Fri 0600-1900 Saturdays 0600-1800 Sun. & holidays 0600-0700 0800-1130 1600-1730	**Marine operations**
		6204	**0900-1600**	South Pacific emergency frequency. The first three minutes of every hour and half-hour are silent periods reserved for distress calls.
YJB 1	17°26'S 168°20'E	1420 kHz	1100-1400 1745-2145	Commercial broadcast
YJB 4		3945	"	Commercial broadcast
YJB 7		4975	"	Comercial broadcast
Radio Tanafo	Espiritu Santo	3990 kHz	0730-0830	Commercial broadcast

Part III -
Islands of Micronesia

- **Mariana Islands**
  - *(a) Guam*
  - *(b) Northern Mariana Islands*
- **Trust Territory of the Pacific Islands**
  - *(a) Marshall District*
  - *(b) Kosrae District*
  - *(c) Ponape District*
  - *(d) Truk District*
  - *(e) Yap District*
  - *(f) Palau District*
- **Kiribati**
- **Republic of Nauru**

Micronesia is a Greek term for "small islands" and that is what they are. There are 1400 of them with a total land area of only 1060 square miles covering about four million square miles of ocean. Except for Kiribati, they all lie in the Northern Hemisphere and span the International Dateline. Largest of the islands and the most populated is Guam made of coral limestone terraces on top of a submerged volcano. Most of the islands are, however, true atolls. The climate is warm but tempered with the tradewinds and rain is adequate but not abundant. In the western part of Micronesia, typhoons are common and can occur the year around.

The Micronesian evolved from the Asian corridor area of Malaysia and is generally more like the Polynesian in features and way of life than the Melanesian. In the far western part of Micronesia, the peoples are very similar to the Filipino. There are eight identifiable cultural areas thoughout Micronesia: the Mariana Islanders also known as Chamorros; the I-Kiribati; the Marshallese; the Eastern Carolinians; the Central Carolinians; the Yapese, the Palau islanders; and the Southwest islanders. The Micronesians were good navigators like the Polynesians roaming at least within their island groups so that the Micronesian culture and society has some homogeneous features. There are few natural resources on these islands and atolls so the people are predominantly agrarian and fishermen.

Most of Micronesia (in fact, all but Kiribati, Nauru and Guam) is part of the Trust Territory of the Pacific Islands administered by the United States since the end of World War II. Micronesia has had a succession of rulers — Spain, Germany, Japan, and the United States. All of these masters have left their trademarks in language and culture plus limited development of economic "centers" in each of the groups.

Island Groups
of Micronesia

Island Group	Number of islands	Land area sq. mi.	Population (1967/71)	Government
Guam	1	209	87,000	United States Territory
Northern Marianas	14	185	12,300	United States Commonwealth
Marshall Islands	33	70	20,200	Trust Territory of United States
Caroline Islands	47	462	69,800	Trust Territory of United States
Kiribati (incl. Banaba)	17	117	46,400	**An independent republic within the British Commonwealth**
Nauru Island	1	9	7,000	An independent republic within the British Commonwealth

Chapter 23

MARIANA ISLANDS CHAIN

The farthest north islands of Micronesia and those closest to the Asian mainland are the Mariana Islands. They are the southern end of a long chain of submerged seamounts extending south from the Japanese archipelago. Originally called the Ladrones Islands by Magellan in March 1521, they extended from Guam on the south to Maug Island in the north, a distance of 520 miles.

The largest of the Mariana Islands is Guam at the southern end. It is composed of coral limestone terraces built on top of a submerged volcano. The islands to the north are of similar geologic formation but younger in age so that less weathering has occurred to create fertile soil. In fact the northernmost islands cannot support any population.

As a result of Magellan's early voyage, the Spanish took great interest in the western Pacific. Spanish priests ac-

companied the early explorers and they established missions in the Mariana Islands in the sixteenth century. The Catholic priests immediately set to converting the Chamorros to Christianity but were hampered by native revolts. The Spanish soldiers took a hand in rounding up most Chamorros, putting them on Guam where they could be better controlled. Some, however, escaped to nearby Rota while the islands of Tinian and Saipan and others to the north were left uninhabited. In the process of controlling the native Chamorros, half of them were killed leaving only 1700 on Guam. From then on there was a mixing of the races and it would be hard to find a true blooded Chamorro today. Descendants of the Chamorro number in the thousands and occupy Guam, Rota, Tinian, and Saipan.

The United States involvement with the Mariana Islands came about as a result of the Spanish American

A monument has been placed at Umatac as the historical landing spot of Ferdinand Magellan, the first European explorer to cross the Pacific Ocean. He landed on Guam in 1521.

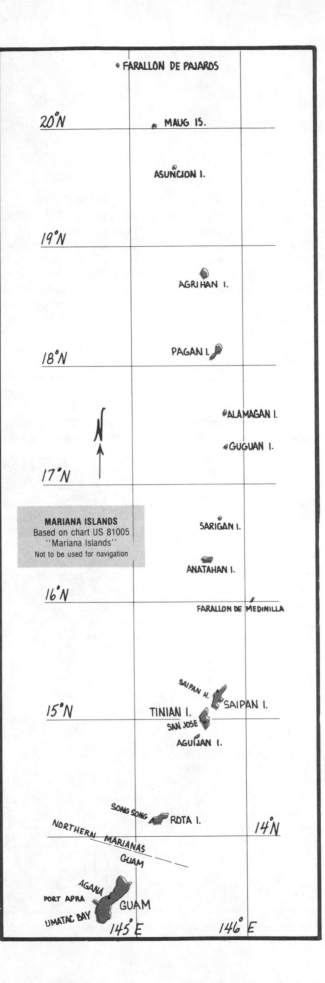

FARALLON DE PAJAROS

20°N · MAUG IS.

ASUNCION I.

19°N

AGRIHAN I.

PAGAN I.

18°N

ALAMAGAN I.

GUGUAN I.

17°N

N

MARIANA ISLANDS
Based on chart US 81005
"Mariana Islands"
Not to be used for navigation

SARIGAN I.

ANATAHAN I.

16°N

FARALLON DE MEDINILLA

SAIPAN H.
SAIPAN I.
15°N TINIAN I.
SAN JOSE
AGUIJAN I.

SONG SONG ROTA I.
NORTHERN MARIANAS 14°N
GUAM

AGANA
PORT APRA GUAM
UMATAC BAY 145°E 146°E

Wherever coral reefs give protected waters you will find the outrigger canoe used for fishing or for fun.

War which was fought primarily in the Philippines as far as Pacific involvement was concerned. The United States took over Guam which at that time seemed to be the only island worthwhile in the group, especially from a naval harbor standpoint. Spain recognizing the end of its Pacific colonial empire, then sold the rest of the Mariana Islands to Germany as well as the Caroline and Marshall Islands. This, then, was the political status of the Mariana Islands up to World War I.

The German Oceanic empire was based mostly on commercialism and included holdings in New Guinea as well as the island groups of Samoa, Marshall, Carolines and Marianas. Germany's goal was commercial expansion initially and much of the administration of her colonies was in the hands of copra and trading company officials. Political expansion would naturally follow on the heels of successful commercial ventures. It probably would have, too, except World War I interfered with it and Germany lost all of her Pacific holdings.

New Zealand took over Western Samoa, Japan seized control of the Marianas (except Guam), the Marshalls and the Carolines, and Germany's interest in New Guinea was absorbed by Australia. Between wars the Pacific was administered in four political parts — the French and British had the South Pacific, the Dutch had New Guinea, the Japanese had Micronesia, and the Americans had Hawaii.

But Japan was not satisfied with her gains from World War I so she precipitated World War II in the Pacific with aggressive land, sea, and air action that took the Imperial forces as far south as New Guinea before being stopped by the Pacific Allied forces. It took several years but Japan was militarily defeated and all of her holdings outside of the Japanese islands, themselves, were put in various forms of trusteeship under the victorious Allies. Guam

was returned to the United States and the island groups of Marianas, Carolines, and Marshalls were made into the Trust Territory of the Pacific Islands to be administered by the United States until self-determination by the peoples themselves could be resolved.

The Northern Mariana Islands were the first to resolve their choice and in January, 1978 they became a territory of the United States in the same political status as Guam. Therefore, there are now two Territories of the United States sharing the islands of the Mariana chain. Although the Commonwealth of the Northern Mariana Islands governs itself independent of the Trust Territory, the headquarters of the Trust Territory continues in residence at Saipan and will stay there until the remaining members of the Trust Territory decide on their future political status.

The Weather

The islands of the Marianas chain have similar weather conditions. Under ordinary circumstances, the wind and seas in the vicinity of Guam are easterly due to the northeast trades. Westerly winds are at times experienced during the summer months as Guam is within the limits of the southwest monsoon. These winds are, as a rule, light. In the vicinity of Guam, northeasterly and east-northeasterly winds prevail 65 percent of the time between December and May and are strongest during these months.

Gales occur occasionally in the areas northward of Palau and Guam Islands, chiefly in winter, due to the strengthening of the northeast monsoon and trades. Sometimes, however, they occur at other seasons in connection with typhoons. Between June and November, the

269

surface winds are quite variable. Calms are rare. In the southern islands, the winds show a slight southerly trend as early as May.

In the vicinity of the islands of Saipan and Tinian, the steadiest winds occur when the winter monsoon and the northeast trades reinforce each other. Between November and April, northeasterly to easterly winds prevail seventy percent of the time at speeds of 10 to 12 knots. During the summer monsoon (May to October) easterly winds predominate, but southerly to westerly winds also occur. Wind speeds are about 10 to 11 knots from May to July, and 8 knots from August to October. Land mass effect modifies the maritime diurnal variations so that the surface winds are strongest at 0300 and weakest at 1400.

In the vicinity of Pagan Island, the winds are steadiest during the northeast monsoon (November through March). They blow mostly from the northeast at an average speed of 15 knots. From April through June, the monsoon weakens and the prevailing winds become more easterly. During the wet season (June through November), easterly winds continue to predominate, but with considerable percentages from southerly to westerly directions. The winds are mostly light, the only strong winds occuring with typhoons.

Typhoons sometimes form southward of the Mariana Islands and occasionally pass in the vicinity of these islands. They are apt to occur more often during the summer months and are accompanied by high winds and torrential rains. They seldom occur during the winter months. Typhoon Olive swept over the Mariana Islands on 30 April 1963 causing severe damage to the islands of Saipan, Rota, and Tinian.

Tropical disturbances sometimes occur in the vicinity of Guam; the frequency is about once every 2 years. The storm center is usually small at the early stage of development, which is usual in this area. Typhoons are most common between April and November because of the greater incidence of mid-ocean low-pressure areas during the period. There are usually several typhoons each year. These commonly have winds of 80 to 100 knots moving around a central eye of total calm.

Tropical disturbances occur between August and January in the vicinity of the islands of Saipan and Tinian. Records show one storm a year originating in or passing over this area. The storm center is from 50 to 100 miles in diameter at the time of passage and is quite intense near the center.

Tropical disturbances usually pass well to the southward of Pagan Island, but several have been experienced. August, September and October are the most likely months. January through April is the only period believed to be entirely free of such storms. Probably not more than one a year passes close enough to effect Pagan Island.

Gales seldom occur in the vicinity of the islands of Tinian and Saipan. Winds reach gale force in the vicinity of Pagan Island from two to four percent of the time.

Thunderstorms occur frequently from July to the early part of November. December through May are the months that are relatively free from thunderstorms.

In the Mariana Islands, the rainy season attends the summer monsoon at which time thunderstorms are fairly common. The wet season (July through October) has a mean monthly average of 10 inches of rain or more. The major rainfall consists of heavy showers. As a rule, the rainfall dimishes as the latitude increases.

The rainy season at Guam is from the first of July until the early part of November, with a monthly average of 8 to 15 inches. January through May is the dry period with an average monthly fall of 2 to 3 inches. April is the driest month. The mean average rainfall is about 70 inches annually.

The rainy season at the islands of Saipan and Tinian is from July to November, the dry season lasts from December through June. During the rainy season, with the doldrum belt lying almost directly over these islands, there are increased showers and numerous thunderstorms and squalls. The dry season is characterized by fair weather, interrupted by fronts associated with northerly low pressure centers and some showers. Saipan Island has an average rainfall of 86 inches per year with a monthly average of 13 inches. During the rainy season (July through October) it averages 13 inches per month. Throughout the rest of the year, the average is about 4 inches per month. April is the driest month with an average of about 3 inches.

Pagan Island has an average annual rainfall of 60 inches. Since the mean position of the doldrum belt is always southward of this island, rainfall and cloud cover is somewhat less than over the more southerly islands. This belt lies closest to this island between July and September, bringing a maximum development of the northeast monsoon from November through March, the average rainfall then being 2 to 3 inches per month. Some rain will fall during weak cold fronts which drift slowly across this region about twice a month. These rains are usually of short duration. Rainfall increases somewhat as the wet summer season is approached. During this season the rainfall is estimated to be about 10 inches monthly, decreasing somewhat in October and November.

In Guam, the average mean temperature is 81°F, the mean maximum is 90°F, and the minimum is 70°F. The temperatures for the rest of the Mariana Islands are quite uniform throughout the year. January and February are the coolest months. The nights are cooler in the northern islands. Temperatures above 87°F normally occur from 13 to 22 days a month between April and August. The daily minimums seldom fall below 74°F during the summer months. The yearly range of temperatures is 3°F in the south and 7°F in the north. The daily range is about 10°F.

Humidity is high throughout the year, but there is somewhat less humidity from December through May. The yearly average is about 76 percent, the January average is 68 percent and the June average is 84 percent.

Fog and mist are rarely reported in the Guam, Saipan-Tinian areas. Visibility of less than 1¼ miles can be expected on less than one day per month.

The yearly average cloud cover is about 7/10. The maximum coverage of 8/10 to 9/10 occurs during the summer months (July to October). Cloudiness is higher over the islands than over the adjacent seas. Clouds are more frequent during the daytime.

Chapter 23-A

GUAM

The Country

Guam is located in the western Pacific 13° north of the equator. It is the most southern, most populous, and largest island of the Marianas chain. The island is 30 miles long and ranges from 4 to 8½ miles in width. It has a total land area of about 209 square miles.

The land mass was formed by the successive upheavals of a submarine volcanic mountain range and the limestone beds of the coral reefs surrounding the range. The northern end of the island is a plateau of rolling hills set on vertical cliffs rising 300 to 500 feet above sea level. The cliffs are marked with crevices, and small caves are found at various heights in the cliffs. These caves were formed by the breaking of the surf against what was once the sea-level line. The island narrows in the middle around a low dome-shaped mass of land that the islanders named the island's belly.

The tropical climate yields a lush vegetation, including vines, savanna grass, and various species of palm and other trees that would rapidly cover most of the island if not constantly cut back. The vegetation cover of the northern half of the island has a lower crown height than that of the south. The winds on the east coast of the southern half of the island have reduced vegetation on the coastal slopes, and in several places these have seriously eroded.

Trees found on the island include coconut, breadfruit, banyan, ironwood, banana, and several types of flowering species. Coconuts, supplemented by rice, were used as the major food staples before the arrival of the Spanish. Wild orchids are found as well as frangipani. Flame tress and hibiscus were introduced from the other islands.

The island has a limited range of animal life. There were no quadrapeds indigenous to the island, and the only indigenous mammals that have been found are two species of bats. Rats and small large-eared mice abound. Small deer were introduced by the Spanish in the 1770's.

The bird population suffered, as did most island animals, during the war. There are numerous shorebirds, such as the reef heron and varieties of the rail. The only true bird of prey is a short-horned owl. The only true songbird is a member of the warbler family. There are many varieties of dove, one species of tern, and no sea gulls.

There are no snakes of the usual kind on the island, although there is a six-inch long scaled worm with microscopic eyes. Sea turtles are common visitors to the island. Insect life is minimal save for the many species of mosquitos, none of which are malarial. Non-poisonous but painful scorpions and centipedes are common. Large spiders sometimes reach six to ten inches in diameter.

Three different types of lizards are found on the island. The most formidable in appearance is the iguana. Although reaching larger sizes elsewhere, on Guam the iguana usually grows to more than four to six feet in length. It preys on small birds, eggs, and chickens. It has been known to attack small dogs when cornered but generally flees when encountered.

Carbon dating from cooking pits shows the presence of man as early as approximately 1320 B.C. Potsherds,

Guam

A territory of the United States

Port of Entry:

Apra Harbor   13°27'N, 144°40'E

Distances between ports in nautical miles:

Between *Apra Harbor* and:

Funafuti, Tuvalu	2460
Honolulu, Hawaii	3320
Kwajalein, Marshall Islands	1410
Lae, New Guinea	1320
Malakal, Palau Islands	710
Nonouti, Gilbert Islands	1980
Noumea, New Caledonia	2530
Ponape, Caroline Islands	910
Rabaul, New Britain	1190
Selwyn Bay, Solomon Islands	1760
Suva, Fiji	2780
Talomako, New Hebrides	2180
Tinian, Mariana Islands	130
Truk, Caroline Islands	590
Wake Island	1330
Wotje, Marshall Islands	1550
Yap, Caroline Islands	460
Tokyo, Japan	1340

Standard time:

10 hours fast on GMT

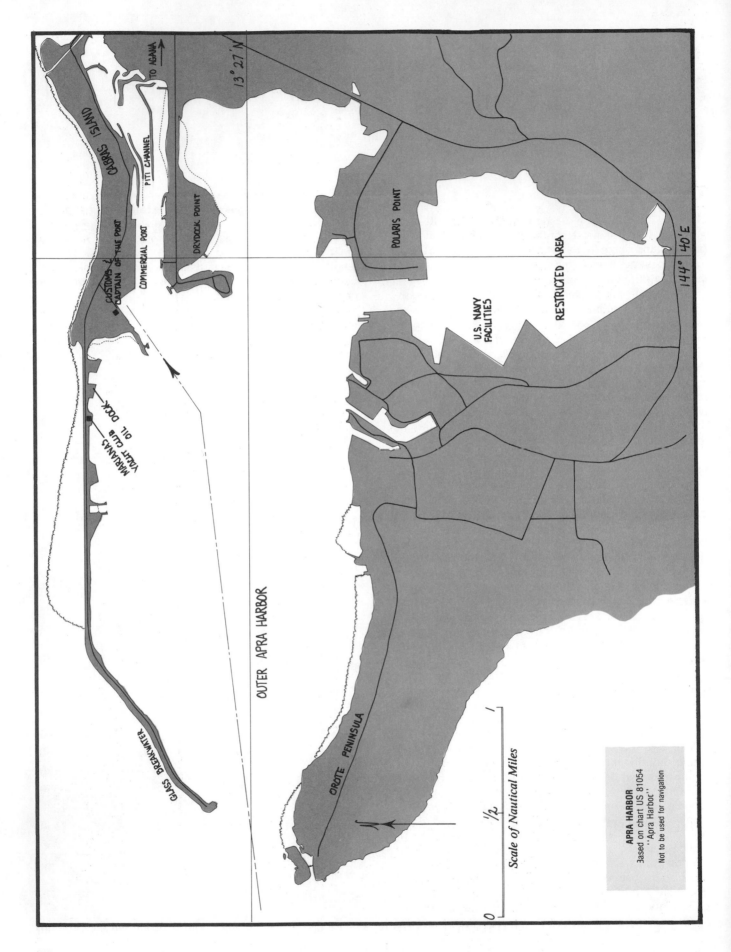

CABRAS ISLAND

TO AGANA

13° 27' N

PITI CHANNEL

COMMERCIAL PORT

CUSTOMS & CAPTAIN OF THE PORT

DRYDOCK POINT

POLARIS POINT

U.S. NAVY FACILITIES

RESTRICTED AREA

144° 40' E

MARIANAS YACHT CLUB OIL DOCK

GLASS BREAKWATER

OUTER APRA HARBOR

OROTE PENINSULA

N

½   1

Scale of Nautical Miles

0

APRA HARBOR
Based on chart US 81054
"Apra Harbor"
Not to be used for navigation

stone tools, and weapons found in archeological diggings indicate that the island was well populated at least 3,000 years ago and became at some time the major population and trade center for all of the Mariana Islands.

Although the origin of the Chamorros is still uncertain, on the basis of their languauge and way of life they are believed to be Malayo-Polynesian. They are the only oceanic people who have cultivated rice. On the basis of such evidence as this, most anthropologists agree that if the Chamorro did not themselves have origins in southeast Asia, they had prolonged contact and mixed with people that did.

The arrival of Ferdinand Magellan in 1521 brought the first contact with the west. During the second half of the 17th century, the Spaniards established the first permanent European settlement on Guam. The religion of the Chamorros was supplanted by Christianity. The many wars between the Spanish and Chamorros, coupled with smallpox and typhoons, resulted in the decimation of the population from an estimated 50 to 100,000 natives in the early 1600's to about 5,000 in the late 1690's.

Spain continued in possession of Guam until the War of 1898 with the United States. At that time the Spanish not only gave up Guam and the Phillipines to the United States, but they sold the rest of their possessions in the Pacific, namely the rest of Micronesia to Germany.

In World War I Guam became involved by the sinking of the German cruiser *Cormoran* in Apra Harbor by its own crew. Between the two world wars the island made substantial economic strides and contacts with other parts of the world increased.

When World War II broke out in the Pacific, Guam was virtually defenseless and the Navy commander surrendered to the Japanese on December 10, 1941. The Japanese removed all Americans from the island and for a period of 31 months the Guamanians were subject to heavy demands by the occupying Japanese forces. On July 21, 1944 American reoccupation forces landed on the beaches. Major enemy resistance ceased on August 18, 1944.

The population in 1969 stood at 104,000 of which about 40 percent represented United States military personnel and their dependents. The population centers are concentrated on the coastal or narrow middle areas of the island. The capitol, Agana, and its suburb, Agana Heights, are located on the western side of the middle of the island and had a combined population of 6,200 persons in 1968.

At the time of the arrivals of the Spanish, most Chamorros on Guam lived in small villages of wood and thatch dwellings along the coast. The basic social unit was the family. Although marriages were relatively easily terminated, each man had but one wife at a time. Concubines were permitted, and unmarried males were allowed considerable sexual freedom. After puberty all males lived in the village clubhouse until they married. Each clubhouse had its secret rituals and festivals.

As a result of the initially rapid conversions to Christianity and the later reduction of the population, the values and structures of Chamorro society were rapidly eroded. By the time the Spanish lost possession of the island there were no genetically pure indigenous people, and the islanders had lost almost all traces of their Chamorro culture. Even the structure of their language had assimilated many Filipino and Spanish elements.

Although the maintenance of the Spanish traditions among the old, partcularly in regard to religion, has continued, by 1970 this was a marginal aspect of society. The majority of Guamanians reflect the basic culture, society, and values of mainland Americans.

United States administration of the Territory of Guam is provided under the 1950 Organic Act and its amendments. The Territorial Government of Guam is the only administrative unit on the island. All Guamanians are citizens of the United States. They do not, however, participate in national elections, nor are they represented in the United States Congress although there is a representative of Guam in Washington.

The government of Guam is composed of three branches: the executive, the legislative, and the judicial. The executive branch is headed by a governor, assisted by the secretary of Guam. Both serve four year terms. The first Guamanian governor, Manuel L.F. Guerrero, was appointed in 1963 with the confirmation of the Senate. Under the Guam Elective Governship Act of 1968, provisions were made for the popular election of the governor and the lieutenant governor.

The judicial branch is composed of two courts—the District Court of Guam and the Island Court. The District Court possesses the jurisdiction of a judicial court of the United States. The Island Court possesses jurisdiction over claims under $5,000 involving domestic relations, domestic probates, claims against the government, and in criminal cases not involving felonies. It also has jurisdiction over tax cases.

Yacht Entry

U.S. citizens will require a passport if not arriving directly from the U.S. (Hawaii). A visa is not required. There is no limit on the length of stay for U.S. citizens.

Non-U.S. citizens will need a passport for entering Guam and a permit can be obtained after arrival for a stay of not more than 30 days. Persons planning to stay longer than 30 days will need to apply for a visa which should be done ahead of time.

Yacht Facilities

Tides and heavy swells make anchoring around the periphery of Guam very hazardous. The only natural bay of commercial value is Apra Bay, formed in the San Luis de Apra Basin on the upper western coast of the island. Farther down the coast are Agat Bay and Umatac Bay.

Apra Harbor, an improved natural harbor, is located off the northeast side of Orote Peninsula. Cabras Island and a breakwater that extends along Luminao Reef form the north side of the outer harbor. The commercial port for Guam is located on Cabras Island and is the major transshipment port for the Pacific Islands Trust Territory. Apra inner harbor contains extensive berthing facilities but is a restricted area.

Agana, a modern city in a tropical setting. It is located about 10 miles northeast from Apra Harbor, the Port of Entry. Most provisions can be obtained here but boat hardware is scarce.

The harbor is extensive and safe except during the typhoon season. There is a possible hurricane hole for small boats in Piti channel beyond the commercial wharves. It has about 6-feet of water in it. The worst typhoon months are August through November although they have been known to occur during any month.

Contact with the Harbor Master on VHF channel 16 is recommended when approaching Apra Harbor. Customs clearance can be obtained at commercial Wharf Foxtrot. Immigration must be handled at the Agana Airport.

There are some moorings available at the Marianas Yacht Club in the northeast corner of the outer harbor along with telephone and showers. This is within walking distance of the Customs Office.

Most supplies including diesel fuel and gasoline are readily available at the harbor and in the town of Agana.

All harbor operations are under U.S. Naval control but the Port Security Officer at Commercial Port issues all clearances for that port.

Agana Bay is an open roadstead with a very steep-to bottom and great depths near the reef. A small craft harbor is located in Agana Bay but the reef passage and channel are narrow and very dangerous for mariners without local knowledge. Mariners unfamiliar with the channel should not attempt entry without assistance or during other than daylight hours with favorable conditions. Assistance can be requested from the Agana Harbor Patrol. The boat basin has 42 slips up to 45 feet LOA. Water, electrical, and telephone services are available.

Umatac Bay on the southeast corner of Guam is a particularly scenic port of call but exposed to westerly winds.

Medical Memo

Immunization requirements:

Smallpox vaccination is required if travel does not originate in the United States or its possessions. Immunization against cholera and yellow fever are required if you have transited or visited within the last six days an area currently infected. Typhoid, paratyphoid and tetanus shots are recommended.

Local health situation:

Guam is free of all communicable diseases.

Health services:

There are numerous public, private and military hospitals in Guam. The large Guam Memorial Hospital can provide all needed medical services. There is an island-wide system of health care centers.

Dental and optical services are both available at the Guam Memorial Hospital but there is a scarcity of trained medical personnel.

Drug stores carry a full line of non-prescription and prescription drugs. Prescription drugs are sold only on the order of a doctor.

Water:

Tap water from the public supply is reported to be safe but all other water should be considered suspect and treated.

Jetsam and Flotsam

Currency:

Guam uses United States currency.

Language:

English is the common language in Guam but you may occasionally hear bits of Chamorro spoken. Today's Chamorro language is no longer pure having been modified with Filipino and Spanish words.

Electricity:

110 volt, 60 Hz AC

Postal Address:

Yacht (   )
General Delivery
Agana, Guam 96910, USA

or, if you are at the yacht club

Yacht (   )
c/o Mariana Yacht Club
Agana, Guam 96910, USA

External Affairs:

United States embassies or consulates

Information Center:

Guam Visitors Bureau
P.O. Box 3520
Agana, Guam 96910, USA

Cruising Library:

Guam Past and Present, Charles Beardsley; Charles E. Tuttle Co., Rutland, VT 05701, USA
A Complete History of Guam, Paul Carano and Pedro C. Sanchez; Charles E. Tuttle Co., Rutland, VT 05701, USA, 1964

The small craft harbor at Agana requires local knowledge to enter because of the narrow channel through the fringing reef.

Radio Communications

Station name and call	Location	Frequency Transmit/Receive	Service hours LMT	Type of service
Harbor Master	Apra	VHF channel 16	Continuous	Port operations
Agana Harbor Patrol	Agana	2136 kHz	0600-0200	Harbor assistance
Coast Guard - NRV		2670 kHz-ssb	1005-2205	Western Pacific weather
Radio Guam - KUAM	Agana	610 kHz 93.9 MHz (FM)	Continuous	Local storm & small craft advisories Commercial broadcast
KATB	Agana	570 kHz		Commercial broadcast

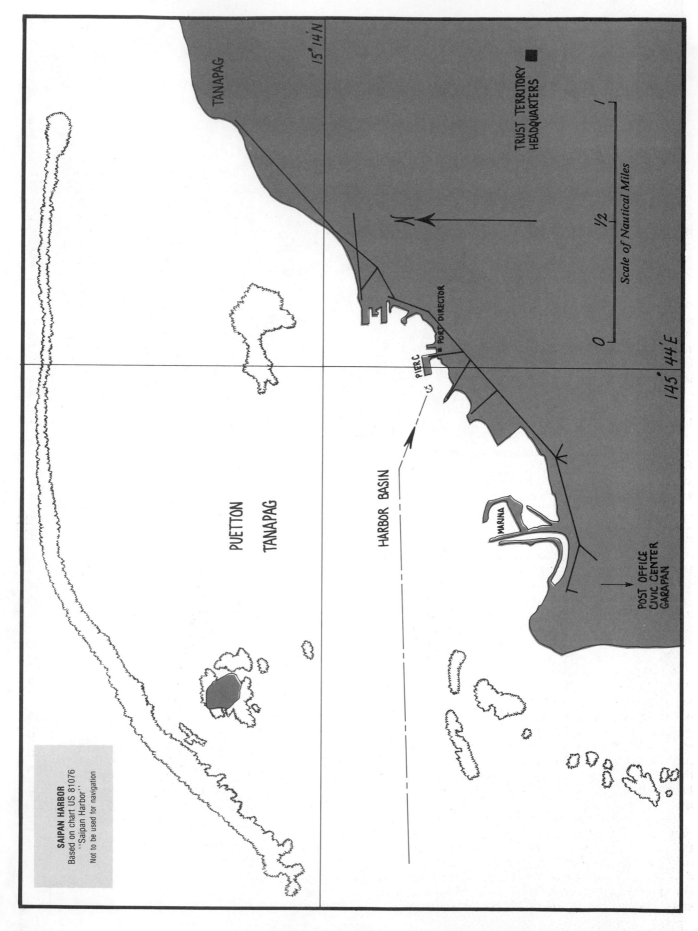

SAIPAN HARBOR
Based on chart US 81076
"Saipan Harbor"
Not to be used for navigation

TANAPAG

15° 14' N

TRUST TERRITORY
HEADQUARTERS

Scale of Nautical Miles

0   ½   1

145° 44' E

PORT DIRECTOR

PIER C

PUETTON
TANAPAG

HARBOR BASIN

MARINA

POST OFFICE
CIVIC CENTER
GARAPAN

278

Chapter 23-B

COMMONWEALTH OF THE NORTHERN MARIANA ISLANDS

The Country

Stretching more than 400 miles from the Territory of Guam to the lonely volcanic peaks of the northern islands, the Marianas constitute the highest slopes of a massive mountain range rising six miles off the floor of the Marianas trench. Here lies the boundary between the Pacific Ocean and the Philippine Sea.

They contain fourteen major units (twenty-one individual islands) having a combined land area of 183.6 square miles. Although the entire chain is composed of high volcanic types, it is often discussed in terms of a northern section of nine and a southern section of five island units because of differences in the size, altitude, and soil covering of their respective components.

The five islands of the southern section are Saipan, Tinian, Rota, Aguijan, and Farallon de Medinilla, which together have a land area twice as great as that of the northern section. Saipan has a land area of 46.5 square miles and is the largest of the Mariana group. Tinian and Rota are the second and third largest, respectively. Aguijan and Farallon de Medinilla are uninhabited and of little significance.

The southern section, although larger in overall land area, is generally lower than the northern section, but for the most part the islands are greatly rolling rather than mountainous. Although the islands are volcanic in origin, there has been no such activity for a long time, and their cores are largely covered with limestone terraces, representing former stands of the sea that were upthrust in the distant past. The erosion of this limestone has produced a covering of excellent topsoil, and the well-watered islands have a good growth of vegetation.

The nine islands of the northern section consist of Farallon de Pajaros, Maug, Asuncion, Agrihan, Pagan, Alamagen, Guguan, Sarignan, and Anatahan. Except for Maug, which is a cluster of three miniscule islands connected by a common base beneath the water, all are single islands that rise precipitously as mountain peaks of rocky, volcanic materials. All are quite high, and Agrihan's peak of 3166 feet is the highest in Micronesia. Some of the peaks are active volcanoes, which have erupted on Farallon de Pajaros, Asuncion, Pagan, and Guguan islands.

The rugged terrain, lack of easily eroded materials to provide soil cover, and insufficient amounts of rain make the northern section unsuitable for habitation. Actually, only five islands (Anatahan, Sarigan, Alamagan, Pagan, and Agrihan) are permanently inhabited, and they contain less than 250 people or less than two percent of the entire Mariana population of 15,000 persons.

Coconut palms are found on most of the islands. They grow along the coasts of the dry islands but sometimes form extensive woods, such as are found on the great plains of Pagan island. Occasionally in the interior of the islands, more or less open woods are found and even on the coast, dense forests with little undergrowth are found. Bush-like casuarina trees grow on dry and sandy shores.

From land covered with tall grass, coconut palms, breadfruit trees and Areca palms rise above the mangroves in the ravines. More widely distributed than the forest is the savannah with its shrubs and bushes. This is the case particularly on Tinian island where oranges, citrons, guavas, and other fruit trees are found.

Saipan is an oblong island dominated by the rock-green slopes of Mount Tagpochau and it has a population of over 12,000 persons divided among eight villages. The largest of these, Chalan Kanoa, is a dense concentration of metal and wood houses, here and there interrupted by

Northern Mariana Islands

A United States Commonwealth

Port of Entry:

Tanapeg Harbor, Saipan   15°14′N, 145°44′E

Distances between ports in nautical miles:

Between *Saipan* and:

Agana, Guam	120
Honolulu, Hawaii	3230
Jaluit, Marshall Islands	1550
Johnston Island	3230
Kwajalein, Marshall Islands	1510
Majuro, Marshall Islands	1780
Palau, Caroline Islands	900
Ponape, Caroline Islands	1000
Truk, Caroline Islands	610
Tokyo, Japan	1460
Yap, Caroline Islands	630

Standard time:

10 hours fast on GMT

Saipan was the last big island battleground of World War II. Just one month before the end of the war, the Japanese defenders of Saipan moved their surviving forces to the north end of the island for a suicidal last ditch stand. This was their last command post. Saipan is a treasure trove of war relics but it is also the capital and Port of Entry for the Northern Mariana Islands and the Headquarters of the Trust Territory of the Pacific Islands.

the restored concrete shells of surviving Japanese houses or the more typhoon-proof pillbox-like residences recently erected by the more affluent Saipanese. The main road through Chalan Kanoa, like all of the major arteries around the island, has a smooth macadam surface, and slowly but surely, the interior grid of narrow, dusty, pot-holed roads is experiencing the face-lifting effects of hot mix and steam roller.

The proximity of houses, the hordes of children, the rusting auto bodies sitting in front yards, and the friendly congestion of it all suggests something of a Puerto Rican barrio. The landscape and atmosphere is generally Hispanic, with occasional evidence — a water cistern, a Shinto shrine, a snatch of song — of the thirty-year

Japanese mandate. With the inevitable exception of the Micronesian/American government housing perched atop Capitol Hill (headquarters of the Trust Territory executive branch and Congress) and a few other government housing areas, the other communities of the island differ but little from Chalan Kanoa.

Saipan island is the major producer of livestock in all of Micronesia. Swine, poultry, carabao, goats and ducks are found on the southern islands. Considerable vegetables are grown on Saipan, Tinian and Rota for local use as well as shipment to Guam. Trochus shells are found in the southern Mariana Islands.

The Commonwealth of the Northern Marianas is self-governing with their own elected governor and a legislature in the same manner as Puerto Rico. Full United States citizenship, however, must wait the end of the trusteeship of the United States over all of Micronesia which is now fixed for 1981.

Yacht Entry

U.S. citizens will require a passport if not arriving directly from another political entity of the United States. A visa is not required and there is no time limit on the length of stay for a U.S. citizen.

Non-United States citizens will need a passport for entering the Mariana Islands and a permit can be obtained upon arrival for a stay of not longer than 30 days. Persons planning on staying longer than 30 days will need to apply for a visa ahead of time at a United States consul or embassy.

Yacht Facilities

Saipan Harbor consists of two anchorages, the outer anchorage known as Garapan anchorage and the inner harbor called Puetton Tanapag. The inner harbor is protected by a barrier reef. Both are too far away from port facilities so yachts are advised to head straight for the L-shaped Pier C and tie up along the south (inside) face of the pier. The Harbor Master's office will be found at the base of the pier.

If you cannot remain alongside the pier, anchor a short distance out. There is good holding ground throughout most of the harbor and it is relatively free of coral heads.

There are no particular facilities for yachts in this harbor, only those that service the small working boats. Diesel fuel and gasoline are available at the dock as is fresh water. Deck and engine supplies are available only in

Jetsam and Flotsam

Currency:

The Northern Mariana Islands use the United States dollar.

Language:

The official language is English. Many persons can speak Japanese fluently and a few can speak the native Chamorro tongue.

Electricity:

Electric power is 110 volt, 60 Hz AC

Postal Address:

Yacht ( )
General Delivery
Saipan, Northern Mariana Islands 96950 USA

External Affairs Representative:

United States consulates and embassies

Information Center:

Marianas Visitors Bureau
P.O. Box 861
Saipan, Northern Mariana Islands 96950, USA

limited amounts. Repairs of a minor nature can be made including some electronic repairs.

Saipan is a fairly large island with government and commercial activities spread over much of it. About six miles south of the commercial docks are the post office and civic center in the area called Chalan Kanoa. The second business and government area is located at mid-island in the Garapan-Tanapag area. There you will find the Trust Territory headquarters on Capitol Hill along with other government functions.

Provisions are available in limited selection. Beef, pork and fresh vegetables and fruit are obtainable as well as staple goods.

Medical Memo

Immunization requirements:

Smallpox immunization is required if travel does not originate in the United States or its possessions. Immunization against cholera and yellow fever are required if you have transited or visited within the last six days an area currently infected. Typhoid, paratyphoid and tetanus shots are recommended.

Local health situation:

The Northern Mariana Islands are free of all communicable diseases.

Health services:

Major medical services are available at the main hospital on Saipan. There is a field hospital located on Rota and five dispensaries located throughout the other islands. All facilities and medical services are provided by the government. Fees are less than those charged in the United States. Limited dental and optical services are also available.

Prescription and non-prescription drugs are available at the hospital and dispensaries.

Water:

Tap water from the public supply is supposedly safe. All other water should be considered suspect and treated.

Radio Communications

Station name and call	Location	Frequency Transmit/Receive	Service hours LMT	Type of Service
WSZE	15°07′N 145°29′E	1050 kHz 93.9 MHz (FM)	0600-2300	Commercial broadcast
KJQR	16°N 144°E	1350 kHz	0600-2400	Commercial broadcast
Radio Saipan (KUP - 71)	Garapan	2182/2182 kHz 2724/2724 7935/7935	24 hours	Government maritime

Chapter 24

TRUST TERRITORY OF THE PACIFIC ISLANDS (TTPI)

The Country

The two archipelagoes now comprising the TTPI, (Marshall and Caroline Islands) involve about 90 island units that contain several times that number of individual islands; many units are complex groups of separate landforms collectively called by a common name. Truk island in the Caroline group, for example, is really a cluster of 98 associated islands, and Ulithi, in the same archipelago, is an atoll having 49 islets around its central lagoon.

All islands and island units in the territory are small, ranging downward in size from Babelthuap in the Palau cluster, which has a total land area of 153 square miles. to countless others that are mere specks of coral and sand occupying less than one square mile of the ocean's surface. The islands are so uniformly tiny in fact that despite their incredible number, the total land area of the present TTPI aggregates only 528 square miles.

The islands may be classified as high or low, depending on their altitude, and as continental or oceanic, according to their geological substructure. The Palau cluster, and the island of Yap in the Carolines are high types of varying elevation. These islands are also continental because they are formed by the exposed peaks of the submerged mountain range extending from Japan to New Guinea, which represents the easternmost limits of the Asian continental shelf. The outermost reaches of this shelf seaward of the islands are delineated by deep ocean trenches, which contain some of the most profound depths ever sounded. The Nero Trench between Yap and Guam, for example, has been measured at more than 36,000 feet.

Truk, Ponape, and Kosrae islands in the Eastern Carolines are also high islands, having maximum elevations of about 1,500, 2,500, and 2,000 feet respectively. They are classified as oceanic rather than continental, however, because their substructure is not associated with the land mass of Asia but with great piles of lava extruded from fissures in the floor of the sea itself.

All other islands in the TTPI, regardless of the archipelago in which they are located, are low types that rise only six to eight feet above the surface of the water. These islands are formed by coral growths capping submerged peaks of the continental shelf or oceanic lava piles that do not quite reach the surface. Most of these coralline formations are atolls; that is, they consist of a barrier or a fringing reef, or both, enclosing a number of tiny islets around an interior lagoon. Some, however, such as Lib island in the Marshall group, are single islands that have neither reefs nor lagoons. Still others, such as Fais Island near Ulithi, are raised atolls; that is, they are atolls that have been thrust upward by upheavals in the ocean floor so

that their lagoons as well as their encircling reefs are fully exposed. In the elevating process their lagoons are often drained away, leaving a shallow, saucerlike, and usually marshy depression in their centers.

The territory as a whole is so large and complex that for purposes of orderly presentation it is discussed in terms of six component areas or districts. The relatively compact Marshall archipelago constitutes a separate district by itself. The larger and more dispersed Caroline group, however, is subdivided into five districts, each centered on and named after the most significant island in the area.

Virtually all islands of the territory have a lush and varied covering of vegetation because of the warm and humid climate. The types of plant life vary considerably between the high and low island forms, although coconut and breadfruit trees and two varieties of bamboo are common everywhere. Hibiscus trees can also be found throughout the territory except on the driest atolls.

Vegetation on the low Caroline islands is usually limited to coconut palms, breadfruit, casuarina, pandanus, creeping vines, sedges, and associated strand growth. The high islands are marketed by three distinct types of growth. The coastal flats have dense coverings of broadleaf forest in which mangroves predominate. The mangroves are often interspersed with nipa palm and other salt-resistant vegetation. Inland from the tidal flats coconut trees predominate but give way on the lower slopes to dense rain forests of exceedingly varied composition in limestone areas or to scrubby growth and grassland in volcanic soil regions. The upper slopes of high volcanic islands usually have thin, leached soils that do not permit the growth of tall trees and are covered with wet, mossy scrub forests and an undergrowth of ferns so thick that a path must be cut through them.

The only indigenous land animals in the territory are believed to be four species of bats. Two species are fruit eaters, and two are insect eaters; they are prevalent both on the high and the low islands. All other land animals were introduced by original inhabitants of the area or were brought in later by European and Asian immigrants. Among the introduced animals are dogs, pigs, several species of rats, horses, cattle, water buffalo, goats, and cats. Of special interest also are deer, which were brought to the Marianas and a few other high islands by the Japanese. These ruminants have multiplied so rapidly on Ponape that they constitute a real threat to native gardens.

The islands are usually free from harmful reptiles, but two species of crocodiles and two types of venomous sea snakes are occasionally found in the Palau district. One specie of these snakes is also present in the Marshall

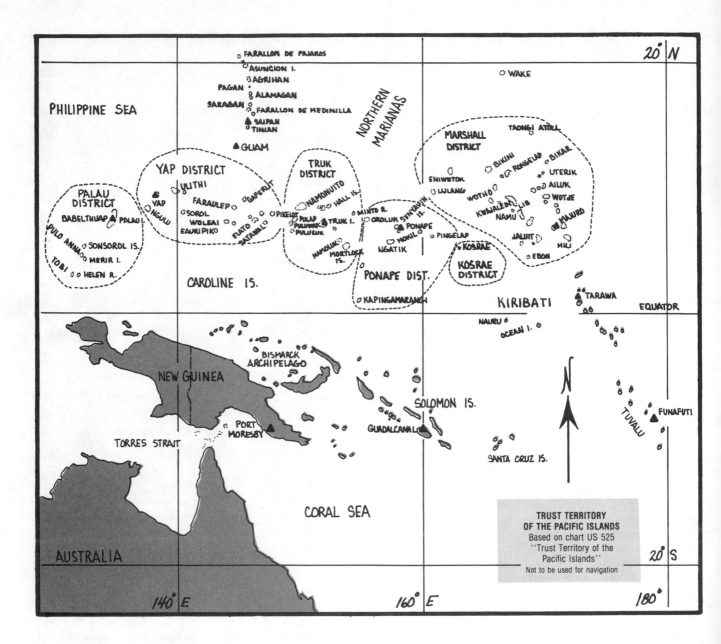

PHILIPPINE SEA

FARALLON DE PAJAROS
ASUNCION I.
AGRIHAN
PAGAN
SARAGAN
ALAMAGAN
FARALLON DE MEDINILLA
SAIPAN
TINIAN

GUAM

NORTHERN MARIANAS

WAKE

MARSHALL DISTRICT

TAONGI ATOLL

PALAU DISTRICT

YAP DISTRICT

YLITHI

FARAULEP
YAP
NGULU
SOROL
WOLEAI
EAURIPIKO

GAFERUT

TRUK DISTRICT

NAMONUITO
HALL IS.

PIKELOT
PULAP
PULUWAT
PULUSUK
ELATO
SATAWAL

TRUK I.

MINTO R.
OROLUK SENYAVIN IS.
PONAPE

BIKINI
ENIWETOK
UJLANG
WOTHO
KWAJALEIN
NAMU
LIB

RONGELAP
BIKAR
UTERIK
AILUK
WOTJE
MAJURO

BABELTHUAP
PALAU
PULO ANNA
SONSOROL IS.
TOBI
MERIR I.
HELEN R.

CAROLINE IS.

NAMOLUK
MORTLOCK IS.
MOKIL
NGATIK

PONAPE DIST.

PINGELAP

JALUIT
MILI

KOSRAE

KOSRAE DISTRICT

EBON

KAPINGAMARANGI

KIRIBATI

TARAWA

EQUATOR

NAURU
OCEAN I.

NEW GUINEA

BISMARCK ARCHIPELAGO

SOLOMON IS.

GUADALCANAL

N

TUVALU
FUNAFUTI

PORT MORESBY
TORRES STRAIT

SANTA CRUZ IS.

CORAL SEA

AUSTRALIA

20° N

20° S

140° E

160° E

180°

**TRUST TERRITORY
OF THE PACIFIC ISLANDS**
Based on chart US 525
''Trust Territory of the
Pacific Islands''
Not to be used for navigation

group. Palau also has a few non-venomous snakes, including a tree snake, a mangrove snake, a boa, and a rare golden burrowing snake. Several species of lizard, including the large monitor variety that reaches a length of six feet, are abundant on many high and low islands alike.

There are relatively few land birds in Micronesia, but marine and shore birds are abundant. These include tern, albatross, booby, frigate, plover, cormorant, and several kinds of heron. The Palau cluster is noted for one specie of rare fresh-water duck. Many other varieties of birds, both land and marine, can sometimes be seen in the islands, but they are migratory rather than resident.

An estimated total of about 7,000 varieties of insects can be found in Micronesia. Approximately half of the different species are known to exist in the territory as a whole; many of the others are endemic only to specific areas.

Marine life in Micronesia is rich in both number and variety. The reefs, lagoons, and shore areas, as well as the open sea, teem with game and food fish and other forms of marine life. All types characteristic of tropical Pacific waters are represented, including bonito, tuna, albacore, barracuda, shark, eel, snapper, flounder, and sea bass. Many highly colored small fish inhabit the reefs, as do octopus, squid, jellyfish, and sea slugs *(trepang)*. There are also many kinds of mollusks and crustacea, such as crabs, lobsters, longusta, shrimp, oysters, and clams. Of special interest is the giant tridacna clam, whose heavy, fluted shell is prized by decorators. Marine mammals include the porpoise and the sea cow, or dugong, which once was plentiful in the Palau district but now is becoming quite scarce.

Since first being sighted by sixteenth century voyagers, Micronesia has known a succession of foreigners. Spain's rule, beginning in the eighteenth century, was ended by the Spanish-American war, German's hegemony ended with the appearance of Japanese gunboats in 1914, and Japan's mandate was finished (and America's begun) with the events of World War II. Each of these nations left its mark—in language, architecture, and religion. And, just as important, each contributed to the considerable, still growing, poise with which Micronesians confront visitors today. Far from naive in their response to foreigners, sometimes more sophisticated than the foreigners themselves, citizens of Micronesia have undergone a continuing informal education in the ways of the world.

Today, little physical evidence remains of the Spanish administration—a moss-covered wall in Ponape, a stone foundation in Yap—but the Spaniards did leave behind one item of continuing strength: the Roman Catholic faith, which approximately half of the Trust Territory's population continues to embrace.

Towards the close of the nineteenth century, Germany showed a mounting interest, commercial and political, in Micronesia. Attracted by the lucrative copra trade and desirous of attaining status as a colonial power, Germany took advantage of Spain's withdrawal from the Pacific after the Spanish-American War, purchasing control of the islands. The German period was short, lasting only until the outbreak of World War I, when the Japanese seized the islands without opposition. The Germans are still remembered, however, for their vigorous efforts to expand trade, augment copra production, and for the stern discipline of their colonial administrators. One German, named Winkler, has passed into Palau folk history as a legendary authoritarian character named "*Binklang*". Many elderly Micronesians still possess a surprisingly good command of German language (and songs and dances) after sixty years of absence.

In 1914 began the long period of Japanese control in Micronesia. The islands were formally entrusted to Japan under a League of Nations mandate in 1920. Today's islanders look back upon these years with mixed emotions. Most adults still speak Japanese, many have Japanese names, many reveal evidence of Japanese blood. Throughout the Territory there remains evidence of Japanese activity: visitors to Ponape will find lengths of roadway which girded the island in Japanese times—the road now being vigorously reclaimed from the jungle. Strollers on the island of Dublon in the Truk Lagoon will come across the massive remains of a Japanese hospital—in its time one of the most impressive facilities in the Pacific. Koror, in the Palau district, still boasts several seaplane ramps, football fields of concrete sloping into water. Elsewhere, throughout the territory, countless docks, foundations, water cisterns, roadways, testify to Japan's attachment to the Trust Territory, and some Micronesians enjoy looking back upon the days when Koror, Garapan, and Dublon were thriving, modern settlements with the amenities of Japanese life. In terms of population and economy—though not political development, the Japanese period marked a high point in Micronesian history. Despite the wartime harshness and discipline which marred the Japanese' closing years, and the almost total destruction which accompanied the conquest of the islands, (along with considerable loss of life to Micronesians), many islanders look back upon the Japanese period with a cautious nostalgia.

"The United States Trust Territory of the Pacific Islands"—this lengthy title was first attached to Micronesia in February 1947, when the United Nations awarded the U.S.A. a trusteeship over the territory. Naval administration of the Carolines and Marshalls lasted until 1951.. In the Marianas (excepting Guam, of course) it lasted until 1962. Appointed by the President, the High Commissioner maintains headquarters on "Capitol Hill" on Saipan. In Washington, Trust Territory affairs are a concern of the Department of the Interior. Moreover, the administration makes annual reports to the Trusteeship Council of the United Nations and every three years is subject to the very close scrutiny of a United Nations Visiting Mission.

Below the High Commissioner is a network of department directors and division chiefs, and in each district a district administrator. The judiciary is separately administered by a Chief Justice and associates appointed by the Secretary of Interior.

Elected by the citizens of the Trust Territory and first

convened in 1965, the Congress of Micronesia has met and surpassed expectations. Confounding observers who had predicted it would amount to nothing more than a showpiece, the congress exercises growing legislative authority. Moreover, delegates from different districts have shown a surprising solidarity and common interest, overcoming (or at least controlling) their traditional regional loyalties.

The trusteeship administration of Micronesia by the United States is not and never was intended to be a permanent arrangement. Although timetables vary, it is understood that by 1981 Micronesians will vote on the political fate of the islands. Alternatives now officially being discussed range from outright independence to a still loosely-defined "free-association" with the United States. Meanwhile, the responsibility for administration of the Trust Territory rests with the United States, committed to strengthen the economic, social, and political development of Micronesia. Lacking the missionary zeal of the Spaniards, the stern bearing of the Germans, the aggressive economic program of the Japanese, America may hope to be remembered as the nation which worked with and for Micronesians. And Americans may hope that, if and when they depart, they leave more than a colony behind.

The name Micronesia, "small islands", refers to more than the diminutive land mass of the Trust Territory. It could apply as well to the experience, outlook, and commitment of many island dwellers. They live in a world of islands . . . and, often, these islands are their entire world. Their allegiance is to a village, to a home island or, at most, to a group of adjoining, related islands. The concept of a nation, let alone one as sprawling an entity as Micronesia, is recent and unfamiliar.

Moveover, the name Micronesia, considered either as a place name or an ethnic description, has its failings. Ethnically, the term Micronesian does not fit the colony of 1000 Polynesians on Kapingamarangi and Nukuoro islands in the Ponape district. And, conversely, the residents of Guam, Northern Marianas, and the Kiribati Islands are considered Micronesians, although they are not a part of the Trust Territory. Little wonder, then, that an islander would balk at identifying himself as a Micronesian. But, though somewhat blurred at the edges, the term Micronesian will serve as a convenient umbrella under which to discuss the inhabitants of six different districts, speakers of at least nine district languages.

There is something of a common background. The original homeland of the Micronesians was very likely somewhere near Malaysia and long, hazardous sea voyages brought them to these islands. Archaeological investigations in recent years indicate that the settlement of Pacific islands was much earlier than previously estimated. Dates as early as 1500 B.C. have been suggested through the carbon dating of artifacts found in the Marianas. Anthropologists shy away from the notion that there was ever a golden age, a formidable vanished civilization, in Micronesia. Still, the ruins of Nan Madol in Ponape—a channeled Venetian city built of basalt logs

lining artificial canals—suggest the presence of an impressive, industrious society at sometime in Micronesia's past. And experts do agree that today's indigenous population is still well short of what the islands once supported. Scholars have estimated that Palau, which today boasts an indigenous population over 13,000 once supported five times as many people.

Micronesian Beauty and the Beast.

Micronesians are characterized by medium stature, brown skin, and straight-to-wavy black hair. A slight physical variation tends to exist from district to district, so slight, indeed, that few outsiders can be entirely certain about detecting it. In general, the people of the Caroline Islands tend to show a stronger relationship to Malaysian types than the residents of the Marshalls.

Whatever curent nuances of appearance may distinguish citizens of one district from citizens of another, all have felt the impact of western rule. The inhabitants of the Mariana Islands, the present-day Chamorros, differ considerably from their ancestors, whose skeletal remains indicate they were tall and large-boned. Modern Chamorros actually are the descendants of an indigenous population which has intermarried over the past three centuries with Spanish, Filipino, Chinese, German, Japanese and American strains, producing the modern

Many of the islands of the Trust Territory are beautiful atolls so familiar throughout Oceania. Coral reefs, sparkling sands, motus, coconut palms and friendly native peoples set upon the azure blue of the world's largest ocean. It's enough to make a blue water cruiser out of any sailor.

Chamorro physical type. The same sort of ethnic mixing can be found, perhaps in lesser degree, throughout all the districts of the Trust Territory. The inhabitants of Kosrae Island, for instance, still bear traces of visits by whalers during the nineteenth century.

Traditional customs differ from district to district (and within districts) since each of the scattered, isolated islands have produced local adaptations and inventions of their own. The differences in culture and language are not inconsiderable, and residents of each district take pride in the customs of their home islands. They make much of their district's character. Yet, though differences like this can distinguish (and divide) the districts, the similarities between the districts are also great. They are all islanders, all residents of relatively small villages on relatively small tropical islands. Most of their societies make complex class distinctions, create narrow political loyalties, hold close kinship ties, respect the memory of the ancestors, and acknowledge traditional as well as elected leaders. But Micronesians have more than their island environment in common: they have shared similar destinies. However great the distance from Saipan to

Palau, from Yap to the Marshalls, these islands have known a common history, have witnessed a succession of foreign flags. Today, many islanders, while proudly insisting on the distinctions between districts, accept that the islands of Micronesia are united by common interest, if not by indentical cultures or languages.

Certainly the main barrier between interdistrict communication is language. We can talk of Micronesia, we can describe Micronesians. But what is the language of Micronesia? At least nine major languages, with regional dialect variations, can be differentiated. Two of these languages are classified as "Malaysian" in type: Chamorro and Palauan. Yapese, Ulithian, Trukese, Ponapean, Kosraean and Marshallese are deemed "Micronesian" languages, while Kapingamarangian and Nukuoroan are Polynesian tongues. Add to this the fact that district languages vary from island to island; even from village to village on the same island.

Some administrators argue that the solution to this babel of tongues is the introduction of a common foreign tongue. The argument is not a new one. During their thirty year mandate, the Japanese pressed Micronesians to learn Japanese and the evidence is that their efforts succeeded. Certainly, a forty-five year old Chamorro would have no way of communicating with a forty-five year old Palauan save in Japanese. And, chances are, they'd get along quite well that way. Under the United States administration vigorous efforts are being made to establish English as a common languge. Wherever possible, English is used in Trust Territory schools. But visitors soon will discover that the addiction to local languages is strong and pervasive. Away from American administrators, outside of government offices, the local tongues still prevail.

The biggest business enterprise in Micronesia is the business of government, with the Trust Territory administration employing about 7,000 Micronesians and several hundred Americans. Another 8,000 Micronesians work for wages in private businesses. Added emphasis is being given to the development of a viable, self-sustaining private sector. The Territory's decision to accentuate vocational education reflects its concern that white-collar workers be matched by blue-collar (or no-collar) workers.

Away from governmental headquarters and district centers, the traditional cashless life of fishing and food gathering continues, with only occasional and partial concessions to the twentieth century's money-oriented, job-centered economy. In the past, those businesses which prospered were closely related to conventional island patterns; the manufacture of copra (fluctuating in its cash value), gathering of World War II vintage scrap (almost depleted), and handicrafts (picking up all the time). All these enterprises demand a minimum of capital, no formal training, only slight equipment, and absolutely no 7:30-4:30 regimentation. All three can be undertaken at the worker's convenience and, likewise, dropped at will.

Doubtless, there will (and, perhaps, should) always be torpid islands where the "economy" is negligible, where life is a matter of spearing fish, wrenching out taro roots, retrieving fallen breadfruit, and picking coconuts. But in much of Micronesia this simple style of life is changing, and will continue to change. The attraction of life in district centers, the prospect of cars and movies, Polaroids and transistors, high fashion and cold beer, is luring many Micronesians off outlying islands, and introducing them (for better and for worse) to a more aggressive business-oriented world. District centers (Kosrae, Koror, Majuro, Kolonia-in-Ponape, Colonia-in-Yap, Moen in Truk) boast a growing number of retail outlets, ranging from hole-in-the-wall operations selling little more than canned mackerel and cigarettes, to million-dollar-a-year enterprises like the Truk Trading Company.

As district centers become more crowded and the need for dollars grows more imperative, Micronesians are seeking employment for wage-employment outside of government. Chances are they will find it in tourism and fishing primarily (now emerging as the major economic possibilities) as well as in agriculture. Few visitors who visit Micronesia fail to notice the irony that, amongst some of the richest fishing grounds on earth, Micronesians persist in favoring canned fish, fish caught off Micronesian shores by foreign vessels, shipped to other countries for processing, then returned for retail sale. In Palau the Van Camp fishing and freezing plant marks the beginning of a major fisheries development in the Trust Territory.

A specialist in tropical disease, a connoisseur of rampaging infections and maladies would not find Micronesia an exciting opportunity. As tropics go, Micronesia is quite a healthy place, with most of the hot weather villains either absent altogether or well under control and none of the temporary unpleasantness often experienced by tourists. Yellow fever, malaria, and cholera are unknown, tuberculosis is controlled and leprosy, even of the mildest sort is on the edge of extinction. Infections and parasites are among the more troublesome disorders remaining in the Trust Territory, both are often related to the consumption of contaminated food or water. Visitors who follow tourist trails will find water safe to drink in all district centers, bottled or canned soft drinks are on sale almost everywhere and drinking coconuts also are excellent thirst quenchers.

Micronesia is not a plague-ridden jungle, in fact, it's one of the healthiest climes in the world. True, infant mortality is slightly higher than in the United States but so, too, is life expectancy. Despite a seeming lack of variety in diet, despite a disappointing affection for canned food and an indifference to what Americans call "greens", studies indicate that the average Micronesian has entirely adequate nutrition.

It's fortunate that there are no critical health problems in Micronesia because, until now, hospital facilities have been distinctly modest. A new 125-bed hospital has been completed in Truk and another, slightly smaller, is planned for Ponape. In the district centers, hospitals can be relied upon for routine medical problems and outlying dispensaries (more than 150 of them) bring a measure of rudimentary medical service to outlying areas. A visitor can be assured of competent treatment in Trust Territory hospitals. He will not, on the other hand, elect to make a prolonged stay in any Trust Territory medical facility.

Although American doctors have recently been contracted for assignment in district centers, the burden of medical treatment in Micronesia still falls on "Medical Officers" or "M.O.'s." These doctors are generally graduates of the Fiji School of Medicine, specially trained to practice medicine on tropical islands. They have earned the confidence of local residents.

Stretched over 3,000 miles between Hawaii and the Philippines, Micronesia comprises thousands of islands divided into six administrative districts. The islands are governed by the U.S. under a United Nations Trusteeship, with the six districts administered through a presidentially appointed High Commissioner. Micronesia geographically includes Guam, however, politically Guam and the Trust Territory are separate, with Guam being a full-fledged Territory of the United States.

On March 24, 1976, the President of the United States signed the "Covenant to establish a Commonwealth of the Northern Mariana Islands in political union with the United States." The Covenant will not come fully into effect until the Trusteeship is terminated for all of the Trust Territory, most likely by the end of 1981. Some of the Covenant's provisions, however, including those calling for a locally approved Constitution and an elected governor, became operational in the fall of 1977.

The island of Kosrae, formerly administered as a subdistrict of Ponape, became a separate district on January 1, 1977. In addition, the Congress of Micronesia as well as some of the individual districts are considering various political status options for the era following the termination of the Trusteeship. Although the future political status of Micronesia is uncertain, the United States has set 1981 as the target year of stepping out of its Trusteeship.

The Weather

The climate of the TTPI as a whole is tropical and maritime, characterized by high temperatures and humidity and by generally heavy rainfall. There are some seasonal variations, but they are small and of little consequence. It is a few degrees hotter, and rainfall is slightly higher in the months of the northern summer. (May through October). Temperatures, however, vary little from the territory's annual mean of 80°F, and the humidity is constant at about 80 percent. Annual mean temperatures are 80°F in the Yap, Palau, and Ponape districts and 81°F in the Truk and Marshall districts.

Within each district there is also a slight increase in temperature as one travels from the northern to the southern portions.

Annual rainfall is consistently high but shows some variation among the districts. Except for the northern portion of the Marshall district, where annual precipation is about 82 inches, all other sections of the territory have 100 inches or more. Annual rainfall is about 155 inches in the Palau, 119 inches in the Yap, 127 inches in the Truk, 185 inches in the Ponape, and 158 inches in the southern Marshall districts.

Weather conditions are generally good in Micronesia but are subject to frequent and rapid changes. A fine day may suddenly give way to one of torrential rains, strong winds, squalls, and occasional thunderstorms. Most of these conditions are related to the interplay of complex wind systems that prevail in different parts of the territory. Islands east of about 150° east longitude are under the influence of steady northeast trade winds most of the year. In summer, however, the intertropical front moves northward, and in southern areas the southeast trades prevail. When these trade winds meet along the front, they give rise to weak cyclones, which bring heavy

Jetsam and Flotsam

Currency:

All parts of the Trust Territory use the United States dollar.

Language:

The official language is English but there are indigenous tongues unique to each district. In addition, Spanish, German and Japanese are often heard reflecting past masters of these islands.

External Affairs Representative:

United States consulates and embassies

Information Center:

Government Office of Tourism
Trust Territory of the Pacifc Islands
Saipan, Northern Mariana Islands 96950, USA

Cruising Library:

Pacific Adventure, Willard Price: John Day Co., New York, USA 1936.
America's Paradise Lost, Willard Price; John Day Co., New York, USA, 1966.
Japan's Islands of Mystery, Willard Price; John Day Co., New York, USA 1944.
Micronesia, I.G. Edmonds; Bobbs-Merrill Co., Indianapolis, IN, USA 1974.

sporadic rains. The cyclonic storms generally move westward, gathering strength and intensity as they go. They then curve northward from the equator sometimes, bringing much destruction to islands in their paths.

West of 150° east longitude, the pattern of the trade wind is broken by seasonal changes over Asia. In the summer months low pressures over the continent draw in air from Micronesia, resulting in prevailing winds from the southwest and the south. In the winter, continental high pressures reverse the flow. Winds blow out from Asia as the northwest monsoon and strong typhoons strike the western Caroline island groups. Typical of these great storms was Typhoon Jean, which struck the Carolines in 1968 and reached its maximum intensity in the southern Marianas. It caused damage amounting to about $16 million and was so destructive to Saipan that the island was declared a disaster area by the President of the United States.

Yacht Entry

All yachts, even those of United States registry, must have a vessel permit and individual personal entry permits to enter the waters of the Trust Territory. These can be obtained by writing to:

Chief of Immigration
Trust Territory of the Pacific Islands
Office of the High Commissioner
Saipan, Mariana Islands 96950, USA

A copy of the required Vessel Entry Permit (TT-1124A) and the Personal Entry Permit (TT-AGE-097) are shown here for information. Copies of the vessel entry permit should be sent ahead to each district center that you intend to visit.

Note that each personal application must be submitted with the applicant's police abstract or clearance. If you are able to secure one in person, fine, if not, have your police department mail it directly to the above address with a note that it is submitted in conjunction with your Entry Permit Application. Return all papers to the Chief of Immigration at the above address.

United States citizen tourists entering the Trust Territory need proof of citizenship while non-US citizen

Medical Memo

Immunization requirements:

Smallpox immunization is required if travel does not originate in the United States or its possessions. Immunization against cholera and yellow fever are required if you have transited or visited within the last six days an area currently infected. Typhoid, paratyphoid and tetanus shots are recommended.

Local health situation:

All of the districts of the Trust Territory are generally free of communicable diseases. The island of Ebeye in the Kwajalein atoll is reported to have recurrent epidemics of influenza and diarrhea due to extreme sanitation problems in an overcrowded area. The bacteria in the lagoon is reported to be 25,000 times the safe level established by the World Health Organization.

Health services:

There are no private doctors, dentists or service facilities in the Trust Territory. There is one general hospital offering both hospital and outpatient care in each district center. In addition there are dispensaries located on many other islands: 44 in the Marshall, 11 in Palau, 12 in Ponape, 53 in Truk, and 14 in the Yap district. Fees are less than those charged in the United States. Limited dental and optical services are also available.

Prescription and non-prescription drugs are available at the hospitals and dispensaries.

Water:

Tap water from the public supplies at the district centers is reportedly safe. All other water should be considered suspect and treated. It has been reported from Palau that hookworm larvae have been found in the water.

APPLICATION FOR VESSEL TO ENTER TRUST TERRITORY

Date: _____

APPLICATION MUST BE IN BLOCK LETTERS OR TYPED

I hereby apply for permission for the following vessel to enter the Trust Territory at all official ports of entry and in support of my application, submit the following:

Name of Vessel: _____

Place of Registry: _____

Registry Number: _____

Operator's Name: _____

    Nationality: _____

        Address: _____

Owner's Name: _____

    Nationality: _____

        Address: _____

Call Sign: _____ Length: _____ Breadth: _____ Depth: _____

Last Port of Call: _____

I also understand that permits are granted subject to the following conditions:

1. The appropriate District Administrator, or District Administrator's Representative shall be notified in writing or by cable well in advance of the estimated date and time of arrival of the vessel in order that appropriate authorities can be at the port to meet the vessel.

2. Payment is made of all docking fees and port charges.

3. No commercial cargo or paying passengers shall be carried on board the vessel.

4. The master, crew and all passengers shall have in their possession valid entry permits or Form TT-958, whichever is applicable, to enter the Trust Territory.

I certify that the facts hereinabove set forth are true and correct to the best of my knowledge and belief; and it is fully understood that while this vessel is in the Trust Territory, it is subject to the above conditions and all of the rules, regulations, and laws of the Trust Territory.

_____
Applicant Signature

Vessel Entry Permit for the Trust Territory (TT-1124A)

TRUST TERRITORY OF THE PACIFIC ISLANDS
OFFICE OF THE ATTORNEY GENERAL
DIVISION OF IMMIGRATION
SAIPAN, MARIANA ISLANDS 96950

ENTRY PERMIT APPLICATION

DATE _____

APPLICATION MUST BE IN BLOCK LETTERS OR TYPED

I hereby apply for permission to enter the Trust Territory of the Pacific Islands and in support of my application, submit the following:

NAME: _____

(LAST) _____ (FIRST) _____ (MIDDLE)

HOME ADDRESS: _____

MAILING ADDRESS: _____

CITIZENSHIP: _____ DATE & PLACE OF BIRTH: _____

PASSPORT NO: _____ DATE & PLACE ISSUED: _____

OCCUPATION: _____ SOCIAL SECURITY NO: _____

NAME & ADDRESS OF EMPLOYER: _____

MARITAL STATUS:

SEX:

Single ☐   Divorced ☐   Widowed ☐   Male ☐

Married ☐   Separated ☐   Female ☐

MEMBERS OF SAME FAMILY ENTERING FOR THE SAME PURPOSE AS APPLICANT:

NAMES: RELATIONSHIP: DATE & PLACE OF BIRTH: CITIZENSHIP:

_____

_____

_____

HAVE YOU EVER APPLIED FOR TRUST TERRITORY ENTRY PERMIT BEFORE?   Yes ☐   No ☐

IF YES, WHEN & FOR WHAT PURPOSE: _____   PHOTOGRAPH OF APPLICANT:

WAS THE ENTRY PERMIT:

Granted? ☐   Denied? ☐   Revoked? ☐

IF GRANTED, WHAT IS THE ENTRY PERMIT NO: _____

DATE OF EXPIRATION: _____

LABOR I.D. NO: _____
(If applicable)

DATE OF EXPIRATION: _____

POLICE RECORD FROM YOUR PLACE OF RESIDENCE
MUST BE ATTACHED TO THIS APPLICATION.

PHOTO

1½ x 1½

Must be signed
by the applicant

PURPOSE OF ENTRY: _____

APPLICANT must furnish information regarding purpose of entry, description of business to be transacted, names and address of company, firm or business you represent and products or services involved, and names and addresses of persons or firms to be contacted (in detail) _____

PLACES TO BE VISITED: _____   LENGTH OF VISIT: _____   EXPECTED DATE OF ENTRY & CARRIER: _____

I certify that the facts hereinabove set forth are true and correct to the best of my knowledge and belief and it is fully understood that throughout the period of my visit I am subject to all of the rules, regulations, and laws of the Trust Territory. If my permit is withdrawn for any reason or expires while I am in the Trust Territory, I agree to leave said Territory by the first available transportation at my own expense.

_____
Signature of Applicant

(U.S. CITIZEN SUBMIT IN SINGLE COPY)
(ALL OTHERS SUBMIT IN DUPLICATE)

Personal Entry Permit for the Trust Territory (TT-AGE-097)

tourists must have a valid passport and Multiple Entry Visa to the United States. Check the latest tourist entry requirements for non-US citizens from your country of origin.

All persons entering the Trust Territory for more than 30 days or for purposes other than tourism must have a Visitor Entry Permit obtained in advance from the Chief of Immigration. A valid ticket for passage out of the Trust Territory (non-refundable within the area) is required. Kwajalein and Johnston Islands are not open to tourists.

In certain Trust Territory districts a drinking permit is required for all persons and this is administered solely by the local government. This includes visitors who wish to consume any alcoholic beverage. The fees vary from $1.00 to $3.00 and the permit is good for 30 days. If you carry liquor in your boat's stores it should be used with care during your stay in one of these controlled drinking districts.

Vessels with valid entry permits for both vessel and crew should make formal entry at the District Center (Port of Entry) for the island district involved. This process must be repeated as you travel from one district to another. When you wish to stop at an island enroute before reaching the District Center, you can notify the appropriate District Center by radio. In essence, they want to know where every visiting yacht is and it may also be good for your own safety as well as legality to keep them informed.

The TTPI liaison office in Hawaii is located in Suite 4106 in the Federal Building at Ala Moana and Punchbowl Streets. The address is:
P.O. Box 50026
Honolulu, HI 96850 USA

There is also a TTPI liaison office in Guam in the CGIC Building in Agana.

Yacht Facilities

The Trust Territory is north of the common route of around-the-world cruising boats. Hence, it has few facilities for yachts but at the same time it is unspoiled by itinerant sailors living off the goodwill of the local people. Let's keep it that way by being responsible yachtsmen.

All of the district centers have deep water commercial ports. There are no such things as slips and dock-side tie-ups are very limited. There is good sand bottom anchorages in all the lagoons.

Fuel, both gasoline and diesel, can be obtained at the district centers of Majuro, Kosrae, Koror, Kolonia, Moen, and Colonia. Foodstuffs and other provisions are also obtainable at the district centers. Marine suppliers are few and far between although Majuro has a fiberglass boat factory and can make fiberglass repairs. All of the islanders are sailors by heritage and necessity and we are told that they make very good crew members.

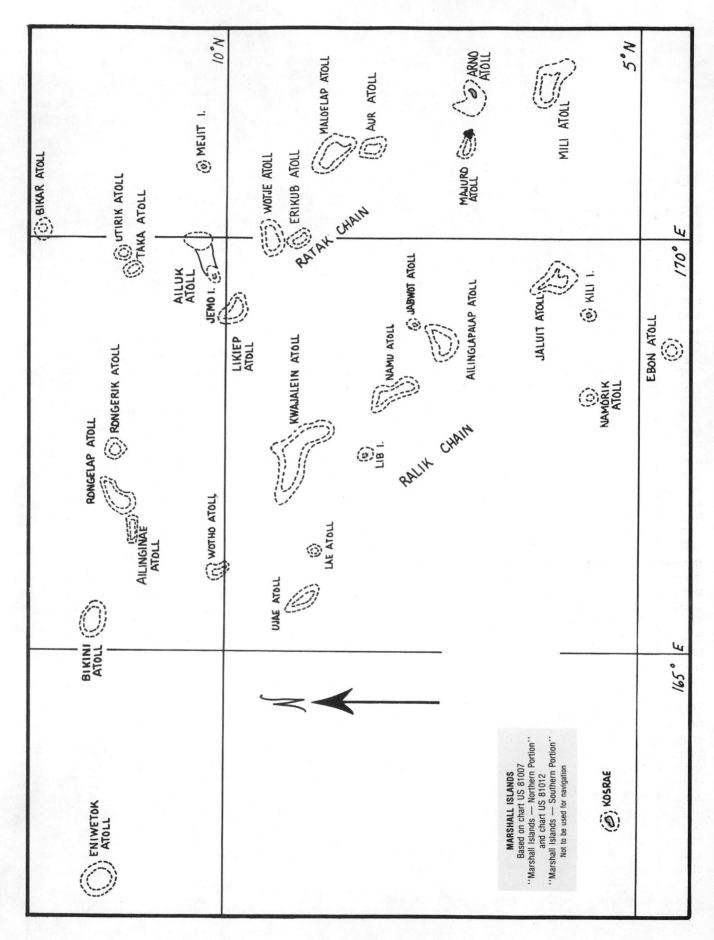

MARSHALL ISLANDS
Based on chart US 81007
"Marshall Islands — Northern Portion"
and chart US 81012
"Marshall Islands — Southern Portion"
Not to be used for navigation

10° N

5° N

170° E

165° E

BIKAR ATOLL

UTIRIK ATOLL

TAKA ATOLL

MEJIT I.

AILUK ATOLL

JEMO I.

LIKIEP ATOLL

WOTJE ATOLL

ERIKUB ATOLL

MALOELAP ATOLL

AUR ATOLL

ARNO ATOLL

MAJURO ATOLL

MILI ATOLL

RATAK CHAIN

BIKINI ATOLL

RONGELAP ATOLL

RONGERIK ATOLL

AILINGINAE ATOLL

WOTHO ATOLL

KWAJALEIN ATOLL

UJAE ATOLL

LAE ATOLL

LIB I.

NAMU ATOLL

JABWOT ATOLL

AILINGLAPALAP ATOLL

JALUIT ATOLL

KILI I.

NAMORIK ATOLL

EBON ATOLL

RALIK CHAIN

ENIWETOK ATOLL

KOSRAE

N

294

Chapter 24-A
MARSHALL DISTRICT

The Country

The Marshall Islands archipelago consists of thirty-three major island units located in the eastern part of the TTPI between 162° and 174° east longitude. These units contain 1136 individual islands of low, oceanic, coral formation, they are so tiny they have a combined land area of only about 68 square miles. The group is arranged in two parallel chains about 150 miles apart running generally southeast to northwest for some 800 miles between 4° and 14° north latitude. The eastern, or *Ratak* (sunrise), chain contains fifteen island units of 570 individual islands and a land area of 34 square miles.

There are no high islands in the entire group. Most island units (twenty-eight) are atolls of the classic type having large lagoons and a varying number of encircling islets. Kwajalein in the *Ralik* (sunset) chain has the largest lagoon (839 square miles); its number of component islets, 97, is second to Mili atoll, which has 102 islets around its 295-square-mile lagoon. The smallest atoll, also in the Ralik chain, is Namorik, whose two islets enclose a lagoon of only 3¼ square miles. Five of the island units are single islands—Mejit and Jemo in the Ratak chain, and Lib, Jabwot, and Kili in the Ralik chain.

The district's population of about 25,000 persons is fairly evenly divided between the two chains, although the Ratak group has about 1000 more inhabitants than the Ralik section. Only Arno (1095) and Majuro (8000) in the Ratak chain and Kwajelein (3702) have more than 1000 inhabitants. Five island units in the Ratak chain (Taongi, Bikar, Taka, Jemo, and Erikub) and three in the Ralik chain (Ailingnae, Rongerik, and Eniwetok) are uninhabited. Eniwetok was the site of early United States nuclear tests and the island unit is still contaminated with radioactivity.

Dotting the Pacific between the Caroline Islands and Hawaii, the Marshalls provide a striking contrast to the high volcanic islands east and west. Mere etchings of coconut palms and coral, the Marshalls have produced fierce warriors, have survived the ravages of war and the shock of the atomic age, and still manage to epitomize the ideal of a tranquil island society. The Marshalls are administered from the district center of Majuro. But some of the remote islands are 600 miles away from the district center, and many of the 25,000 Marshallese are tied to Majuro by tenuous, occasional shipping service. With 70 square miles of dry land laced over 180,000 square miles of ocean, the Marshalls constitute the eastern gateway to Micronesia.

From all over the Marshalls, even from Kiribati and Fiji, islanders come to Majuro, a melting pot of island peoples. The sea around Majuro, particularly the lagoon, reminds visitors that the island once was called "the pearl of the Pacific." And the sea is a welcome and inevitable companion on any visit to Majuro, for the district center (like all Marshall islands) is a mere fingering of land stretched like a thin earthen dam between ocean and lagoon. Majuro is composed of several islands welded together years ago with Navy muscle and mountains of coral.

The Weather

The Marshall Islands are climatically divided by the effects of the North Equatorial Current and the Equatorial Counter Current into the Northern and Southern Marshalls with approximate boundary at the parallel of 8°30' North.

The northeast trade flows persistently into the Marshall Islands group. The trade blows strongest from December to March during which time it runs steadily over the

Marshall Islands
A Trust Territory District

Port of Entry:

Uliga, Majuro   7°06'N, 171°22'E

Distances between ports in nautical miles:

Between *Majuro* and:

Agana, Guam	1820
Honolulu, Hawaii	2280
Johnston Island	1450
Kwajalein, Marshall Islands	280
Palau, Caroline Islands	2500
Saipan, Mariana Islands	1780
Tokyo, Japan	2800
Truk, Caroline Islands	1330
Ponape, Caroline Islands	900
Yap, Caroline Islands	2250

Standard Time:

12 hours fast on GMT

Residential suburbs on atolls are not unlike their counterparts on the continents, only here the tradewinds forever clear the air and breathe a rustle of contentment through the palm trees.

whole area, but it becomes weaker and is much less steady over the south and west portions of the group from July to November. It is weakest in September and October. At this time considerable percentages of southerly and southeasterly winds are experienced. The trades are strengthened to Beaufort Force 7 with considerable frequency during the winter months, but winds of Force 9 or higher are rarely experienced. Calms are also rare throughout the area. Lowest wind speeds occur in August.

In the southern Marshalls, the northeast trades predominate from December to April, with moderate speeds from points between east and northeast. In some years, however, the trades fail, or appear only sporadically, and are replaced by moderate east to southeast winds. From May, east to southeast winds increase in frequency. becoming predominate in the autumn months. In this season the winds are light and changeable, frequently interrupted by calms. However, sudden violent west to southwest winds occasionally reach gale force.

The winds tend easterly at Jabor and attain speeds of 11 knots in December and 4 knots in August. Calms occur on the average of 4 to 6 percent of the time over the south portion.

In the northern Marshalls, the winds blow chiefly from

the east and northeast throughout the year. These trade winds are more constant in direction during the winter months, from December through March. Their speed then is about 18 knots. During the remainder of the year when the trade wind belt has shifted northward, the winds are generally lighter and more variable both in direction and velocity.

The winds are mostly easterly in the vicinity of Eniwetok atoll. A maximum speed of 39 knots has been reported in December. At this time a maximum speed of 19 knots was reported at Ujelang atoll. Lowest wind speeds occur in August. At this time Ujelang atoll reported a speed of 8 knots. Eighty-five percent of the winds in the vicinity of Utirik atoll blow between north-northeast and east throughout the year. Calms are rare over the northern Marshalls.

Observations of the field of motion over the Marshall Islands show that tropical disturbances tend to originate in the region. Stations in the eastern Marshalls show wind changes before those in the west, that is, the disturbances move from east to west. Records show typhoons seldom ever originate in or move over the Marshall Islands.

In the northern Marshalls, gales are infrequent, but if they occur, they usually happen during the summer and autumn, and they come from the southeast. In January

1978 a tropical storm of short duration with winds of 40-45 knots was located 150 miles south of Eniwetok moving northward.

Thundersqualls are fairly common, except in January and February when they are relatively infrequent. In the southern Marshalls thundersqualls are most common during the interval between July and November. Most are of light to moderate intensity, often accompanied by heavy rainfall. Jabor reports a mean maximum of 3 days per month with thundersqualls in July.

Precipation is at a minimum from December through May. Winter and spring are considered to be the dry seasons; the exception being Jaluit atoll. Rainfall increases from the north to the south part of this area. Precipitation increases during the summer months. The period of maximum rainfall extends from July through November, except at Jabor.

Rainfall is heavy in the southern Marshalls. It reaches an annual average of 159 inches, with every month averaging more than 9 inches. April and May have over 16 inches and September has 13 inches. January and February are drier, averaging about 9 inches. Cloudbursts, in which more than 1 inch of rain falls, are frequent. Rainfall usually occurs as moderate to heavy showers or squalls.

Rainfall is heavy and well distributed through all months at Jaluit atoll, where rain occurs on an average of 20 days per month, except in February, which is usually the least rainy month of the year. Jabor, on Jaluit atoll, records the highest annual rainfall, over 150 inches. At Jabor, high monthly readings occur during the period April through July.

In the northern Marshalls, the rainfall is lowest during the time of trade winds, when it averages about 3 inches

Jetsam and Flotsam

Currency:

The Marshall Islands use the United States dollar.

Language:

The official language is English and is spoken by everyone. The native tongue is Marshallese which is spoken by the elders of the community.

Electricity:

Electric power is 110 volt, 60 Hz AC.

Postal Address:

Yacht (   )
General Delivery
Majuro, Marshall Islands, TT 96960, USA

External Affairs Representative:

United States consulates and embassies.

Information Center:

Marshall Islands Tourist Commission
Majuro, Marshall Islands, TT 96960, USA

Majuro Atoll is the District Center for the Marshall Islands District and its Port of Entry. Most government functions are located on the island of Uliga shown here. The old port is at the center of the picture.

The longest road in all of the Trust Territory extends for about 30 miles connecting the "urban" east end of Majuro Atoll with the rural western end.

per month. The heaviest rain occurs from September through November. At Ujelang atoll the average annual rainfall is 83 inches and farther northward at Bikini atoll it is less. The mean amount at Eniwetok atoll ranges from 1 inch in January to 8 inches in September, and also records the lowest annual rainfall of about 45 inches.

Temperatures are relatively constant throughout the year, with the high mean being 83°F and the low being 81°F. During the dry season (December through May), temperature extremes range from a minimum of 71°F to a maximum of 98°F; during the wet season (June through November) temperature extremes range from a minimum of 67°F to a maximum of 98°F.

Relative humidity is high during all months. During the day, the relative humidity ranges from about 89 percent at 2100 to 73 percent at 1400.

Cloudiness reaches a minimum during the winter months, averaging 4/10 at Ujelang atoll. The maximum is reached at Eniwetok atoll during the summer months, when the average cloud cover is 7/10 through the year.

Visibility is usually good to excellent, except during heavy rain squalls. Fog occurs very rarely.

Yacht Facilities

Majuro lagoon is a large natural harbor which has been wire-dragged to remove isolated coral heads. The principal anchorage is off the island of Dalap in the southeastern corner where protection is offered from the prevailing northeast trades. Boats with some local knowledge can also anchor in the far western end of the lagoon off the island of Laura which is called Majuro's "outer island" and has a small village and a smattering of stores.

The majority of the population and business activity on Majuro takes place on the three islands of Darrit, Uliga, and Dalap which are linked together by a causeway. Ad-

Even atoll dwellers must get away from it all and those on Majuro visit the "outer island" of Laura for relaxation on the beach.

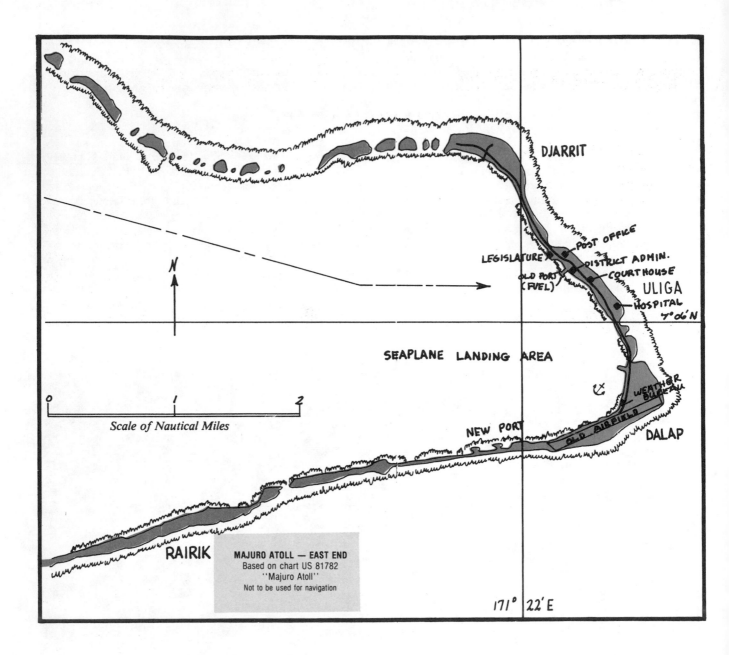

MAJURO ATOLL — EAST END
Based on chart US 81782
''Majuro Atoll''
Not to be used for navigation

ministrative headquarters is on Uliga and there you will find the District Administrator, post office, bank, and what stores there are of significance. The main harbor facility on Majuro is located at Uliga and it is an 862-foot long concrete T-head pier which can be used for a temporary tie-up while checking in, fueling and provisioning. (A new port development is taking place toward the western end of Dalap on the way to the new airport.) There is a charge of $5.50 per day to use the Uliga pier. Fuel is available from Mobil Oil at the dock. Fresh water is also available at a cost of one cent per gallon with a

minimum of 1,000 gallons. Provisions such as fresh vegetables, staples, and fish are available in limited quantities.

There is a small marine railway available which can handle vessels to 60 feet. General repairs of a minor nature can be made but yacht hardware is non-existent. A small fiberglass boatbuilding factory is located here which can do minor fiberglass repair work. Some electronic repairs can also be accomplished.

There is a yacht club at Majuro made up mostly of Hobie Cat sailors.

Radio Communications

Station name and call	Location	Frequency Transmit/Receive	Service hours LMT	Type of service
WSZO	7°N, 170°E	1100 kHz	0600-2400	Commercial broadcast
Radio Kwajalein	Kwajalein	1220 kHz 100 MHz	24 hours	Armed Forces radio
Radio Majuro (KUP-66)	Majuro	2182/2182 kHz 2724/2724 7935/7935	24 hours	District administration
Kwajalein Control	Kwajalein	2716/2716 kHz	24 hours	U.S. Navy net control

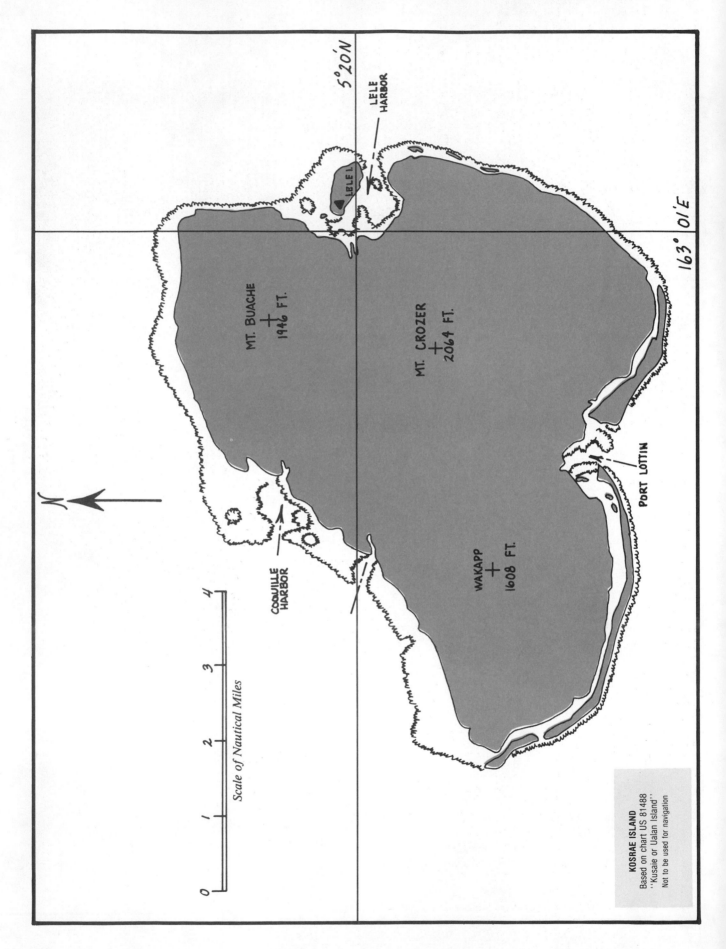

Scale of Nautical Miles
0 1 2 3 4

N

5°20'N

163° 01'E

LELE I.

LELE HARBOR

MT. BUACHE
1946 FT.

MT. CROZER
2064 FT.

WAKAPP
1608 FT.

COQUILLE HARBOR

PORT LOTTIN

KOSRAE ISLAND
Based on chart US 81488
"Kusaie or Ualan Island"
Not to be used for navigation

Chapter 24-B

KOSRAE DISTRICT

The Country

Kosrae island is the easternmost island of the Caroline group and was made a separate district of the Trust Territory in 1978. It is a high triangular island measuring 42 square miles in area. The interior of the island is mountainous with the highest peak to the north, Mount Buache, rising 1946 feet and the highest peak of all being Mount Crozer at 2064 feet in the middle of the island. Between the two is a lush valley spanning the island with Lele Harbor at the eastern end and Coquille Harbor at the western end of the valley.

Overall the island is hilly and covered with dense forests. It is composed of basalt and is so fertile that almost any tropical plant can be grown there. Kosrae is said to be one of the most beautiful islands in the Pacific. Among the valuable forest products are timber which in days past was eagerly sought after for shipbuilding.

Kosrae island is fringed by a reef extending offshore up to one mile on its northwestern side. After heavy rains, muddy waters extend far offshore making it difficult to identify the reefs. Inside the reef are many islets composed mostly of mangroves. The coastal lowlands are narrow in most areas. There is no lagoon but three harbors of significance. Lele is the principal harbor and once was a rendezvous point for American whaling ships operating in the Pacific. It was also the temporary home of the pirate Bully Hayes who lost his ship on the reef and settled there until driven away by a British warship.

Kosrae supported a large population in the 17th and 18th centuries which dwindled away to a low of about 1200 persons early in the 20th century. The population has since recovered and in 1970 there were 3740 persons on the island.

Principal agricultural products are bananas, sugar cane, taro, breadfruit, papaya, copra, and forest products.

The Weather

The eastern Caroline Islands are swept by the northeast trades. East-northeast or east winds blow almost constantly from December through April at an average speed of 9 knots. From May until December, east to southeast winds increase in frequency and predominate in September through November, with an average speed of 5 knots. These averages are for land stations and winds over the open water would be slightly higher in speed. Gales rarely occur. Over the open sea, winds are usually strongest about 0300 and lightest about 1400.

Kosrae island located on the south margin of the northeast trades, which dominate from December to April inclusive, is swept by northeasterly winds of 10 to 15 knots. The northeast trades shift northward in June and July and light variable winds and calms prevail until the southeast trades become dominant. The winds during the latter period are less strong and constant than those of the northeast trades. In November and December the wind systems shift southward and the island has another period of the doldrums. Typhoons sometimes have occured over Kosrae island but they are rare during the winter months.

Rain is heavy at Kosrae island averaging 10 to 20 inches per month throughout the year. It is fairly evenly distributed throughout the year and at Lele an average of 176 inches of rain falls in one year.

Yacht Facilities

There are three harbors on Kosrae—Lele to the east, Port

Kosrae Island

A Trust Territory District within the Caroline Islands

Port of Entry:

Lele, Kosrae   5°20′N, 163°01′E

Distances between ports in nautical miles:

Between *Lele* and:

Agana, Guam	1210
Apia, Western Samoa	1900
Honolulu, Hawaii	2470
Kolonia, Ponape	320
Majuro, Marshall Islands	520
Noumea, New Caledonia	1720
Pago Pago, American Samoa	1870
Tarawa, Kiribati	650

Standard time:

11 hours fast on GMT

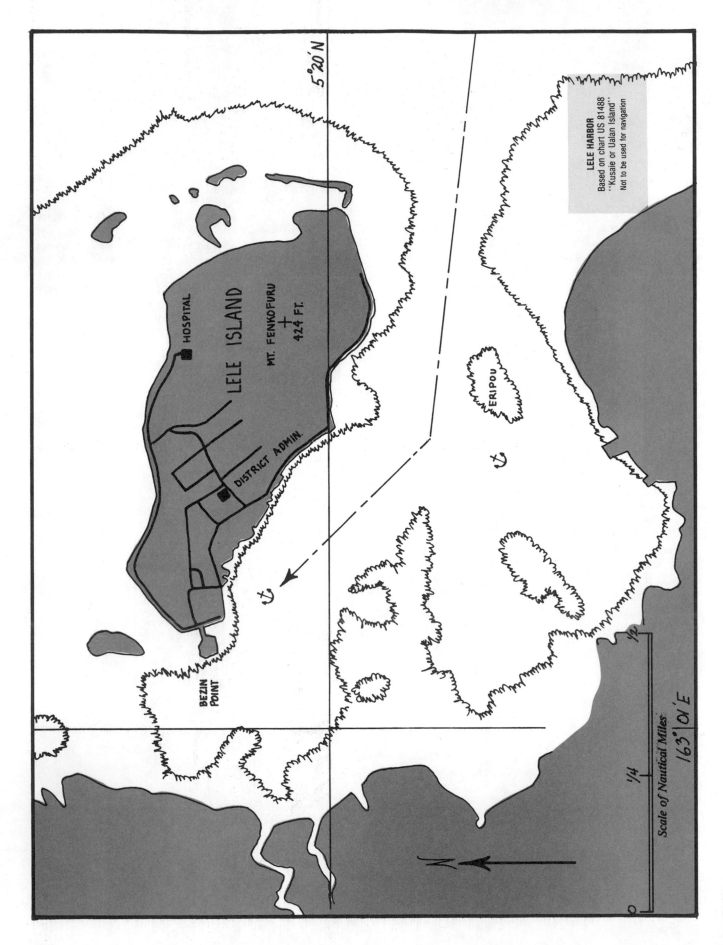

LELE ISLAND

HOSPITAL

MT. FENKOFURU
424 FT.

DISTRICT ADMIN.

BEZIN
POINT

ERIPOU

5°20'N

163°01'E

Scale of Nautical Miles

1/4   1/2

Lottin on the south and Coquille on the west. Lele, the principal harbor, is sheltered from southwesterly winds by the mountains of the interior and from northwesterly winds by Lele island on which Mount Fenkofuru rises to 424 feet. Mangroves and fringing reefs border the harbor. Depths in the harbor range between 28 and 100 feet and the reefs are steep-to. The best anchorages during prevailing northeasterly winds are off the village of Lele in 45 feet of water with a fine black sand bottom.

Lele is the district center and is located on the southwest side of Lele island. A commercial dock and new pier are located at Lele. Some provisions and water are available. Diesel fuel and gasoline can also be obtained but virtually no equipment or engine supplies.

Jetsam and Flotsam

Currency:

The United States dollar is the official currency.

Language:

The official language is English and is spoken by everybody. The native tongue is Kosraen which is spoken by the elders of the community.

Electricity:

Electric power is 110 volt, 60 Hz AC

Postal address:

Yacht   (   )
General Delivery
Kosrae, TT 96944 USA

External Affairs Representative:

United States consulates and embassies

Information Center:

Kosrae Tourist Commission:
Kosrae, TT 96944, USA

Radio Communications

Station name and call	Location	Frequency Transmit/Receive	Service hours LMT	Type of service
KUSI	Lele	1500 kHz	1000-2200	Commercial broadcast

Chapter 24-C
PONAPE DISTRICT
(Senyavin Islands)

The Country

The Ponape district is in the easternmost part of the Caroline archipelago. It consists of nine island units that contain 163 individual islands and a total land area of 133 square miles. Ponape is a high oceanic formation that completely dominates the district, accounting for all but four square miles of its land area and more than 80 percent of its population. The other eight units making up the 163 islands are all low coral atolls of insignificant size. About 20,000 people live in the Ponape district.

Ponape island, the administrative center of the district, is a rugged mountain peak rising to an altitude of 2579 feet. It has fertile soil and abundant rainfall that results in a dense covering of luxuriant tropical growth. Under Japanese administration the island underwent intense agricultural development and in 1970 still produced large quantities of coconuts, breadfruit, bananas, taro, and yams.

The eight atolls all have populations of less than 1000 except Oroluk and Ant islands, which are uninhabited. The two atolls of Kapingamarangi and Nukuroro, isolated in the southern portion of the district, are unique in that their inhabitants are physically and culturally Polynesian rather than Micronesian.

From the thatch-roofed, coral-floored Polynesian atolls of Kapingamarangi and Nukuroro, where graceful outrigger canoes sail over emerald water, to the tall, massive island of Ponape, with high waterfalls and fresh water streams, Ponape epitomizes every ideal of a South Seas paradise. Visitors count Ponape among the most beautiful islands in the world. Of the three other populated atolls in the district, Ngatik is culturally fairly close to Ponape, having been resettled by Ponapeans in 1837 after all the former male inhabitants were massacred by the crew of a British whaler. Mokil and Pingelap are heavily populated atolls whose alert, disciplined residents have supplied many of the district's leaders.

The barrier reef surrounding most of Ponape island is roughly pentagonal. Inside this reef is a lagoon which ranges from one to five miles across. Much of the island's shoreline is separated from the lagoon by a mangrove swamp. On the southwest side of the island, in Kitti municipality, the swamp is as much as a mile wide, and can be penetrated by canoes or small boats which wind their way along serpentine channels among towering black trees, accompanied by the screaming of swamp birds. Because of the mangroves, Ponape island has few beaches although numerous lagoon islands offer sites for picnicking. Most Ponapeans, however, prefer to picnic alone, and swim in the many fresh water streams which come gliding and falling toward the ocean off the massive, wet and lush mountains of the interior. Estimates vary as to how much rain it takes to keep these rivers flowing. The weather station in Kolonia records an average of 182 inches a year, but the interior of the island probably gets about twice that. All this rain, feeding hundreds of streams, has pretty well gouged up the island, making road building and maintenance a real headache. The Japanese did complete a belt road which was open to vehicle traffic about three-quarters of the way around the island and this roadway now is being reclaimed from twenty years of hungry vegetation. Even so, most travel outside the district center is by small boat or outboard powered canoe. Kolonia resembles nothing so much as a frontier town out of the old west: a wide, clay-red street, maybe a quarter of a mile long, lined by two movie theaters, numerous small to middle-sized general stores, several restaurants, and a long row of bars. When it's dry for too long dust covers everything. But usually rain showers are frequent and short. Clothes dry out fast.

Ponape

(Senyavin Islands)
A Trust Territory District within the Caroline Islands

Port of Entry:

Kolonia, Ponape   7°N, 158°13′E

Distances between ports in nautical miles:

Between *Kolonia* and:

Agana, Guam	1010
Honolulu, Hawaii	2840
Johnston Island	2350
Kwajalein, Marshall Islands	650
Kosrae, Caroline Islands	320
Majuro, Marshall Islands	900
Palau, Caroline Islands	1620
Saipan, Mariana Islands	1000
Truk, Caroline Islands	430
Tokyo, Japan	2290
Yap, Caroline Islands	1370

Standard time:

11 hours fast on GMT

Ponapeans learned long ago that travel by water was far superior to attempting overland journeys on their rugged island. An almost continuous barrier reef provides quiet waters for canoe travel.

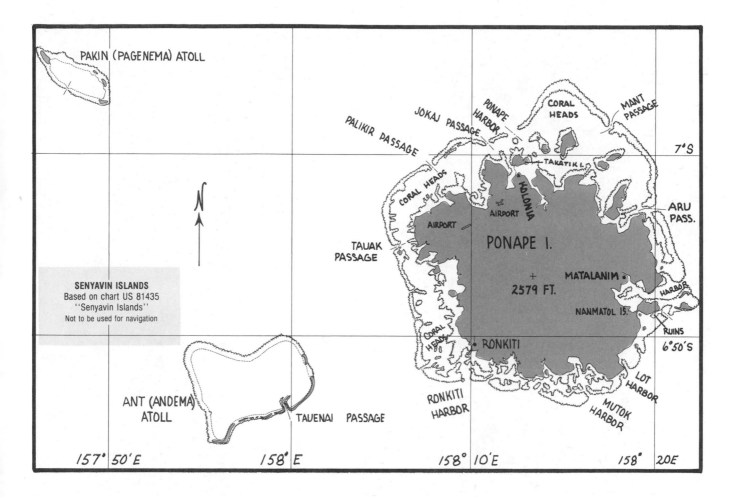

Another of the great archeological mysteries of the Pacific Basin is the ruin of Nan Madol. Located at the southeast edge of Ponape island these striking and baffling ruins are all that remain of an advanced but ancient civilization. Situated on tidal flats, nearly 100 semi-artificial islets framed of columnar basalt resting on the coral reef. The stone city was complete with residences, altars, food storage centers, security tunnels, and burial sites. The Venice-like city flourished in the 11th century but vanished as a living thing leaving nothing but these mysterious ruins.

The Weather

The eastern Caroline Islands are swept by the northeast trades. East-northeast or east winds blow almost constantly from December through April at an average speed of 8 knots. From May until December, east to southeast winds increase in frequency and predominate in September through November, with an average speed of 5 knots. The average speeds are for land locations and winds over the open sea are usually stronger. Gales rarely occur. Over the open sea the winds are strongest about 0300 and lightest around 1400.

In the vicinity of Ponape island the northeast trades predominate at all seasons of the year, and blow with great steadiness over the northern part of the area be-tween November and April. Winds are more variable and are marked by occasional shifts to southeasterly and southerly between July and November, although easterly winds still predominate.

The northeast trades blow from December to March over Ponape island. Gales have been reported during the trades, but are estimated to occur less than 5 percent of the time. During April, east to southeasterly winds increase in frequency and become predominant in September and October. During this season the winds are light and variable with frequent calms. Sudden violent westerly to southwesterly winds sometimes occur with the better developed storms and they occasionally attain gale force.

The doldrums belt moves northward over Ponape island in June and July when the northeast trades give way to the southeast trades. A maximum of squalliness and rainfall occurs at this time over the open sea. The doldrums move southward in November and December and cause a secondary increase in squalliness and precipitation.

Showers and squalls are frequent and occur at any time of the year. Squalls are sometimes violent and have an average duration of 20 minutes. Thick cumulonimbus clouds immediately precede these squalls, bringing gusty winds and heavy rain. Thunderstoms are rare with an annual average of about 17 distributed throughout the year.

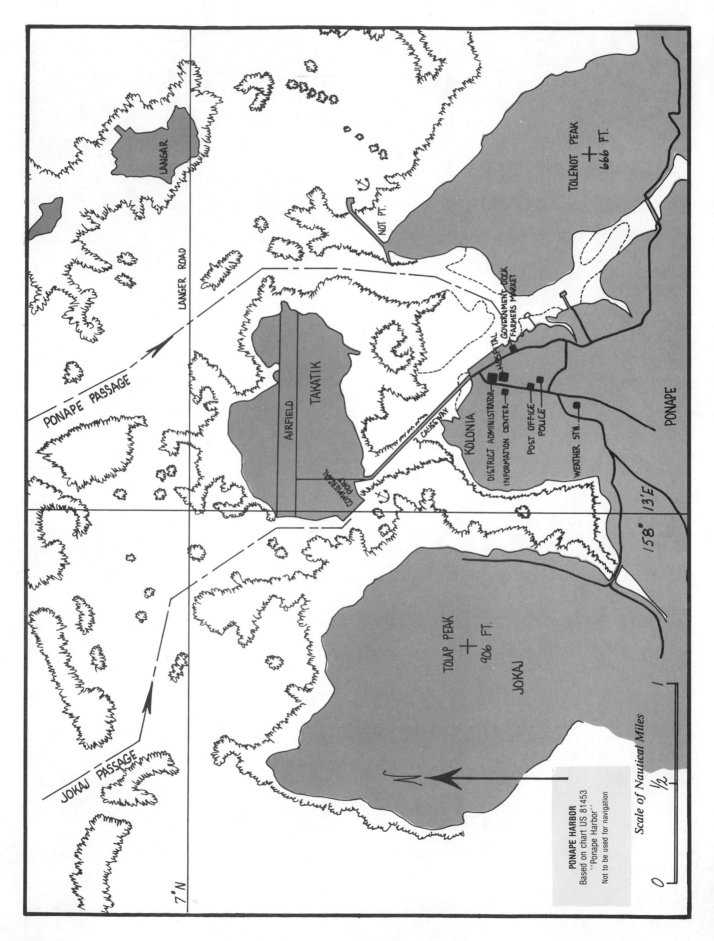

LANGAR

TOLENOT PEAK
+ 666 FT.

NOT PT.

PONAPE PASSAGE

LANGER ROAD

AIRFIELD

TAKATIK

CAUSEWAY

COMMERCIAL PORT

GOVERNMENT DOCK
FARMERS MARKET
HOSPITAL

KOLONIA

DISTRICT ADMINISTRATOR
INFORMATION CENTER
POST OFFICE
POLICE
WEATHER STN.

PONAPE

158° 13' E

7° N

JOKAJ PASSAGE

TOLAP PEAK
+ 906 FT.

JOKAJ

PONAPE HARBOR
Based on chart US 81453
"Ponape Harbor"
Not to be used for navigation

Scale of Nautical Miles

0   ½

310

Abundant rainfall on the mountainous interior of Ponape produces many sparkling waterfalls used to advantage by the Ponapeans.

Typhoons have sometimes occured over Ponape but they are rare during the winter months.

Ponape island is very wet with rain falling practically every day from March to December. One inch of rain falls on about 5 days of each month. January and February, the so-called dry months, have in excess of 9 inches. On the average, the rainfall amounts to 10 to 20 inches per month the year around.

Yacht Facilities

The port for the village of Kolonia, the district center for Ponape, is located at the southwest corner of Takatik island with access to Kolonia by way of a causeway.The deep water channel through the reef on the north side of Ponape is well marked and boats can usually sail in on a broad reach. Check in with the port officials at the main pier and then anchor out away from possible ship traffic.

The main pier at Takatik is almost 1000 feet long and water is available on it. The Not (Net) Point pier is about 250 feet long and diesel fuel can be obtained from there. On the east side of Kolonia is a 270-foot long pier and several small jetties which can be used by small boats. Gasoline is available at the Kolonia pier.

The District Administrator is located in Kolonia near the start of the causeway to Takatik Island. Within walking distance you will also find the post office, bank, handicraft co-op, and miscellaneous stores. The farmer's market is located near the Kolonia pier.

Some fresh fruits and vegetables are obtainable in Kolonia along with a limited selection of staple goods. There are no boat repair facilities or supplies.

The ruins of Nan Madol on Ponape Island remain as a monument to a lost civilization. Believed to have been occupied as late as the 11th Century AD, Nan Madol occupied 100 semi-artificial islets framed of basalt "logs".

Jetsam and Flotsam

Currency:

The United States dollar is the official currency.

Language:

The official language is English and it is spoken by everybody. The native tongue is Ponapean which is spoken by the elders of the community.

Electricity:

Electric power is 110 volt, 60 Hz AC

Postal Address:

Yacht (   )
General Delivery
Ponape, TT 96941, USA

External Affairs Representative:

United States consulates and embassies

Information Center:

Ponape Tourist Commission
Kolonia, Ponape, TT 96941, USA

Radio Communications

Station name and call	Location	Frequency Transmit/Receive	Service hours LMT	Type of service
WSZD	7°N, 158°E	1450 kHz	0600-2400	Commercial broadcast
Radio Ponape (KUP-66)	Kolonia	2182/2182 kHz 2724/2724 7935/7935	24 hours	District administration

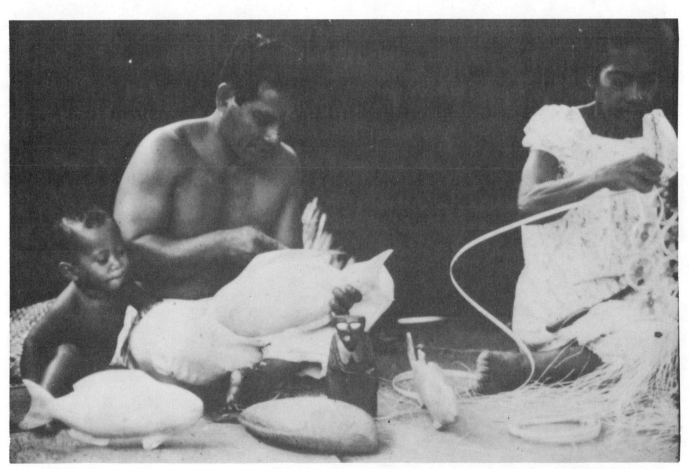

The forests of the interior provide good materials for Ponapean handicrafts. Excellent wood carvings are made by the Polynesians from Kapingamarangi Atoll who now live in Kapingamarangi Village on Ponape.

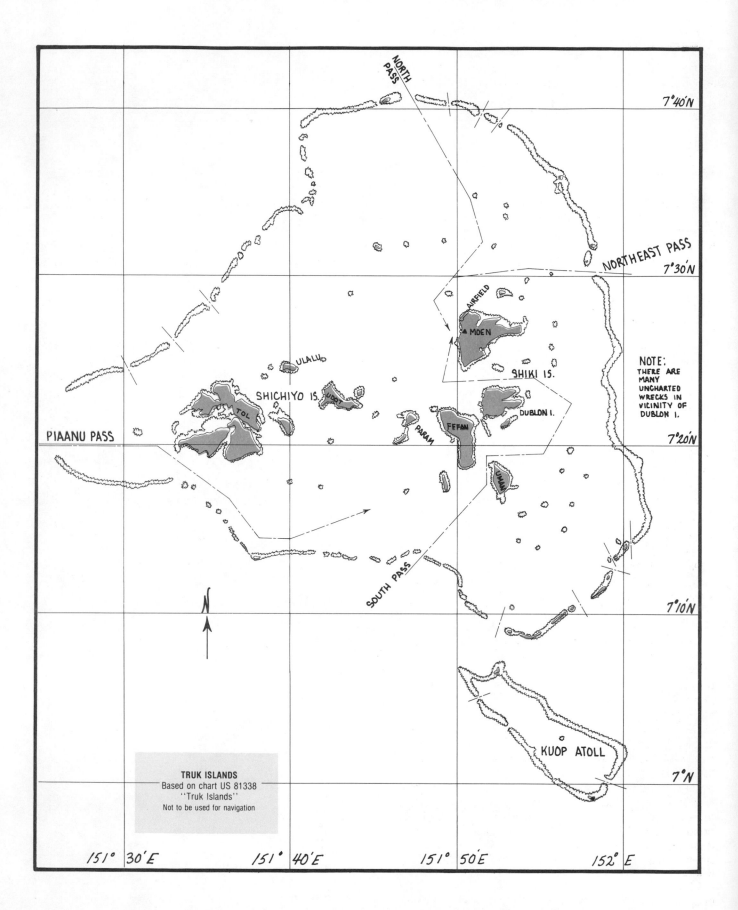

NORTH PASS

7°40'N

NORTHEAST PASS

7°30'N

AIRFIELD

MOEN

SHIKI IS.

ULALU

SHICHIYO IS.

UDOT

TOL

DUBLON I.

PARAM

FEFAN

NOTE:
THERE ARE
MANY
UNCHARTED
WRECKS IN
VICINITY OF
DUBLON I.

PIAANU PASS

7°20'N

UMAN

N

SOUTH PASS

7°10'N

KUOP ATOLL

7°N

TRUK ISLANDS
Based on chart US 81338
''Truk Islands''
Not to be used for navigation

151° 30'E   151° 40'E   151° 50'E   152° E

Chapter 24-D

TRUK DISTRICT

The Country

The Truk district consists of fifteen major island units made up of 290 individual islands with a combined land area of 49.2 square miles. About 40 of the islands are inhabited, and many of the rest are used as food islands, that is, they are used by inhabitants of nearby islands to grow crops and to raise livestock. Excluding Truk itself, all the island units are low coral formations of undistinguished configuration; 12 are typical atolls, and two, Nama and Pulosuk, are single islands.

Truk, which accounts for about 75 percent of the district's total land area, is an interesting complex of eleven high volcanic islands enclosed by a coral ring that is broken into eighty-seven tiny, low coral islets. The formation is comparable to that of an atoll, but the presence of the high islands within the lagoon rules out the use of that term. The encircling reef, which in places has a diameter of forty miles, contains several passages into the lagoon affording excellent anchorage for large ships.

The islands of Moen, Dublon, Fefan, Uman, Udot, and Tol are the major interior high islands of Truk. All are mountainous and heavily wooded, except in a few places where cultivation, fire, and erosion have reduced them to grasslands. Tol island, which has a peak rising to over 1400 feet is the highest. About two-thirds of the district's total population lives on these six high islands.

At one time millions of years ago Truk atoll was one big island, a rolling mountainous hulk with today's Udot island at its approximate center. Slowly, the island sank (and is still sinking though at an infinitesimally slow rate). Now only the highest peaks of the prehistoric mountains remain. The result is the mighty Truk lagoon, forty miles across, with eleven main islands and numerous satellites caught in a coral circle; three-peaked Udot; rolling agricultural Fefan (named for its resemblance to a reclining woman); the abandoned naval base of Dublon, its peak resembling a transplanted Mount Fuji; and, not least of all, there is the ominous peak of Tol, a tropical Matterhorn with a height of 1400 feet—tall enough to attract and hold rain clouds on otherwise sunny days. Outside the lagoon are smaller island groups, low atolls even farther advanced in geological age; the Halls and the Mortlocks, Namouitos and Westerns. With just forty-six square miles of land, the Truk District has the largest population of all six districts, more than 32,000, and, doubtless, when Micronesia begins to feel the pinch of overpopulation, Truk will be one of the first districts to wince.

Moen is the district center for the Truk Islands. The heart of town is the so-called "saddle"—a dip between two steep knobby hills where stand the hospital and the district administration, the Truk high school and courthouse, all in their newly constructed high style finery. Farther down along the shore, there is a mixture of architecture with new metallic post office and warehouse and concrete bank and office spaces blending with old metallic and driftwood-finished structures. But a visitor who looks beyond this drab vista, out upon the lagoon, will find himself gazing at a breath-taking gallery of mountaintop islands—Tol, Udot, Dublon, and others, all at anchor in the lagoon. A memorable demonstration of the fact that a district center is as much a jumping-off place as a destination.

The Weather

The Caroline Islands are under the influence of the doldrums belt from June through November. During this period, heavy rains, thunderstorms, and violent squalls will sometimes offer hazards. Cumulus and cumulonimbus clouds with ceilings sometimes reduced to 500 to 1000 feet for short periods, poor visibility, lightning, and confused seas accompany the more intense of these storms. Most are of short duration and seldom cover an

Truk Islands
A Trust Territory District within the Caroline Islands

Port of Entry:

Moen, Truk   7°27'N, 151°50'E

Distances between ports in nautical miles:

Between *Moen* and:

Agana, Guam	630
Honolulu, Hawaii	3370
Kwajalein, Marshall Islands	1070
Majuro, Marshall Islands	1330
Manila, Philippine Islands	2100
Palau, Caroline Islands	1180
Ponape, Caroline Islands	430
Rabaul, New Britain	710
Saipan, Mariana Islands	660
Tarawa, Kiribati	1440
Tokyo, Japan	2080
Wake Island	1095
Yap, Caroline Islands	950

Standard Time:

11 hours fast on GMT

area larger than 20 or 25 miles in diameter. The storms usually move from east to west and occur most frequently in the day at about 0600.

Northeasterly trades blow almost constantly from December to May over Namoi islands and Truk islands. The average speed is about 15 knots with an occasional gust of 30 knots. Light variable winds can be expected from July to December. The influence of the doldrums is felt for a longer period (June to November) over Nomoi island. During May and June, the trades decrease in force and intensity, with increasing east-southerly winds.

As a rule, the winds increase during the morning hours and decrease during the night.

In the Truk group the northeast trades are very steady. Between November and June 85 percent of the winds flow from north-northeast to easterly directions. By July, however, the indraft of the summer monsoon carries easterly to southerly winds from this area into Asiatic waters, and thereafter through October, the trade winds are overshadowed by various southerly to westerly breezes with an average 13 percent of calms.

A region of typhoon development is located north-

The "high islands" inside the Truk lagoon have all of the beauty of tropical Oceania.

Meeting houses are an important facet of community life and they are built with consideration of traditional design.

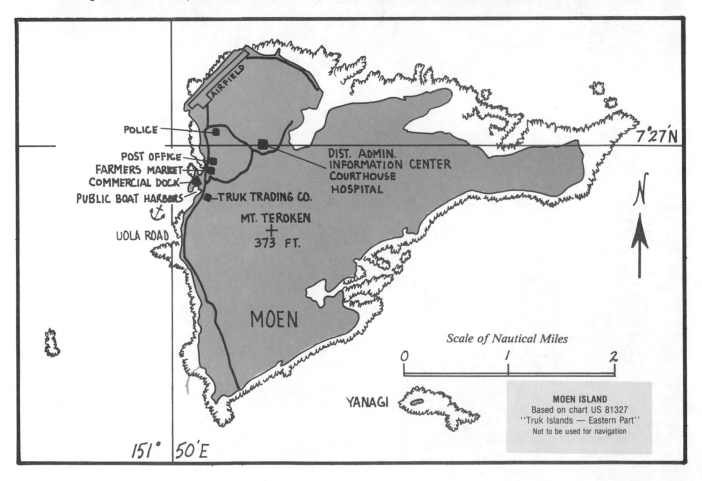

POLICE

POST OFFICE
FARMERS MARKET
COMMERCIAL DOCK
PUBLIC BOAT HARBORS

UOLA ROAD

AIRFIELD

DIST. ADMIN.
INFORMATION CENTER
COURTHOUSE
HOSPITAL

TRUK TRADING CO.

MT. TEROKEN
+
373 FT.

MOEN

7°27'N

N

YANAGI

151° 50'E

Scale of Nautical Miles

0   1   2

MOEN ISLAND
Based on chart US 81327
''Truk Islands — Eastern Part''
Not to be used for navigation

The atoll of Namonuito lies about 150 miles northwest of Truk atoll. The barrier reef is awash in most places and entry to the lagoon should be made only at known deep passes. Most of the population of about 300 persons live on the reef island of Ulul.

ward of Truk islands. As a rule, however, such storms do not reach full development until they pass westward of Guam. They occur most frequently in late summer or autumn.

Much rain occurs in all months in the eastern Caroline Islands. Truk Islands averages 121 inches annually with a maximum of 12 inches per month occuring in July and August and a minimum of 6 inches in January. January, February and March show average rainfall somewhat under 10 inches per month. Thunderstorms are quite common between May and October.

Nomoi island usually has its heaviest rainfall between June and October. Winter and early spring, the so-called dry season, has an average of 7 or 8 inches of rainfall per month. The rain falls mostly at night with a maximum during the early morning hours, usually decreasing rapidly after sunrise. Minimum rainfall and cloudiness can be expected between 0900 and 1400.

Yacht Facilities

The district center for Truk is located on Moen island near the northeast pass to the lagoon. There is no detailed chart of this area because the United States is still using primarily Japanese chart information. Japanese headquarters before and during World War II were on adjacent Dublon island and the principal ship anchorage then was Eten anchorage which is well charted.

Today's Truk Harbor is located on the west side of Moen island in an area called Uola Road. Caution must be used when approaching Moen island for, as the U.S. Sailing Directions say, "Moen island is fringed with reefs and fronted by dangers". Besides the reefs there are innumerable wrecks of Japanese warships in these waters.

The principal harbor facility, Baker Dock, has a 300-foot long pier at its north entrance where a visiting yacht can tie up to check in with the District Administration and for purposes of reprovisioning. Some dockage facilities also exist, inside the south entrance to the harbor.

District Administration, hospital, and some stores are located a short distance to the northeast of the harbor in a saddle between the hills. The famous Truk Trading Company, a general store with a surprising line of merchandise, is located across the road from Baker Dock as is the post office and some additional stores.

Some fresh foods can be obtained at Moen and many canned products are available. While most personal needs can be satisfied at the Truk Trading Company, few boat supplies are available any place in Truk. Gasoline, diesel fuel, and potable water are available at the docks. There are no repair facilities.

Radio Communications

Station name and call	Location	Frequency Transmit/Receive	Service hours LMT	Type of service
WSZC	7°N 151°E	1300 kHz	0600-2400	Commercial broadcast
Radio Truk (KUP-67)	Moen	2182/2182 kHz 2724/2724 7935/7935	24 hours	District administration

The most famous general store in the Trust Territory.

Jetsam and Flotsam

Currency:

The United States dollar is the official currency

Language:

The official language is English and it is spoken by everybody. The native tongue is Trukese which is spoken by the elders of the community.

Electricity:

Electric power is 110 volts, 60 Hz AC

Postal address:

Yacht   (   )
General Delivery
Moen, Truk, TT 96942, USA

External Affairs Representative:

United States consulates and embassies

Information Center:

Truk Tourist Commission
Moen, Truk, TT 96942, USA

Chapter 24-E
YAP DISTRICT

The Country

The Yap district consists of sixteen island units that contain 145 individual islands and a total land area of 46 square miles. The units include the Yap islands proper, five single-island formations, and ten atolls. Four of the island units, Gaferut, West Fayu, Pikelot, and Olimarao, are usually uninhabited, as are many of the small island components of other units. About 65 percent of the district's total population of 6870 resides on the Yap islands proper.

The Yap island unit is a group of four major and six minor high islands surrounded by fringing and barrier reefs. The main island in the group is 585 feet high and, since it rises from the Asian continental shelf, is classified as continental rather than oceanic. All other islands of the district, except Fais, which is a raised atoll, are low, lagoon-type atolls.

The Yapese have long fascinated anthropologists studying what is changing and what is unchanged in the most reserved, most socially complicated of the Trust Territory's six districts. But you don't have to be a scholar to wonder at Yap or to speculate about what is past or passing and to come. The district center of Colonia is a study in contrasts, with the properties of modern life—motorcycles, beer, and jukeboxes absorbed into a culture of grass-skirts, loin-cloths, and betelnut. Away from Colonia, and not far away at that, life continues little changed in a world of tranquil beaches, thatched roofs, stone money and ceremonial dances. And on such "outer islands" as Ulithi, Faraulep, Woleai, Eauripik and Satawal, life goes on as it did a half century ago.

Yap islands "proper" is a complex of four separate islands—Rumung, Map, Gagil-Tomil, and Yap. Rumung is reached only by boat. Colonia, the district center, is the only settlement which could be considered even partially modern. The mixture of Americans, Yapese from nearby villages, more primitive "outer islanders" and a lively expatriate Palauan community create a somewhat cosmopolitan atmosphere. Away from Colonia's stores, its gas pumps, electricity, water, and tiny hotels, most of Yap's people continue to subsist on an economy of gardening, food-gathering, and fishing. Main crops include taro, yams, sweet potatoes, and bananas. Moreover, Yapese betelnut and coconut are both reputed the best in the Trust Territory and enjoy continuing popularity as export products.

The areca palm, a source of betelnuts, was probably not an indigenous plant but was introduced from other places well in advance of the arrival of the Spanish. Betelnuts are about the size of a small chicken egg, orange in color and covered by a fibrous husk. The meat of the nut is wrapped in a leaf of the pepper vine with a small amount of quicklime. The action of the lime and betelnut produces a blood-red color. Betelnut chewing results in a discoloration and eventual destruction of tooth enamel. It has a mild narcotic effect on the chewer and also kills certain intestinal parasites.

Yap is probably best known for its stone money. They vary in size from six inches in diameter to wheels 12 feet in diameter. The money is always circular with a hole through the center in order to carry it on a pole. The material is aragonite which has a crystalline pattern and the hardness of marble. The raw material for these stone wheels was, surprisingly, not found on Yap but on the island of Palau almost 300 miles away. The effort required to quarry the stone, carve it into wheels, and transport it to Yap is what gave the money its value.

You might think that stone money was a difficult medium of exchange to handle but it really wasn't. Stone

Yap Islands
A Trust Territory District within the Caroline Islands

Port of Entry:

Colonia, Yap	9°30'N, 138°08'E

Distances between ports in nautical miles:

Between *Colonia* and:

Agana, Guam	510
Honolulu, Hawaii	4150
Kwajalein, Marshall Islands	1980
Majuro, Marshall Islands	2250
Manila, Philippine Islands	1060
Palau, Caroline Islands	280
Ponape, Caroline Islands	1370
Rabaul, New Britain	1140
Saipan, Mariana Islands	630
Truk, Caroline Islands	950
Tokyo, Japan	1800

Standard Time:

10 hours fast on GMT

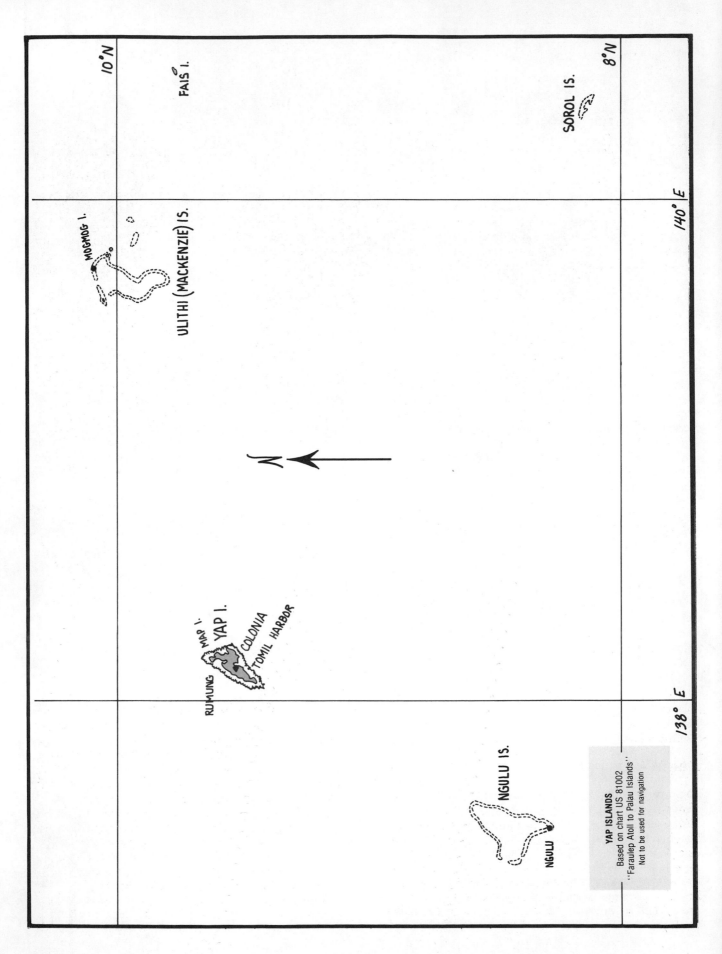

YAP ISLANDS
Based on chart US 81002
"Faraulep Atoll to Palau Islands"
Not to be used for navigation

10°N

8°N

FAIS I.

SOROL IS.

140° E

MOGMOG I.

ULITHI (MACKENZIE) IS.

N

RUMUNG I.

MAP I.

YAP I.

COLONIA

TOMIL HARBOR

138° E

NGULU IS.

NGULU

Yapese tradition calls for the older people to perform the dances of their villages, but on great occasions the youngsters also have an opportunity. This trio was waiting its turn during the dedication of the new Yap Legislature Building.

money was rarely handled or moved from its place of "deposit". It was really more a measure of the wealth of the individual and was highly visible to all.

The Weather

The winds at Ulithi atoll 80 miles to the east of Yap are dominantly the northeast trades, which blow from later November to May, with greatest force from December to February when the trades are reinforced with the northeast monsoon. In May through July the wind is east and long periods of calm occur. From the end of July to the end of September, the southwest monsoon prevails. From September to November calms occur. Typhoons are known in this area. Six of ten typhoons that passed between Guam and the Palau islands in 1951 and 1952

passed to the northward of Ulithi atoll. Two passed directly over the atoll and the remaining two passed to the southward of the atoll.

Japanese sources state that from November through March easterly winds generally prevail. April through June, and September through October, have northeast to southeast winds and are comparatively calm. In July and August the wind direction is changeable; south winds come up quickly and die away in one night. A shifting from north to west is said to be a sign of bad weather.

The doldrums belt oscillates back and forth over the Yap islands area from July through September, being the principal climatic control during this period.

The northeast trades are best established in January, when northeast or east winds blow 89 percent of the time with an average speed of 6 knots, and occasionally ex-

A local sailor takes advantage of the tradewinds and calm waters inside the barrier reef of the Yap Islands.

ceeding 25 knots. The trades prevail from February through May, with a gradual decrease in frequency to 68 percent in May, and with a slight decrease in speed.

During June the trades weaken, and winds veer toward the southeast. In July through September light variable winds, mostly with a southerly component, and frequent calms are prevalent; strong and gusty winds occur with brief periods of squally weather. In October, light southwest winds prevail, although northeast and east winds are almost as frequent. The northeast trades become reestablished during November and December.

Gales average one a month in March, and may occur occasionally at other times. Wind speeds during the entire year are somewhat higher over the open sea.

Typhoons sometimes occur in the Yap island area, usually in May and June, or in the last three months of the year.

The average path of typhoon centers is north of Yap; however three or four per year pass close enough to affect the weather, usually from September through November. Typhoons centered north of Yap cause heavy showers and increasing winds from the westward. The swell is heavy from the northwest, and results in a heavy confused cross-sea.

Much rain occurs throughout the year in the western Caroline Islands, but there is a definite increase between May and October. Thunderstorms are failrly common from June to November.

Ulithi atoll has the heaviest rainfall (15.6 inches) in January. December with 3.6 inches is the month with least rainfall. In general, precipitation is greatest during calms.

There is a distinct seasonal variation at Yap Islands, the wettest season being from July through September, with an average of 16 inches per month. Heavy rains are most frequent during the early morning.

The driest season is February through March, when the monthly average is 6 inches. The rain during these months is usually of the shower type.

Temperatures at Ulithi atoll average about 81°F throughout the year. The daily maximum occurs at noon, when the temperature reaches 90°F. The minimum, at night, is around 75°F.

Fog is virtually unknown, and visibility is usually very good except during heavy rains. It has been estimated that visibility below 1¼ miles occurs once or twice a month from July through September and not more than once a month during the remainder of the year.

Jetsam and Flotsam

Currency:

The United States dollar is the official currency

Language:

The official language is English and it is spoken by everybody. The native tongue is Yapese which is spoken by the elders of the community.

Electricity:

Electric power is 110 volts, 60 Hz AC

Postal address:

Yacht (   )
General Delivery
Colonia, Yap, TT 96943, USA

External Affairs Representative:

United States consulates and embassies

Information Center:

Yap Tourist Commission
Colonia, Yap, TT 96943, USA

Cruising Library:

His Majesty O'Keefe, Klingman and Green; Charles Scribner's Sons, New York, USA, 1950.

A village in the Yap Islands.

Weather in the Vicinity of Woleai Atoll

The weather at Woleai atoll, 360 miles east-southeast of Yap, is controlled partly by the doldrums belt. In June it moves northward across this area, accompanied by frequent showers and squalls; poor visibility, lightning and rough seas accompany the most intense of these squalls. From mid-July to mid-September, when the doldrums lie to the north, winds from the southerly quadrants prevail and showers are frequent. In October the doldrums belt moves southward across the area, squally, rainy weather being interspersed with periods of good weather. From November through May, the relatively dry northeast trades predominate, with brief showers.

The islands are situated southward of the usual track of typhoon centers, but an average of three a year pass close enough to affect the weather, with the greatest frequency in May and June and again during October and November.

Visibility is generally good, being limited only by rain. Fog does not occur. Temperatures average 80°F with little seasonal variation; relative humidity is high throughout the year, averaging about 85 percent.

From November through May, northeast and east winds prevail 78 percent of the time, with an average speed of 10 to 12 knots. In June, winds are mostly from the northeast, but begin veering toward the east during the latter half of the month; speeds average 10 knots. From July through September, southerly winds prevail with speeds averaging 8 knots, and calms occur 6 percent of the time. During this period there are occasional brief periods of squally weather. In October, winds begin backing toward the east with southeast being the prevailing direction; speeds average 10 knots.

Precipitation in the Woleai atoll area is heaviest from June through October, when it averages 13 inches per month and is primarily heavy showers. The drier season is from January through March with a monthly average of

The stone money of Yap is personal property not to be moved or sat on. It is a symbol of the owner's wealth. This piece is on display at a Yap church.

6 to 7 inches. In November, April, and May, rainfall averages 9 inches. The number of rainy days varies from 15 in January to 22 in July.

Yacht Facilities

The main port for the Yap District is at Colonia on Yap island. It is reached through a 1½-mile long passage bordered by fringing reefs making it imperative to hold to the designated channel. There are numerous fish weirs and traps along the sides of the channel.

The main wharf at Colonia is 230 feet long and a 200 foot long barge has been permanently tied up to it. Space permitting, yachts can tie up alongside the barge while going ashore to check in with the District Administrator. There are also several smaller piers which can be used. Diesel fuel, gasoline, and fresh water are available at the main wharf. There are no slipway facilities nor boat hardware available. Government workshops may be able to assist with minor boat or equipment repairs.

The village of Colonia is very small and everything is within walking distance of the dock. The District Administrator, post office, bank and hospital are all located along the southern edge of the town where the port facilities are. Across the narrow peninsula are the farmer's market and handicraft center. Fresh fruits, vegetables, and staple goods are available.

Yap, more than any other district in the Trust Territory, maintains its traditional culture and with it taboos which should be recognized by the yachtsman visitor. Here are a number of them:

Whistling is not done in public

Women should not wear skirts or shorts that expose the leg above the knee

Do not sit or stand on stone money

Never step over a person's outstretched leg

Do not step over another person's personal belongings

Do not pat a child on the head

Avoid pointing at other persons

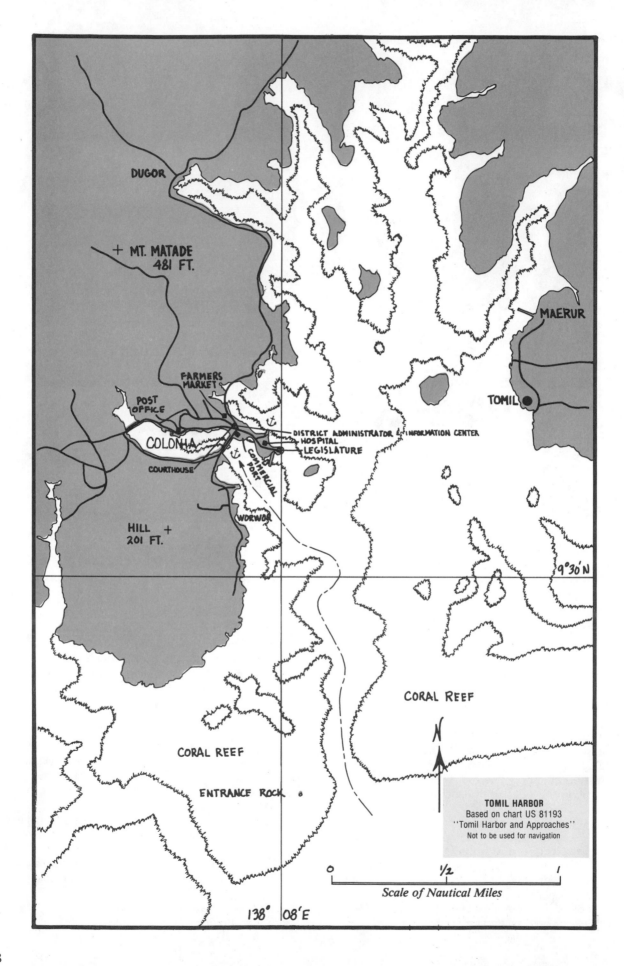

DUGOR

+ MT. MATADE
481 FT.

MAERUR

FARMERS
MARKET

POST
OFFICE

TOMIL

COLONIA

DISTRICT ADMINISTRATOR & INFORMATION CENTER
HOSPITAL
LEGISLATURE

COURTHOUSE

COMMERCIAL PORT

HILL +
201 FT.

WORWOR

9°30'N

CORAL REEF

N

CORAL REEF

TOMIL HARBOR
Based on chart US 81193
''Tomil Harbor and Approaches''
Not to be used for navigation

ENTRANCE ROCK

0   ½   1

Scale of Nautical Miles

138° 08'E

Radio Communications

Station name and call	Location	Frequency Transmit/Receive	Service hours LMT	Type of service
WSZA	10°N 137°E	1480 kHz	0600-2400	Commercial broadcast
Radio Yap (KUP-69)	Colonia	2182/2182 kHz 2724/2724 7935/7935	24 hours	District administration

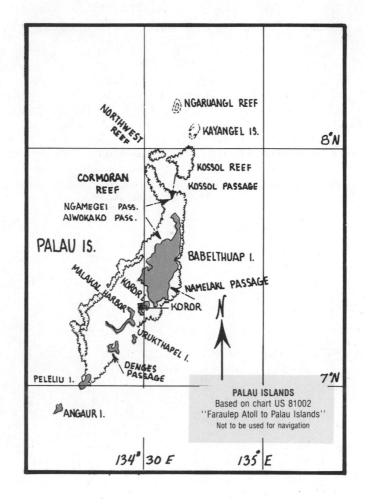

NORTHWEST REEF

🌀 NGARUANGL REEF

🌀 KAYANGEL IS.

8°N

CORMORAN REEF

KOSSOL REEF

KOSSOL PASSAGE

NGAMEGEI PASS.

AIWOKAKO PASS.

PALAU IS.

BABELTHUAP I.

MALAKAL HARBOR

KOROR

NAMELAKL PASSAGE

KOROR

N

URUKTHAPEL I.

DENGES PASSAGE

PELELIU I.

7°N

🌀 ANGAUR I.

PALAU ISLANDS
Based on chart US 81002
''Faraulep Atoll to Palau Islands''
Not to be used for navigation

134° 30 E

135° E

Chapter 24-F
PALAU DISTRICT

The Country

The Palau district is the westernmost administrative component of the Caroline archipelago and consists of six island units that include 349 individual islands involving a total land are of 191 square miles. The group is formed directly by the exposed peaks or indirectly by coral capping on still-submerged elevations along the outer edge of the Asian continental shelf. Thus all its islands are classified as continental rather than oceanic in form.

The major island unit is the one known as the Palau cluster. Its main elements are Babelthuap, Koror, Peleliu, and Angaur islands, which are high volcanic types, and Kayangel island, which is the district's only true atoll. The cluster also includes 338 tiny rock islands of little significance. Only the 5 main islands and 3 of the lesser ones are permanently inhabited, all but 192 of the district's total population of 11,904 is concentrated on them. All the islands except Angaur and Kayangel are enclosed within a single barrier reef.

Babelthuap is a sizable island that dominates the cluster. It is about 27 miles long, and its area of 153 square miles make it the largest single land mass in the entire Trust Territory. Although classified as a high island, Babelthuap is not mountainous. It is, rather, an area of gently rolling hills, which reach a maximum height of about 700 feet. The island also has one of the few real lakes in the Trust Territory, Lake Ngardok, which is 3000 feet long and 1000 feet wide with a depth of 11 or 12 feet. Most of Babelthuap is composed of volcanic materials, but its southeastern corner is raised coral limestone.

Koror, which is the capital of the district, Peleliu, and Angaur islands south of Babelthuap are high, rugged formations of raised limestone, which nevertheless have considerable portions of exposed volcanic materials. Like Babelthuap, they are covered with a dense growth of trees and bushes in great variety. Kayangel island is located twenty-eight miles north of Babelthuap and is a typical low coral atoll having a number of islets encircling its well-protected interior lagoon.

The five other island units of the Palau district are the tiny islands of Sonsorol, Pulo Anna, Merir, Tobi, and Helen. They are isolated in a string extending southwest from the Palau cluster almost to New Guinea. All, except Sonsorol, which has two components, are single islands of raised limestone formation. Merir and Helen islands are uninhabited; Sonsorol, Tobi, and Pulo Anna have populations of 55, 75, and 13 persons respectively.

Far to the south, within two hundred miles of New Guinea, are the sparsely populated islands of Sonsorol and Tobi, the sand spit of Helen Reef (inhabited by birds and turtles) and the mosquito-infested islet of Merir (shore parties are counseled to wear long-sleeve shirts!) Hundreds of miles northward is the picture-perfect atoll of Kayangel, of which all who visit speak in superlatives. But most of Palau's 191 square miles of land are concentrated in a central cluster of islands stretching 125 miles from the northern tip of Babelthuap to the south beach of Angaur. Babelthuap, largest island in the Trust Territory, with ten villages hugging its coastal plains and almost no one, including Palauans, has ventured far into the interior of the mighty jungled island. And just off the southern flanks of Babelthuap is a quite different array of islands—a gay flotilla of emerald hillocks, formerly called the Rock islands but now more aptly termed the Floating Garden islands—dozens and dozens of them laced across the sea. And, still farther south, are the hot war-littered islands of Peleliu and Anguar.

Palau Islands

A Trust Territory District within the
West Caroline Islands

Port of Entry:

Koror, Koror Island   7°20N, 134°29′E

Distances between ports in nautical miles:

Between *Koror* and:

Agana, Guam	800
Honolulu, Hawaii	4450
Majuro, Marshall Islands	2500
Manila, Philippine Islands	920
Ponape, Caroline Islands	1600
Rabaul, New Britain	1240
Saipan, Mariana Islands	900
Truk, Caroline Islands	1180
Tokyo, Japan	1970
Yap, Caroline Islands	280

Standard Time:

9 hours fast on GMT

Outrigger canoes are great for fishing the lagoon of the Palau Archipelago.

Of all the Trust Territory's district centers, Koror with its population of around 7000 may be the settlement with the most distinctive individual character. To be sure, the houses, by and large, rely on the corrugated metal and tin which are so incongrously commonplace throughout Micronesia and the roads are just now beginning to see paving over the lengths of pitted obstacle course. But about Koror there linger the traces of a distinguished pre-World War II community and it may be that this sense of the past renders the present tolerable and future promising. For Palauans can—and do—remember when Koror, with a population almost six times the current figure, was the bustling administrative center of the Japanese Trust Territory. Today only remains are left—a sadly abbreviated stretch of paved road called "geisha lane," a Shinto shrine, seaplane ramps, Japanese-type houses or—more likely—tin and wood shanties perched on much wider concrete foundations and entered by a flight of imperial steps. In Japanese times the population of Koror was overwhelmingly non-Palauan but, after the invasion, Palauans moved into the ruined colonial city and claimed it as their own. Today Koror is a growing commercial center with hotels and movie theaters, numerous bars, countless stores, and a growing sense of its own potential. Fishing and tourism both have firm footholds in Palau today and chances are that Palau will become one of the most rapidly developed of the six districts.

The Weather

The Palau District is under the influence of the trades and monsoons with northeasterly winds in the winter months and winds tending westerly in the summer. In the traditional Palauan calendar the winter months are known as "Ongos", meaning "northeast" which is the direction of the prevailing winds at that time. The summer period is known as "Negebard", meaning "southwest" or the direction of the prevailing monsoonal wind in the summer.

The Palau islands lie on the east edge of the monsoon belt where the northeast trades and the northeast monsoons merge creating winds of 12 to 14 knots on the open ocean in the winter and spring months of December through April. In May the winds over this area diminish and blow mostly from the east at which time the southwest monsoon is beginning to set in. In summer and in early autumn, July to October, the southwest monsoon prevails over the area. In October and November the northeast trades again become established setting up winds of 12 to 14 knots during the winter months. Between the periods of the northeast trades and the southwest monsoon the winds may be variable.

Rain occurs at all seasons in the Palau island area, but is at a minimum during the period of the northeast monsoon. Squally conditions, however, appear to occur more frequently from November to January, as the northeast monsoon is gradually established against the variable south to easterly drift of preceding months. Thunderstorms are rare from January to April and fairly common from May through August.

At Palau island, 148 inches of rain occurs on an annual average, with 20 inches in July and slightly over 7 inches in March. Rainfall is somewhat lighter over the open sea. Precipitation occurs on about 50 percent of the days from February through April and on approximately 75 percent during July through September. The heaviest rains occur during the early morning with a secondary maximum soon after sunset.

While gales seldom occur in the Palau area, typhoons do and there is an average of two typhoons a year affecting the area. September is the most common month but July, August, and October have almost as many. Typhoons are least frequent during the month of February. The normal typhoon path is just northward of the Palau islands heading west at 12 to 13 knots. The typhoon diameters are usually small if that is any consolation.

Yacht Facilities

One finds in the Palau islands an endless array of islands, harbors and passages, most of which can be visited by the cruising yacht exercising due care for the fringing reefs throughout the area. But before any visiting is done, en-

Jetsam and Flotsam

Currency:

The United States dollar is the official currency.

Language:

The official language is English and is spoken by everybody. The native tongue is a Micronesian dialect which is still spoken by the elders of the community.

Electricity:

Electric power is 110 volts, 60 Hz AC

Postal address:

Yacht (   )
General Delivery
Koror, Palau, TT 96940
USA

External Affairs Representative:

United States consulates and embassies

Information Center:

Palau Tourist Commission
Koror, Palau, TT 96940, USA

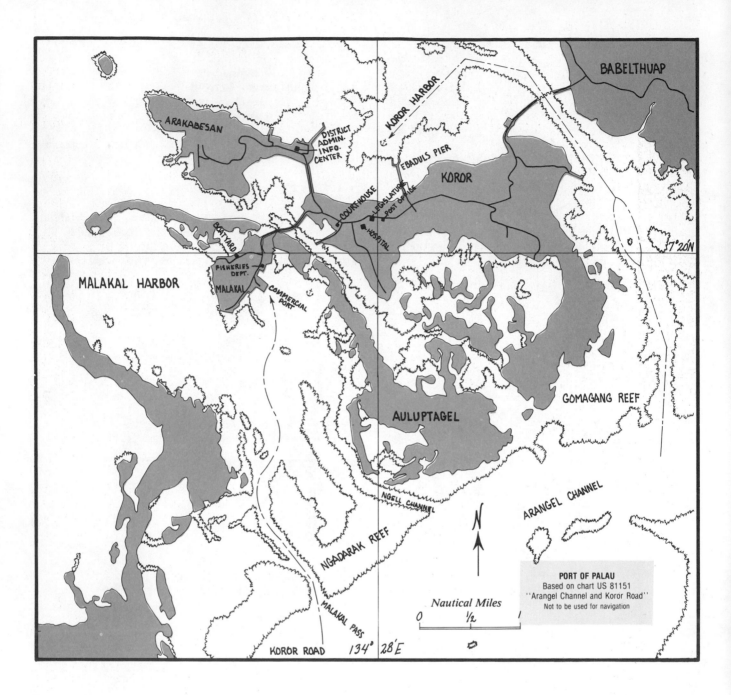

PORT OF PALAU
Based on chart US 81151
"Arangel Channel and Koror Road"
Not to be used for navigation

try should be made at the District Administrative Center which is located on Arakabesan island. You can bring your yacht into either Malakal or Koror harbors which will get you within walking distance of the Administrative Center.

The larger of the two harbors is Malakal harbor and it is the Port of Palau. Harbor facilities are located on the east side of the island and consist of one main wharf about

500 feet long and several smaller ones plus a number of deteriorated ones now unuseable. Diesel fuel, gasoline, and fresh water are available here but the water should be heavily chlorinated as it has been reported that there are hookworm larva in it. There is a boatyard on Malakal island which can handle fishing boats up to 100 tons and they have some miscellaneous boat hardware but little of the yacht variety. The Fisheries Department alongside

Koror, the District Center of Palau. Ebadulis Pier and Koror Harbor are visible on the far side of the island.

the main wharf has some additional supplies. It is not advised to lie along the main wharf overnight because sudden high winds and rain squalls may buffet your boat against the wharf. You are better off to anchor clear of the wharf and shoreline.

The harbor at Koror is smaller and used primarily by the interisland trading boats. A small craft basin exists between the two arms of the pier extending from Ebadulis pier and you can tie up here for business ashore.

The commercial center of the Palau district is located on Koror island and there you will find stores, post office, laundromat, bank, and a hospital. Causeways connect the islands of Arakabesan, Malakal, Koror and Babelthuap and your immediate business and supply needs can all be taken care of on foot.

After you have officially entered Palau and wish to cruise to the other islands of the group, get permission from the District Administrator and the principal chief of the group. You will find diplomacy a great ally in enjoying these islands.

The waterfront at Koror.

Radio Communications

Station name and call	Location	Frequency Transmit/Receive	Service hours LMT	Type of service
WSZB	Koror	1500 kHz	0600-2400	Commercial broadcast
Radio Palau (KUP-68)	Koror	2182/2182 kHz 2724/2724 kHz 7935/7935 kHz	24 hours	District administration

Chapter 25

KIRIBATI
(Gilbert Islands)

The Gilbert Islands became an independent republic on 12 July 1979. They continue in full association with the Commonwealth of Great Britain. The name of the new republic, Kiribati, is pronounced "Kiribas" and the people of Kiribati do not refer to themselves as Kiribatians but as I-Kiribati. In the Gilbertese alphabet there is no letter S but T followed by I is pronounced as S. The main island of Betio in the Tarawa atoll is pronounced "bay-sho."

The Country

Kiribati occupies a vast, irregular shaped area of over 200,000 square miles in the central Pacific. Its eastern components, the Phoenix group and three atolls of the Line island group are in Polynesia; its western portion, the Gilbert group, is located in Micronesia. Despite the extent of the ocean area which it occupies, the total land area is only 117 square miles. Its population of a little over 45,000 persons is Micronesian.

Islands of the territory are low atolls, except for Banaba (Ocean Island), which is a raised atoll. Banaba is one of two phosphate islands in the Pacific actively being mined. Profits from the enterprise are paid to the Banabans who are in the most part living on Rabi island in the Fijis. The reserves of the island are rapidly approaching extinction and the long term future of the island and the Banabans is not settled.

All the rest of the islands are coral atolls whose soil is a porous mixture of decomposed coral and sand that is incapable of retaining what moisture it does receive. Only pandanus, casuarina, sedges, and the ubiquitous coconut palm can survive, and even these are sparse. Sometimes the islanders dig pits in which they are able to accumulate sufficient compost to make a soil which is planted with taro root. But generally the population in the drier parts of Kiribati subsist on fruits of the pandanus, on coconut and palm products and on fish that abound in the lagoons and surrounding ocean. Pressure on the land is sometimes overtaxing, and groups of people must remove to other areas where food is more plentiful and varied.

Kiribati consists of 17 atolls lying roughly between 4°N and 4°S latitude just west of the 180th meridian. Except for Banaba island, which was a rich but now declining source of phosphate, they are economically important only as producers of moderate amounts of copra. Two of the atolls in the northern Gilberts (Butaritari and Tarawa) were famous battleground during World War II.

The Phoenix group, and Enderbury Islands consist of six small atolls located just below the equator at about the 175th west meridian. Individually named Phoenix, Hull, Sydney, McKean, Birnie and Gardner, they are economically unimportant, and many of their inhabitants have been migrating to the Solomon Islands where better living conditions are available.

Three of the atolls in the northern Line group, Washington, Fanning, and Christmas complete the territory of Kiribati. Christmas island is the largest in the group being 140 square miles in area. It has no indigenous population but is inhabited by about 700 I-Kiribati brought in to work the coconut plantations. Fanning and Washington islands are much smaller than Christmas and are also inhabited mostly by the plantation workers.

Since the Guano Act passed by Congress in 1856

Kiribati

An independent republic with the British Commonwealth

Ports of Entry:

Tarawa	1°21'N, 172°55'E
Banaba (Ocean) Island	0°52'S, 169°35'E

Distances between ports in nautical miles:

Between *Tarawa* and:

Apia, Western Samoa	1285
Agana, Guam	1830
Funafuti, Tuvalu	695
Honolulu, Hawaii	2100
Levuka, Fiji	1310
Ponape, Caroline Islands	1000
Banaba Island	240

Between *Banaba Island* and:

Honolulu, Hawaii	2480
Pago Pago, American Samoa	1410
Papeete, Society Islands	2610
Suva, Fiji	1210

Standard time:

12 hours fast on GMT

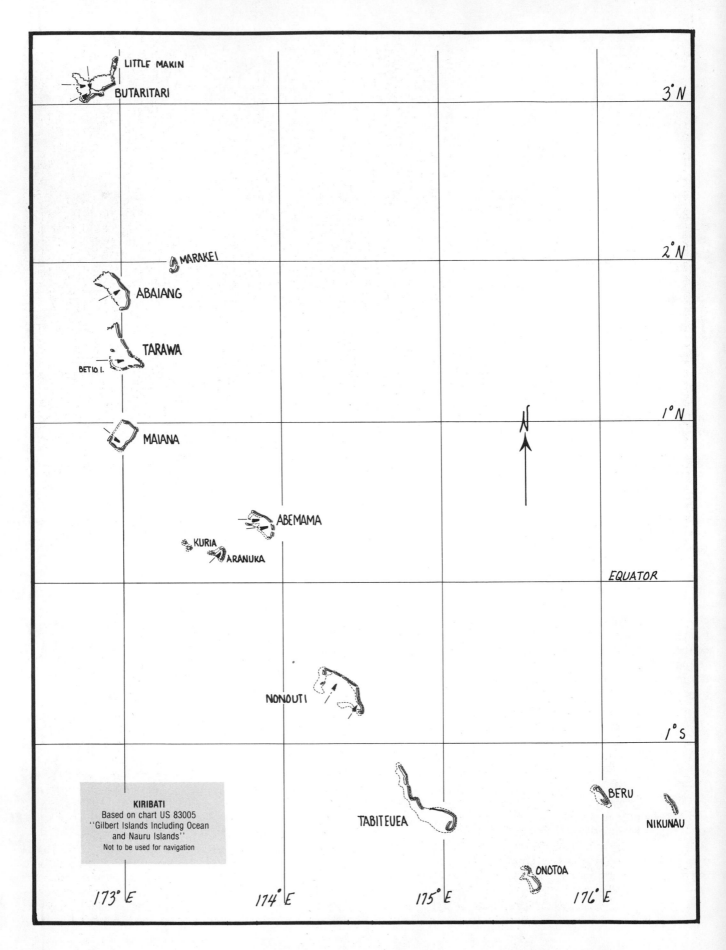

LITTLE MAKIN

BUTARITARI

3° N

MARAKEI

2° N

ABAIANG

TARAWA

BETIO I.

1° N

MAIANA

ABEMAMA

KURIA

ARANUKA

EQUATOR

NONOUTI

1° S

BERU

NIKUNAU

KIRIBATI
Based on chart US 83005
''Gilbert Islands Including Ocean
and Nauru Islands''
Not to be used for navigation

TABITEUEA

ONOTOA

173° E

174° E

175° E

176° E

A modern frame dwelling on Tarawa Atoll.

there has been a friendly controversy with Great Britain regarding ownership of eight islands in the Phoenix group and six in the Line group. In 1979 the United States relinquished claim to all of them and they are now an unquestioned part of Kiribati. These islands are Caroline, Christmas, Flint, Malden, Starbuck and Vostock in the Line group and the atolls of Birnie, Gardner, Hull, McKean, Phoenix, and Sydney together with the islands of Canton and Enderbury in the Phoenix group. The United States will, however, continue some joint ventures on the island of Canton.

Although the I-Kiribati believe that they are descendents of Samoans there is little real evidence to support that or any other genealogical theory. The first Europeans to see the islands were the Spanish and it is believed that de Quiros sighted Butaritari in the year 1606. Captain Byron stopped at Nikinau in 1765 but it was a random process of discovery for the other islands spanning about 50 years. The island group was originally named after the British Captain Gilbert who stopped there in 1788 in the company of Captain Marshall after whom the Marshall Islands are named.

The waters of Kiribati were a favorite sperm whale hunting ground and many of the early traders were deserters from the whale ships. Blackbirding (slave procurement) ran rampant in the 1850 to 1875 period and it led to the creation in 1877 by Britain of the office of the High Commissioner for the Western Pacific to settle differences between native peoples and the traders. It was later joined with the Ellice Islands to forms the Gilbert-Ellice Islands Colony which lasted until the present when the Ellice Islands separated to form Tuvalu.

The Weather

The southeast tradewind season extends from March to November. It is characterized by more or less steady tradewinds blowing from the east-southeast and very little rainfall. There is actually no specific doldrum period although calms and cat's paws occur quite often in June and July.

The westerly season occasionally extends from November to March although there is no certainty that actual west winds will develop in any force. The westerly season is the rainy season although it doesn't rain every day. With the exception of Butaritari and Little Makin, Kiribati can be said to be in the dry zone. Rainfall at Tarawa is about 55 inches annually but there are occasional drought years when the rainfall may be as low as five inches.

Island contours are too low to provoke much precipitation from the clouds borne by the constant southeast tradewinds that blow over them and, consequently, fresh water is usually at a premium. The territory is too far east to be effected very much by the northwest monsoon. It does, however, lie within the narrow belt of the intertropical front where cyclonic storms originate and from which occasionally heavy rain will fall.

The climate is uniformly hot, seldom varying more than a degree or two from an annual mean in the mid 80's. The southern islands are drier than the northern islands. Except on calm days which are somewhat oppressive, the heat is tempered by the tradewinds. Nights are generally cool and comfortable.

Gales are rare and the region is outside of the usual belt of tropical storms. Only one hurricane has been known to cross Kiribati and that occurred in December 1927 at 3°N and 173°E.

Yacht Entry

There are four Ports of Entry to Kiribati—Betio on

Jetsam and Flotsam

Currency:

Kirbati uses Australian currency. At press time the rate of exchange was $US1 = $A.85.

Language:

Gilbertese is the indigenous language of the islanders but English is the official language understood by just about everybody.

Electricity:

Where electricity is available, it is 240 volt, 50 Hz AC.

Postal Address:

Yacht (   )
Poste Restante
Betio, Tarawa
KIRIBATI

External Affairs Representative:

Australian consulates or embassies

Cruising Library:

Astride the Equator: An Account of the Gilbert Islands, Ernest Sabatier; Oxford University Press, Melbourne, Australia, 1977.

Tarawa is the main port for all Kiribati; Banaba, Christmas and Fanning islands are their own Ports of Entry. Yachts checking in at any of these ports must observe the normal customs, immigration and health formalities.

Visas are required of all persons except citizens of the United Kingdom and British commonwealths. Visas are good for four months and they should be obtained from a British Consulate before entering Kiribati waters. A cruising permit covering the entire group can be obtained from the Department of Customs at Tarawa.

Yacht Facilities

Tarawa: The main anchorage at Tarawa is in the southwestern part of the lagoon off Betio island. There is a turning basin at the southern end of the harbor and a 425-foot long wharf with depths of 10 feet alongside. A mooring buoy is stationed in the anchorage but it is mainly used by the Government marine training ship, *M.V. Teraaka* when in port.

Visibility in the waters of the lagoon is generally poor because of coral particles carried in suspension. This greatly reduces the value of eyeball navigation from the spreaders so greater care must be used when moving about. The main ship channel into Betio is well buoyed and beaconed.

There is a slipway available for boats up to 90-feet long and 45 tons. Both mechanical and electrical workshops

Medical Memo

Immunization requirements:

Immunization for smallpox, cholera and yellow fever are required if you have transited or visited within the last six days (smallpox 14 days) an area currently infected.

Local health situation:

Sanitation standards at Tarawa are poor even to this day and there was a mild cholera epidemic experienced in 1977. Yachtsmen are advised to have cholera vaccinations and observe good health practices while in Kiribati until this sanitation problem has been corrected.

Health services:

There is a central hospital on Tarawa staffed by medical officers and a number of assistants. There are small hospitals on other islands staffed by assistant medical practitioners. On Banaba Island the British Phosphate Commission maintains a general hospital for their employees. District nurses visit outlying villages every few months.

No dental or optical practice exists and the only drugs available are at the Tarawa hospital.

Water:

All water should be considered suspect and treated before use.

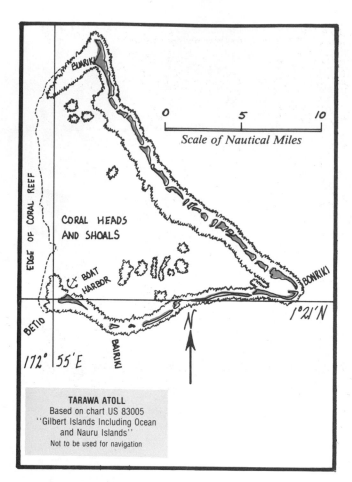

Scale of Nautical Miles

TARAWA ATOLL
Based on chart US 83005
"Gilbert Islands Including Ocean
and Nauru Islands"
Not to be used for navigation

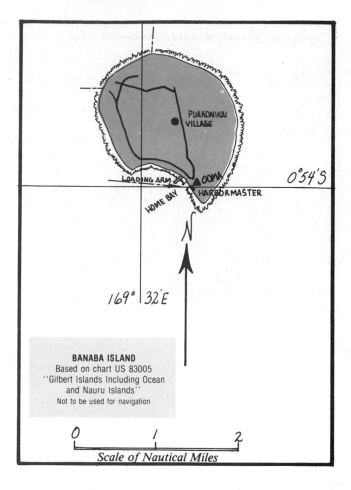

BANABA ISLAND
Based on chart US 83005
"Gilbert Islands Including Ocean
and Nauru Islands"
Not to be used for navigation

Scale of Nautical Miles

are available to help with repairs. Diesel fuel is available as are limited quantities of potable water. Some provisions may also be obtained at Betio.

The port is reasonably well protected from all winds but westerlies may require you to move to the lee of a small island since the harbor is essentially open to the west.

Banaba: This port is controlled jointly by the Kiribati government and the British Phosphate Commission. Ships moor to deep moorings outside of the reef and are serviced by lighters which pass through a man-made cut in the reef. Yachts can also come into the inner harbor but it is too deep to anchor so you must tie up at a mooring. Permission to use the mooring must be secured ashore at the Harbor Master's office. The harbor is shelted from north to east to east-southeast but exposed to the westerlies. The Harbor Master's office is located at the base of the southeastern breakwater.

Diesel fuel is available and some provisions. Minor boat repairs can be affected at the island.

Coconut Body Armour

Gilbert Islands **35c**

The small harbor at Betio on Tarawa Atoll is a beehive of activity. Large ships anchor outside but yachts can enter the harbor and tie up at the dock for clearance purposes.

Radio Communications

Station name and call	Location	Frequency Transmit/Receive	Service hours LMT	Type of service
Tarawa Radio (VSZ)	1°27′07″N 172°55′18″E	470/500 kHz 500/500 2182/2182 6204	Continuous Continuous Continuous Continuous	CW-marine operations CW-marine operations RT-marine operations RT-marine operations
Station Tarawa (VSZ-1)	1°19′36″N 172°59′42″E	844 kHz	Mon-Fri 0630-0800 1200-1400 1830-2130 Sat 1200-1400 1830-2145 Sun 1830-2130	Commercial broadcast
Ocean Island (VQK)	0°52′S 169°35′E	500/500 kHz	1030-1300 daily	CW-marine operations
Ocean Radio	″	6204/6204	daily	RT-marine operations

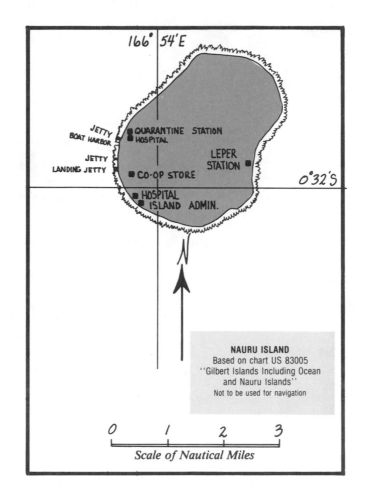

166° 54'E

JETTY
BOAT HARBOR
■ QUARANTINE STATION
■ HOSPITAL

JETTY
LANDING JETTY
■ CO-OP STORE

LEPER
STATION ■

0°32'S

■ HOSPITAL
■ ISLAND ADMIN.

N

NAURU ISLAND
Based on chart US 83005
''Gilbert Islands Including Ocean
and Nauru Islands''
Not to be used for navigation

0   1   2   3

Scale of Nautical Miles

Chapter 26

REPUBLIC OF NAURU

The Country

Nauru is an oval shaped island in the west-central Pacific lying 32 miles south of the equator. It is about 12 miles in circumference and contains eight square miles of land. It is one of three great phosphate islands in the Pacific, the other two are Ocean Island in the Gilbert group and Makatea Island in French Polynesia.

The island is slightly domed with a narrow band of coastal lowlands about 300 yards wide encircling the cliffs of the dome which reach about 200 feet high. The level plateau thus formed is the floor of the former atoll lagoon and contains deposits of phosphate that are 50 feet deep in some places. A narrow reef also encircles the island whose outer edge drops off sharply to the floor of the sea and provides no inlet or safe anchorage for vessels that arrive for cargoes of phosphate.

Because the top of the plateau is open mined for phosphate, it is deeply gouged, leaving no room for villages or farms. These are located on the narrow coastal rim where a belt of light but fertile soil produces coconut palms, casuarina, a few root crops, and the usual strand vegetation. In the interior of the island there is a small brackish lagoon which is slightly above sea level.

The population includes about 4,000 indigenous Nauruans, 1,800 I-Kiribati and Tuvalu islanders, 1,100 Chinese, and 500 Europeans. They live in small settlements scattered throughout the island. The Nauruans are a mixture of the three Pacific racial groups: Melanesian, Micronesian, and Polynesian. Their origin and how they came to the island are unknown. Their language, Nauruan, gives no clue as to their origin, its structure and many of its words have no relationship to either Polynesian or Melanesian languages. Most of the people speak English and all understand it. Nauruans are all professing Christians.

The first European to visit Nauru was Captain John Fearn on the British whaling ship *Hunter* in 1798. He named it Pleasant Island. Little contact was made with the island by Europeans for the next 90 years. In 1888, however, Nauru was annexed by the German Empire. Under German rule, Christianity and schooling were introduced and the translation of the bible into Nauruan gave the language its standard form.

In 1900 an employee of the British-owned Pacific Islands Company, working guano deposits in the Pacific, discovered that a piece of petrified wood from Nauru was actually high grade phosphate rock. When it was confirmed that both Nauru and Ocean Island had large amounts of phosphate deposits, The Pacific Phosphate Company (also British owned) was formed and started mining Nauruan phosphate. In 1914 an Australian detachment took over the island in the name of the British Empire.

Nauru's constitution, adopted by an elected Constitutional Convention in 1968, established a republic with a parliamentary form of government. The president (Chief of State) is elected by the parliament from among its own members for a three year term corresponding to that of parliament. He in turn appoints four or five members of parliament to serve concurrently as cabinet ministers. The cabinet is responsible to parliament and is obliged to resign as a body in the event of a no-confidence vote.

The unicameral parliament consists of 18 members elected by universal adult suffrage.

A supreme court was established by the Constitution and parliament may create lower courts and courts of appeal.

Nauru has no capitol city as such. Parliament House and government offices are located in the Yaren District on the ocean and opposite the airport. Locally, Nauru is divided into 14 districts which are grouped into eight electoral districts.

Republic of Nauru

An independent republic within
the British Commonwealth

Port of Entry:

Nauru (Aiwo District)   0°32′S, 166°55′E

Distances between ports in nautical miles:

Between *Nauru* and:

Funafuti, Tuvalu	890
Honiara, Solomon Islands	675
Honolulu, Hawaii	2450
Kosrae, Caroline Islands	420
Majuro, Marshall Islands	490
Ocean Island	160
Suva, Fiji	1270
Tarawa, Kiribati	400

Standard time:

11 hrs. 30 min. fast on GMT

The taming of frigate birds is an ancient tradition on Nauru. Prize birds are passed on from father to son. Special perches are built near the beach for the birds.

Jetsam and Flotsam

Currency:

Nauru does not have its own currency but uses Australian dollars. At press time $US1 = $A.85.

Language:

Nauruan is the indigenous language but English is spoken by nearly everybody.

Electricity:

Unknown

Postal address:

Yacht ( )
General Post Office
Republic of NAURU

External Affairs Representative:

Australian consulates or embassies

Cruising Library:

Nauru, Nancy Viviani; Univerity of Hawaii Press, Honolulu, HI 96822 USA.

Nauru's economy is based almost totally on the mining of high grade phosphate ore. It exports about 2 million tons a year and its gross national product varies with the world market price of phosphate. Its per capita income is exceeded only by the Persian Gulf oil states. Phosphate resources total some 45 million tons. At the present rate of extraction, these resources are expected to be exhausted in the next 20 years. Revenue from the phosphate is invested in long term trust funds that have been established to take care of the Nauruans when the phosphate has been depleted.

There are no taxes and the costs of government and the large statutory trust fund are paid from phosphate revenues. The government subsidizes all imports so that food and other necessities are available at a nominal cost. Virtually everything must be imported including fresh water which is brought from Australia as ballast in the vessels that take the phosphate from Nauru.

The Weather

The prevailing winds during the months of March through October are from the northeast to east and rarely stronger than Force 4 or 5. Winds are often light and, surprisingly, affected by the island with winds stronger near shore and especially at night. Nauru is not in the normal hurricane belt but occasionally south-westerly storms do occur.

Nauru's wet season occurs between November and February and the average annual rainfall is 80 inches. Extremes reached a low of 12 inches in 1950 and as much as 180 inches in 1930 and again in 1940.

Being on the equator the climate is naturally hot but tempered by the tradewinds. In the shade the temperatures range between 76°F and 93°F with a humidity between 70 and 80 percent.

The best time to visit Nauru is during the dry season

In lush contrast to the barren phosphate fields which surround it, Buada Lagoon serves Nauruans as a swimming pool and a place to breed fish to fill the need for protein in the diet.

when the tradewinds are the steadiest and safe moorage can be had in the lee of the island.

Yacht Entry and Yacht Facilities

Visas are required for extended stays and they can be obtained through Australian Consulates.

Yacht facilities are almost non-existent with anchorage impossible around the fringing reef because of the great depths. A small boat basin has been blasted out of the coral reef for use of cargo boats, launches, and the local fishermen.

Provisions can be obtained in limited quantities including meats, vegetables, and bread. Some fresh water is available as is a limited supply of diesel fuel. There are no repair facilities or parts available.

Medical Memo

Immunization requirements:

Smallpox vaccinations are required of all visitors and cholera and yellow fever certificates for persons coming from or transiting an infected area.

Local health situation:

No reported medical problems.

Health services:

There are two hospitals on Nauru — one for the Nauruans and one for the personnel of the phosphate industry. Some dental care is also available.

Water:

The water should be treated before use.

Radio Communications

Station Name and call	Location	Frequency Transmit/Receive	Service hours GMT	Type of service
Nauru Radio (VKT)	Nauru	1320 kHz	1900-2200	Commercial broadcast
			0100-0200	Commercial broadcast
			0515-1100	Commercial broadcast
			2200-0100	Relay of Radio Australia
			0200-0515	Relay of Radio Australia

Part IV -

Islands of the Eastern Pacific

•Galapagos Islands

Part IV -
Islands of the Eastern Pacific

One need not venture far into the Pacific Ocean to find tropical islands. Several exist just 600 miles off the west coasts of the Americas. Unfortunately, they are not the types of islands of which Paradise is made. Instead they tend to be rocky, barren and without comfortable harbors.

Off the coast of Mexico are the Revilla Gigedo Islands which are a possession of Mexico and uninhabited except for a small village on Isla Socorro which is the largest of the four island group. The islands are of volcanic origin and the only vegetation is low cactus, sage and some grass. There are no true harbors but adequate shelter can be found in a number of coves and dinghy landings can be made in moderate weather on sandy beaches.

Farther south is Clipperton Island, a dependency of France but not part of French Polynesia. It is an atoll with an enclosed lagoon of brackish water. At one time there was believed to have been a useable passage into the lagoon. The island is about five miles in diameter and is covered with low brush, some coconut palms, and has wild pigs and birds in abundance. At various times it has been inhabited but with no degree of permanency. As many as 100 people lived on it in the early 1900s when a

British firm was mining phosphate there. Anchorage can be taken off the northeast side in a coral sand bottom but a capable crewman should be left on board for security.

Most famous of the Eastern Pacific island groups are the Galapagos Islands which straddle the equator on the route from Panama to French Polynesia. They are worthy of a cruising stop if you can get official permission and details of them are given in this chapter.

South of the Galapagos and out of the tropics, but still in a region of good weather, are the Juan Fernandez Islands, a possession of Chile. These islands have long been used as a watering stop for sailing ships coming up the coast from Cape Horn. The main island of Isla Mas a Terra was made famous as the setting of the popular fictional book *Robinson Crusoe* and it is often referred to as Robinson Crusoe Island. Today there is a Chilean Air Base on Isla Mas a Terra with about 500 persons living there. Water and some provisions are available.

Except for the Galapagos, these islands are rarely visited by cruising yachts and may just be of interest to the adventurous yachtie who is exploring the West Coast of the Americas.

Chapter 27
GALAPAGOS ISLANDS
(Archipielago de Colon)

The Country

The Galapagos Islands is a group of 13 major islands and several minor ones. They are volcanic in origin and are geologically very young. Darwin estimated the number of extinct volcanoes at 2,000. The oldest rocks found in the Galapagos are about five million years old and the youngest about one million years old. The physical characteristics of the islands are very dramatic with striking lava flows, interesting basalt formations, and beautiful sand beaches. The principal islands are:

Island	Size	Area	Height
Isabella	74 x 45 mi.	2249 sq.mi.	4900 ft.
Santa Cruz	17 x 23	389	2835
San Salvador	20 x 13	203	2974
Fernandia	15 x 18	245	4900
San Cristobal	26 x 10	195	2350

The Galapagos lie astride the converging El Nino current from the Gulf of Panama and the Humboldt current from the south. The currents flow side by side to the west northwest around the islands but not always maintaining the same position. The waters of the northern islands could have temperatures as high as 80°F while the waters around the southern islands could have temperatures as low as 60°F.

Coastal areas and the small islands are covered with bushes and small trees. The most striking plants are the cacti. After rains, which are scarce, desert annuals will spring up, flower and quickly die. There is a striking contrast between vegetation of the dry coastal areas and the dense growth on the heights. Fog, rain, and mist create a forest of ferns, lichens, orchids and creeping plants—a true rain forest only miles from desert land.

It is usually the fauna that one thinks of when the Galapagos Islands are mentioned. Native land mammals are limited to two species of the rice rat, all others having been introduced by visitors to the islands. Marine mammals, however, are plentiful including sperm and killer whales which are occasionally sighted off the northern coast of Isabella island. In addition, there are the bottlenose dolphin and common dolphin. The cold water of the Humboldt current supports colonies of two species of sea lions. Fur seals, at one point on the verge of extinction, can now be seen around some of the islands.

Reptiles are probably the most dramatic of the native animals. Even the name Galapagos suggests a reptilian world since its Spanish translation means giant tortoises. All of the reptiles on the islands, except the sea turtles, are indigenous only to the Galapagos. Among the reptiles found on the islands are the giant tortoise, lava lizard, and the land iguana. Along the coasts one finds many kinds of sea turtles and the marine iguana.

There are a variety of both land and sea birds. Although some are found in other tropical lands, there are some very unusual birds found only here. Among these are the Galapagos penguin and the flightless cormorant. Nearly all of the land birds are unique to the islands. Darwin noted 23 different species on San Salvador and commented that they were incredibly tame. There are still many who have no fear of man.

Due to their location in relation to the plankton-rich Humboldt current, fish thrive around the waters of the archipelago. Large sharks, tuna, lobster and crayfish abound.

The Galapagos Islands were discovered by Tomas de Berlango, Bishop of Panama, in 1535 when his ship was caught in a current that pulled him off course in his voyage from Panama to Peru. In his accounts to Emperor

Galapagos Islands
(Archipielago de Colon)
A Province of Ecuador

Ports of Entry:

Wreck Bay	0°54'S, 89°37'W
Academy Bay	0°45'S, 90°18'W

Distances between ports in nautical miles:

Between *Wreck Bay* and:

Callao, Peru	1000
Guayaquil, Ecuador	660
Honolulu, Hawaii	4220
Easter Island	1950
Nuku Hiva, Marquesas Islands	2750
Panama, Panama	650
Pitcairn Island	2760
San Diego, California	2590
Seattle, Washington	3770

Standard Time:

5 hours slow on GMT

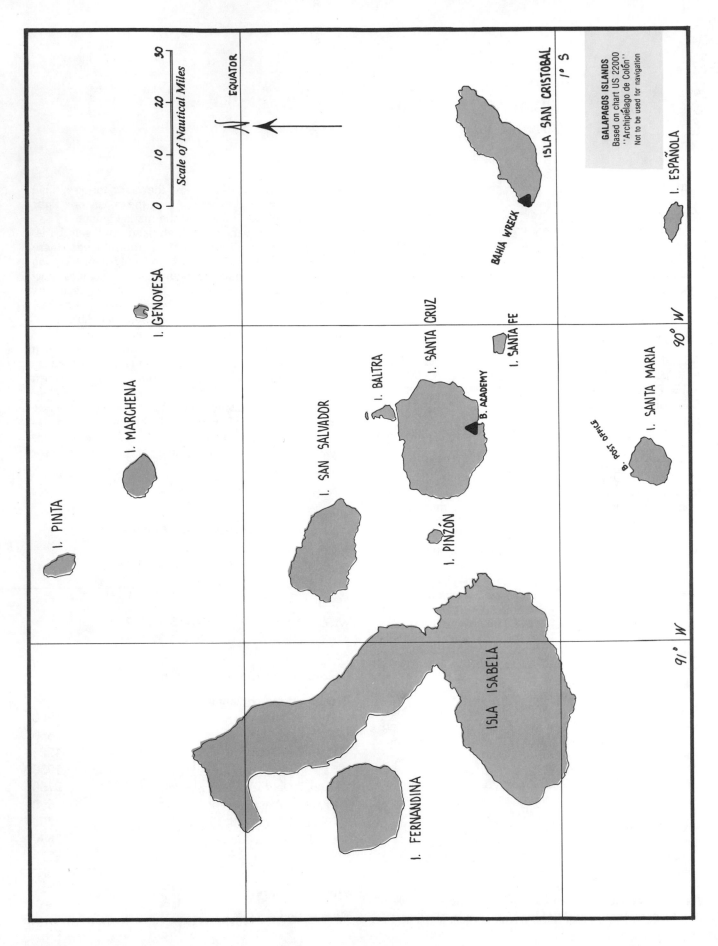

Scale of Nautical Miles

0 10 20 30

EQUATOR

N

I. PINTA

I. MARCHENA

GENOVESA

I. SAN SALVADOR

BALTRA

I. SANTA CRUZ

B. ACADEMY

I. PINZÓN

SANTA FE

ISLA ISABELA

I. FERNANDINA

B. POST OFFICE

I. SANTA MARIA

90° W

91° W

BAHIA WRECK

ISLA SAN CRISTOBAL

1° S

I. ESPAÑOLA

The land iguana is an ugly, lethargic creature which crawls slowly along the ground dragging its tail and belly. It will stop and doze for a minute or two with its eyes closed and legs outspread.

Carlos V of Spain, he includes descriptions of the incredibly tame wildlife, the huge tortoises, and unusual iguanas. In the decades that followed, the archipelago received the name "Islas Encantadas" (bewitched islands), because of the currents that tricked navigators and make the islands appear and disappear unpredictably. During the 17th century, English pirates found the islands to be a useful refuge, and therefore made visits to restock their vessels with food and water. They in turn stocked the islands with goats, pigs, and cattle so that they could resupply themselves with fresh meat when returning. Unfortunately, they also found the giant tortoises an excellent source of fresh meat and they took thousands of these defenseless creatures to sea, storing them in their hulls until they required fresh meat at sea. The effect on the tortoise population was devastating and

some species are now extinct. The others are carefully protected and are being raised in controlled conditions at the Darwin Research Station at Academy Bay on Santa Cruz island.

From 1780 to 1860 the islands were visited by many British and American whalers who killed thousands of the Galapagos fur seals. These visitors also captured and stored the tortoises in their ship's holds for fresh meat supplies, and again the population of these giant mammals suffered.

Ecuador annexed the group in 1832 and attempted to use it as a colony and a penal settlement but without much success. Charles Darwin was serving as naturalist on the British ship "H.M.S. *Beagle*" when it visited the Galapagos in 1835 and he was the first person to recognize their significance in understanding the evolu-

The most famous native of the Galapagos Islands is the huge land tortoise. During Darwin's visit to the islands he estimated that the large ones weighed as much as 500 pounds. They were almost decimated by whaling and other ships that stopped at the Galapagos specifically to capture them for fresh meat on their continuing voyages.

tion theory of life. In the early 1930's a group of Germans attempted to set up a colony which failed in part but some of their descendants are still on the islands. Today the Galapagos archipelago is a national park of Ecuador.

There are no indigenous people in the archipelago. It has an approximate population of 2,000 Ecuadorians and 100 permanent foreign residents. Most of the Ecuadorians live a subsistence life but with more government employment available and the flourishing biological research station at Academy Bay, there promises to be some improvement in the standard of living. Ecuador has, since 1959, denied any more permanent residency permits to non-Ecuadorians.

The Galapagos Islands are a province of Ecuador administered by the Ecuador Forestry Service. The seat of

government is at Progreso, San Cristobal Island. All native mammals, reptiles and birds are protected. In 1959 the government of Ecuador and the internationally recognized Charles Darwin Foundation with the help of UNESCO and other scientific organizations, established a biological research station at Academy Bay, Santa Cruz island.

The Weather

Although the island group lies on and near the equator, the climate is tempered by the cold Humboldt current.

The southeast tradewind is the prevailing wind and blows between southeast and southwest. From April to December the tradewinds blow with great regularity and gales are unknown. Calms are frequent from January to April with occasional light squalls from the northwest. Heavy rollers occasionally break upon the northern shores during the rainy season, but no wind of any consequence accompanies them.

Thundershowers occur between November and March but the rainfall is unequally distributed with most falling at higher elevations of the larger islands. The greater part of the islands are, in general, embraced in a dry zone which rises to about 800 feet. Maximum rainfall is 48 inches per year at the wettest point. Fog and occasional drizzles may be found at the lower levels. Because the rains are brought by the southeast trades, the fertile land is all on the southeast sides of the islands and at the higher levels. Fresh water supplies for yachts are very limited.

Thick fog has been reported at sea near the archipelago in April and September.

The preferred season for visiting the Galapagos is between December and May. Then there is more sun with only occasional downpours but, unfortunately, light

Jetsam and Flotsam

Currency:

The Galapagos Islands use Ecuadorian currency. The Ecuadorian dollar is called a sucre and it is equal to 100 centavos. At press time the rate of exchange was $US1 = 28 sucre.

Language:

The official language of the Galapagos Islands is Spanish. English is spoken by many people in the business and official world.

Electricity:

Where electricity is available it is 110 v, 60 Hz AC.

Postal address:

Yacht (   )
Poste Restante
Wreck Bay, San Cristobal Island
ECUADOR

Note:

An historic communications means exists at Post Office Bay on the north coast of Santa Maria Island. This was a crossroads in the whaling days and the location of an old barrel in which whalers put letters to be picked up later by some homeward-bound vessel. It is still in use today.

External Affairs Representative:

Ecuadorian consulates or embassies.

Information Office:

Ecuadorian Tourist Commission
P.O. Box 2454
Quito, ECUADOR

Cruising Library:

The Galapagos, R.I. Bowman; University of California Press, Berkeley, CA, USA, 1966.
Floreana Adventure, Margret Witmer; E.P. Dutton & Co., New York, USA, 1961.
Galapagos: The Flow of Wildness, Eliot Porter; Sierra Club, San Francisco, CA, USA, 1968.

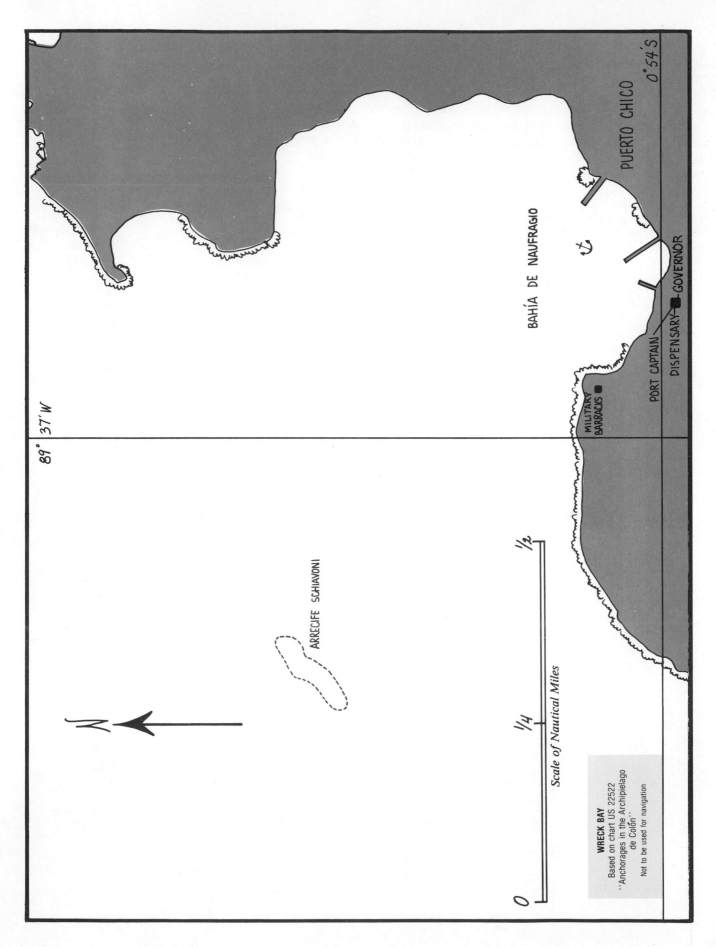

89° 37' W

N

0° 54' S

PUERTO CHICO

BAHÍA DE NAUFRAGIO

ARRECIFE SCHIAVONI

MILITARY BARRACKS

PORT CAPTAIN

DISPENSARY GOVERNOR

0   ¼   ½

Scale of Nautical Miles

WRECK BAY
Based on chart US 22522
"Anchorages in the Archipielago
de Colón"
Not to be used for navigation

winds. The poorest month is September when it is overcast with drizzles and is relatively cool. This is known as the Garua season. Commercial travel is at a low ebb at this time.

Yacht Entry

For centuries the Galapagos Islands have been an attraction to seafarers. Initially as a place of refuge and reprovisioning for explorers, pirates, and ships of commerce and, more recently, as a port of call for cruising yachts. At one time yachts could stop at the archipelago without prior arrangements and visit all of the islands. But the very popularity of the archipelago caused the Ecuadorian government to take a more active administrative control. Now they have made it a national park and placed it under the jurisdiction of the Forest Service in order to preserve its unique and fragile ecology.

Along with this formal administration went severe restrictions on casual yacht visits. Yachts desiring to visit the Galapagos must now obtain prior permission from the Ministry of Defense. Requests for a "Navigational Permit for the Galapagos Islands" should be submitted well in advance of a desired trip to:

Ministro de Defensa Nacional
Quito, ECUADOR

The request should state a good reason for the visit, its duration, and the specific islands of interest. Along with this it should identify the crew and their nationalities,

specify the official and visual description of the boat, and contain a statement relative to the skipper's responsibility for the crew and vessel while in Ecuadorian waters. Above all, it should be written in good Spanish.

It will take several months to get a response and it may be negative. But don't blame the Ecuadorian government, just remember the problem the United States has with its national parks. If a navigational permit is granted, United States citizens will not need a visa (for up to 90 days)—just a passport and a smallpox innoculation.

There are now two official Ports of Entry—Wreck Bay on San Cristobal and Academy Bay on Santa Cruz. The official name for the Port of Entry at Wreck Bay is Puerto Chico. The capital of the archipelago is also located on San Cristobal at the town of Progreso. Academy Bay on Santa Cruz is the location of the biological research station established by the Charles Darwin Foundation in 1959.

When you get there you will be in for a surprise. It will cost you $US20 in port charges every time you arrive and depart these two ports. Charges are more on weekends and holidays or for entry outside of normal office hours. And that isn't all. You cannot visit other islands in the archipelago without taking on a guide arranged through the Park Service. He will accompany you on board and you will pay him $US8-10 per day. Most of these guides do not speak English but there are trained nature guides available who do speak English and they charge $US15-20 per day. (It has recently been reported that yachts can stay only three days for which there are charges of up to $US50. Naturalists guides can no longer

Medical Memo

Immunization requirements:

Vaccinations for yellow fever and smallpox are required if you have transited or visited an infected area within the last 14 days (yellow fever six days).

Local health situation:

The climate of the Galapagos is healthy and there are none of the diseases common to the tropics. Although the parent country of Ecuador is a malaria risk, it does not extend to the Galapagos Islands.

Health services:

There is dispensary service at both Ports of Entry but major medical problems as well as dental and optical would have to be taken care of at Quito, Ecuador. Air service is available for an emergency. Limited drugs are available in the dispensaries.

Water:

Water is in limited supply and that which there is may be brackish. All water should be considered suspect and treated before use.

be hired to cruise with you to other islands.)

Many yachts recently have just been "dropping-in" on the Galapagos, some claiming a measure of distress. The Ecuadorian government has been very tolerant of this questionable practice and they have allowed yachts to stay up to three days at one or the other of the Ports of Entry. The boats and crews are not allowed to travel to any other islands but they can go ashore on the one island.

For the present, yachties will have to content themselves with making a formal request for a visit and hope that it will be granted.

Yacht Facilities

There are no special facilities for yachts in the Galapagos Islands, only those that are shared with the ships that come there from Ecuador. At Wreck Bay yachts anchor out and crews take their dinghies into a small pier. Water is available at the town dock but it is not potable without first boiling. Potable water can be obtained from private residences or Forrest Nelson's hotel at four cents per gallon. There are no slipways, bulk fuel, or marine supplies available. Small quantities of fuel may be purchased locally depending on the island supplies.

Facilities at other islands are virtually nil.

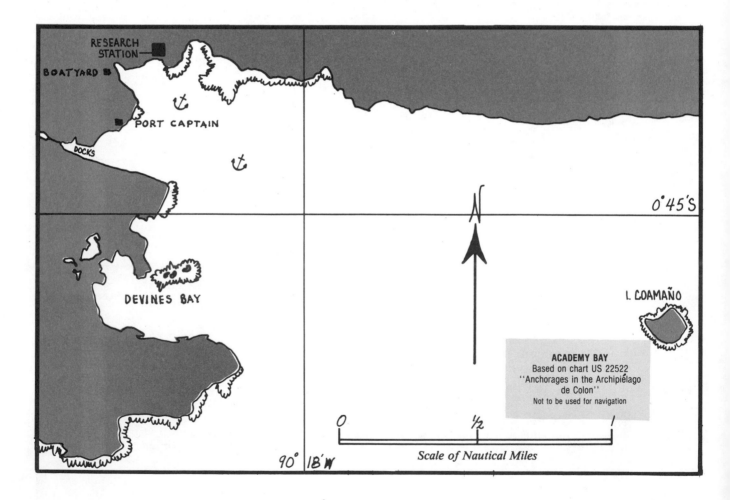

RESEARCH STATION

BOATYARD

PORT CAPTAIN

DOCKS

DEVINES BAY

N

0°45'S

I. COAMAÑO

ACADEMY BAY
Based on chart US 22522
"Anchorages in the Archipiélago de Colon"
Not to be used for navigation

0   ½   1

Scale of Nautical Miles

90° 18' W

Radio Communications

Station name and call	Location	Frequency Transmit/Receive	Service hours LMT	Type of service
Galapagos Radio	Puerto Chico	8450/8450 kHz		Maritime business
(VG 8)	Isla San Cristobal	1410 kHz 4810	0715-2300	Commercial broadcast

Appendices

Appendices
(a) Tri-Language Dictionary for Port Entry
(b) Glossary of Cruising Words
(c) Mastering the Three Rs at Sea
(d) Amateur Radio Operation in Foreign Waters
(e) Charter Boats in the Pacific

Index

TRI-LANGUAGE DICTIONARY FOR PORT ENTRY

COASTAL NAVIGATION

English	French	Spanish
anchorage	mouillage	fondeadero
bay	baie	ensenada
beacon	balise	baliza
black	noir	negro
breakers	brisants	rompiente
broad (wide)	large	vasto
cape	cap	cabo
channel	chenal	canal
coast	cote	costa
coral	corail	coral
cove	anse	caleta
current	courant	corriente
east	est	este
flat	basse	plano
gulf	golfe	golfo
harbor	port	puerto
head	tete	cabeza
headland	nez	promontorio
high	haut	alto
hill	colline	cerro
hill, bluff	morne	escarpa
house	maison	caserio
island	ile	isla
islet	ilot	islote
lagoon	lagon	laguna
landing place	debarcaderie	disembarcadero
large	grand	grande
lighthouse	phare	faro
low	bas	bajo
mountain	mont	monte
north	nord	norte
pass	passe	paso
peak	pic	pico
peninsula	presqu'ile	peninsula
point	pointe	punta
quay	quai	embarcadero
red	rouge	rojo
reef	recife	arrecife
river	riviere	rio
roadstead	rade	rada
rock	rocker	roca

sand	sable	arena
sea	mer	mar
shoal	haute-fond	bajio
shoal bank	banc	bajio
small	petite	chico
south	sud	sur
tower	tour	torre
town	ville	ciudad
valley	vallee	valle
village	village	pueblo
white	blanc	blanco
west	**ouest**	ceste

ENTERING A FOREIGN PORT

English	French	Spanish
accident & illness	accidentes et maladies	accidentes y efermedad
Act of God	fortune de mer	accidents
anchorage	mouillage	fondeadero
appeal	appel	apelacion
bill of health	patente de sante	patente de sanidad
bonded stores	provisions entreposees, en franchise, sous douane	viveres precintados
certificate of clearance		zarpe
certificate of registry	certificate de francisation	patente de navegacion
cook	cuisinier	cocinero
courtesy ensign	pavillon de courtesie	bandera de cortesia
crew	equipage	tripulacion
customs clearance	libre-sortie, conge de douane	despacho de aduana
customs office	bureau de douane	aduana
doctor	medecin	medico
flags	pavillons	banderas
harbormasters office	bureau de capitaine de port	commandancia de marina
insurance certificate	certificat d'assurance	poliza de seguro
man overboard	homme a la mer	hombre al agua
mate	second, chef de quart	segundo, piloto
navigator	navigateur	navegante
passport	passeport	pasaporte
pilot	instructions nautique	derrotero
Q signal: My vessel is healthy and I request free pratique (health clearance)		
ships articles	role d'equipage	rol
ships company	L'equipage	compania naviera
ships log	livre de bord	cuaderno de bitacora
ships papers	papiers de borde	documentacion
shipwreck	naufrage	naufragio
skipper	chef de bord	capitain

SERVICES IN A FOREIGN PORT

English	French	Spanish
accident	accident	accidente
auxiliary	auxiliaire	auxiliar
baker	le boulanger	panadero
bank	la banque	banco
butcher	boucher	carnicero
chandlery and ships chandler	quincaillerie, accastillage et fournisseur de marine	**pertechos y almacen de** efectos navales
careening grid	**gril de car'enage**	dique de peine, carenero
dairy	la laiterie	lecheria
dentist	dentiste	dentista
diesel engine	moteur diesel	motor diesel
diesel oil	gas-oil, mazout	gasoil
doctor	m'edecin	medico
drinking water	l'eau potable	aqua potable
electrical system	syst'eme electrique	instalacion electrica
engine oil	huile	aceite de motor
fish market	le marchand de poisson	pescaderia
gasoline	essence	gasolina
gasoline engine	moteur a essence	motor de gasolina
greengrocer	le marchand de le'gumes	verdulero
grocer	l'epicier	tendero de comestibles
hospital	hôpital	hospital
illness	maladies	enfermedad
ironworker	la quincaillerie	ferreteria
kerosene	petrole	petroleo
maintenance	entretien	mantenimiento
outboard engine	moteur hors-bord	motor fuera de bordo
painting	peinture	pintado
pharmacist, chemist	pharmacien	fermac'entico
post office	la poste	correo
sailmaker	voilier	velero
shipyard	chantier naval	astillero
slip, slipway	cale de halage	veraddero
stamps	destimbres	sellos

GLOSSARY OF CRUISING WORDS

Anchorages:
Examination anchorage - An anchorage at which boats wait until entry examination is complete.
Quarantine anchorage — An anchorage set aside for ships in quarantine. Q flag is flown here.

Archipelago:
A large geographically related group of islands.

Atoll:
An annular-shaped coral reef enclosing a lagoon. There may or may not be islets on the reef.

Atollon:
A small atoll on the periphery of a larger one.

Barrier reef:
A coral reef roughly paralleling the shoreline and separated from it by a channel of water.

Coastal plain:
That strip of flat land running along the coastline separating water and mountain.

Coral:
The hard calcareous substance secreted by the marine polyp for the purpose of providing it a home.
Coral may be dead or alive.

Coral island:
An island principally made of coral. It may be a full atoll, a solid island or simply an accumulation of debris on a coral reef.

Coral reef:
A reef principally composed of coral growth.

Fjord (Fiord):
A long narrow arm of the sea between high cliffs.

Free port:
A port where the host country has waived import and export duties, usually to expand trade.

Fringing reef:
A coral reef adjacent to land with no navigable water between it and the shoreline.

Grid:
Parallel timbers laid on the shoreline on which small boats can be grounded at high tide and left high and dry at low tide so that bottom work can be done on them between tides.

Haven:
A place of refuge for vessels away from the fury of wind and waves. Usually accessible under all conditions of weather.

Hurricane:
A cyclonic storm with winds in excess of 64 knots. Also called a typhoon.

Island:
A land area smaller than a continent and entirely surrounded by water.

Lagoon:
The area of water within an atoll. It may be salt water due to a connection with the ocean or it may be brackish due to fresh water mixing with salt water seeping through the annular reef structure.

Marina:
A man-made area with berths and facilities for maintaining and storing yachts.

Motu:
An islet with some vegetable growth situated on a reef.

Passage:
A channel for navigating a boat through a reef. Also a sea journey between specific points.

Pidgin:
A simplified language form used by islanders in conversing with English-speaking people.

Port of Entry:
A port where officials of a country exam a vessel and grant entry of goods and people to that country.

Pratique:
Permission granted to a vessel to enter a country after determining that the vessel has a clean bill of health.

Quarantine:
The isolation of a vessel until it is determined that it is a healthy vessel and can be granted pratique.

Quay:
A stone or masonry structure along a shoreline against which vessels moor to transfer cargo.

Reef:
A localized area of rock or coral which is a hazard to navigation. It may or may not be above the water.

Shoal:
A localized shallow area which is a hazard to navigation. Usually sand or mud.

Slipway or slips:
A marine railway built to haul small vessels out of the water for repairs.

Tropics:
That portion of the earth situated between the Tropics of Cancer and Capricorn and spanning the equator.

Tropical storm:
A cyclonic storm with winds between 35 and 64 knots.

Tsunami:
Fast moving waves caused by a submarine earthquake which are capable of traveling thousands of miles. Erroneously called tidal waves. Sometimes called seismic waves.

Vigia:
An uncertain or hidden danger previously reported in a general area. Both existence and position are doubtful.

Voyage:
The full length of a sea journey, made up of one or more passages.

Waterspout:
A tornado over the ocean in which a funnel-shaped pendant descends from a black cloud and with violent rotating motion draws up water or anything else from the surface of the ocean.

Zarpe:
A departure clearance usually given by the Customs officials which gives your vessel permission to leave and, in effect, is a letter of introduction to your next port of call.

MASTERING THE THREE Rs AT SEA

There is no better schoolroom than the world of nature and the child traveling in the Pacific with his parents is probably the luckiest of all students. He gains an intimate knowledge of living a life of self-sufficiency with his playground the ocean blue. The clean life of sailing and the adventure of visiting new lands will give a depth of learning and appreciation for life not attainable in a classroom. What better way is there for a child to understand the meaning of One World than to mingle with his peers in the other lands and learn about their way of life?

But there is one drawback for the school-age child and that is an absence of formal education needed to prepare him to compete in today's sophisticated society. While it may be fun to sail the oceans of the world, it is not fun to return home and find yourself unprepared for the job market or without educational prerequisites for college. Cruising parents must give serious thought to filling the academic educational gap which their children could suffer.

Fortunately, a number of qualified academic institutions in the United States (and probably elsewhere) have prepared correspondence courses equivalent to classroom studies and these have been accredited by national and state educational boards. They are made specifically for the student who must study away from the classroom for a variety of reasons and have proven useful to the cruising student. The following pages summarize the programs of four recognized correspondence schools serving student needs up through high school. With these courses taken at sea and the actual experience of visiting the countries of the Pacific Basin, the cruising child will have a more satisfying education than could be provided in any classroom.

CALVERT SCHOOL
Tuscany Road, Baltimore, MD 21210, USA
Grades: Kindergarten through 8th

"The Calvert Home Instructions Courses are built from the regular Day School curriculum of the Calvert School - a distinguished independent school in Baltimore, Maryland. Consequently, the teachers who prepare these courses are in daily touch with the student problems and are in a position to advise the parents in practically every matter pertaining to the student's education.

No teaching experience or training on the part of the parent or home teacher is necessary. A specially prepared manual is supplied with every course, showing the parent exactly what to do every step of the way and giving helpful guidance and encouragement for both parent and child.

Calvert School was founded in 1897. In 1908, through the establishment of its Home Instruction Department, the benefits of Calvert education were extended to parents and children everywhere."

How it operates
Each grade is planned for a school year of about nine months. Due to the individual instruction which you will give your child, however, you will be able to make the schedule flexible and may adapt the courses to the needs and abilities of the child. The daily amount of time you will need will vary, but it is well to plan upon three and one-half to five hours, depending upon the pupil and the grade. If your child needs as much as two years for the completion of a single course, the School permits that length of time, but most pupils complete each course in a school year by following a regular schedule that occupies the morning hours.

Texts and Materials
This is a totally packaged course including lesson manual, textbooks, workbooks, and supplies for the school year. The average weight of a Calvert Course is 20-22 pounds. Tuition fee includes shipment of course materials by book post or parcel post. If foreign delivery by air express is desired, additional funds must be sent.

Tuition Fees
Kindergarten	$ 80.00
Grades 1 through 7	140.00
Grade 8	150.00
Advisory Teaching Service	70.00 (each grade)

Special Services

Individual subject courses are also offered for the 8th grade student which may be taken for separate credit or collectively as the complete 8th grade course noted above. Individual courses offered are English, History, Mathematics, Reading/Literature, and Science. The Advisory Teaching Service is also available for the individual course.

INDEPENDENT STUDY HIGH SCHOOL
UNL Division of Continuing Studies,
511 Nebraska Hall, University of Nebraska, Lincoln, NE 68588, USA
Grades: 9th through 12th

"The Independent Study High School has been in existence since 1929. The program is fully accredited by the North Central Association of Colleges and Schools and by the Nebraska State Department of Education. This accreditation allows us to grant a high school diploma upon completion of specific requirements. Courses may also be taken for personal interest or to supplement the local school curriculum.

Each student that enrolls in one of our courses must have a local supervisor. The supervisor is an important person in the student's relationship with the Independent Study High School. Supervisiors are not teachers and need not have the background to help the student with the subject matter of the course."

How it operates

Each course is planned for 18 weeks - a semester's work. A schedule of estimated time for each unit is listed in the Material for the Student at the beginning of each unit. If the student expects to complete the course in 18 weeks, he should follow this schedule closely. The minimum time requirement for the completion of a one-semester course is five weeks from the time the first lesson is received by the Division of Continuing Studies.

The registration for an independent study course is one full year. At the end of the year the student must pay a renewal fee if he is to continue his work in good standing.

The supervisor receives materials, sets specific study times, monitors examinations, reviews with the pupil the corrected examinations, and maintains a working paper file for the student's use. In addition, the supervisor provides encouragement to the student. The supervisor is the important connecting link between the student and the instructor at the Independent Study High School.

Texts and Materials

The necessary materials (texts, kits and other supplies) are available from the school or can be procured separately in the case of textbooks. Course material is normally shipped by surface means but airmail is also available at an extra cost. Air freight shipment is recommended for overseas delivery. Material lost in shipping will normally be replaced at no cost, after the appropriate waiting period, but transportation costs will be assessed to the customer.

Tuition Fees

Tuition is indicated below for each one-semester (5-hour, ½ unit) course and each one-half semester (2½ hour, ¼ unit) course:

Non-resident tuition for ½-unit course	$33.00
Non-resident tuition for ¼-unit course	$24.00

Special Services

Tuition can be refunded on a pro-rated basis for legitimate reasons submitted by the supervisor. Textbooks furnished by the school, in good condition and not outdated will be repurchased by the school at 60 percent of the original price. Records, tapes and kits are non-refundable.

INDEPENDENT STUDY BY CORRESPONDENCE
University of Florida, Division of Continuing Education,
2012 West University Avenue, Gainsville, FL 32603, USA
Grades: 9th through 12th

"Independent Study by Correspondence is designed for a large number of individuals for whom no other means of guided learning is practicable. For any of a number of legitimate reasons many persons find it impossible to enroll in scheduled classes. The educational needs of these persons are very real and to deny them is unwarranted. For these educationally disadvantaged persons, Independent Study by Correspondence seeks to provide those learning opportunities which are essential in assisting each individual to make the greatest possible contribution to society. For those unable to avail themselves of classroom instruction, Independent Study by Correspondence fills a void.

In addition to the many specific opportunities provided by this widely accepted method of instruction, this method is believed to aid in the development of self-discipline, desirable learning habits and the ability to organize thinking and utilize knowledge resulting from study."

How it operates
Each course is designed to include the subject content of one semester's work in a comparable high school class. Consequently, each course carries ½ unit of high school credit. If a full unit is desired, then two sequential courses in the one subject representing two semesters of work must be completed.

A period of one year from the date of enrollment is allowed for the completion of a course. An expired enrollment may be reinstated for a period of six months by paying a fee of $5.00. No enrollment may be continued in force for more than 30 months. The minimum time for completion of a course is one month. A maximum of four lessons per week will be accepted for grading.

Only two correspondence courses may be carried simultaneously. It is recommended, however, that only one be taken and completed before enrolling in the other.

Each course is based on a study guide and is made up of sixteen written assignments. Each assignment contains a written portion which is prepared on special paper and sent to the instructor for grading. Unsatisfactory assignments must be reworked before credit can be given for the course.

Texts and Materials
The required texts and materials can be purchased from independent distributors or ordered from the school as part of the registration. The school will send courses overseas but no information is available on shipping method or charges. Used books are available at reduced cost.

Tuition Fees
The enrollment fee for each half-unit course is $25.00. Textbooks and other materials are in addition.

Special Services
Partial refund of tuition will be made within three months of starting the course, nothing thereafter. Used books still being used in the correspondence courses and in usable condition will be purchased back. This does not include phonograph records.

Independent Study by Correspondence courses are also available at the college level.

HOME STUDY INSTITUTE
Takoma Park, Washington, DC 20012
Grades: Preschool, Elementary, and High School

"Home Study Institute offers instruction to children who are unable to attend class or choose this alternative. Children who are in foreign countries, who are in isolated areas, who need to keep up with school while they travel with their parents, and children who need Christian education when no school is available. A New York Court has stated: "It is settled law that a parent need not avail himself of formal education facilities for a child in order to satisfy the requirements of the law, it being sufficient that a systematic course of study be undertaken at home and that the parent render qualified quality instruction".

How it operates
Ordinarily students are advised to enroll for one course at a time. However, the student doing full-time correspondence study may carry more than one course. A student may enroll for either or both semesters of any subject if course prerequisites are met. Students enrolling for quarter credit must specify first quarter, second quarter, or third quarter.

From the date of registration the Home Study Institute allows one year for the completion of a correspondence course. A student who is unable to complete a course within one year may request an extension of time for a period of one year upon payment of a $5.00 fee.

Most HSI courses yielding semester credit have a midterm and a semester examination for each semester. Courses giving quarter credit have examinations at the end of each quarter.

The mother (or some other person chosen) is the teacher. She uses plans prepared and presented in the syllabus for the specific grade. Frequent messages from the HSI supervisor encourage a high level of work and this supervisor grades all test papers sent in for each six-week period. It is not necessary to maintain the schedule suggested by the syllabus, but it is the best plan.

Texts and Materials
The tuitiion rates include the cost of syllabus or study guide but not the cost of textbooks, supplies, or shipping charges. All textbooks and supplies are handled on a cash basis. Overseas shipments are sent registered surface mail unless otherwise indicated. Airmail transmittal of lessons and books can be done for minimal additional cost.

Tuition fees
Kindergarten	$ 15.00
Grades 1 through 6	$135.00 (Full year, all subjects)
Grades 7 and 8	$402.00 (Full year, 5 subjects)
High School	$120.00 per unit

Special service
A number of college-level courses are also offered in Religion, Business Administration, Education and Psychology, English and Speech, History, Geography and Sociology, Languages, Mathematics, and Science.

Used textbooks may be returned and HSI will refund 85% of the list price on new (unused) books and 50% on used books received in good condition.

AMATEUR RADIO OPERATION IN FOREIGN WATERS

You cannot operate your ham rig within the territorial limits of another country unless you are in possession of a guest or reciprocal operating permit issued by that country. These permits also specify the permissable operating frequencies which you can use while in that country's waters.

Following are the addresses of the official contacts for obtaining such permits:

HAWAII
District Field Office
Federal Communications Commission
Federal Building
P.O. Box 1021
Honolulu, HI 96808, USA

FRENCH POLYNESIA
Direction de L'Office des Postes et Telecommunications
Papeete, Tahiti
FRENCH POLYNESIA

EASTER ISLAND
Radio Club de Chile
Casilla Postal 13630
Santiago
CHILE

PITCAIRN ISLAND
Tom Christian, VR6 TC
Box 1
Adamstown
PITCAIRN ISLAND

COOK ISLANDS
See New Zealand

WESTERN SAMOA
See New Zealand

TOKELAU ISLANDS
See New Zealand

NIUE
See New Zealand

TONGA
The Superintendent
Telegraph and Telephone Department
Nuku'alofa
TONGA

NEW ZEALAND
Director General
Radio Division
General Post Office
Wellington
NEW ZEALAND
   (For general information on Amateur
   radio in New Zealand write: New Zealand
   Association of Radio Transmitters, P.O. Box
   1459, Christchurch, NEW ZEALAND)

FIJI
The Secretary for Posts and Telecommunications
Department of Posts and Telecommunications
P.O. Box 40
Suva, FIJI

WALLIS AND FUTUNA GROUP
Service des Postes et Communications
Mata Uta,
TERRITORIE DES ILES WALLIS ET FUTUNA

PAPUA NEW GUINEA
Department of Posts and Telegraphs
Port Moresby
PAPUA NEW GUINEA

SOLOMON ISLANDS
The Secretary for Posts and Telecommunications
Department of Posts and Communications
Honiara, SOLOMON ISLANDS

NEW CALEDONIA
Direction de L'Office des Postes et Telecommunications
Noumea
NEW CALEDONIA

NEW HEBRIDES
The Secretary for Postes and Telecommunications
Department of Posts and Telecommunications
Vila
NEW HEBRIDES

TRUST TERRITORY OF THE PACIFIC ISLANDS
High Commissioner
Trust Territory of the Pacific Islands
Office of the Director of Communications
Saipan, Mariana Islands 96950, USA

KIRIBATI
The Secretary for Communications, Works and Utilities
P.O. Box 487
Betio, Tarawa
KIRIBATI

NAURU
Director of Telecommunications
REPUBLIC OF NAURU
Central Pacific

GALAPAGOS ISLANDS
Guayaquil Radio Club
Casilla Postal, 5757
Guayaquil
ECUADOR

CHARTER BOATS IN THE PACIFIC

It is not necessary for you to have your own cruising boat to sample the delights of the waters of the Pacific Ocean. Charter boats are becoming increasingly available in the islands and, with air transportation as good as it is, you can take a vacation cruise there as easily as any place in the world. The big difference is that you will not be one of thousands doing the same thing. Yours will be an individual adventure into unspoiled, uncrowded waters much the same as if you were using your own boat.

There currently are charter cruising boats available in Hawaii, French Polynesia, Tonga, New Zealand, Fiji, and the Marshall Islands. The sailing grounds range from the lush green of New Zealand's Bay of Islands to the shimmering atolls of the Marshalls. With the exception of French Polynesia, all of the charter areas are English-speaking and even in French Polynesia those associated with the tourist trade can speak English.

But you are not going to the Pacific to simply extend your hometown way of life, so once on your boat you will head for neighboring islands to live the carefree life of the cruising yachtie. Here in the Pacific as no other place in the world, you can escape the bonds of civilization by exploring virgin anchorages and islands.

Some of these areas are so primitive and challenging to navigation that the charter agency includes a skipper in the plan to assure fun without risk. This skipper is a local person who will enlighten you on the traditions and lore of the area and even teach you some of the culture. Other charters offer the typical bareboat arrangement where, if you can show evidence of adequate sailing experience, you can skipper your own boat and really be free of the rest of the world.

In either case the boats come fully equipped with linens and all necessities of the galley. Provisioning, however, varies between areas. Hawaii and New Zealand have adequate markets to ensure that you can provision your vessel with considerable ease after arrival. In other areas the boats come fully provisioned because a first-time visitor would have difficulty in expeditiously locating supplies. It is not uncommon for a full-time cruising boat crew to take several days to find its way around a new island and that would be prohibitive for a vacation charter. The charteree is also in a much better position to be able to blend native and imported foods to give meals with a touch of island magic.

Fishing, swimming and shelling are all part of the cruising life and most itineraries are planned to give these without spending too much precious vacation time sailing to new anchorages. Most boats come equipped with fishing and snorkeling gear and several are equipped for SCUBA diving. If you are a qualified SCUBA diver, you will have an unbelievable adventure in diving the coral reefs of the Pacific islands.

You don't have to follow the sun to charter in the Pacific. Being mostly in the Tropics, it is good the year around. Outside of the Tropics, in New Zealand, you will find seasonal charter rates because the local people are back at work in the Southern Hemisphere during the months of April to November and competition for charter boats is lessened.

You may want to consult the section on weather to see what season has the greatest preponderance of tropical storms in the area in which you wish to charter. While no charteree would let you go out with a storm brewing, you likewise wouldn't want your cruise to be constrained to a port during your vacation. Some areas like French Polynesia and the Marshall Islands generally have good weather the year around.

LANDFALLS OF PARADISE has assembled the most complete and up to date list of charter boats available in the Pacific. The agencies listed are believed to be reputable and stable and the information furnished by them correct at the time of printing. There are other boats in the Pacific offered for charter but they are not fulltime enterprises and might be difficult to deal with.

If sailing in an unspoiled part of the world is your vacation goal, then look to one of these charter boats to introduce you to the world's largest ocean. The airlines can get you there quickly so don't worry about miles. Just go and enjoy the pristine beauty of cruising away from it all.

Charter Opportunities in Hawaii

HAWAIIANA YACHT CHARTERS - This charter agency has been doing business in the Hawaiian Islands since 1972 and offers both bareboat and crewed boats in a variety of sizes. Boats are in a ready-to-sail condition with linens, dishes, charts, cooking utensils, full tank of fuel, and all safety gear. On request they will also procure food and beverages of your choice.

Associated with the charter company is the Hawaii Sailing Academy which offers basic and advanced sailing courses in four 2-hour sessions each. Tuition is $US85 per first adult and $US35 for each accompanying person. There is also an intensive one day course with 2 classroom hours and 6 sailing hours which is offered for $US89 per first adult and $US35 for each accompanying person.

Fleet boats: Cal 2-24, Columbia 30, Columbia 34, Columbia 36, Down East 38, Coronado 41, CT 41, and Columbia 43

Rates ($US):

	Bare boats		Crewed boats (a)	
	Columbia 34	Coronado 41	Columbia 36	Columbia 43
5 charter days	$ 650	$ 865	$ 900	$1250
10 charter days	$1200	$1465	$1700	$2350

(a) Crewed boats include cost of one crewman
(b) Rates are for parties of 6 people. Additional persons will be charged $5 per day each.
(c) Provisioning charges are at food and beverage costs plus a $25 service charge.

Contact: Hawaiiana Yacht Charters
P.O. Box 8231
Honolulu, HI 96815, USA

LANAI SEA CHARTERS - This agency operating from the Island of Lanai offers both bareboat and skippered charters. The boats are docked at Manele Bay and you can fly from Honolulu to Lanai Airport where the agency will meet your airplane. If you want some landtime, the agency has a four bedroom house for rent on the outskirts of Lanai City or can make reservations for you at the local lodge.

Charter boats come equipped with Avon dinghy, alcohol stove, ice chest, head compartment, dodger sunshade, two-way radio, charts, dishes, linens and all required safety equipment.
Fleet boats: Cal-28 *Makani,* Ranger-33 *Hornblower,* Coronado-35 *Stacked Deck.*

Rates ($US):

	Daily rates (a)		
	Cal-28	Ranger-33	Coronado-35
Bareboat (b)	$ 70	$ 95	$110
Deluxe cruise (c)	$200	$225	$240

(a) Plus a one-time setup fee of $100.
(b) Bareboat charters can engage a skipper for the first day at a cost of $60 to familiarize the charterer with boat and local waters.
(c) Deluxe rates are for two people; for each additional person, add $15 per day. The deluxe cruise includes captain, cook, food, beer, wine and incidentals.

Contact: Lanai Sea Charters
Box 401
Lanai City, HI 96763, USA

SEABERN YACHTS - This agency operates out of the old whaling center of Lahaina and offers both bareboat and skippered charters. Bareboat charters are restricted to areas in the vicinity of Lahaina, Lanai, and Molokai. Provisions can be obtained from nearby stores which are well stocked but more expensive than mainland stores. Charters of one week or longer have guest privileges at the Lahaina Yacht Club.

The charter boats come equipped with safety gear, sunshade, trolling gear, charts and compass, ice chest, tool kit, head compartment, and AM/FM radio. Sail inventories include reefing mainsail, 120 and 150% Genoas, and a working jib. The boats also come with ice, fuel, dishes, utensils, stove, and bedding.

Rates ($US):

Boat	Daily	Weekly
Newport-20	$ 55	$330
Santana-22	$ 60	$360
Cal 2-24	$ 65	$390
Pearson 26	$ 75	$450
Ranger 33	$110	$660
Columbia 43	$160	$960

(a) Includes checkout of boat, harbor and entrance area
(b) Inquire about cost for skipper services
Contact: Seabern Yachts
P.O. Box 1022
Lahaina, Maui, HI 96761, USA

VIOLANTE BOATS AND CHARTERS - This agency offers the 50-foot steel hull sloop *Mae Ya Nang II* for skippered charter in the Hawaiian waters. *Mae Ya Nang II* has separate staterooms for three persons each plus quarterberths for the two paid crew. Linens are furnished as well as fishing and snorkeling gear, and foul weather gear.

The boat is fully provisioned according to a list prepared beforehand by the charterer. Food and beverage costs are billed at actual purchase cost to the charterer but keep in mind that food prices in Hawaii are higher than on the mainland.

Specifications:
LOA - 50 feet
Hull material - steel with teak decks
Spar material - spruce
Cabin material - mahogany
Auxiliary power - 65 hp Ford diesel

Equipment:
Avon Sportboat with 10 hp outboard motor
VHF and short wave radios
Pressure water system
Full emergency equipment

Rates ($US):

No. of Weeks	Cost (a)
1	$1250
2	$2250
3	$3000
Full month	$3500

(a) Includes Coast Guard licensed skipper and a cook.
Contact:
Violante Boats and
Charters
P.O. BOX 8656
Honolulu, HI 96815, USA
or:
Violante Boats and Charters
3316 Keneth Drive
Palo Alto, CA 94303, USA

HONOLULU SAILING CRUISES - This fleet of Cal sailboats is available for bareboating around the island of Oahu or on longer voyages to the neighbor islands. Boat pickup or dropoff can be made at Honolulu or Lahaina for weekly charters. Crewed boats are also available.

Rates ($US):

	Cal 20	Cal 25	Cal 27	Cal 2-30	Cal 40
Daily	$ 50	$ 70	$ 85	$100	$185
Weekly	$275	$375	$450	$550	$975

An outer island sailing cruise is available aboard the Cal 40. This five day, all inclusive cruise is $350 per person (up to six persons).
Contact: Honolulu Sailing Cruises
1667 Ala Moana Boulevard
Honolulu, HI 96815, USA

Charter Opportunities in French Polynesia

Danae III - An 18 meter ketch offered for skippered cruising in French Polynesia. It has three individual cabins sleeping a total of eight persons. Each cabin has its own washstand and there is one shower and water closet for passengers. The messroom has a bar and stereo music. Enroute charter activities include sailing and navigation lessons and arrival activities feature fishing, SCUBA diving, and shelling. One hostess on board.

Typical 5-day itinerary includes Huahine, Raiatea, Tahaa, and Bora Bora with possibility of a "Tamaaraa" (Tahitian feast).

Danae III can also be chartered for a diving safari to the Tuamotu Islands. Rates on request.

Specifications: LOA - 18 meters
Beam - 5 meters
Draft - 2.8 meters
Displacement - 52 tons
Sail area - 185 sq. meters
Auxiliary power - twin diesel engines of 85 hp each

Equipment: Zodiac boat with engine and sails
SCUBA equipment for six persons (compressor on board)
Snorkeling gear

Rates: CFP 33,000 per day for 3 to 6 persons (including 3 meals and all the wine and beer you can drink!)
CFP 28,000 per day for one couple
Minimum length of any cruise is 5 days.

Contact: M. Claude Goche
Fare, Huahine
FRENCH POLYNESIA

Aita Peapea - A Columbia 56 ketch with four separate cabins sleeping two persons each plus berthing for two more in the lounge. Boat is equipped with showers and hot water, freezer and washing machine.

Classic itinerary includes Huahine, Raiatea, Tahaa and Bora Bora. Boat is offered with crew of two, three meals a day, drinks, water activities, and transfers between airport, hotel and boat.

Specifications: LOA - 56 feet
Beam - 13 feet
Draft - 8 feet
Displacement - 27 tons
Auxiliary power - 115 hp Westerbeke

Equipment: 11 kw Onan 115v AC generator, life raft, inflatable boat with outboard.

Rates:

No. of passengers	Cruise length	Price per day
4 (minimum)	unlimited	CFP 36,250
5	"	CFP 38,250
6	"	CFP 42,400

Contact: Mr. Michel Ventre
P.O. Box 110
Uturoa, Raiatea
FRENCH POLYNESIA

Charter Opportunities in Tonga

SOUTH PACIFIC YACHT CHARTERS – One of the few places in the Pacific where bare-boating is possible is the Vava'u group of Tonga. These are fiberglass boats built by the CSY yacht builders in Tampa, Florida, USA, which builds many of the charter yachts for the Caribbean charter trade. These are all new boats built specificlly for Tonga charter service and were delivered on their own bottoms in January 1979.

The SS 44s accommodate six persons in two separate staterooms plus a convertible saloon. There are two head compartments plus a stall shower and 400 gallons of fresh water.

Specifications:

LOA 44 feet	Draft-6 feet 6 inches
LWL-36 feet 4 inches	Displacement-37,000 pounds
Beam-13 feet 4 inches	Sail area-1060 square feet

Auxiliary power: diesel engine with 100 gallons of fuel

Rates ($US)

For 5 charter days for up to 8 people - $1116
For 10 charter days for up to 8 people - $1860
Full provisions must be taken at an additional $10 per person per day.

These rates include dinghy with outboard, snorkling gear, linens, ice, fuels, and trash bags. A charter captain can be hired for $25 per day including his meals.

Contact: South Pacific Yacht Charters
P.O. Box 6
Smithfield, UT 84335
USA

Charter Opportunities in New Zealand

RAINBOW CHARTERS - This agency offers bareboat charters with 20 and 26 foot boats in the Bay of Islands. Both boats accommodate five persons and are completely fitted out with toilets, water tanks, electric lighting, lifelines, boom tents, navigation needs, and safety equipment required by the government. Overseas visitors are supplied with sleeping bags, pillows, chilly bins and wet weather gear at no additional cost.

Your cruising area is the Bay of Islands with 100 or more islands and over 50 smaller bays or inlets. Around the Bay are the small historic towns of Russell, Waitangi, Paihia, Kerikeri and Opua where you can provision at costs quite modest. Fishing is also good in the Bay.

Specifications:

	Tracker 7.7 (keeler)	Davidson M20 (centerboard)
LOA	25 ft. 5 in.	20 ft.
Beam	8 ft. 2 in.	8 ft.
Draft	4 ft. 8 in.	11 in.
Auxiliary power	8 hp outboard	5 hp outboard

Equipment: Dinghy with each boat.

Rates: ($NZ):

	Peak season (15 Dec.-Easter)	Mid-season (Easter - 31 May) (1 Oct. - 14 Dec.)	Off season (1 June - 30 Sept.)
Davidson M20			
per day (a)	$ 45	$ 40	$ 30
per week	$275	$225	$150
Tracker 7.7			
per day (a)	$ 65	$ 55	$ 40
per week	$375	$325	$225

(a) minimum of two days

Contact: Rainbow Yacht Charters and Sales
Opua, Bay of Islands
NEW ZEALAND

BLUE HORIZONS, LTD. - This agency offers a Cavalier 39 equipped to accommodate six persons but can be handled by two persons. It is offered for bareboat charter and a skipper can be supplied if wanted. Sails include mainsail, trisail, Genoa, jib and storm jib. The boat is fully equipped with pillows, cutlery, crockery, and cooking utensils. Normally persons supply their own bedding and food, but other arrangements can be made for overseas visitors.

The boat is fitted with a BMC 1500 diesel giving a top motoring speed of 8 knots.

Equipment: Radiotelephone, deepfreeze and gas stove

Rates ($NZ)

	Off season (Apr. - Nov.)	In season (Dec. - Mar.)
per day	$ 70	$ 80
per week	$450	$500

A skipper can be provided for $25 per day

Contact: Blue Horizons, Ltd.
P.O. Box 4210
Auckland
NEW ZEALAND

Shiokaze - This registered yacht is offered for skippered charter out of Auckland cruising the nearby Hauraki Gulf or extended cruises up to the Bay of Islands.

Shiokaze is 44 feet long, ketch rigged, center cockpit and equipped with a 75 hp diesel auxiliary engine. Accommodations include berths for eight persons in three cabins; there are two toilets, one with a cold shower, and complete cooking facilities including refrigerator.

Rates ($NZ): $25 per day per person with a minimum of 5 persons. All food is included but no liquor.

Contact: W. Mark Robson
P.O. Box 17-207
Auckland
NEW ZEALAND

Charter Opportunities in Fiji

Longships - A 50-foot catamaran built in Bristol, England, in 1966 by her present owner, Merv Lippiat. Merv sailed it across the Atlantic and spent two years chartering in and around Antigua in the West Indies before heading into the Pacific. *Longships* sleeps six guests in two cabins, each with its own washroom and wardrobe. The saloon seats 10 persons around a central table. As in all catamarans, the deck space is extensive for outdoor living.

While owner Merv Lippiat regales you with sea stories stretching half way around the world, his wife Fannie, will whip up delicious Fijian cooking from a modern galley with gas stove, oven and refrigerator.

Longships carries two dinghies, a self-inflating life raft, and radiotelephone.

Specifications:

LOA-50 feet	Draft-3 feet 4 inches
LWL-43 feet	Sail area-1000 square feet
Beam-20 feet	

Auxiliary power: 30 hp Ford diesel engine

Construction: Double skin mahogany on iroko stringers

Rates ($F)

$160 per day for four persons (minimum). This includes captain, crew, food laundry, and snorkeling gear.
$20 per day extra for each additional person.

Rendezvous rates available if you want *Longships* to meet you at any other place than its home port in the Fijian archipelago.

Contact: Mr. Merv Lippiat
            The Regent of Fiji Hotel
            P.O. Box 678
            Nadi, FIJI

Tau - A 90 foot steel ketch with twin bilge keels built in 1972. The entire standing rig was built by Alspar in Australia and the sails are from Hood in New Zealand. *Tau* commenced charter operations in 1974.
   Accommodations include three twin-berth cabins with shared washroom facilities and a master stateroom with two ¾ berths and its own washroom. Fresh water showers in all facilities.
   Equipment includes VHF radio, autopilot, echo sounder, and 240v AC electricity.

Specifications:

LOA-90 feet	Draft-7 feet
Beam-17 feet 6 inches	Sail area-2500 square feet

   Auxiliary power: 172 hp Gardner diesel engine with 700 gallons fuel.
   Fresh water: 1600 gallons

Rates ($F)
   $500 per day which includes captain, crew, food, laundry, snorkeling/spearfishing gear. Up
      to eight guests.
   Long term charters are available within the Fiji group or to neighboring Pacific islands.

Contact: Mr. Colin E. Philp
            Tradewinds Marine, Ltd.
            P.O. Box 3084
            Lami, Suva, FIJI

Sta Reta - A 40 foot motorsailer which sleeps 5 persons. It is available for general charter as well as diving charters. Accommodations include shower and toilet facilities and a galley.

Rates ($F)
   $120 per day for up to four persons
   $25 per day for each additional person.

Contact: Mrs. L. Evans, Director
            Scubahire, Ltd.
            GPO Box 777
            Suva, FIJI

Index

Boldface type refers to illustrations and charts.

Academy Bay 351, 353, **358**
Acapulco 36
Agana 273, **274**
Agana Bay 275, **277**
Ahe **91**
Aitutaki 127
Ala Wai Boat Harbor **61,** 70
Alofi 170
American Samoa: country 48, 131, **133,** 135,
    currency 138; entry regulations 137; language 138;
    medical 139; Port of Entry **134,** 135, **137, 140;**
    radio 141; yacht facilities 137; other 16, 34
Apataki 77
Apia **142, 144, 146,** 147, **148**
Apra Harbor 271, **272**
Archipielago de Colon 351
Argentina 64
Atolls 88
Atuona **82**
Auckland 173, **182, 185,** 190, **191**
Austral Islands: country 48, 75, 105; entry
    regulations 77; medical 77; weather 107;
    yacht facilities 109
Australia 15, 64, 167, 259, 340, 346, 348
Austrialia del Espiritu Santo 257
Avatiu 121, **126, 128, 129**

Bahama Islands 65
Banaba 337, **342**
Bay of Islands 173, **177, 178,** 187, **188**
Bermuda 65
Bora Bora 75, **101, 102**
Bounty, H.M.S. 75, 105, 116, 121, 155, 156

Cabo San Lucas 36
Canada 65
Canton 339
Caroline Islands 266, 283, **284,** 303, 307, 315,
    321, 331
Chile 111, 350
Christmas Island 135, 337, 341
Clipperton Island 350
Club Nautique de Caledonie **250,** 254, 255
Coconut crabs 91
Coconuts 88, **91**
Colonia (Yap) 321, **328**
Cook Islands: country 48, 121, **122;** currency 125;
    entry regulations 126; language 125; medical 127;
    Port of Entry 121, **126, 128, 129;** radio 130;
    weather 124; yacht facilities 127; other 178
Cook, James 52, 98, 105, 121, 155, 170, 175, 245

Crew 43
Cruising license 64

Dangerous Archipelago 88
Darwin, Charles 351, 354
Doldrums 23

Easter Island: country 48, 111, **112;** currency 113;
    entry regulations 114; language 113, medical 114;
    Port of Entry 111, 114; weather 112; yacht
    facilities 114
Ecuador 351
Ellice Islands 165
Entry procedures 18, 34

Fakarava 88, **94**
Fanning 337, 341
Fatu Hiva **82**
Fidgee 199
Firearms 65, 78, 126, 137, 207, 241
Fishing 51, 67, 92
Fiji: country 198, **200;** currency 203; entry
    regulations 205; language 203; medical 206; Ports
    of Entry 199, **201, 208, 209, 210;** radio 212;
    weather 204; yacht facilities 208; other 36,
    237, 288
France 75, 198, 213, 245, 257, 350
French Polynesia: country 48, **74,** 75; currency 76;
    entry regulations 77; language 76; medical 77;
    Port of Entry 75; other 16
Friendly Islands 153
Funafuti 165, **168**

Galapagos Islands: country 351, **352;** currency 355;
    entry regulations 357; language 355; medical 357;
    Ports of Entry 351, **356, 358;** radio 359;
    weather 354; yacht facilities 358
Gambier Islands 88, **89,** 95
Gilbert Islands 337
Gizo 235, **239,** 242, **243**
Graciosa Bay 235, **242**
Great Britain 15, 64, 116, 165, 173, 198, 199, 235,
    257, 337, 345
Guam: country 266, 267, **268,** 269, 271; currency
    276; entry regulations 273; language 276; medical
    275; Port of Entry 271, **272;** radio 277; yacht
    facilities 273; other 34

Ha'apai 153, 164
Ham radio 39, 41, 118
Hanalei Bay 71

Hanga Roa 111, 115
Harvey Islands 121
Hawaii (Island) 51, **66,** 67
Hawaii Yacht Club 71
Hawaiian Islands: country 48, **50,** 51; currency 58;
    entry regulations 61; language 58; medical 62;
    Ports of Entry 51, **52, 53, 55, 61, 63, 64, 65,
    66, 68, 69, 70, 73;** radio 72; weather 59;
    yacht facilities 67; other 34
Heyerdahl, Thor 88
Hilo **52, 53, 66,** 67
Hiva Oa 75, **82, 84**
Honduras 64
Honiara 235, **237, 240,** 242
Honolulu **61, 63, 64, 69,** 70
Hoorn Group 213
Howland 149
Huahine **99**
Hurricane 25
Hurricane Warning System 28

International Association for Medical Assistance
    to Travelers (IAMAT) 62
International Date Line 13
Isla de Pascua 111

Jamaica 65
Juan Fernandez Islands 350

Kahului **55,** 67, **68**
Kauai 51, **60,** 71, **73**
Kavieng 219, 233
Keehi Lagoon 70
Kermadec Islands: country **194,** 195; Port of Entry
    195; weather 195; yacht facilities 195
Kieta 219, 233
Kira Kira 235, 243
Kirabati: country 266, 337, **338;** currency 340, entry
    regulations 340; language 340; medical 341; Ports
    of Entry 337, **342, 343;** radio 343; weather 340;
    yacht facilities 341
Kolonia (Ponape) 307, **310,** 311
Kona **54,** 59
Koror 331, **334, 335, 336**
Kosrae District: country 283, **284, 302,** 303; currency
    305; entry regulations 290; language 305; Port of
    Entry 303, **304;** radio 306; weather 303; yacht
    facilities 303
Kwajalein 295

Lae 219, 221, **222,** 230
Lahaina **56,** 68
Lautoka 199, **210**
Lele Harbor 303, **304**
Levuka **207, 208,** 210, **211**
Liberia 65
Line Group 337
Los Angeles 36
Loyalty Islands 252
Luganville Bay 256, 260

Madang 219, 221, **225,** 230
Magellan, Ferdinand 13, **267,** 273
Mail 17
Majuro 295, **298, 300**
Mangareva 78, 88, **89**
Manila 321
Manua Islands **133,** 139
Maoris 121, 175
Mariana Islands Chain: country 267, **268,** 269, 283,
    286; weather 269
Marquesas Islands: country 48, 75, 79, **80, 83, 84;**
    entry regulations 77; medical 77; Ports of Entry
    75, **81, 82;** weather 79; yacht facilities 79
Marshall District: country 266, 283, **284, 294,** 295;
    currency 297; entry regulations 290; language 297;
    Port of Entry 295, **298, 300;** radio 301; weather
    295; yacht facilities 299
Mata Uta 213, **216**
Maui 51, **57,** 67
Maupiti **103**
Melanesia 13, **14,** 197
Micronesia 13, **14,** 265, 286
Moen 315, **317**
Money 18
Moorea 95, **98,** 99
Mururoa 78, 88

Nan Madol 286, 309, **312**
Nauru: country 266, **344,** 345; currency 346; entry
    regulations 348; language 346; medical 348;
    Port of Entry 345; radio 348; weather 347
Navigator Islands 131
Nawiliwili **65, 70,** 71
Neale, Tom 121
Neiafu 153, **158,** 162, **163, 164**
Netherlands 65
New Caledonia: country 198, 245, **246;** currency 253;
    entry regulations 254; language 253; medical 254;
    Port of Entry 245, **248, 249, 250;** radio 255;
    weather 252; yacht facilities 255; other 34, 213
New Hebrides: country 198, **256;** currency 259; entry
    regulations 258; language 259; medical 260; Ports
    of Entry 257, **261, 262, 263;** radio 264; weather
    258; yacht facilities 259
New Zealand: country 48, 173, **174;** currency 179;
    entry regulations 65, 182; language 179; medical
    184; Ports of Entry 173, **176, 182, 183, 185,
    188, 189, 191;** radio 187, 192; weather 180,
    187; yacht facilities 185, 187; other 15, 36,
    116, 121, 149, 170, 172, 195
Nila 235
Niue: country 170, **170;** currency 172; entry
    regulations 171; language 172; medical 172; Port
    of Entry 170; radio 171; weather 171; yacht
    facilities 171; other 178
Norfolk Island 116, 155
Northern Mariana Islands: country 266, 267, **268,**
    279, 288; currency 281; entry regulations 281;
    language 281; medical 282; Port of Entry **278,**
    279; radio 282; yacht facilities 281
Noumea 245, **247, 249,** 250

Nouvelle Caledonie 245
Nuku Hiva 75, **83**
Nuku'alofa 153, **155, 156, 161,** 162
Nukunonu 149, **151**

Oahu 51, 70
Ocean Island 337
Opua 173, **176,** 187

Pacific Ocean 13
Pago Pago **134,** 135, **137, 140**
Palau District: country 283, **284, 330,** 331; currency
    333; entry regulations 290; language 333; Port of
    Entry 331, **334, 335, 336;** radio 336; weather
    332; yacht facilities 333
Panama 36, 79, 88, 95, 116, 121, 173, 351
Papeete 75, 95, **97, 100,** 103
Papua New Guinea: country 198, **218,** 219; currency
    223; entry regulations 227; language 223; medical
    228; Ports of Entry 219, **220, 222, 227, 229,**
    231, 232; radio 233; weather 224; yacht facilities
    228; other 35, 235
Papua Yacht Club 228
Passage lengths 36, 37, 51, 79, 88, 95, 105, 111,
    116, 121, 135, 143, 149, 153, 165, 170, 173,
    195, 199, 213, 219, 235, 245, 256, 271, 279,
    295, 303, 307, 315, 321, 331, 337, 345, 351
Passport 17
Paumotu Archipelago 88
Penrhyn 121
Pets 67, 185, 208, 258
Phoenix Group 339
Piracy 43
Pitcairn Island: country 48, 116, **117, 119;** currency
    120; entry regulations 118; language 120; medical
    118; Port of Entry 116, **119;** radio 118; weather
    117; yacht facilities 118
Point Cruz Yacht Club 242
Polynesia 13, **14,** 48
Ponape District: country 283, **284,** 307, **309;**
    currency 312; entry regulations 290; language 312;
    Port of Entry 307, **310;** radio 313; weather 309;
    yacht facilities 311
Port Allen **73**
Port Moresby 219, **220,** 221, **224,** 228, **229**
Pratique 18
Puntarenas 36

Rabaul 219, 221, **227,** 230, **231**
Rabaul Yacht Club 233
Radio 37, 39, 41, 118
Raiatea 95
Raivavae 105, **107, 108, 109**
Rangiroa 75, **89, 90, 94**
Raoul Island **194,** 195
Rapa 105, 107, 111
Rapa Nui 111
Rarotonga 121, **123**
Rhinoceros beetle 126, 160, 207, 217
Ringi Cove 235
Rose Island 136, 139

Royal Suva Yacht Club **202,** 208
Rurutu 77, 107
Russell **177, 178,** 187

Samoa Islands: country 131, **133;** weather 131;
    social customs 131
San Diego 36
San Francisco 36
Sandwich Islands 51
Santo 257, 260, **261**
Savai'i 147
Senyavin Islands 307
Seven Seas Cruising Association 44
Slocum Society 44
Society Islands: country 48, 75, 95, **96;** entry
    regulations 77, 99; medical 77; Port of Entry 75,
    97, 100; radio 104; weather 95; yacht facilities 98;
    other 34
Solomon Islands: country 198, **234,** 235; currency
    241; entry regulations 241; language 241; medical
    239; Ports of Entry 235, **237, 240, 242, 243;**
    radio 244; weather 238; yacht facilities 242
Stevenson, Robert Louis **144**
Suva 199, **201,** 205, 208, **209**
Suvarov 121
Swains Island 136, 139

Tahiti 95
Taiohae Bay **81,** 85, **85**
Takaroa **93**
Tanapeg Harbor **278,** 279, 281
Tanna Papua 219
Tarawa 337, 341, **342, 343**
Tauranga 173, 186
Ten-Minute Form 45, 46
Tokelau Islands: country 48, **149;** currency 150; entry
    regulations 152; language 150; medical 152; Port
    of Entry 149, **151;** weather 151; yacht facilities
    152; other 178
Tokyo 279, 307, 321
Tonga: country 48, 153, **154;** currency 159; entry
    regulations 160; language 159; medical 160; Ports
    of Entry 153, **156, 161, 163, 164;** radio 164;
    weather 158; yacht facilities 162; other 178
Tongatapu 153
Tradewinds 23, 24
Tropical cyclones 25, **26, 27, 29, 30, 31,** 60, 125,
    151, 159, 181, 195, 205, 215, 226, 258, 270,
    311, 316, 325, 333
Truk District: country 283, **284, 314,** 315; currency
    320; entry regulations 290; language 320; Port of
    Entry 315, **317;** radio 320; weather 315; yacht
    facilities 318
Truk Trading Co. 288, 319, **320**
Trust Territory of the Pacific Islands: country 266, 269,
    282, 283, **284;** currency 289; entry regulations
    290; language 289; medical 288; weather 289;
    yacht facilities 293
Tsunamis 60, 186
Tuamotu Archipelago: country 48, 75, **86, 87,** 88;
    entry regulations 77; medical 77; Ports of Entry 75,
    89; weather 92; yacht facilities 92

Tubuai 105, **106**
Tutuila 135, 137
Tutukaka 181
Tuvalu: country 48, 165, **166;** currency 167; entry
    regulations 165; language 167; medical 169; Port
    of Entry 165, **168;** radio 169; weather 165;
    yacht facilities 165
Typhoon **27,** 28, 29, **30**

Ua Pu 77
Ulithi 283, **322,** 325
Union Group 149
United States 15, 51, 135, 271, 279
Upolu 143

Vancouver 36
Vanua Levu 199
Variables 24, 25
Vava'u 153, 162, **163**
Vila 257, 259, **262, 263**
Visa 17
Viti Levu 199

Wake Island 52, **284**
Wallis and Futuna Islands: country 198, **214;** currency
    215; entry regulations 215; language 215; medical
    217; Port of Entry 213, **216;** yacht facilities 215
Washington Island 337
Waterspouts 165
Weather 23, 35
Wellington 173, **186**
West Germany 65
Westerlies 24, 25
Western Samoa: country 48, 131, **133,** 143; currency
    145; entry regulations 144; medical 146; Port of
    Entry **142,** 143, **146;** radio 148; yacht facilities
    147; other 178
Whangarei 173, **183,** 187, **189**
Woleai Atoll 326
World Health Organization 17
Wreck Bay 351, **356**

Yap District: country 283, **284,** 321, **322;** currency
    325; entry regulations 290; language 325; Port of
    Entry 321, **328;** radio 329; weather 323, 326;
    yacht facilities 327; social customs 327
Yslas de Salamon 235